ISBN: 0-9759129-8-4

Copyright © 2006 by Stan Russo

Published by:

Inklings Press
2 N. Lincoln Ridge Dr. #521
Madison, WI 53719

www.inklings.com

All rights reserved. No part of this publication may be reproduced, stored in a retrieval system or transmitted in any form or any means (electronic, mechanical, photocopying, recording or otherwise) without prior written permission. Permission is granted for the quoting of brief passages for review or educational purposes in compliance with Fair Use.

THE 50 BEST MOVIES

FOR THE MOVIE FAN

Stan Russo

~ Inklings Press ~

INTRODUCTION

What is the point of a movie? To be more specific, what is a movie designed to do? That is a difficult question and one with many answers. Some will say that the job of a movie is to enlighten people to the situations around them. Others might say the job of a movie is to reveal and showcase technical innovations within film. There are even some that have the ridiculous notion that movies are meant to entertain the audience. I am part of that last group.

The utmost job of a movie *is* to entertain its audience, regardless of whether it is a documentary, an action film, a gripping drama, a comedy or even a combination of all the genres just listed. Movies should always create a feeling that a person was glad they saw what was placed upon the screen, even if the material is of a depressing nature. When I go to a movie I am looking for some kind of escapism along with entertainment, whether it is of the action, comedic or dramatic variety. If a movie is not entertaining, whatever message it is trying to get across in its story, or lack thereof, winds up completely lost on me. I can read the newspapers if I want to learn about the current political climate in South America or the plight of the weeping juniper swallow from Antarctica. If a filmmaker wants to make me aware of those things then they should do it in a way that is entertaining and keeps my focus, even if they choose to present it in a documentary account.

That is all that movies really are to me. They are a means of escapism into a magical world of wonder, even if the world depicted happens to be my specific neighborhood. My neighborhood has been the setting for a number of movies such as *State of Grace* and *Daredevil*. I would much rather be transported to a galaxy far, far away, yet I have no objections with being taken on a ride within my own backyard, as long as it is an entertaining ride.

The first movie I can remember seeing in the theaters was *Stir Crazy*. Even though I was nine years old and the material was of an adult nature, with a probable PG-13 rating now, the movie was hysterical and my parents were there with me. They both loved the comedy team of Richard Pryor and Gene Wilder. After that movie so did I. Something else happened after seeing that movie. I was hooked. I spent many a weekend watching movie after movie after movie in the multiplexes of Brooklyn. When I saw the early show of *Raiders of the Lost Ark*, I enjoyed it so much that I stayed for the next two shows to see it again and then again. Come to think of it now, movies may have been my original introduction into writing. I always had an affinity and desire to create stories and I probably have movies to thank for that.

Once a person develops a taste for movies it is generally because of a few films that have affected that viewer in a profound manner. Everyone loves movies, yet there are people who understand what being a true movie fan really means. For me, there were a couple of movies that turned me from audience member to fan to serious fanatic. Those films have still remained as some of my favorites. A chapter will be presented in this book, chapter 2, which shall speak a bit about some of the movies I consider my favorites.

Each one of them touched me in a specific way and I don't mean in a Roman Polanski sort of way. As you read on you will understand what I mean by that. My favorites are an eclectic variety of films that generally correlate to my personality, yet my affinity for them could have been something as simple as the mood I was in. As a self appointed critic of film, I try to allow my intellect to guide those choices, yet some of the great movies I include among my favorites simply hit home with me when I saw them.

The point of this book is to discuss and debate movies. I find no better mechanism for debate than a ranking system. This affords the readers two separate possibilities to differ with my opinion. After all, the main list of this book presented in chapter 1 is my opinion. What you will come to hopefully realize is that my opinion is subjective, yet not arbitrary. If it were arbitrary, I would have put any movie on the list I wanted, without the painstaking hours it took to finally arrive at the finished list.

There are a couple of basic rules with regards to the main list. The first rule is that a movie must have had a theatrical release. The second rule is that the movie must be a full-length feature. The third rule is that movie must not be a documentary. With respect to that last rule, a movie can tell the life story of an individual or depict historical events, yet must not be considered a film that is of the documentary style of filmmaking. *Bowling for Columbine* is a documentary. *Ray* and *The Aviator* are not. I believe those three simple rules are easy enough to accept. The fourth rule may be a little tougher to handle.

The fourth and final rule is that each movie available for selection among the main list must be an English language film. There is a specific reason for that. With so many movies made each year, it is almost impossible to keep up. The average number of movies made has drastically risen over the past few years thanks to the advent of the independent film. An independent film is one that can be made on a smaller budget and therefore by a smaller studio. With smaller studios popping up everywhere, the number of movies made each year naturally increases. What that does is make it increasingly harder to see every movie that comes out each year. Now take that model to a foreign or international level.

With hundreds of countries making a number of films each year, it would be theoretically impossible to see every one of them, along with seeing the multitude of English language films. By that rationale it is unfair to include foreign films among the main list. There are some popular foreign films, such as *Life is Beautiful*, *Hero* and *Crouching Tiger, Hidden Dragon*, all of which have been featured in American cinemas due to their popularity and American distribution. Who is to say that they are the best the world has to offer? Perhaps there is a foreign film from the country of Iran that cannot be seen in America due to political embargos. One would never know until years from now. As a result, foreign language films have been excluded from the main list. A number of them shall be discussed in chapter 6, but there are still other foreign film gems that have yet to discovered.

Speaking of not having the ability to see every foreign film made, simply due to the mathematical implausibility of the situation, I will not claim to have seen every single English language movie that has ever been made. I have seen a great majority of them, but I have not seen every single one. To illustrate this issue I offer the movie *Air Bud*.

The 1997 movie *Air Bud* is a tale of a boy who befriends a stray dog. Sounds sweet enough, albeit a bit of a kid's movie. There is nothing wrong with that though because plenty of movies made specifically for children have become classics. Wait a second. I forgot to include the other major plot point in *Air Bud*. The dog can play basketball. That last sentence should be enough to have made my point, yet I will go on a little further. *Air Bud* is a movie for kids, but not really for kids so much as to distract kids. It is typical of the kind of marketing that studios utilize to increase merchandising revenue. Let's make a movie where a dog plays basketball, the kids will love it. Even though that is a sad statement on the intellect of children in America, the movie still has its audience and the toy stores will stock up on *Air Bud* mini basketballs.

I did not have to see *Air Bud* to realize the movie was an utter piece of trash. The next step would be to have a gorilla play third base for a minor league baseball team. Already done. That was the theme of the movie *Ed*, another movie meant for kids who will someday be referred to as *'special'* and another film I did not have to see to realize it was a total piece of garbage. Selection plays an important role in seeing movies, specifically with so many movies made each year. If a movie that I did not have the ability to see is even remotely good I will hear about it and go see it. I have seen some real stinkers as well though. That is the price we must all pay for those rare treasures of cinema, many of which will be among the main list.

After the main list and the chapter on my favorite films are presented, there will be five additional chapters. They will contain a large number of movies within them, all with the express purpose of giving the reader a broader range of movies to discuss and debate. These chapters have the movies within them critiqued as a companion and comparison to the main list. Every list should have at least another prominent list to compare itself too. I have chosen two lists and offered a history of the Best Picture winners from the Academy Awards as my comparison pieces.

In assessing and contrasting the lists side by side, the reader should notice similarities, which does in fact add to the credibility of each list. If I were to present fifty movies on my main list that never won or were nominated for any Oscars, were never mentioned or nominated by the American Film Institute for inclusion among their 100 greatest films or rated highly by movie fans across the world on the Internet Movie database, then my list should be one that becomes immediately suspect. You will see that even if you disagree with my main list, as most will because everyone has a different idea of which movie is better than another, you can not deny its credibility as a list or that the list possesses cinematic integrity, when you compare it to the other pieces within the book. If I ranked *Air Bud* as #12 and *Ed* as #6, then my list would suck. I did not.

To reiterate, all I am trying to do here is present the reader with another option to discuss and debate the movies that they enjoy. I understand that movies are a visual event and are much more enjoyable when they are seen rather than talked about. That is a given. Ask yourself one thing though. Who among you has never seen a movie, enjoyed it and then not discussed it with your friends or family? The answer to that question is no one. Everyone loves to talk about the movies they enjoyed with friends, family or whomever. We even like to talk about the movies we did not enjoy or downright hated with those same groups. This book is another opportunity to do that. You might even read about a few movies you have never seen and will want to see because of the write-ups in this book. That makes the entire process I went through all worth it.

4

Chapter One:

The List

6

50

ALL THE PRESIDENT'S MEN
1976

Often times, the story of the investigation behind the story is far more intriguing than what has been found out. I understand that may sound strange to some, but for anyone who has seen *All the President's Men*, it makes perfect sense. The story of the break-in at the Watergate Hotel in 1972 began as a simple robbery. It was nothing significant that the Watergate was where the Democratic National Headquarters was housed. Enter two reporters at the *Washington Post*, Bob Woodward and Carl Bernstein, who uncovered the truth behind that robbery. Assigned to what was originally viewed as a basic robbery, Woodward and Bernstein knew there was something bigger behind it all.

Based upon the 1974 book, *All the President's Men* is a fantastic inside look at what it takes to get a high profile story, which became one of the stories of the century. Fully detailing the lengths that Woodward and Bernstein had to go to in order to finally write this story, which eventually brought down the White House and prompted the resignation of President Nixon. *All the President's Men* is an insightful look at the deep investigative techniques required, displaying the full gamut of thorough journalism. They could not just go on what they knew, which their investigations clearly led them to believe. They needed the hard facts from people who were willing to go on the record for them. In that political climate, those kinds of people did not come forth for fear of their own safety.

A masterful and unique detective story, it is almost as unbelievable as any detective story coming from the halls of fiction. The more Woodward and Bernstein delved into the issues the more the pieces began to unravel. Knowing now that the conspiracy went all the way up to the President does not diminish the film at all. It is fascinating to see how two journalists merely doing their job brought down those men. It is noteworthy to state that without the articles and subsequent book the entire criminal conspiracy conducted by the Republican Party might have gone undiscovered. This brilliant movie clearly defines the reporter's struggles in uncovering an immense political scandal.

Filled with magnificent performances all around, capped off by an Oscar winning supporting performance by Jason Robards as *Washington Post* Managing Editor Ben Bradlee, *All the President's Men* is clearly an ensemble piece. Nobody denies that Robert Redford and Dustin Hoffman, as Bob Woodward and Carl Bernstein respectively, are the two true stars of the film. This movie however, lives and dies with the supporting players, who compliment this piece in every way.

At the time, the Watergate scandal and subsequent resignation of President Nixon was still fresh in the minds of the American people, yet many of them did not know the complete story behind it. Almost everyone knew about the scandal, but this was not just a rehashing of those basic events. *All the President's Men* is an inside look at what it took to get a story that important and the levels to which those in power would go to keep the throne. A better look at what goes into getting a story this important has never been presented on film before or since. The unique feel of the film transports the audience into the world that Bernstein and Woodward lived during their investigatory journey.

49

AIRPLANE!
1980

As you shall see in the upcoming one page analyses, movies generally have sub-textual messages or meanings. They are not simply about a basic storyline presented as a means of escape into a world of wonder. The movies that go deeper than what is merely presented upon the screen usually tend to stand the test of time. They present a certain quality that lives on in the minds of the viewer, way past the time that the movie has ended. Almost always, movies that do not possess that quality fade out of memory and into obscurity. *Airplane!* is one of the few exceptions to that rule.

Having a simplistic premise about it, this movie makes a gigantic comedic statement. This statement does not come from formulaic comedy, but rather from the exact opposite, deriving its meaning out of off the wall hilarity. Generally, comedic movies are designed to have specific staged comedic bits. However, with *Airplane!*, its comedy comes from the absurd. Staged comedy provides a general situation and then works toward arriving at a comedic setup. This movie does not do that. *Airplane!* actually creates comedy out of nothingness. The comedy comes from presenting what appears to be a dramatic situation and then turns upside down to deliver unexpected comedy. It is as if the relative shock of the comedy provides this movie with its most memorable moments.

The rudimentary story follows an ex-fighter pilot turned cab driver chasing after his former lover, a stewardess about to fly away and out of his life. He buys a ticket and boards the plane with the hopes of winning her back. During the flight, all three pilots contract food poisoning and he is summoned to land the plane and help save the day. He succeeds and wins the girl back in the end, despite all the odds against him. The actual plot of the film is not the real story of the movie though.

When *Airplane!* came out in 1980 it was a definite jolt to the way comedy could be shown on film. The farcical nature of the movie went beyond anything that had been done before. The creators, Jim Abrahams, David and Jerry Zucker, were fresh off their hysterical yet underrated sketch film *The Kentucky Fried Movie* and ready to take that next step in their planned evolution of the comedic film. *Airplane!* completed what was attempted in that first film, a fully cohesive story based on numerous ridiculous premises all blended into one full movie, resulting in a classic.

The true story behind the greatness of *Airplane!* lies in the many sight gags, mixture of reality and ridiculousness and the many one liners. Brilliant one-liners such as *'stop calling me Shirley'*, *'looks like I picked the wrong week to quit sniffing glue'* and perhaps that best of the bunch, *'excuse me stewardess, I speak jive'*, are among many that give this movie extended life. It is a spoof taken to the umpteenth level, shaping the way filmmakers could present lampoon style efforts in the future. If there is any real message to the movie then it has to be that no one should take themselves too seriously. No person or group is spared here. Therefore, anyone that takes these insults to heart does not understand the true meaning, everything and everyone is fair game.

48

THE PRINCESS BRIDE
1987

What classifies a movie as timeless? Is it as simple as breaking through the generation gap of moviegoers over a distinct period of time? Could it be the mere fact that it gets better and becomes more appreciated with age? One thing is for certain, a movie that is in consideration as a timeless classic must bypass a single specific genre, so as not to be pegged as one particular type. A movie that falls under that category generally fails to hold continual appeal for audiences as the genre advances and evolves throughout time. *The Princess Bride* is one of those rare movies, transcending genre and generations to become one of the few movies that all ages can appreciate.

Consisting of pirates, battles, multiple chase sequences, magnificent sword fights, evil princes, revenge, brute squads, redemption, castle storming, kidnapping, miracles, a battle of wits (to the death), the fire swamp, the pit of despair, true love, a six-fingered man and one enormous giant, not to mention a grandfather sharing a family tradition with his sick grandson, *The Princess Bride* is a magical journey for even the most disheartened moviegoer. As with any great story, one of the key elements to a great movie is turmoil, existing throughout. Once true love is discovered, it is immediately lost through the false notification of death, whereby the plot then falls into place.

The journey that occurs, to recapture that true love, leads the main character into a variety of adventures. They take him to the brink of death, more than once and back again to where the story originated from. *The Princess Bride* is a beautiful work of symmetry, mixed with heart, comedy, redemption and adventure, which will leave the moviegoer wanting more. Movies that are able to achieve that feat are few and far between. Just when the story ends and your heartstrings are tugged, it is shown that all one has to do to relive the magic is come back again and have the story read to you again tomorrow. It is a grand metaphor for watching the movie over and over.

Directed by former television star Rob Reiner, *The Princess Bride* has an all star cast of supporting players, each contributing to the magical nature of this film in their own special way. The most famous person in the cast was probably the massive Andre the Giant, who plays Fezzak, the brute with heart. Newcomers Robin Wright and Cary Elwes are now familiar faces, starring in such big name films as *Forrest Gump* for Wright and *Glory* for Elwes. They careers began with this film. Smaller roles were filled by standouts Billy Crystal, Christopher Guest and a great Wallace Shawn.

The story of true love that one unconditionally has for another, triumphing above all is at the epicenter of this magical tale of wonder. Not even death can stop true love here, even the true love that an old timer has for his sick grandson. *The Princess Bride* was a critical and public success, but few truly understand its hold on a generation of moviegoers. It is a movie that can be seen over and over again, without any fear of getting stale. This movie's appeal reaches out to everyone, watched and enjoyed by fans of all cultures, genders and most importantly, generations.

47

BREAKING AWAY
1979

    What is the next step in life after high school is over? One year after graduating, a group of four teenagers search for their own identities while struggling to remain together. Individual ambition, as well as a lack thereof threatens to break up the group, which focuses on one of the members desire to become a champion cyclist. It is the cyclist's story that becomes the primary driving source of the film. When he is ultimately let down by his heroes, who he has spent the last part of the year trying to emulate, a moving realization occurs to him that it is better to be yourself and respect where you come from, as opposed to trying to be something you are not.

    Four local Indiana teens come to grips with their friendship and life, in the face of growing up. Each one them has a different story. Dave has dreams of becoming a champion cyclist. Cyril's failures drive his aspirations. Moocher suffers from an inferiority complex due to his height and Mike longs for the time, not long ago, when he was looked up to as the high school quarterback. Despite the trials and tribulations they go through the real challenge comes from their confrontations with the local college kids. The differences are clearly evident among the two groups, providing the basis for the mutual dislike, conflict and emerging competition between them.

    Dave's disillusionment reaches its peak when his heroes cheat by jamming a rod into his wheel during a bicycle race. The injury he receives is a minor one, yet the damage has clearly been done. His dreams, for the moment, are shattered. This causes him to reexamine his life, which includes revealing the fact that he is not actually an Italian exchange student to a college girl he has been courting and entering into the college fraternity bicycle race. During the finale, the bicycle race, Dave is a shoo-in to win it for his team. His injury forces the four men to work together as a team. Their teamwork shows that even while growing up their friendship will always remain intact.

    In a year dominated by the gripping family drama *Kramer vs. Kramer*, which came as close to sweeping the five major awards at the Oscars as a movie could without achieving that feat, *Breaking Away* clearly showed that a small film could make a difference. Its impact is based upon its gentle message. Only rewarded with a Best Original Screenplay Oscar victory, *Breaking Away* has unfortunately become a forgotten gem. This film deserves to be remembered among the greats that cinema has offered over the years. I challenge anyone to watch it through without becoming a fan.

    Clearly an ensemble piece of acting, *Breaking Away* examines rural values versus privileged society, lifelong friendships and parental relationships. Dave's bond with his parents, a loving mother, Barbara Barrie, in an Oscar nominated role, and a grumpy father, Paul Dooley, robbed of a deserved nomination, supply that stabilizing factor in this gem of a story. *Breaking Away* is not about bicycling, in the same way that a film like *Rocky* is not about boxing. Those aspects merely serve as a backdrop for a small movie that is equal parts emotional, uplifting and heartwarming.

46

FARGO
1996

If kidnapping were so simple more people would do it. This is what should have been explained to the criminals in *Fargo*. Based on true events, or so we are led to believe, the levels to which some will go for money is truly shocking. There must have been great artistic licensing taken with this film because the events depicted are way too far fetched for anyone to believe they actually occurred. There is the old axiom that truth is stranger than fiction, yet this kind of fiction is actually much more bizarre than the truth could have ever been. One must wonder that if the stranger parts of this movie were actually based on real events how these central figures made it that far in life?

Car salesman Jerry Lundegaard hires two men to kidnap his wife. The ransom is to be paid by his father-in-law. The plan, in Jerry's own mind, is foolproof. That is where things always seem to take a sharp turn down the wrong way of a one way street. The two men Jerry hires bungle every aspect of the job, as well as Jerry's father-in-law insisting he take control of the ransom drop off. That screws up Jerry's plans as he has badly short changed the two men on their cuts. Once things go wrong, the events keep spiraling out of control, inevitably crashing down upon all involved.

The real nuisance in the criminal's side is the pregnant chief of police, Marge Gunderson. After three murders occur in her county she is on the case, using all of her prowess/ineptitude to somehow unravel what is going on. One of the more compelling investigative moments/blunders is when Marge relaxes enough to allow Lundegaard to flee the interview, to her amazement. Frances McDormand's performance is brilliant. I remember seeing the movie for the first time and remarking how she was going to win an Oscar even though the movie debuted in February. What I did not expect was for her to win a Best Actress Oscar. In a ninety-seven minute movie her character does not appear until the thirty-first minute and is on screen for less than thirty-three minutes. To me, that should have qualified her as a supporting actor, yet the Academy works in mysterious ways.

Some may say that the true star of this amazing movie is the gratuitous violence, meant to play as a deterrent. Others will say the snowy landscapes are the focus, showing the isolationism of the area that drove those men to commit such indecent acts. I believe it is the language and authentic regional manner of speaking that sets this movie apart from any other. It is what is most remembered about this movie, becoming a character itself. It is perhaps the greatest achievement of the film, how the quasi-retarded mannerisms of that culture were showcased to effectively parody.

Fargo, at its core, is a comedy. The fact that many cannot see this is due to its depictions of a specific region of America and the exposing of their apparent eccentricities. More than simply that, the writing is crisp and the storyline works. It does not go overboard on comedy to sacrifice story aspects, but rather skillfully intertwines both elements together. The Coens are an integral part of why *Fargo* is so great. They are immersed in every aspect of the film, which translated into a labor of love rather than another ordinary film, the opposite of the dull stuff pumped out all the time.

45

ROCKY
1976

What good are a man's dreams if there is no one there to share them with him? One of the great misnomers of cinema is that *Rocky* is a movie about boxing. It is not. What makes *Rocky* such a great film is its detailed character depictions, specifically in how they overcome the monotonies of life. No one can argue that boxing is the main attraction, but it is the character interaction that raises *Rocky* above other formulaic movies that deal with the fight game. Anyone can throw a couple of fighters into the ring and show action. It has been done over in many films before *Rocky* and many films since. Those types of films come and go, because they do not have special qualities. It is from *Rocky's* heart and character interaction that the film transcends genre.

Rocky Balboa is a bum, make no mistake about it. Another way to describe him would be to call him a loser. Even when he wins, as is shown in the opening scene where he defeats 'Spider' Rico, he loses. He somehow cannot seem to escape it until he falls for someone exactly like him, the shy and quiet Adrian. In her, he sees a way to share his life with someone who seems the same as him. Rocky's courtship of Adrian is the true heart of the film. Two lovable nobodies who find happiness in each other, showing that everyone deserves someone, no matter what life has done to them. It is always better to be with someone than to be alone, out of which true love can eventually take form.

Everyone knows that part of the charm of *Rocky* is that special underdog versus champion element. Due to a fighter's injury and a marketing opportunity, Rocky is given the chance to step in and fight Apollo Creed for the heavyweight title. It is the opportunity of a lifetime. The pre fight training scenes are almost as legendary as the entire series has become. It does not matter that he loses. It only matters that he gives it his all and in the end is rewarded with true happiness. With Adrian by his side, victory is achieved. That more than anything is the point of this bittersweet film.

Just like the story of the great underdog rising up and battling the Goliath, in the form of Apollo Creed, *Rocky* went up against the powerhouses of film on Oscar night. This time it was *Rocky's* turn to triumph, taking home the top two awards at the most prestigious ceremony in movies. Although receiving four separate acting nominations not one actor or actress would claim victory on that night. Looking over the particular categories, only one of the four performers had a legitimate grievance in not claiming victory, Talia Shire, who lost to Faye Dunaway from *Network*.

Gotcha. Made you think *Rocky* would not be included on this list, after reading the final paragraph of the *Breaking Away* write-up. I am not sure why one would not expect this fantastic underdog story, with more heart than many romance movies made to provoke emotions and twice as much character to make a list such as this. I understand why some will undervalue this movie. It is primarily because of its many sequels, which at the time of this write-up another one is scheduled to be made. The negative opinion of *Rocky* is a direct result of the sequels produced to capitalize on box office profits.

44

THE NIGHT OF THE HUNTER
1955

What would a movie look like if it were directed by Captain Bligh? Not the Captain Bligh from history, yet rather the Captain Bligh portrayed in the famous book *The Mutiny on the Bounty*, later turned into a movie that depicted Captain Bligh as a tyrannical monster. Any movie directed by that character would play like some sort of nightmare. In 1955, those who love nightmares and frightening visuals got their wish. Actor Charles Laughton, the man who played the maniacal Captain Bligh to cruel perfection, directed his only movie, *The Night of the Hunter*.

Not so much a nightmare, the film was more of an adult fairy tale gone haywire. *Night of the Hunter* plays as if told by the Brothers Grimm and not *dumbed* down or *happied* up for children by Walt Disney. The film is shot in what one can only call a perpetual darkness. A dreamlike state is induced from watching, where comparisons to fairy-tales are immediately made, with the characters coming off at times as if they are in a comatose trance. This film has arguably the creepiest character in cinematic history, the evil preacher Harry Powell played by Robert Mitchum. While presenting a façade of pleasantness, Powell's evil nature shines through, as he gets angrier and angrier at the sin committed in front of his eyes. He actually believes that it is his duty to rid the world of sin by committing it himself.

During his time in prison for robbery Powell shares a cell with a man who was arrested for robbing a bank. He learns that the money is hidden somewhere with the man's family before he is executed for murdering two people. Once released, Powell finds the family, tricks his way into marrying the widow, murders her and then finds out where the money is, hidden in the young girl's doll. After the kids escape from the preacher and flee upriver, he eventually tracks them down, only to encounter his own downfall at the hands of the lady who takes the children in.

When the movie came out, the world did not seem ready for a movie with the feel and look of *The Night of the Hunter*. Some might say that the subject matter, a demented and villainous preacher tormenting and chasing after two innocent young children caused the backlash and complete ignoring of this movie for all major awards. There was not one nomination for any of the American Academy Awards for the movie, but additionally it was totally shut out for all awards. The American ignorance of the tense subject matter may have played a part. In 1992 however, the movie was somewhat vindicated with a National Film Registry Award, albeit too little and too late.

The Night of the Hunter is one of the most misunderstood movies ever made, in a variety of ways. Most do not see it as one of the strongest arguments against religious zealotry, despite its reliance upon Biblical stories and images. Many cannot understand the statement it makes that evil incarnate masquerading in the form of good can turn the hearts and minds of people to do their bidding. It was also both a financial and commercial failure, more than likely because it was so misconstrued We have cinema historians to thank for reminding the world about this brilliant movie, which is so unique in its look and feel that there may never be another film like it again.

43

JFK
1991

 Where were you when President John Fitzgerald Kennedy was shot? There are only a few moments in American history that are as remembered as vividly as the Kennedy assassination. Oliver Stone veered his already heralded career into an altogether fantastical direction with *JFK*, his ode to the bevy of suspicious events surrounding the investigation of the Kennedy assassination. If there were not enough conspiracy nuts in America, this spawned an entirely new generation of them. Based upon a fusion of two nonfiction books, *JFK* has not only changed the way we think, but also provided a thought provoking film that challenges us to question what is offered as truth. One of the primary themes of the film is that challenging accepted truths is not just our right, but also our duty.

 New Orleans D. A. Jim Garrison reopens the investigation into the Kennedy assassination, three years after the government determined that Lee Harvey Oswald acted alone. *JFK* is the absolutely mesmerizing account of one man's passion for finding out the truth regarding what was probably the worst event in America in over a century. Once Garrison's investigation goes public, his office is immediately turned into a circus by media and kept under surveillance by certain unnamed government agencies. Stone links the assassination, through Garrison's investigation and the nonfiction work of author Jim Marrs, all the way up to the White House.

 JFK clearly elucidates major inconsistencies and questions further debatable data, most notably the historic magazine cover photograph of Oswald holding a rifle, presumably the rifle that fired the 'magic' bullets. According to forensic analyses this appears to have been a doctored photo based upon shadows and inaccurate light configurations. This, among many other irregularities will always place doubt upon what exactly took place leading up to that horrible day in history. More than any other account of the assassination, this film shows that doubt will always exist as to what happened. That goes for even those who may or may not have been involved.

 The amazing cast is full of one fantastic performance after another. Listing the stars of this movie would take up an entire page and then some. Kevin Costner brings the perfect demeanor needed to play the main character, who becomes more and more distraught the more he learns about what can actually happen within the country he believed in. Tommy Lee Jones was the sole Oscar nominee and his performance is a sight to see. In comparison to the acting job of Joe Pesci though, who has numerous scenes with Jones, one has to wonder how Pesci was overlooked in favor of Jones.

 From a cinematic sense, it is Stone's innovative use of inter cutting thousands of non-linear scenes that provide essential background and create incredible suspense. Editing played such a major part of this movie that it seemed to be a character unto itself, deservedly rewarded with an Oscar for the magnificent and breakthrough look of the film. Oliver Stone has created a work of art wrapped inside an intellectual exploration for answers that may not even be there. I hate destroying the mystery of a list such as this, but *JFK* is simply the best work Stone has ever done.

42

TWELVE ANGRY MEN
1957

It is not easy to stand alone. When eleven men believe in the guilt of a boy and are prepared to send him to his death, one man has the courage to at least force a discussion of the case. *Twelve Angry Men* is a masterful story of what should go on inside a jury room, yet unfortunately probably never does. While the facts are discussed, the story allows and depends upon the revealing of the individual personalities of the jury members. It is these twelve men who clearly display how personal beliefs often affect or cloud the judgment of those that are given an incredible responsibility.

Juror number eight has the idea of spending a few moments to discuss the points of the case that has just been tried. His objections are not based upon hard facts, at first, but rather the idea that everyone deserves the right to have their case discussed. One by one, his arguments and points begin to expose flaws in the case against the defendant and win over members of the jury to his way of thinking. During this process, the jurors who were originally so convinced of his guilt begin to question and pose their own issues with the case, snowballing into further insights and discussion.

Throughout the deliberation, there are three members of the jury who are consistently against juror number eight, despite all the relevant issues brought up by the other members. Juror number three hates kids. This derives from his relationship with his son, which affects him so negatively that he has become a sadist. Juror number ten is a flat out bigot. Almost every comment from his lips is about the defendant's background, as opposed to remarking on the salient facts of the case. His prejudices, the story intimating that they were ingrained in him from early on, forbid any ability to analyze a situation in a clear manner. Juror number four is portrayed as the intellectual of the three guilty mainstays. His eventual transformation marks the changing point of the case.

This is a fictitious setting, yet the film points out the true flaws of the jury system. The larger implications from this story are that convenience often outweighs the greater responsibility of jurors to ponder the true merits of a case. Lumet's crafty direction within a single location, the jury deliberation room, is as close to art as this medium allows. The movie never seems confined. In fact, the opposite is true. As the story unfolds, despite the single cramped setting, a definitive feeling of openness is presented. *Twelve Angry Men* is stereotypical in its presentation of the jury members, yet it is truly ambitious in its belief system where intellect triumphs over predetermined biases.

Twelve Angry Men was another in the long line of those pesky little movies that reach the zenith because of their excellence only to be swatted down by the grand sweeping epic. It was a fore drawn conclusion that *Twelve Angry Men* was going home empty handed, yet what is more important is the statement, rather than the Oscar wins. That small victory was achieved by simply getting two major nominations, although Henry Fonda was mysteriously passed over for his amazing acting. Despite losing all three awards, *Twelve Angry Men* has grown to become a definitive fan favorite.

41

FIELD OF DREAMS
1989

"If you build it, he will come". The mystery of who the baseball field is actually built for is what makes *Field of Dreams* such a fantastic story. An absolute tale of majesty and wonder akin to a modern day fairy-tale, *Field of Dreams*, told from a human perspective, highlights that time honored theme of redemption. The movie also incorporates additional idealistic subject matter such as censorship, personal privacy of the famous, the symbolism of 1960's counter culture versus Midwestern core values and that one last shot at glory, albeit in a lesser capacity. It is truly that second chance at redemption that the movie emulates. After all, everyone deserves a second chance.

Iowa farmer Ray Kinsella begins to hear ghost like voices in his cornfield, instructing him to perform a number of tasks, most notably to plow under his corn and build a baseball field. Once he builds the field, his finances begin to become a worry for him. Kinsella additionally questions his faith and sanity. Then one night, legendary but banned former baseball player 'Shoeless' Joe Jackson shows up on the field. It is one of those memorable scenes in cinema, played flawlessly by Kevin Costner, wearing all the necessary emotions of amazement, apprehension and anxiousness upon his face. Once Ray has helped 'Shoeless' Joe back on the field, the voice then asks for more.

Thus begins a magical road trip of discovery earnestly challenging his resolve. The first stop is Boston where Ray must enlist the services of famed writer and recluse Terence Mann. Ray finally convinces Mann to attend a baseball game with him, where a voice gives them both further instructions. Their next stop is Minnesota, where they are to locate a man named Archibald Graham. When they arrive they learn that 'Doc' Graham has been dead since 1972. With faith on their side, not even death can stop their mission. On the way back to Iowa they pick up a young Archie Graham. Graham proves his worth, on the field and in his choice of going into medicine. However, the voices heard by Ray were not really about helping Jackson or Graham.

While it is true that many actors would say it is merely performing their craft that brings them the most pleasure and greatest rewards everyone knows that the Oscars are what most strive for. That recognition reaffirms the fact that they are doing not only solid work, but also exemplary work within their chosen profession. It does not really matter who wins, but the recognition of a job well done is something that pleases everyone, despite the few out there that choose to make specific statements about the process. The Academy missed three great performances in this fantastic film, James Earl Jones, Kevin Costner and Burt Lancaster as the elder 'Moonlight' Graham.

Bringing together two great American traditions, baseball and family, *Field of Dreams* uses a number of different plot mechanisms to arrive at its grand theme of redemption, between a father and son who had too little time together. Regardless about whether you like baseball or not, this movie is about something more. It is about hope. Family, faith, idealism and even baseball all have their roots in hope, making for one of the great endings in cinema, where hope is ultimately rewarded in a truly unbelievable manner.

40

REDS
1981

    Many say that *Doctor Zhivago* is the single greatest love story set during the turbulent times of the Russian Revolution. This idea may have been true when that book won the Nobel Prize in 1958, or when the movie came out in 1965. In 1981 though, that idea was strongly challenged by the retelling of the enthralling romance between Americans John Reed and Louise Bryant, played by Warren Beatty and Diane Keaton. A gripping love story set among the backdrop of the formation of American socialist politics, Beatty crafts an amazing piece of intellectual Americana. The characters are richly layered, man of them challenging the notions of a country that thrusted beliefs upon them.

    A fantastically crafted tale on the courage of conviction in the face of anxiousness over the specter of emerging communism, *Reds* offers a great narrative of political history. Told from the side of the radicals who theorized about economic ideologies, this multi-layered account involves the creation of a political party, its subsequent fracturing and the roadblocks that are presented by those with differing beliefs, specifically within the framework of their own party. One of the best critiques of the difficulty in transference of politics across cultural boundaries, it is incredibly moving to watch Reed's transformation from journalist to political activist. His journey takes him to the center of Eastern European socialism, realizing that problems exist everywhere regardless of culture.

    It is not easy to challenge the system, especially when the country you grew up in and belonged to was acting in direct opposition to what you believed. The foundation of the United States was built upon freedom of thought, one of the fundamental ideals of democracy, yet during this turbulent time those in power felt the need to disregard those ideals in favor of oppressing conflicting thought, despite fighting enemies who engaged in the same activity. It was ambitious to create a movie that showcased the darker side of an otherwise beloved period in American history. *Reds* was critically acclaimed upon its release, yet due to its politics has become widely underappreciated.

    The true magnificence of *Reds* though, is the sweeping romance between Reed and Bryant. It is their mutual intellectualism that brings them together and keeps them coming back to each other. Despite stints apart, where loneliness drives Bryant into the arms of famous playwright Eugene O'Neill, they always find the road back to each other. No matter what the stakes of their own beliefs and how far they are willing to go to see them come to fruition, their longing for one another always rises above everything else. Nothing can stop them from being together, including a final journey leading up to one of the magical moments of cinema history, their reuniting in Russia.

    Filled with amazing acting and writing, *Reds* has become a forgotten masterpiece. It lost to the British import *Chariots of Fire* in the Best Picture race. It had been dominated in the public eye by the Spielberg adventure thriller *Raiders of the Lost Ark*. It failed to wrest the top two acting awards from screen legends Henry Fonda and Katherine Hepburn. All these elements worked against this perfectly balanced historical treasure, helping to keep its greatness in relative obscurity.

39

REBECCA
1940

Can a man get past the loss of his wife? Will a new marriage suddenly breathe life into him? Or will the loss disturb him until the end of his days? *Rebecca* is a haunting tale of love lost but not forgotten and the effects it has upon the man's second wife as she struggles through life in their grand estate. *Rebecca* has the distinction of having been the first American film directed by Alfred Hitchcock. Remarkably, the film was nominated for eleven academy awards, yet only won two. One of those was the Best Picture award though, toppling a variety of great films in the process.

While vacationing in Monte Carlo, Max De Winter plans to end his life. He has recently lost his dear wife, Rebecca, and he may not be able to go on without her. De Winter meets a young American woman who revives his spirit for life. They marry and return to his ancestral home, Manderlay. The new Mrs. De Winter meets Mrs. Danvers, the woman who runs the house and has a strange way about her, specifically in her loyalty to the first Mrs. De Winter, in an Oscar nominated and creepy scene stealing performance by Judith Anderson. The new Mrs. De Winter also learns that Rebecca, the first wife, still has a hold over not only the servants, but the entire house as well.

As time goes by, the new Mrs. De Winter discovers the strange occurrences within the house, marked by the memory of Rebecca. The strain eventually becomes too much on her as her mind begins to give way. She believes that the ghost of a dead wife is haunting her, whether simply in memory or in actuality. At the same time, Mrs. Danvers, loyal to Rebecca, constantly torments her. The only one she feels close to is Max, yet his despair over Rebecca and what occurred almost a year ago not only worries her but is beginning to frighten her. Rebecca still has a deep hold over him also.

Both Laurence Olivier and Joan Fontaine are excellent as the tragic couple, yet as stated earlier, Judith Anderson steals the show. Olivier lost to Jimmy Stewart for *The Philadelphia Story*, while Fontaine lost to the equally beautiful Ginger Rogers for *Kitty Foyle*. Stewart's win was clearly a makeup award for his performance the previous year, yet Rogers was a well deserved winner. Anderson also lost, yet to an actress who gave a clearly better performance. Although the movie took home the Oscar for Best Picture, Hitchcock mysteriously lost the Best Director Award to John Ford. Ford would also win the following year becoming the first director to accomplish that feat.

This able retelling of Daphne du Maurier's gothic masterpiece shows the inner workings of a relationship that appears doomed from the start. Not just a story about relationships, *Rebecca* is equal parts ghost story and mystery, told in that grand style of eerie suspense that evokes memories of a time past. There is no need for blood soaked victims or gory encounters. The true key to a suspense mystery is what is not shown, but rather offered up to make the audiences respond on a visceral level. The moviegoer becomes a part of the film, feeling both their pain as he copes with the loss of Rebecca and she struggles to keep the love of her husband, while keeping her sanity. Only one thing can save them, revealing the secret of Manderlay, presented in that classic Hitchcock style.

38

HIGH NOON
1952

What would you do if you knew someone was coming to kill you, on the day of your wedding? Does a man leave town and run in fear for the rest of his life or stay to fight his battle, even though the odds are stacked against him? Those are the questions that bind this magnificent tale together. *High Noon* is not about a great showdown, unlike *Gunfight at the OK Corral*, or the more modern version, *Tombstone*. It is about character, plain and simple. Every single person in the story is making a decision based upon their internal makeup, not right or wrong, but merely how they view themselves. That is what true character is, a decision one makes based upon his beliefs. This is evident as Gary Cooper's marshal searches for assistance, which goes surprisingly unfulfilled.

Three men ride into town, awaiting the arrival of the noontime train. Across town, the marshal weds a Quaker, played by Gary Cooper and Grace Kelly. The couple is getting ready to leave town, with the new marshal on his way the next day. A telegram arrives explaining that a man the marshal put away five years ago was just pardoned. The three men are awaiting his arrival, for the opportunity to take revenge. While almost completely out of town, the marshal and his bride turn the carriage around and head back to town. After returning he learns that nobody will help him and that his new bride will leave him if he stays to fight. It is not in his character to just leave.

As stated earlier, this movie is all about character. In the face of eminent danger, there are those that will rise up to the occasion and those that will run for cover and hide. The town is made up of both kinds of people, with the marshal as the only kind that shall stick to his guns and stay the course. Only his bride, an outsider to the town, comes back to help save him just before her train, the noontime train, leaves the station. The marshal realizes that the only people he can count on in the town are himself and his bride. It is a stark lesson to learn, but one that matures him as to the true nature of people. His final act is to throw his badge down and leave in disgust.

Some call *High Noon* the performance of Gary Cooper's career. That is tough to agree with since Cooper has been nominated for so many great performances throughout his career, winning a Best Actor Oscar for *High Noon* and *Sergeant York*, the first man to win Best Actor Oscars in consecutive decades. A nomination in 1936 for *Mr. Deeds Goes To Town* made Cooper only the second man to be nominated in three consecutive decades. The only thing for certain is that his role as the Marshal who refuses to run from danger is merely one in an amazing and storied career. Kelly's performance is overshadowed by the great cinematography, almost a character itself.

The Western genre was transformed by *High Noon*. No longer did this type of movie require a battle against marauding Indians, knock-down saloon fights shown in high speed motion for effect or formulaic quests for glorious land. This was an internal story of bravery, courage and a man sticking to his convictions despite all that is against him. Marshal Will Kane is not just a hero because he stayed and won, but simply because he stayed. That is enough to make him a hero.

37

ON THE WATERFRONT
1954

Should life imitate art? The best art comes from life. It is derived out of life experience. Some experiences are not as pleasant as others. This is the unfortunate nature of life, providing the story behind the story for this heralded movie. The back story might be as fascinating as the movie itself. Director Eliza Kazan used the story within this film to justify his actions. Kazan was tabbed as a communist. In 1952 he appeared before the committee on un-American activities, announced he was a Communist and named names of other members and party sympathizers. Eventually, the ideology of communism wore off for Kazan. Perhaps it was the stigma attached to it or he evolved in his own socio-economic outlook. *On the Waterfront* was Kazan's justification for his actions.

An ex-prizefighter turned longshoreman named Terry Malloy, in an amazing Oscar winning performance by Marlon Brando, witnesses the death of a longshoreman named Doyle. Doyle made the mistake of speaking to the police regarding waterfront corruption. Malloy was indirectly involved, as he was told to send Doyle up to the rooftop, where he was to be thrown off for talking to the cops. Once another longshoreman, who plans on talking to the police, is also murdered right in front of Malloy's eyes, this only helps add to Malloy's confusion about the situation.

To make matters worse, Malloy falls for Doyle's sister. Along with the parish priest she is intent on not only finding Doyle's murderer, but also putting an end to the corruption on the docks. Confusion on whether or not Malloy will testify against the mob boss after receiving a subpoena arises, so a decision is made to take him out. Charley, Terry's brother, who also works for the mob boss, can not go through with the murder. As a result, Charley is murdered. Insistent upon revenge, Terry is talked out of violence, but also talked into testifying against the mob boss. Terry is now all alone, considered as a traitor by his friends until he proves he was right in speaking the truth.

For three straight years Marlon Brando had been nominated for a Best Actor Oscar. He lost in 1951 for his terrific performance in *A Streetcar Named Desire*, perhaps the best of his career. He lost the following year for *Viva Zapata!*. In 1953, another loss came for his role in *Julius Caesar*. One can only imagine how Brando must have felt when he was told of a fourth straight nomination, especially since he was up against two former winners and screen icons, Humphrey Bogart and Bing Crosby. Thankfully Brando won, as did Eva Marie Saint for playing his love interest.

From what I know about Kazan, it is hard not to see him as a coward. He turned his back on his friends, named their names to an unconstitutional committee and then tried to validate his betrayal by stating his beliefs were incorrect. Kazan saved his own ass, nothing more, nothing less. *On The Waterfront*, despite its hidden subtext and its petty attempt at ego validation, is an amazing film. Regardless of what drove Kazan to create this masterpiece, *On The Waterfront* should not be forced or subjected to any external ideologies. It is a movie and should stand on its own merit.

36

NETWORK
1976

    Television could not possibly be as crazy as real life, could it? Actually, it can be even crazier. Television is reflective of the realities of life and wholly indicative of the culture that is entrenched by it. That ideal has never been clearer than in the reality laden model of television dominating the air waves currently, highlighting misery, idiocy and human despair. The audience keeps watching, so the networks keep showing these reality shows of wretchedness and feeble minded or unconscionable people as pseudo-stars. Sometimes they get lucky and the depraved miscreants possess both qualities, making the show's ratings even better. That's what it is all about: ratings.

    Anchorman Howard Beale is fired after a long and glorious career. He is fired due to poor ratings. On what was to be his final broadcast, Beale states that he is going to kill himself on air. After an on air apology goes awry the following night, the spinning of the network wheels commence. Beale is seen as a cash cow for the failing news division of the network, which causes the firing of long time newsman Max Schumacher and installing of the head of programming into his role.

    Network is a visionary, yet highly satirical combination of the two main divisions of a network, programming, designed for profit, and news, historically a negative cash flow division, to maximize profit margins. Although the behind the scenes aspects of the network are fascinating to witness, specifically Ned Beatty's tyrannical deliberation of modern economics, the true wonder is in the all too brief showcases of the terrorist programming meetings, where a pseudo-communist faction argues over revenue sharing, distribution costs and foreign rights. The fantastical irony of a militant organization quarrelling over definitively capitalistic concepts defines this movie as whole. It plays as over the top farce. Even in farce, the reality of truth escapes and seeps its way inside.

    Network is what many movies are not, incisive and intelligent. Often times, those that try to make these types of statements forfeit story for sermonizing. This movie does not, creating both clever insights and marvelous storytelling. It has been called a scathing attack on the immoral aspects of corporate television. I see it differently. To me, it is the precursor toward the creation of reality television, predicting its arrival, its absurd glorification, its rise to prominence and lastly, its inevitable implosion. Such is the nature of life and culture, which is always going to be reflected in the television programming that will be produced. *Network* is cynical, but that is an understatement.

    It is tough to state what aspect of *Network* is the best; the acting, the direction or the script. Three of the four acting Oscars were won by this movie as well as the award for Best Original Screenplay. *Network* received five acting nominations in all, becoming one of only less than ten movies to achieve that feat. Peter Finch, Faye Dunaway and Beatrice Straight were the three actors who won, with Finch's award having been the first posthumous Oscar ever awarded that was not a lifetime achievement or humanitarian award. Paddy Chayefsky won his third Oscar for writing, yet Lumet is the best part of *Network*. Once again he is responsible for creating an absolute classic.

35

CHINATOWN
1974

Private eye Jake Gittes takes a routine case, to spy on a husband and catch him with another woman. It was the type of case he had done numerous times before. From his own admission it was his specialty. The only problem; it was not the man's wife who hired Gittes, as he would soon find out. That meant one thing, not only was the man being setup, but so was Gittes. In seeing the main character for only a brief moment on screen, one immediately understands that this is unacceptable to him. He will not allow himself to be made a sucker. It is not in his personality.

The movie masterfully transports the audience back to Los Angeles of the 1930's, when it was still primarily an emerging desert community. It was a time when opportunities were seized by those with wealth, strictly for the purpose of obtaining more wealth. This is something that Gittes does not understand, providing one of the great back and forth dialogues of the movie, with the eccentric character played by legendary film director John Huston. It is also one of the primary themes of the movie. Those with power feel they can get whatever they want, regardless of who it affects.

Chinatown is more than just the wealthy pulling strings and using their power to attain more wealth. Starting out with the standard detective noir, the movie delves into numerous sub-stories, all blending into one cohesive plot. There are double crosses, red herrings, police corruption, murders, land scandals, intrigue at every level of the story, plot twists that continually change the flow of the story (in a positive and clever way) all that masterfully lead up to the grand finale, where the whole story is ultimately explained. Gittes, the fast talking and wise-cracking private eye who wants to help those in need, eventually finds himself back in the one place he does not want to be, Chinatown.

Chinatown is director Roman Polanski's crowning achievement in cinema. He will never come close to anything as brilliant as this again. One reason why is because he cowardly fled the United States of America over a criminal case, so the projects for him are limited. Polanksi, forty three at the time, had drugged and raped a girl of thirteen years old under the guise of taking sexually explicit pictures of her. Despite consent, there exists a humane law to protect children from sexual predators such as Polanski. His indecent acts were of a harsh felonious nature. Needless to say, Polanski's career never returned to the glory of *Chinatown*, although in 2002 he was awarded a Best Director Oscar for *The Pianist*. Too bad he could not come to America to receive his Oscar.

Any analysis of *Chinatown* should include a discussion of the two leads, Jack Nicholson and Faye Dunaway. Neither of them won acting awards for this movie, yet many critics and film historians feel that their Best Actor and Actress victories, in 1975 for *One Flew Over the Cuckoo's Nest* and 1976 for *Network* respectively, were makeup wins for their performances in *Chinatown*. I completely agree that the Academy is notorious for handing out makeup Oscars, yet I completely disagree that their victories resulted from *Chinatown*. Both winning acting performances are the high points of their storied careers. The Oscars they received were absolutely warranted. Nicholson could have easily won for both performances. Dunaway's loss is more acceptable to handle though.

34

THE MALTESE FALCON
1941

Why would someone remake a movie based upon a detective novel that had already been made twice before, within the last decade? The answer is, because he could. John Huston chose the Dashiell Hammett novel to make his directorial debut. He saw what had been done to Hammett's famous novel before, most recently in 1936, yet marveled at the possibilities. What this story called for was a fast talking, hard nosed main character who was both good and alternatively outside of the law, what Hammett depicted. The original move to polish up the story, making the movie seem more formulaic, took away the greater texture of the plot. *The Maltese Falcon* relied upon detective Sam Spade portrayed as a main character who was not the average hero. Hollywood had been used to the typical detective who went by the book and solved the crime in a perfect gentlemanly manner.

The Maltese Falcon is an anything but standard detective story. A mysterious girl hires two detectives, yet one of the detectives is murdered at the beginning of the story. This act sets the story in motion, which includes the police element. The police suspect one detective for murdering his partner because they discover he might have been sleeping with his partner's wife. As Spade searches for the truth he stumbles upon an even greater mystery, the search for a mysterious jewel encrusted falcon. That relic is worth more than the lives of the people that have been killed over it.

The mysterious falcon eventually arrives at Spade's office, after there are many encounters with those who know its value. The final confrontation occurs at Spade's apartment. Rather than the standard revelation of whodunit in many detective movies a mutual agreement is met by almost all parties regarding the falcon. Once an important discovery is made about this falcon, the quest must be continued. After seventeen years of searching, failure is not an option for this lot. Despite the fact that Spade appears to have become one of the villains, it was all done to save his own neck.

Two important film elements were created with this groundbreaking work, the creation of the *'film noir'* picture and the use of the anti-hero. The anti-hero is that strangest of fictional creatures who acts in a negative manner in order to achieve good. Villains are usually the more exciting characters in any given story, because what drove them to their way of thinking shapes their actions. With the advent of the anti-hero a new character was born who was just as interesting as any villain. In many cases, the anti-hero is actually more intriguing than any villain.

The Maltese Falcon was a landmark film in a many other ways. It can be best remembered for introducing two legendary icons to the status of cinematic stardom. Humphrey Bogart, who played Sam Spade, was toiling as the gangster in numerous low budget B-class pictures. There was the opinion in Hollywood that he could not carry a picture with his acting. *The Maltese Falcon* proved that notion wrong. His performance in this highly successful and innovative film led to Bogart becoming a leading man, which in turn led to *Casablanca*. The other icon to emerge from this film would be director John Huston, who would also gain immensely from this film's success.

33

THE CONVERSATION
1974

Francis Ford Coppola's *The Conversation* is not your average movie. Delving into the world of high tech surveillance, Coppola's story is a tale of personal claustrophobia gone awry. The setting is designed as tight to show the main character's personality as well as personifying the world that he lives and works in. It is a world where anyone can know everything about you. There is no privacy if someone is only an earshot away from knowing all your secrets. This in turn promotes the kind of world the main character lives in. It appears as if his work has taken over every aspect of his life, creating an emptiness filled only by what comes naturally to him, listening to other people lives.

Surveillance expert Harry Caul is hired to spy on two people. It appears to be a basic job. One of the rules that Harry lives by is that it is not his business to care what the conversations are about, only to get them on tape. Once he starts to get emotionally involved, as has happened before, that is when the trouble usually starts. Harry does not want to make that mistake again.

Unable to help himself, Harry becomes involved in his current job. Immediately, things in his sheltered life begin to unravel. As a result of a past assignment, people were murdered. This fact continues to haunt him, shaping the way he lives his life. Because of the past Harry feels it is his duty to do whatever possible to insure that it does not happen again. The key now is to study enough about the conversation to prevent any wrongdoing, although that is not as easy as it may seem.

The Conversation is a unique character study. The main character is isolated because he chooses to be. He has only the most basic of relationships. There are those he chooses to hire for jobs and those he gets involved with until the time has come where he must reveal personal information or leave. He feels more comfortable leaving a situation as soon as it reaches that level. The only true friend he has is his close associate, yet Harry's cold demeanor drives him to work for a competitor.

This movie is not for everyone. It is often purposefully repetitive and slow, functioning that way for the benefit of the story. Although there is a developing sense of intrigue and suspense as the movie builds, there is almost no action, relying on the developing story to drive the movie. This is not a flashy film. It is one that challenges us to think. Coppola's best original film is an expose into acute paranoia. There is a valid argument that this amazing film showed the promise of what Coppola could have accomplished had he not been held up to the high standards of the Godfather films.

The Conversation was shut out on Oscar night by *The Godfather II*. Despite both films having been directed by Coppola, few remember this one. Fewer know that it was written and directed by Coppola, the director of mega hits and epic blockbusters. This small movie with the deep inner message won the prestigious Golden Palm award at the Cannes Film Festival. When the Oscars came around, many thought that *The Conversation* had no chance of receiving any accolades. There was the possibility that Coppola could win both writing awards. Sadly, he did not. *The Conversation* went down as a film that would forever be overshadowed by another directed by the same man.

32

TOUCH OF EVIL
1958

    There are myths that develop among some of the Hollywood films. The disputes that exist over a director's vision and the studio's desire for profit are that of legend. Orson Welles' *Touch of Evil* is one of those stories. Welles came out publicly to thoroughly disown the film, after studio executives forced re-shoots, added shots and cut or re-edited the film to their own specific standards. When the butchered studio version was released in 1958, it failed miserably. Recently, a fifty-eight page memo was discovered outlining Welles' complete editing instructions of the film. This re-cut version, according to Welles' vision, has been hailed worldwide as a noir masterpiece.

    There are multiple stories within this gripping tale of corruption and intrigue in a Mexican border town. It starts out with a bang, literally, as a car explodes. A Mexican narcotics officer, Michael Vargas, happens to be at the scene. He is accompanied by his new bride and quickly becomes involved in the case as an observer. The local police chief, Hank Quinlan, takes charge. His methods immediately arouse suspicion to Vargas. When searching the house of a suspect, evidence is planted and the focus of the story shifts from a murder mystery to a battle between these two men.

    In the meantime, Vargas' bride is harassed by a group of street hoods. These hoods are on orders from a drug dealer whose brother is about to be put away in Mexico by Vargas. For her own safety, Vargas' bride is stashed at a motel. While there, she is terrorized by a wild party going on in the room next door and finally, in an ambiguous manner, is drugged and gang-raped. Framing her for narcotics use and murder leads to Quinlan's downfall. It is his longtime partner that discovers Quinlan is indeed a dishonest officer and behind the whole frame-up.

    Touch of Evil displayed an all star cast, most playing key supporting roles. Charlton Heston played the role of the main character Michael Vargas. Much has been written about his attempts to come off as a Mexican, but that is generally and unfortunately compared to his Oscar winning performance the following year in *Ben-Hur*. Janet Leigh is excellent as Susan Vargas. Add former Oscar winner Mercedes McCambridge as a female gang leader, Akim Tamaroff as the evil but incredibly inept mobster Joe Grandi and the best performance of the lot outside of Welles', Joseph Calleia as Quinlan's partner to the mix and *Touch of Evil* became a wonderfully acted film.

    The true star of the film is Orson Welles. He directed, starred and wrote the screenplay. His utterly disgusting portrayal of Quinlan, a morbidly obese and highly corrupt police officer who would rather plant evidence than chance the guilty going free, provides a stark realism to this gritty thriller. At the heart of this story is his racist cop. It was however, important for Quinlan not to take over the movie, but rather guide the story through the long coming plunge into his own demise. Even after his death at the hands of his longtime partner, it is ironically discovered that his instincts were right on this specific case. There was no need for planting evidence. That is just the core of the misfortune behind this tragic figure of a man, who at the heart of it all had simply lost his way.

31

L.A. CONFIDENTIAL
1997

Does it really matter how the job gets done, as long as it gets done and the criminals are brought to justice? In the Los Angeles Police Department of the 1930's and 1940's, all that mattered were results. A newer style of police was needed to ensure that the public's best interest was at hand. In developing from a cow town to a major metropolitan city, those who were charged with watching over the city desperately needed an image change. It was not easy for many hardnosed traditional officers, leading to an even more important question, how would those officers deal with this change?

Focusing on three officers, *L. A. Confidential* showcases that specific changeover from a corrupt yet effective thug squad to efficient defenders and protectors of the people. The three main officers; the ultra violent yet compassionate Bud White represents the old guard, Ed Exley is the new breed intellectual who does everything by the book and the officer who fits in right between them, Jack Vincennes, the flashy celebrity cop who has all the inside connections and is not above accepting a payoff. These three all form a perfect blend of what a dedicated officer should be. Working together, at different intervals in the story, they find that their individual talents combined achieve far better results than going at it alone, which shows the obvious drawbacks to their personality type.

Three specific events form the basis for this highly entertaining fictional account. The first of these was *"Bloody Christmas"*, where a couple of Mexicans are arrested for assaulting two officers and then beaten by revenge seeking cops at police headquarters. The next event is the massacre at a coffee shop, the Night Owl, where six people are murdered, including a recently fired police officer involved in *"Bloody Christmas"*. The final event, which spans the whole movie, is the murders of organized crime members and stolen heroin, forcing some policeman to make tough choices. All three are connective tissue within a tremendously multi-layered story of corruption gone haywire.

An all star cast highlights this ultra realistic tale. The three main stars are Russell Crowe as Bud White, Guy Pearce as Ed Exley and a highly stylized performance by Kevin Spacey as the celebrity driven officer Jack Vincennes. All three main characters work off each other masterfully, pressing all the right buttons to provide a trio of amazing performances. Longtime actor James Cromwell, as police captain Dudley Smith who knows that a little corruption can go along way and highly underrated actor David Strathairn, as the millionaire pimp Pierce Padgett both shine as usual. The movie is often stolen however, by the diminutive Danny DeVito as a cynical tabloid reporter.

Director Curtis Hanson has created a visual masterpiece, clearly evocative of the times in which the story takes place. It is a neo-noir the likes of *Chinatown* and every bit as creative a detective story. *L. A. Confidential*, while pure enjoyment, is an extraordinary commentary on what is actually necessary to obtain and exemplify justice. The film highlights three extremely different personalities who use dissimilar methodologies to obtain their own brand of justice. It is a terrific indictment of what can happen when justice is taken one step too far, or in this case, over the line.

30

FROM HERE TO ETERNITY
1953

The Japanese bombing of Pearl Harbor on December 7th, 1941 was not the only story of the men and women inhabiting the island of Hawaii. From a novel by James Jones, *From Here To Eternity* offered a multi textured story about numerous characters unprepared for what was to come, not only with the bombing they could not know about, but with their own lives. Offering a unique perspective into the inner workings of an army unit stationed in Hawaii prior to the infamous attack, director Fred Zinneman has crafted one of the great romantic movies of all time.

There are two main characters, Prewitt and Warden, although many of the critical experiences are told through Prewitt's perspective. Prewitt was a former boxer that accidentally blinded a man in the ring. His new commanding officer, Holmes, wants him to fight for their company. Prewitt refuses. As a result, he is tormented by the company boxers on the orders of Holmes. Prewitt takes all they can hand out and more, refusing to give them and Holmes the satisfaction. One true friend, Maggio, helps to keep Prewitt's sanity, in an Oscar winning supporting role played by Frank Sinatra. It is only a matter of time before Maggio finds himself in trouble.

The other main character, Warden, works directly under the command of Holmes. It is Warden who actually runs the company though. Holmes' only concern is with his own advancement and Warden sees him for the goal-oriented officer that he is. From the suffering Holmes imparts upon Prewitt, Warden forms a bond with him. Warden shows that even though he is in command of the men he is just and fair, in direct contrast with Holmes. Warden will later refuse to apply to become an officer for fear of becoming like Holmes, whom he thoroughly despises.

Similar to *Network*, *From Here To Eternity* is one of only a handful of films to garner five acting nominations. Unlike *Network*, one of only two films to win three, it swept the supporting categories, with Sinatra and Donna Reed taking home Oscars. The other three nominees were Montgomery Clift, who played Prewitt, Burt Lancaster, who played Warden and Deborah Kerr in a highly underappreciated role as the wife of Homes who falls for Warden. She has no assumptions about life and plays the role to perfection. Only the budding beauty of Audrey Hepburn playing the role of her lifetime as a princess sneaking away from her privileged life kept Kerr from victory.

The other grand cinematic theme in *From Here To Eternity* is love and tragic love at that. Prewitt develops a relationship with a hooker that will never truly work out because of their differences. Warden has an affair with Holmes' wife, supplying one of the greatest romantic scenes in cinematic history, the storied embrace while lying on the beach as the tide rolls in. All four people know it will end in an unfulfilling way, despite their hopes and aspirations for something better. Even though hope is lost, there is no real time for mourning because the attack on Pearl Harbor begins, ending in the death of Prewitt, who was merely trying to help his unit. The story remains fresh and timeless to this day, marking the second straight year that Zinneman helmed the best film.

29

THE STING
1973

How far would you go to get revenge? Would you risk everything, even your life? The answer is: of course. The key is doing it in such a way that is not only creative, but also in such a way that the person you are getting revenge upon does not come after you again. What *Butch Cassidy and the Sundance Kid* failed to do, *The Sting* more than accomplishes. This is the buddy movie that made the pairing of Paul Newman and Robert Redford a household name, even though they only appeared in two movies together. Although *Butch Cassidy and the Sundance Kid* gets far more credit, it is their chemistry in *The Sting* that is just one of the many reasons why this caper movie works so well.

One of the partners of a small time grifter, played by Redford, is killed by a mob boss after pulling a scam on one of his numbers runners. To exact revenge, he goes to Chicago to set up a big con on the mob boss. Once there, he joins forces with the man who knew his former partner, played by Newman, and they begin the set-up. The con begins by getting into a rigged poker game and breaking it in their favor. This was laying the hook, where the mark, played by Robert Shaw, is prepped for an even bigger takedown. Redford, working with Newman but pretending to be double crossing him for the set-up, convinces Shaw that he wants to take Newman and his operation down.

A test run is tried. It works of course, because it is preset to work. Now the mark is in. In the meantime, Redford is hunted down by a crooked policeman after passing counterfeit bills during a shakedown and a hired assassin. Just when you think you understand, the plot quickly shifts gears. Once the crooked policeman gets too close, the feds make an appearance. Newman has a federal file on him for pulling numerous big time scams, although that is not truly the entire story. Nothing is what it seems in this movie. That provides the primary element of the story, suspense.

One of the most overlooked items with regards to *The Sting* is its spawning of a generation of movies to follow. I am not speaking about the awful sequel, *The Sting II*, but rather of the masses of movies that used the intricate plot gimmick of extreme trickery throughout that was mastered and displayed by *The Sting*. I am referring to a conscious tricking of the audience to believe the plot is moving one way, only to reveal that they have double crossed. Due to the popularity of *The Sting*, even though *Butch Cassidy and the Sundance Kid* is both more popular and critically acclaimed a whole new era of storytelling was created. The new wave of con caper films that followed owes a great deal of gratitude to *The Sting*. It was not the first caper film, but the best of those early efforts.

There are more surprises to come, with numerous twists and turns, double crosses and triple crosses as the audience eventually discovers who is playing who, why and what the big con really entails. Excellent performances all around, with Redford getting an Oscar nomination for his role. The irony here is that in this movie, Newman's performance is the far superior of the two, yet went unrewarded. However, in their first movie together, Redford's performance is the better one, with Newman receiving the praise. That being said, *The Sting* is nothing short of fantastic. It is the classic caper movie, told in such a stylized manner that it leaves you smiling and wanting more of the same.

28

REAR WINDOW
1954

When does voyeurism become dangerous? For a man confined to a chair in his apartment, looking through his binoculars at the world around him is his only outlet. It is a way to live vicariously through the lives of others. Watching their daily routines reminds him of what life was like prior to breaking his leg, when he was a top notch photographer visiting exotic locales and getting into danger with his camera. Why should those binoculars be any different? As he watches the various people come and go, doing the things that he used to be able to do, could his imagination be getting the better of him? That is entirely possible as he believes he has discovered a murder.

L. B. Jeffries, played by Jimmy Stewart, spends his time by peering into the windows of the neighboring apartments. There is the woman that he designates *'miss lonely hearts'*, who has no one and the woman known as *'miss torso'*, who has too many suitors. In these windows, the full gamut of relationships is on display. This was as a metaphor to explain Jeffries' beliefs on his own relationship with a wealthy fashion model who deeply loves him, played by the gorgeous Grace Kelly. It is through staring into one of these windows that he believes a man has murdered his wife. The reporter inside him is now engrossed with the possibility that his neighbor murdered his wife. Kelly simply takes it as another excuse for Stewart to ignore their relationship situation, at first. Soon, she is won over.

To keep closer to him, Kelly begins to aid Stewart in their quasi-investigation into whether a murder took place. His nurse then joins in with them, helping while the plot thickens. A detective friend of Stewart's is called and reacts with obvious skepticism, trying to explain that there must be alternative explanations. Things are not always what they seem, with evidence from the other tenants to prove that. That is, until the finale where the tension builds and the intrigue comes in hordes. The final moments of the film are the most chilling, keeping with that grand Hitchcock style.

Rear Window is Hitchock's second entry on this list. One of his most used actors appeared in this film, James Stewart, working in his second of four films for Hitchcock. Stewart's performance was mysteriously absent among the Oscar nominations, although it was obvious that the Academy owed an Oscar to Marlon Brando and that this would be his year so his absence has never been that big of a deal. Grace Kelly, as Stewart's socialite girlfriend gives another great performance, yet she would win an Oscar for her leading performance that year in *The Country Girl*. *Rear Window* failed to win any of its four Oscar nominations, including screenplay, cinematography, sound and direction.

Once Stewart's observing is discovered by the murderer, the intensity dramatically picks up. For most of the movie it is played as if Stewart is overreacting. This is one of the many reasons why the movie works so well. The audience is taken on a ride from start to finish, where they do not know what is what until the end. Once the murderer sees that Stewart is watching him and he is found out, the taut suspense of him coming after a helpless victim confined to a wheelchair leaves you on the edge of your seat. It is this tension that perfectly culminates a great story and a fantastic movie.

27

THE WIZARD OF OZ
1939

There is no place like home, a theme that rings true in all places and times. This concept is one that must be learned before the journey home can be undertaken. *The Wizard of Oz* is perhaps the most powerfully magical tale ever brought to the screen. Told as a mythical fairy tale/fable, all the elements of great storytelling exist here. There is the child who searches for her way back home, the weird and strange creatures she meets along the journey, the conflict that occurs along the way, the evil villain dead set on stopping the child from getting to safety and the eventual resolution.

A misunderstood and lonely teenager named Dorothy longs to see the world yearning for a better place. Dorothy runs away from home with her dog Toto to escape the clutches of a ferocious neighbor. On her way back home Dorothy gets caught in the oncoming tornado. After finally reaching home, she is struck on the head and knocked unconscious. She wakes up in a magical far off place filled with an evil witch, flying monkeys, a bunch of overly happy, singing and rhyming midgets, talking apple trees and three legendary characters that help her along her journey. Her destination is the grand city where she will come face to face with the all powerful wizard of Oz.

Like all good fairy tales, extreme danger exists along the journey. *The Wizard of Oz* creates one of film's most terrifying villains ever to hit the screen. In the grand old style of the Brothers' Grimm tales of terror, the wicked witch is easily one of the most frightening screen villains, making an indelible impact on the children who watch this classic. Margaret Hamilton is superb, bringing the requisite evil to a gruesome and horrific character. Hamilton, with her hideous green face and hands is equal parts wicked stepmother and Count Dracula. Because there are early scenes that portray the wondrous characters as actual people, the depth of her fright truly reaches another level. One wonders how far apart the malicious Miss Gulch, also Hamilton, and the wicked witch truly are.

Hamilton's absence from the Oscar nominations is an omission that has not gone unnoticed. Judy Garland however, was awarded an Honorary Oscar for her role, which the academy deemed as an outstanding juvenile performance. Makeup is one of the most talked about background elements of the film. The horrors endured by the silver dust to get the Tin Woodsman into character forced actor Buddy Ebsen to leave the production. Interestingly, his voice still remains on some of the songs. This error is such a minute oversight, yet one that is of an interesting and historical nature.

There are those who have taken the movie, told in dreamlike Technicolor cinematography, to subtly stand for the path to psychedelic enlightenment. The mythical nature of the film has allowed it to achieve cult status, although primarily for obscure reasons. People can take whatever they want from it. Recognizing its greatness is what's important. *The Wizard of Oz* is above all a film that must be experienced, but preferably as a rite of passage between parent and child. It is pure family fare and something that should be cherished and shared among and with those you care for.

26

THE SHAWSHANK REDEMPTION
1994

There are only two things that prison cannot take away, hope and your mind. The two must be used in conjunction, or else prison will wear you down. That is what 'Red' thought would happen to newcomer Andy Dufresne when he first arrived. What 'Red', played by Morgan Freeman, would soon find out is that Andy was more than just an average prisoner. Perhaps it was his innocence that set him apart or just his ability to remove himself from the despair. *The Shawshank Redemption* transcended genre as it attempted to send a message to its audience, yet one that was not overtly preachy or superficially religious in nature. The message was that your mind can set you free.

Convicted of murder in 1947, Andy Dufresne, played magnificently by Tim Robbins, is a newcomer to Shawshank Prison. Mainly keeping to himself, he develops a reputation as snobbish. One day he approaches 'Red', the man who can get whatever a prisoner needs inside. 'Red' soon takes a liking to Andy. He sees past what appears to be a better than thou attitude to notice a man who allows himself to not be trapped by his confinement. A friendship naturally ensues.

Throughout Andy's time in Shawshank, he changes that early reputation as a snob into someone who commands respect. A banker in his first life, Andy helps the guards with their finances and tax returns. In return for that help he is given special privileges, which he uses to help his friends and himself escape the harsh realities of their prison sentence, if only for a few moments at a time. Andy is more than just a prisoner, because he uses his mind to think beyond his incarceration.

The story is told about Andy Dufresne, yet the narrator is 'Red'. Even though Andy is far smarter than 'Red', they become close friends. Even though Andy knows more than 'Red', in just about everything, 'Red' is able to pass along lessons that only can be learned through experience. It is their relationship that drives the story. It is important to understand that the redemption does not relate to Andy Dufresne, but rather to 'Red'. His emotional journey is equal to Andy's, if not more.

The success of *The Shawshank Redemption* did not come from its original release in theaters or from a campaign by the studio that helped garner seven Oscar nominations, which included Best Picture, Best Lead Actor (Morgan Freeman) and Best Adapted Screenplay among others. A couple of years went by before this brilliant movie finally got the notice and acclaim it so richly deserves. That occurred as a result of the internet. The Internet Movie Database ranked *The Shawshank Redemption* as the best movie ever made. This ranking resulted from internet voters who were fans of the film. Finally, the movie had caught on in the mainstream and has never looked back since.

From a short story by horror novelist Stephen King, *The Shawshank Redemption* has grown to become one of the most beloved movies of all time. Using the grand themes of hope, survival, salvation and friendship, it is that rarest of films that affects you during every viewing, despite knowing what will happen. It is in the way the material is presented that keeps people hooked. Told with such a quiet grace, this movie gives the subtle impression that hope is out there for everyone.

25

VERTIGO
1958

When does obsession turn into madness? That becomes a trick question throughout the intense and bizarre plot of the Hitchcock thriller *Vertigo*. Is it possible to mold someone into a different person? Should that be done merely for one's own benefit? Hitchcock's most suspenseful film reaches into the very core of psychological despair, presenting an intriguing mystery that some say has no equal. It is equal parts detective thriller and exploration into deep-seeded psychoses.

Recently retired police detective John 'Scottie' Ferguson is asked by an old friend to keep watch over his wife, from afar. The wife may be having spiritual encounters with the dead. Whether she is actually having them or not, the wife believes that she is. As 'Scottie' begins to follow her, he realizes that she is infatuated with the memory of a woman who has been dead for a long time. The man's wife intrigues 'Scottie', to the point where it is becoming a minor obsession for him.

While following her, 'Scottie' saves her from drowning. Immediately attracted to her, 'Scottie' must continue to learn the truth. The more he sees of her the more he becomes obsessed with her. Once they fall for each other, the woman tragically throws herself off the top of a roof, a place that 'Scottie' is unable to follow because of his severe acrophobia. She is gone, along with his sanity. 'Scottie' can not shake the memory of her from his mind, until a replacement is found who looks extremely similar to her. That is not enough for 'Scottie' so he begins to mold her into the exact image of the dead woman. Once this new woman is made over, a shocking secret is revealed.

At the core of *Vertigo* lies a deeply insecure man, suffering from a lack of self-confidence and a severe fear of heights. In finding a replacement for the woman he has fallen in love with, the detective needs to remake her image using a substitute who has a resemblance to the original. It is truly a macabre method of dealing with loss and a man's disturbed desire to recreate what essentially never truly existed. This shall only serve as a momentary respite, until his plan ultimately fails.

Vertigo was Hitchcock's final film with legendary actor James Stewart. Stewart's incredible performance was so misunderstood that the Academy simply ignored him once again. Of all his later films, this was by far Stewart's deepest and greatest acting performance. They ignored Hitchcock and the movie as well. The plot was too complex for the audiences of 1958 to understand. Only recently has *Vertigo* been recognized as an inarguable classic. In missing two of the greatest films ever made, from 1958, the Academy had no choice but to go with the ultra happy yet horrendous musical *Gigi*, showing how awful their judgment was during this year's awards.

Historians state that *Vertigo* was Hitchcock's most personal tale. What he created was an intellectual and deeply gripping psychological thriller that only grows better with age. Shockingly, *Vertigo* was not a success when it was released, in comparison to how well it is received today. A recent poll in a British film magazine ranked *Vertigo* as the second greatest film of all time. While that ranking is a bit high, I am delighted that a new appreciation has grown for this amazing film.

24

THE THIRD MAN
1949

What could be wrong with getting invited to visit an old friend in Austria? First off, when you arrive, your friend is dead. Secondly, your friend is not the same man you remember him as. Thirdly, he is not really dead after all. How well do we really know the people we call friends? Carol Reed's masterpiece, *The Third Man*, challenges our hardened beliefs about friendships and the people we think we know. It is a remarkable examination of loyalty and corruption where nothing is as it seems, until revelations of discovery prove otherwise and tough choices have to be made.

Dime store novel writer Holly Martins arrives in Vienna at the request of his old friend Harry Lime. When Holly arrives, he learns that Lime has just been run over and taken away in a coffin. Distraught at the news, Holly goes to the funeral where he meets the officer in charge. After they go for a drink, the officer reveals that Lime was a master criminal, of the worst variety and urges Holly to return to America. Unsatisfied, Holly decides to stay and investigate further.

During his inquiries, Holly meets a number of associates of Lime. Slowly he is beginning to decipher that the accident that killed Harry may not have been an accident at all. The more he searches, the more puzzling the answers become. New items pop up. One man says he saw the accident and adds that there was a third man. Who was this third man? Now the plot thickens. More is discovered until Holly actually sees the face of his friend out of the shadows, for a brief second. Could it be that the whole thing was a charade? Only one man has that answer.

The scene where Harry Lime shows up to speak with his friend is one of legendary status. Not only does it beautifully throw the entire film into a new mystery while solving the original one. Now it creates a much deeper element of suspense than existed before. This part is of course perfectly workable for the story. This plot construct was completely necessary for the story to function, yet after the now infamous Ferris wheel scene, the movie took on an added depth to it.

In the grand style of Orson Welles himself, Carol Reed had to fight for almost everything that ultimately went into this film. One of those fights dealt with the casting of Welles as the villainous Harry Lime. It is almost impossible to imagine this film without Welles' face peering out of the shadows at Joseph Cotton for the first time or to see anyone else deliver that famous Ferris wheel speech. Reed also received flack from the studio over the setting, which impeccably showcased the tone of the film and the music, which became an immediate sensation. The unique zither sound is one of the few things that immediately pops up when recalling *The Third Man*.

When I say that *The Third Man* was Reed's masterpiece I was being ironic. Reed's only Oscar was awarded for a film that has long been forgotten, 1968's awful *Oliver!* Welles plays the mystifying character of Harry Lime, throwing in his incredible writing talents for that great Ferris wheel scene. It is Welles' acting and presence that helps make this film move from basic to terrific. Add to that a perfect mixture of sound, suspense and pacing to cement this film as a classic.

23

MR. SMITH GOES TO WASHINGTON
1939

    Is it possible for one man to single handedly take on a political machine? That is one of the fundamental principles behind the forming of the United States of America, who took on the mightier machine of England and won their freedom from an oppressive regime. One of the most heartfelt films that Hollywood produced to exemplify this ideology was Frank Capra's 1939 classic *Mr. Smith Goes To Washington*. In a year that has been called the greatest year in the history of cinema this idealistic everyman story struck a chord. It gave people hope and something to count on, despite anything that may be going on behind the scenes, there was a hero watching out for them.

    Following the exploits of a newly appointed junior senator, Jefferson Smith, as he embarks to Washington to serve his country, Smith arrives and is immediately overwhelmed by the history of the area. His enthusiasm gets the better of him, leaving to take a sightseeing tour of the area. Of course, his youthful exuberance for the American ideal makes him an immediate laughing stock to the masses of cynical reporters who choose to exploit him rather than revere him. His secretary, also of the cynical variety, has seen what really goes on behind the scenes. This is something which Smith can not understand, until experiencing it first hand. He will not allow that reality to change him.

    Soon the naïve Smith realizes that the senior senator from his home state, Joseph Paine, is part of a bigger political machine that is involved in corruption, graft and outright crime. When he refuses to go on board with their way of operating, a muckraking campaign is started against Smith. The bill that Smith proposes interferes with their plans for an immense profit so they begin an attack upon his credibility and character, tarnishing his name to the point of prompting his expulsion from the Senate. Smith, however, is too idealistic for them to simply beat down with false accusations. His legendary filibuster, where Smith speaks until collapsing, is one of cinema's most revered moments.

    1939 was the grandest year for cinema. *Mr. Smith Goes To Washington* definitely made a name for itself in this grand year though, receiving nominations in almost every major award category. James Stewart would lose the Best Actor Oscar to Robert Donat from *Goodbye Mr. Chips*. Stewart's performance as the wide eyed junior senator would win raves. The Academy would offer a consolation prize to Stewart the following year though. Claude Rains was also robbed of a well deserved Oscar for his role as the crooked Joseph Paine, yet that oversight was never corrected.

    The naiveté and moral idealism displayed by Smith is not all that unique. It is often shared by many of those who entertain a career in politics. The truth of the matter is that more people end up like Joseph Paine, corrupt and greedy, than sticking to their guns as Smith does. Power corrupts. Those who seek it eventually find that out. *Mr. Smith Goes To Washington* shows the clear distinction between idealism and conformity. In the end, idealism and moral integrity wins out, yet regrettably that is not always the case. While slightly unrealistic, it is an excellent piece of cinematic Americana.

22

SCHINDLER'S LIST
1993

All Germans are evil. That is an untruth that has existed since the 1930s. All Nazis are scum. A clearer truth has never been uttered. There is a distinct difference between a German and a Nazi, the same way there is a distinct difference between an American Southerner and a Klansman. The Nazis were the more powerful European version of the Ku Klux Klan. There have been many movies made with the Holocaust as a backdrop, yet no film has ever been as powerful, as moving or as important in differentiating good versus evil within accepted stereotypes as *Schindler's List*.

Oskar Schindler was a businessman of German descent. He was not a successful one though, but what he had was the ability to manipulate people. It was a certain type of flair for self-promotion that allowed him to succeed during these turbulent times. He has been described as a war profiteer and the early depiction of Oskar Schindler displays a man that is nothing but selfish. He is all about himself, using the masterful skills of self-promotion to further his own gain. It is true that a number of Jews were saved from labor camps early on and benefited from working in Schindler's enamelware factory. Initially, Schindler allowed it only because it served his purpose, himself.

The Holocaust is not the story, although many would disagree due to the horrific nature of what took place. *Schindler's List*, however, is a character study of two opposites. One is an egotistical man who learns compassion and ultimately regret, while the other can only be described as a sadistic animal. Both go through transformations, with Schindler's as the more compassionate. However, the short-lived transformation of the true villain in the movie, the Nazi psychopath Amon Goeth, coming from the verbal prodding of Schindler, is the far more compelling one, because he is evil personified. For a few moments we are lured into the false belief that this madman can evolve.

After three decades in movies, beginning with the ambitious yet less than spectacular *Firelight*, Steven Spielberg finally made a movie so important that the Academy could no longer ignore him as a significant filmmaker. *Schindler's List* was the vindication that Spielberg had long sought after. Regardless of what anyone said about the joy of making films alone, Spielberg had to be thrilled to have this proverbial monkey off his back. In fact, the 1993 Oscars were all Spielberg as movies he directed from that year took home ten trophies, more than all others combined.

I think we all get it. Steven Spielberg hates the Nazis. Often times a filmmaker is clouded by their own history, or in this case the history of his religion's struggles at the hands of an oppressive and psychotic regime. This is not one of those times. In making *Schindler's List*, Spielberg has presented a story that was near and dear to him, yet failed to sacrifice as a filmmaker merely to show his obvious distaste for severely dislikeable fiends. These Nazis are not the bungling villains that Spielberg disintegrated in the much less dramatic or historically significant *Raiders of the Lost Ark*. They are much more real. For this particular movie, that works in an immeasurably better fashion.

21

THE GRAPES OF WRATH
1940

What would you do if you returned to your home after four years and discovered every one was gone? The answer is to go in search of them. That was the easy part. Accepting the fact that while you were away in prison, the farm that you and your family knew and had based their entire existence upon was taken away from you because of technology and bad weather is the hard part. That is exactly what happened during the Great Depression when many farmers from the Dust Bowl were forced to uproot their families and lives in search of work out west. This is the story of one American family's trials and tribulations during this bleak time in American history.

Tom Joad, played by Henry Fonda in one of his two finest performances, returns home from prison only to learn that his family has left the farm they called home. Tom learns from one sharecropper who has remained behind that his family was forced off their land. After catching up with the rest of his family, they all set out for California. Along the way, they suffer hardships, including the death of the two eldest members of the family who were too weak to make the entire trip. When they arrive, they learn that what brought them out there in the first place was all a hoax.

There was no or few great wage paying jobs, what the family based their entire move upon. In trying to find work, the family encounters even more despair. There is little or no work, too many workers to fill those jobs, crooked policemen and constant moves from camp to camp without sufficient money to adequately feed the family. The family runs into a little luck, here and there, but it is only a short time before Tom gets in trouble again and further complicates matters. This new trouble for Tom provides the impetus for him to separate from his family and help others in need.

The 1939 film *Mr. Smith Goes To Washington* had a decided impact upon the main star of this movie, Henry Fonda. James Stewart's makeup Oscar was awarded to him for his role in *The Philadelphia Story*, which came from the same year as *The Grapes of Wrath*. This has caused one of the greatest controversies in Academy Award history. Although no one argues that Stewart did not deserve an Oscar, the general consensus is that Fonda's performance for this film is not only the finest of his career but also far and away the finest that 1940 had to offer. The Academy would wait until 1981 to reward Fonda with an Oscar for Best Actor. On a side note, John Ford would win the first of two straight Oscars for Best Director, the first director ever to accomplish that distinction.

From the John Steinbeck novel about the rough times farmers went through in the previous decade, the film departed from the novel at the end, where the optimism of the human spirit is reaffirmed. Through immense hardships, the loss of loved ones, starvation and all that destroyed their spirit, the Joads are used to define all the families who went through this adversity. There are strong social issues involved, including governmental ignorance to the plight of the common folks, corruption on the corporate level, guerilla tactics to prevent unionization of the workers and a foreshadow to the witch hunt of exposing communism. Key to the central theme of this great film was the importance of keeping the family together, no matter what took place or what was to come.

20

THE FUGITIVE
1993

Hollywood is fueled by money and studios are in the business of turning a profit, which is thoroughly understandable. It was only a matter of time before they would capitalize on television successes for their next endeavors. There is only one answer to the question of what the greatest Hollywood remake of a classic television series was: *The Fugitive*. From start to finish, it keeps you on the edge of your seat, with the suspense of what would happen next. It did not matter that fans of the television series knew the outcome. There was still an unparalleled presentation of mystery and amazing action that made it rise above the rest of those movie adaptations of former television shows.

Dr. Richard Kimble returns home to find his wife murdered. The murderer is a one-armed man whom Kimble struggles with before that man escapes. No one believes him and he is convicted of the crime. On his way to prison the bus transporting Kimble flips over allowing Kimble to escape. After collecting himself, which includes another daring escape from a quickly assembled manhunt, Kimble returns to Chicago to begin his search for the one-armed man who murdered his wife.

With every great protagonist for the audience to follow and root for there must be an antagonist. In *The Fugitive*, that antagonist is the man in charge of his capture, Marshal Samuel Gerard, played by Tommy Lee Jones. The fire that fuels Gerard is the job, his search for a man who has escaped. It does not matter to Gerard that Kimble might be innocent, as he clearly explains to Kimble just before a death-defying dive into a river. This only heightens Gerard's obsession about capturing Kimble. This film, although it can be classified as simply a chase movie, takes great care to develop Gerard as a character. This allowed the audience to identify with him as well. Secretly, we wanted both men to succeed, because neither were villains in the true sense of the word.

How can two characters who are essentially heroes be at constant odds with each other? That was the beauty of the movie. Both men were right. Both men were doing their jobs. In the end, both men came together as equals, independently solving the mystery that the movie is based around and helping each other in more ways than just that. There is no greater cinematic theme than redemption. Dr. Kimble and Marshal Gerard both go through it, but often time a movie can just be enjoyed without taking into account those great emotional triumphs. *The Fugitive* is that type of movie. It is important to understand the emotional arc, but more important to sit back and enjoy.

1993 was the year of Spielberg, with *Schindler's List* and *Jurassic Park* dominating the Oscar ceremonies. Often inappropriately labeled as a popcorn flick, *The Fugitive* was a strong enough film to garner a nomination for Best Picture, even though it had no chance of winning. From this list you can see which movie I believe was the better one. Both films were excellent despite their different genres, yet *The Fugitive* is simply not the type of movie that is rewarded by the Academy. In keeping with that short-sightedness, despite the Best Picture nomination, the director of the film, Andrew Davis, was passed over for a nomination, going to Robert Altman for his film *Short Cuts*.

19

THE GODFATHER II
1974

How does a writer build on the great saga told in *The Godfather*? By telling a mixture of the beginning of the story and the how that story continued. Although the times have changed, the characters, at least the ones who made it out of the first story alive, remain the same. Revealing the history of how Vito Corleone rose to power on the streets of New York City provides extra depth to the original story as well, offering a clearer insight into how one might enter into a life of crime. *The Godfather II* is an interesting combination of the past and the present, portraying many similarities between both periods as well as the evolution of the family during their attempts at legitimization.

Even though it is both prologue and epilogue to *The Godfather*, this movie is technically two separate stories. Beginning in Sicily, young Vito Corleone's passage to America is briefly explained. His father and older brother were murdered by the local Don who ran his home town of Corleone. To save her last remaining son Vito's mother attacks the Don, allowing Vito to escape, where he makes his way to America. After struggling for years to earn a living, Vito, grown up with a family of his own now, murders the local Don and assumes his position. Thus the American reign of Don Vito Corleone begins, starting a new chapter of his life that leads directly into the first movie's story.

In the meantime, inter cut with the background of Vito Corleone's rise to prominence, is the evolution of the Corleone family as headed up by Vito's youngest son Michael. Beginning three years after the story from the first movie ended, Michael finds that legitimizing the family takes as many acts of sheer criminality as what went on during his father's reign. Attempts on his life orchestrated by his own brother, playing sides against one another to ensure business relations and financial security and political corruption for profit are all par for the course. These acts are similar to what went on before Michael took over. Even when things change, they somehow always remain the same.

Like two movies mentioned before it, *The Godfather II* received five separate acting nominations. Of the five nominations the Academy handed out for each of the four awards, three went to *The Godfather II* in the Best Supporting Actor category. It was an impressive race as to who would win of the three. There was the playwright Michael V. Gazzo, who played the troubled mob soldier turned informant Freddie Pentangeli, pioneering acting teacher Lee Strassberg as legendary mobster Hyman Roth, also known as Meyer Lansky, and Robert DeNiro. DeNiro played the young Vito Corleone during his rise to power. Fresh off his star making performance in Martin Scorsese's *Mean Streets*, DeNiro was awarded the first of his many nominations, taking home his first Oscar.

Coming off the great success of the first movie, a morality tale on family, some critics have even gone so far out on a limb as to state that the sequel was superior to the original. This is an impression that is generally unheard of regarding sequels. Only time will tell if I agree with that assessment. Either way, *The Godfather II* is an excellent contrast of old world style and new world modernization. Coppola has crafted another masterpiece. Although dealing with primarily the same characters *The Godfather II* is different from the original, which gives it its own unique presence.

18

BEAUTY AND THE BEAST
1991

Is it fair to include an animated movie on this list? Should there be some sort of distinction due to the obvious differences? My answer is simple. No. A movie is a movie. Regardless of its animated figures, who can actually deliver the material in a far greater fashion than humans ever could, the story is told in such a beautiful and stylized way that it almost becomes lifelike as the audience watches it. There are moments where the animation simply disappears, in favor of the wonder and majesty of the presentation of this timeless classic. It truly is a marvel to see.

Disney's *Beauty and the Beast* is the story of a young woman named Belle who longs for something more in life. With her father missing, Belle sets out in search of him. She wanders through a forest of impending terror until she is saved by a darkly clad figure who takes her back to his castle. Once inside the caste she finds her father, who is kept as a prisoner. In exchange for his freedom Belle agrees to remain in the castle forever. When her father returns to town with the story of a great beast keeping his daughter captive, the townsfolk think he is out of his mind.

Once it is discovered that the Beast exists, the townsfolk, led by the villainous Gaston, set out to kill him. Ironically, it is the Beast's ultimate kindness, allowing Belle to go after her father, which creates this predicament. Belle sets out with her father to help save the Beast. Distraught, the Beast doesn't even fight back when the mob enters his castle. It is not until he sees Belle, who confesses her love for him that he realizes life is worth fighting for. At that moment Gaston attacks, plunging a dagger into him. Only true love is able to save the Beast from death, where it is revealed that he is a handsome Prince. That does not matter to Belle, who has fallen in love with him for his heart.

There is only so much an animated film can accomplish in terms of accolades and Academy Award recognition. The marvelous Disney films of old were usually awarded a special Oscar for their achievement in the overall film process. Animation has become a common medium for storytelling now, so those special Oscars were no longer appreciative, but rather of the handicapping variety. It came time for an animated movie, Disney or not, to be appreciated enough to grant it the highest honor an animated film had ever received, a Best Picture nomination. *Beauty and the Beast* was that film and became the only film to ever receive such praise, despite losing to *Silence of the Lambs*, which would go on to tie a legendary Oscar record by winning all five major awards.

Beauty and the Beast possesses all of the necessary plot elements; danger, mystery, comedy, revenge and true love. Filled with richly crafted characters, such as the absent minded old man who sets the story in motion, comic relief in the form of the villain's piggish sidekick, the evil villain whose treachery threatens the destined happiness, the beautiful young girl searching for something more and the tragic hero who learns from the error of his ways on the path to magical bliss, it is one of the greatest love stories ever told, regardless of format. This beautiful movie is a spectacle of adventure and wonder, of redemption and selflessness and of two kindred spirits finding happiness in each other. This version is the most magnificent one ever told and the best movie of its kind ever made.

17

MIDNIGHT COWBOY
1969

Can friendship survive the rigors and harsh realities of an unforgiving city? *Midnight Cowboy*, a covert term for a male prostitute, is more about the relationship between two losers that no one wants to root for. They are immoral characters, yet not out of malicious tendencies but rather because of their naiveté and downright ineptitude. Neither man is a hero. However, these two characters became archetypal anti-heroes, acting as symbols for perseverance through the concept of mutual dependence. Both men's original goal, to hustle, plays second fiddle to their reliance upon one another as a means of survival. It is a harsh story that makes one thankful for what they have.

Dimwitted and ultra-self confident cowboy Joe Buck prepares to leave his desolate Texas town for the bright lights of New York City. He has plans of making it big as a male prostitute. Once in the city, he quickly discovers the realities that need to be faced. Buck meets another hustler, of a different variety, the grand tragic character of Enrico *'Ratso'* Rizzo. Rizzo hustles Buck out of some money, but is later befriended by him once he is so down on his luck that he has become homeless and compromised his morals to a level he never envisioned. Once the two begin their friendship and mutual dependence, the true nature of the movie becomes realized.

The key to *Midnight Cowboy* may lie within the choices made in the screenplay. There are many opportunities to glamorize the relationship between these two men, yet the story remains steadfast in focusing upon the seedier side of life and their struggles within it. Both characters are given added depth through their individual stories. Joe Buck's story is told through what happened to him in the past while Enrico Rizzo's tale is explained through his dreams of the future. Each of them wants more. Each of them wants something better. Sometimes life does not allow it though. *Midnight Cowboy* did not fall under the spell of depicting the splendor of the city. Instead, it reveled in showing its utter degradations. Using an innovative realism in combination with adult themes, it became the breakthrough movie that realistically fueled and impacted an evolving generation.

In one of the most ironic twists in cinema history, the cowboy icon John Wayne is used in the movie to stand as an example for male virility, yet in real life, John Wayne took the Best Actor Oscar away from one of these emerging stars. It is possible that Jon Voight and Dustin Hoffman were viewed as so equally good that they split the vote, allowing Wayne to surpass them and win his only Oscar, for *True Grit*. Hoffman's performance was far greater than his first role in *The Graduate*, which also earned him a Best Actor nomination. This role took away any notion that was brewing regarding the specific type of character that Hoffman could play. Once *Midnight Cowboy* showed his range he became one of the most sought after and diverse actors in film. Similar to Hoffman in *The Graduate*, this movie was Jon Voight's breakthrough role. Although not Voight's first starring role, it was his third film, but the one that obviously launched his career. *Midnight Cowboy* showcased two of modern cinema's greatest acting talents, becoming the first X-rated movie to win Best Picture.

16

LORD OF THE RINGS III: THE RETURN OF THE KING
2003

It is tough to judge this movie on its own as it is the third part of a more complete story. The first two parts, *The Fellowship of the Ring* and *The Two Towers*, were both good individual movies. I know this has been said before, most specifically for the *Star Wars* trilogy, but if this trio of movies were somehow one singular movie, then that film might have landed at the top spot on this list. The trilogy is that good. It is not one movie though, so each movie must be dealt with on its own. The third and final installment of the trilogy is by far not only the best of the three, but also one of the grandest spectacles ever put on film. Every single aspect of this movie comes off as perfect.

The Return of the King finalizes the long saga of Frodo the Hobbit and his journey to destroy the gold ring that once belonged to the dark overlord Sauron. Sauron is building an army to destroy men and all the creatures that chose to side with them. With the ring in his possession, Sauron would be able to control Middle Earth, where the battle for good and evil is taking place. Along their journey, Frodo and his faithful companion Sam encounter the ring's former owner, Gollum. Gollum is a former Hobbit who has been turned into an evil creature by the ring. In this installment of the trilogy, Gollum attempts to lead the two hobbits to their doom so he can retake possession of the ring.

In the meantime, the fight for Middle Earth has already begun and continues. Aragorn, the rightful heir to the throne of mankind and his devoted friends band together to fight against all odds, battling an army of mercenaries and creatures loyal to Sauron. The grand battle scene where the ghosts who betrayed the former human king fight for the side of good is a marvel to watch. Even though victory is achieved, the forces of good are still thoroughly outnumbered. They fight nonetheless, choosing to go on the attack. All they need to do is give Frodo and Sam that one opportunity to destroy the gold ring and end the war, returning Middle Earth to the forces of good.

In 2001, the first installment of this trilogy was nominated for Best Picture but came up empty. That loss was deserved as a much better film took home the trophy that night. The following year, 2002, the second installment was nominated once again. It also came up short, although this time it lost to a much inferior picture, *Chicago*. That is not to say that *The Two Towers* deserved to win the Best Picture award for that year, because it did not. I am just stating that it lost to a lesser picture. In 2003 the Academy could no longer ignore this fantasy adventure. *The Return of the King* was finally given proper due for the series. This movie was far and away the best film of that particular year.

By itself, *The Return of the King* is an amazing spectacle to watch. The unique style of telling parallel stories to keep everything fresh is brilliant. It is that rare movie that combines almost every known theme in one cohesive story. The trilogy as a whole takes close to eleven hours of viewing time. In my opinion it is absolutely worth it, if only to see this final part of the story. You will be grateful and amazed at seeing the majesty and wonder of one of the greatest stories ever told and possibly the most magical adventure film ever made. It is truly an epic in every sense of the word.

15

A BEAUTIFUL MIND
2001

Is it possible to rationalize the solution to any problem? What if the problem lies within one's own mind? The field of applied mathematics meets the world of schizophrenia in this enormously moving biopic about the tortured genius John Forbes Nash. Nash later won the Nobel Prize, but this film is about his battle with the disorder that affected his brain so severely that he could not function properly and his relationship with the woman who stood by him during that time.

Beginning at Princeton University in 1947, the young mathematical genius from West Virginia sets out in search of the next great innovative idea. Breakthroughs of this variety do not come easy. After struggling long and hard it finally comes to him, which would turn out to be a widely used economic principle. Nash receives help and friendship from his college roommate Charles Herman. It is Charles who helps ease Nash through the long battle of finding his new idea.

Nash's next step is at MIT, where he meets two people that will change his life. One is a mysterious Federal agent named William Parcher and the other is a brilliant student named Alicia. Parcher recruits Nash to perform code breaking work for his undercover project while he starts to date Alicia, which leads to their marriage. The work begins to wear on Nash, causing trouble with his wife due to deep seeded paranoia regarding the enemy coming after him. Are these actual problems resulting from the work he has conducted or is he creating all this within his mind?

The truth is that neither Parcher, nor his college roommate Charles, along with Charles' niece Marcy, ever existed. They are all figments of Nash's schizophrenia, serving a unique purpose to provide praise, friendship and love where he feels none exists. There is a terrific scene where Nash falls back into seeing them once again after he stops taking his medication, yet through the power of his own mind he is able to finally realize that they are creations within his own imagination.

Actor turned director Ron Howard was finally rewarded for his great directing ability with an Oscar. Howard had previously directed such great films as *Splash*, *Backdraft*, *Parenthood* and perhaps his previous best film *Apollo 13*. Jennifer Connelly won a best supporting actress Oscar, yet Russell Crowe was denied what should have been his second consecutive Oscar victory. The award went to Denzel Washington for his role in *Training Day*, a makeup award for his amazing performance two years earlier in *The Hurricane*. In an ironic twist, Crowe's performance in 1999 for *The Insider* was equally as good as Washington's for *The Hurricane*. His sole Oscar to date was for his role in the Best Picture winner *Gladiator*. With more luck Crowe could have won three in a row.

While *A Beautiful Mind* is inaccurate on a number of points regarding Nash's life, the story that is told in the movie is what is important here. With that being said, *A Beautiful Mind* is one of the greatest and most poignant love stories ever told on screen. Alicia's undying devotion to Nash, while a creation of the cinematic story, is so pure that when he finally recognizes it on stage during his Nobel Prize acceptance speech, you cannot help but knowing that something special was witnessed here. The payoff of their love story is one of those truly extraordinary moments in film.

14

TO KILL A MOCKINGBIRD
1962

    This film is generally viewed as one of the great courtroom dramas in movie history, yet that is a misnomer. Only about a quarter of a two hour plus movie is spent within the courtroom. *To Kill A Mockingbird* is not in the style of the grand courtroom melodramas where the entire strategies of the prosecution and defense are played out. This film remains much simpler. Straightforward plainness stands out as one of the key principles that the story is based upon. It is this simplicity that not only presents the impetus for the court case, but also provides the story with its unique flow.

    Why this brilliant movie is so closely connected to the famed cinematic judicial dramas is from the magnificence of that one grand scene and the heroics of Atticus Finch. Atticus is trying to clear the name of an innocent black man in a town where the color of one's skin usually indicates guilt. Played flawlessly by Academy Award winner Gregory Peck, Atticus comes to life as a champion of justice, evoking the kind of man everyone wishes his or her father would be. The image of a crusader for the rights of the little man pops up when reminiscing about this great character. Atticus revels in delivering the truth to the minds of simple folk, even though they do not understand it. Unfortunately, despite being a work of fiction, they do not make their decision based upon it.

    The story is told through the eyes of an eight-year old girl, Scout, the daughter of Atticus. Untarnished by the harsh realities of life, she weaves her way through the story acting not only as a guide but also as an intermediary. Scout provides a much needed voice of innocence that mirrors the ignorance of the simple townsfolk. Her relationship with Atticus frees him up to be the guiding force and the voice of reason and justice to prepare them, her and her brother, along the right path.

    There are two scenes in the movie where Peck brings that vision of a simple man with a wise mind to life. He perfect showcases the ability to control his emotions, display restraint and agree to stick to a concocted story. The latter is specifically crucial as Scout implies that revealing the truth would be like committing another sin. In that culminating scene, Atticus realizes that his daughter has finally understood the concept of justice. This, to him, is an ideal above all. It is a magnificently acted story of a father passing along his principles to his children, set in a backdrop that clearly displays the difference between the thinking man and the ignorant one. The performances, highlighted by Peck, bring this magnificent story to life, a story that holds greater relevance today.

    1962 was all about *Lawrence of Arabia*. David Lean's grand epic swept the top two Oscars for Best Picture and Best Director. It was Lean's second Best Director Oscar in six years. The Oscar domination makes many forget that *To Kill A Mockingbird* was nominated in both categories as well. Most could not even name the director of this film, which happened to be Robert Mulligan. That is less of a shock because, of the nineteen feature films Mulligan directed, the eighteen other films never came remotely close to matching the brilliance of *To Kill A Mockingbird*. What everyone remembers from this film is the performance by Peck, one of five nominations and the only to result in an Oscar.

13

SUNSET BOULEVARD
1950

To what lengths will desperation consume someone? That is the fundamental question at the heart of this dark comedic thriller told in a noir style fashion. The cinematic themes are rampant in this story, which is about not only desperation, but also deep seeded narcissism, ambition, quest for fame, greed and most importantly compromise. At the heart of this film is the conflict between settling and not settling, what people will do to remain faithful to their art or sell themselves for it.

The clash of personality styles between the two main characters, an aging silent film star who will not compromise her standards and the struggling writer who succumbs to giving up his pride and integrity for comfort, make for an engrossing tandem. Their scenes are equal parts engaging and of the variety that makes you want to cringe. Their happiness, her true happiness and his false veneer of happiness, is doomed from the start as the beginning of the film coyly explains.

Out of work and down on his luck writer Joe Gillis wanders into the fancy estate house of Norma Desmond. After a funeral for a monkey Gillis is assigned by her to write her studio picture comeback. Immediately, Desmond takes control of his life, keeping him around as a servant. Soon she makes Gillis her companion, dominating all aspects of his life and becoming jealous of any activity he engages in without her. Her jealousy grows into rage, leading to the downfall of both.

The character of Norma Desmond, played by Oscar nominated actress Gloria Swanson of silent film lore, has been called one of the greatest ever written. Swanson's range of emotional delivery is breathtaking to watch. Her at a moment transformation from sadness into deranged lunacy is almost caricaturish at times, yet breathes life into the role. Desmond comes off as one of the creepiest screen villains ever filmed, yet is never associated with that status. Generally, her character is regarded as tragic rather then villainous, yet considering her duplicitous and underhanded ways, along with the eventual choice she finally makes, her madness definitively borders on villainous.

Swanson had some fierce competition in her category at the Oscars, with Judy Holliday winning for her performance as the ditzy blond in *Born Yesterday*. *Sunset Boulevard* has the distinction of having been one of only a few movies to receive a nomination in each of the four acting categories. All four nominees lost. William Holden won an Oscar three years later for his amazingly cynical performance in another Billy Wilder movie, *Stalag 17*. Nancy Olsen came as close as she ever would and in a better year there would have been no nomination for her. The real error was former director Erich Von Stroheim losing to George Sanders from *All About Eve*. Von Stroheim's only Oscar nomination, a great oversight itself, came and went without the credit and award he deserved.

Sunset Boulevard was a ground-breaking film in terms of style, content and structure. It is widely considered the greatest film ever made that examines the film industry from a behind the scenes viewpoint. The mixing of real life members of the film industry with fictitious characters was so innovative that many have followed its lead. There are many films that do not age well. However, this is that rare type of film that seems fresh today, growing better with age and every screening.

12

RAGING BULL
1980

    The second film on this list that is a character study often mistaken for a boxing picture, *Raging Bull*, is about as different from *Rocky* as night and day. Both movies tell stories about boxers who are tougher than nails in the ring, but that is where the comparisons abruptly end. Jake LaMotta is the antithesis of the fictitious Rocky Balboa outside the ring. It is only in the ring where LaMotta can thrive due to his animalistic nature. This film depicts the inhumane jealous quality that he was known for that would eventually cost LaMotta everything, including his family and dignity.

    This ultra-realistic biopic depicts LaMotta navigating through life while making a name for himself in the world of boxing. LaMotta's atrocious demeanor outside the ring became a definitive reason why he was not more successful throughout his career and after his days as a boxer had ended. There is almost the attempt to blame upbringing on his anti-social behaviors by depicting the neighborhood as a breeding ground for that type of person. What the movie does not do however, is incorrectly identify LaMotta as a sympathetic victim who is just the sum of his surroundings. He is different than those around him, evidenced by the failure of every relationship he ever had.

    Much has been made about the impact *Raging Bull* has had upon cinema, launching its director, Martin Scorsese into the level of super stardom. It is often looked back as the greatest film of its decade, despite losing both the Best Picture and Best Director Oscars to Robert Redford's slice of dysfunctional family life *Ordinary People*. The editing and the acting have been specifically singled out for this film though, garnering *Raging Bull* its only two Oscar victories. Robert DeNiro's portrayal of LaMotta is arguably the single greatest acting performance ever captured on the screen, with only a handful of performances coming close to challenging him for that position. Earning his second acting Oscar, DeNiro solidified his status as one of the greatest actors of his generation.

    The most overlooked aspect of *Raging Bull* is in its perfect setup for the story. The movie begins by showing an aged LaMotta rehearsing for a stage show in 1964. LaMotta is far from the lean fighting machine he was during his dominant times in the ring. DeNiro gained 30 pounds to more accurately depict LaMotta during the later stages of his life, which shows that he deteriorated badly and way past his prime, not only for a boxer but for a human being as well. This scene typifies LaMotta's whole existence. He was merely a caricature of a real person, only truly prolific when he was performing in the ring or hamming it up on stage. It was his persona that outshined his true self.

    Raging Bull distinctly shaped the face of cinema. At the heart of this film was a protagonist who was neither hero nor anti-hero, yet was actually a tragic villain. It was revolutionary for a film to have an audience relate to the plight of a man like LaMotta, while secretly knowing it could not. This great film has been scrutinized, dissected and analyzed past the point of no return, with no real explanation for why LaMotta was the way he was. The sad truth is that he more than likely did not even know himself. It was just in his nature to be the type of animal that was destined for solitude.

11

PSYCHO
1960

How does a director solve the problem of telling the boring tale of a woman who steals money to help pay for her happiness? Easy, kill her and present a totally different story in its place. *Psycho* is not merely known for its creepy motel owner or that one shower scene, but for attempting something as breakthrough as killing off the star early on, just to throw the audience off their guard. This allowed Hitchcock to present almost anything in the moments to come, which is what he did.

The story of Marion Crane is not really boring. Hitchcock makes sure to tell her story as if it were the focal point. He includes all the clever tricks that a master filmmaker knows, specifically suspense. Crane steals $40,000 in cash from her boss, but accidentally gets seen by him as she makes her way out of town. There is a moment where he does not think anything of it, but then realizes something is out of the ordinary. She is also questioned by a policeman who sees her car stopped on the side of the road. The policeman notices that she is acting strange and begins to follow her. What we are presented with here are the beginnings of a standard chase movie, where Crane shall be hunted down for what she has done. That is what we, the audience, is meant to believe will happen.

Tired from driving and thinking about what will happen when her boss finds the money is gone, Crane decides to stop at the Bates Motel for the night. After she shares a brief meal with Norman Bates, the infamous shower scene follows. It is perhaps the most talked about scene in all of cinematic history. The search for Marion Crane now becomes the focal point of the film, with a detective asking way too many questions for Norman Bates' liking. It is eventually discovered that the Bates Motel has its own dark secrets, which when fully revealed are beyond the unthinkable.

Psycho became a ground-breaking film, known all over the world. The secret of Norman Bates' mother is probably known to many now, but at the time was clearly breaking barriers. People will not watch the movie because of that shower scene. What they wind up missing is a fantastic story, deeply disturbing plot and the master at his all time best. It was so brilliant and bizarre that it required an explanation at the end of the movie as to what actually took place. Set into the story, this explanation answered what many people did not want to believe, yet took place right before their eyes. *Psycho* changed the way films were made, responsible for spawning a generation of films that tried to feed of its freshness and originality. Those that followed could not capture its unique quality.

For what I believe to be the third year in a row, Alfred Hitchcock directed the best film that year had to offer. *Psycho* is his fourth and final entry upon this list. *Rebecca* won him his only Oscar for Best Picture, while *Rear Window* is considered his most claustrophobic film and *Vertigo* now believed to have been his ultimate classic. All three films are amazing, as making this list should indicate, yet *Psycho* is by far his greatest film. From the way he manipulated the plot to the obscure delivery of that famous shower scene to the breakthrough use of images and themes that were taboo in American cinema, Hitchcock created a film that was responsible for shaping modern cinema.

10

THE MANCHURIAN CANDIDATE
1962

What if the recent memories of events over a three day period during the war were not as they seemed? It becomes transparently clear that what is remembered by the members of a captured patrol did not actually take place, but instead were fabricated memories created for some particular purpose. That is only the backdrop for the most brilliantly conceived political thriller ever filmed. It is as if that specific genre had been given the detective mystery treatment, with plot twists around every turn and a finale that is both beyond unpredictable and will leave you breathless.

Viewed as a thriller, it is tough to classify *The Manchurian Candidate* into one specific genre. It contains elements from many genres, while focusing on a diverse variety of themes. There was the use of mind control in political warfare, McCarthyism as covert political subterfuge, a puppet leader controlled by a behind the scenes political machine and extremist politics shaping the country in a counter-productive way, more relevant now than ever. This movie has also been classified as satire, yet that is an oversimplification regarding the buffoonery of the weak minded main politician.

The acting performances in this movie are without a doubt some of the finest ensemble acting ever put together. Despite winning the Oscar for *From Here To Eternity*, this is Frank Sinatra's finest, most deeply layered acting work. Add to that two amazing female performances, supplied by Angela Lansbury and Janet Leigh, each unique in their own right yet bonded together by their individual mystery. Finally, the acting of star Laurence Harvey is astonishing to watch. His ability to exhibit over-emotional responses coupled with u-turn maneuvers of blank unemotional presentations breathes the necessary life into the highly complex plot. It is Harvey's performance, so extremely underrated, that allows the serpentine plot to work its way through to tense fruition.

To reveal elements of the story would be doing an injustice to those who have not seen the film. There are specific reasons why this is perhaps the least seen movie of the fifty named here. It was believed that the assassination of JFK clearly echoed the plot points contained within this movie. The movie was removed from circulation as a result. The true story is that Frank Sinatra purchased the rights to the film and withheld it from circulation until 1988 over a contract dispute with the studio that made the film. The JFK assassination storyline plays better in the press than Sinatra exacting revenge on the studio over profit sharing, so that legend surrounding the film remains alive.

No one can argue the roundabout similarities between *The Manchurian Candidate* and the JFK assassination. The problem with any negative feedback from that event hurting this movie is problematic because the film was released in 1962 and the Oscars take place way before November, when the Kennedy assassination happened. The Academy only rewarded this movie with two nominations, for film editing and for Angela Lansbury's flawlessly creepy performance as Raymond Shaw's manipulative mother. She lost to fan favorite Patty Duke for her performance in *The Miracle Worker*. Lansbury's is not only the far better performance but is one of the best acting performances ever given on screen and goes relatively unnoticed as one of the greatest screen villains ever created.

9

THE GODFATHER
1972

Mistakenly called the greatest crime drama ever filmed, *The Godfather* is actually a tale about family. No can deny that there are crimes committed in the movie, yet mainly they are of the unspoken kind. There are acts of gross criminality depicted on screen, yet matching them are tender scenes where family values are taught. Small little scenes exist within this epic tale where those who remain loyal to the family are rewarded, with something as miniscule yet vital as dinner. Beginning with the lavish wedding scene, where Don Corleone's only daughter is married; one principle is made clear, respect and honor your family. Without family, crime does not really matter. These crimes are done for the family, so they seem almost benevolent to the point where they are acceptable.

The popularity of the movie, however, stems from its criminality. While crime seems to be glorified here, it is actually put on trial. The audience is given a prophetic message that crime will always keep you on the edge of your seat. A criminal must always wonder who is waiting around the corner, wishing and scheming to take a bigger piece of the pie than they have been given. One can never truly enjoy the fruits of their labor, because the sad fact that every action promotes a reaction exists, which in turn causes the possibility of all-out war. The movie shifts from the old to the new guard, resulting from an acceptance of the knowledge that the family must evolve to survive.

The transfer of power, from old world ways to new world vision, combines both major elements, criminality and the family. It is the mechanism that connects the entire story. As Don Corleone steps back, the family interests are taken over by his son Michael, who understands the nature of the business, as his father did. Don Corleone knew that in Michael's hands business would remain at the forefront of all family enterprises. It was Don Corleone's wish for Michael to go on to better things, yet he became content that Michael would grow and fulfill that wish in this position.

There are critics and historians out there who consider the sequel to be a better film. While it does present both the prologue and the epilogue to this story, the original is far superior. It is the better story, has at its core the greater theme and compiles an amazing cast that provides some of the greatest cooperative acting in film history. These actors magnificently develop rough edged characters whose values are so disturbing, yet at times so touching that they are almost impossible to root against. They are villains, yet in retrospect one wonders what it would be like to be them.

The Godfather is one of the most cherished and loved films ever. It won the Best Picture Oscar in 1972 and has often been hailed as the greatest motion picture ever made. Few know that the 1972 Oscars were not dominated by *The Godfather*, but rather owned by *Cabaret*. *Cabaret* won a total of eight Oscars that night, almost three times as many as Coppola's masterpiece. Coppola's only Oscar for *The Godfather* was for Best Adapted Screenplay, losing the award for best director to *Cabaret*'s Bob Fosse. It makes little sense that *The Godfather* would win Best Picture but not Best Director, while *Cabaret* would win a total of eight, yet not win the Oscar for best screenplay, losing to *The Godfather*. It seems that the Academy voters had no idea what they were doing this year.

8

ONE FLEW OVER THE CUCKOO'S NEST
1975

Can crazy people be liberated from their own insanity? The arrival of a small time criminal at an Oregonian mental asylum begins to have a serious affect upon the ordinary, yet controlled lives of the inmates. The film was an almost complete derivation from the 1962 novel, where the message was to expose the existence of institutions designed to remove all forms of individuality from society. The change in the story, from the first person character of the giant Indian, 'the Chief', who saw the asylum as mechanism that was in charge of creating social integration, to McMurphy, the quintessential anti-hero, so upset novelist Ken Kesey that he sued the producers over the project.

Randle Patrick McMurphy is sent to a mental asylum from a work farm for observation and evaluation. He believes it is easy time, simply a way to spend the rest of his short sentence in peace. McMurphy, due to his outgoing and boisterous personality, immediately provides a fresh outlook upon the lives of the inmates. From getting the therapy group to unanimously vote to watch a baseball game to escaping for a unscheduled fishing trip to arranging an all night orgy inside the asylum, McMurphy begins to allow the patients, all there at the asylum of their own volition, to achieve the smallest bit of self-confidence and camaraderie. They look up to McMurphy. To them he is a natural born leader, what they are striving to be yet lack the courage to follow through on.

Once McMurphy learns of his new fate, that he is confined to the asylum for as long as the head nurse recommends, he comes to grips with the situation. Finally understanding what must be done, McMurphy sets about escaping. This inadvertently leads to McMurphy appeasing the inmates rather that seizing that one opportunity to escape. Nurse Ratched is perhaps the creepiest nurse in film history. The final confrontation between her and McMurphy has a unique symmetry, ending that conflict and replacing the asylum back to the level of control that existed prior to his arrival.

The end result is a totally subdued McMurphy, a symbol that kept consistent to the novel in the form of organizational control for those who challenge authority. For a short while, the asylum's methods were challenged. That all went by the wayside as the lead antagonist of conformity was finally checked. *One Flew Over the Cuckoo's Nest* is about control. McMurphy's challenging of the system lifts the inmates up, if only briefly. This emotional escapism allows at least one character, 'the Chief', to free himself of the mechanistic, bureaucratic system and take back control of his own life.

One Flew Over the Cuckoo's Nest tied a forty-one year old Oscar record by winning all five major categories, Picture, Director, Lead Actor, Lead Actress and Screenplay. The only other picture to accomplish this feat before 1975 was the 1934 screwball comedy *It Happened One Night*. Four of the five awards were absolutely deserved, although Nicholson's award may have been given for not rewarding his performance the year before in *Chinatown*. The one award of the five that was questionable for this movie was in the Lead Actress category. Louise Fletcher took home the award for her portrayal of Nurse Ratched, but she was technically playing a supporting role in the film. The same type of problem would occur in 1991 when a third movie would win all five major awards.

7

IT'S A WONDERFUL LIFE
1946

Is a person's life really as meaningless as it appears to them? Is the answer as simple as stepping outside yourself to see how many people one individual can affect during a lifetime? This magical fairy tale hits upon every emotion, not only with its main character but with audiences. It is a sentimental roller coaster ride into how the most common of people can impact the world. Today it is mainly considered a Christmas film, yet *It's A Wonderful Life* is not only one of the most beautiful love stories ever set to film, but also one of the darkest tales of a man at the end of his rope, about to end it all. It is not just the heartwarming movie most remember. Its multi-layered plot is what makes the movie so great. Add in a healthy dose of faith and wonder to arrive at absolute brilliance.

George Bailey is contemplating suicide. George has worked hard to achieve his goals, but the death of his father keeps him in his small town, taking over the family business, a savings and loan company. Due to the financial constraints of helping people rather than turning a profit the police are after him for mismanaging funds. After a life spent counting nickels and dimes just to get by, despite dreams of traveling the world and completing immense projects, he is visited by an angel in training at the moment of no return. Clarence, sent down from Heaven to help him, devises a plan to show George how important he is to the world, specifically the impact he had upon his home town. It is a stark treatise on the benefits of settling for the simplicity of life, which has more meaning.

A person does not need to have faith in angels to enjoy this story. The dumbest comment I ever heard about this movie is that it was too unrealistic. Simply stated, movies are not for everyone. Imagination is something that this movie not only requires of its audience but also helps the viewer develop and heighten during the actual viewing. The fairy tale aspect is that George Bailey could not imagine what the world would be like without him. Through the help of those who cared, who prayed for him, he was able to see how different the world would have been without him.

More important than the Oscar nominations it received, five in all without one win, *It's A Wonderful Life* marked an important transformation in the career of its star James Stewart. This was Stewart's first film after returning from duty in World War II. Prior to leaving in order to serve his country, Stewart was the folksy common lovable everyman, highlighted in such great films as *Mr. Smith Goes To Washington*, *The Philadelphia Story* and *Destry Rides Again*. After playing the role of the lovable yet tortured George Bailey, Stewart embarked on a second career of sorts. He still played the folksy everyman, yet now he was tackling roles that gave him a new persona as an actor. *It's A Wonderful Life* was a marked transformation for one of Hollywood's great leading men.

It's A Wonderful Life is the ideal Christmas film, due to its repeated playing at Christmas. As a result, new generations were given the opportunity to appreciate the splendor of this movie. It is rare when a film becomes an icon to be treasured during the holiday season, despite not actually being about that specific holiday. That is a testament to the greatness of *It's A Wonderful Life*. Although the entire movie is great, that final scene never fails to start the waterworks flowing for me.

6

CITIZEN KANE
1941

How does one movie consistently get ranked as the best film ever made? Over the past forty years *Citizen Kane* has topped almost every list that ranked films. Once it was initially praised as the greatest movie ever made, it has uniquely held that status for close to the past half century. One miraculous thing about the stature of *Citizen Kane* is that, despite the evolving views on cinema over time, this movie has managed to remain atop the list. Every time a list of the greatest movies comes out that does not rank it at the top, the detractors always make their presence known.

The grand majestic life of Charles Foster Kane comes to an end. His memory and the way he impacted the world around him shall forever live on. There is a problem. Does anyone know the real Kane, the actual person behind the magnanimous public figure the world saw? This allows for the life story of Kane to be told upon the screen. From a series of flashbacks of his life, the imposing individual's history is revealed. His life is researched because of one reporter's idea that a man's final words can sum up his life, which presents one of cinema's greatest sayings, *'Rosebud'*.

While most know that secret, *Citizen Kane* fashioned itself as the first mystery/biography to be filmed from a fictional setting. That is just one of the major factors of the movie that always seems to be overlooked. One further issue however, Kane's final word, the impetus for the movie to work, is actually never heard by anyone. It is a minor plot hole that gets overlooked by those who choose to wonder at its marvel. *Citizen Kane's* technical brilliance is what is most remembered.

In recognizing the major technical breakthroughs that Welles created with cinematography, editing and story flow for this movie, most disregard how great the actual story is. The combination of a mystery told in a biographical format is fantastic to watch. The pacing gets the audience into the picture, creating the necessary suspense of what the ultimate secret will be. The story element of this movie is an often overlooked item that most critics ignore in favor of marveling at its stature.

When examining *Citizen Kane* most fans of cinema understand that it is generally the most positively regarded movie ever made. This is a distinction that transcends languages, not just an American distinction of excellence. For five straight polls, from 1962 to 2002, *Citizen Kane* has landed at the top spot for the highly revered British film magazine *Sight and Sound*. Most do not know that *Citizen Kane* only won one Oscar: Best Original Screenplay. It did not win Best Picture, losing to John Ford's *How Green Was My Valley*. The difference in greatness between these two movies is so enormous that *Citizen Kane's* defeat has been called the greatest mistake in Oscar history, including the mistakes that never rewarded Welles with any acting or directing Oscars

Orson Welles has masterfully crafted a terrific cinematic tale of a vigorous man's life, his rise to power, his downfall and the grandiose manner in which he embarked upon both. *Citizen Kane* is perceived as a technical wonder, using methods that have become widely used today. Unlike the other films that are remembered only for the technical innovations though, *Citizen Kane* is one of the few that chose not to sacrifice story, acting or any other key element simply for technique.

5

GOODFELLAS
1990

Crime doesn't pay? That is flatly contradicted in the crime thriller *Goodfellas*. For some, crime can be a lucrative business. The money is there, as it always has been, specifically when one belongs to a crew of gangsters. If it were all that easy though, everyone would do it. Like all good things it eventually must come to an end, due to the police, their own suspicions about traitors and their character flaws. It is tough to judge the reasons why someone would enter into a life of crime. This film makes no such judgments, but rather focuses on what happened in the lives of these men and their families. They revel in crime, believing in some deluded way that they are above reproach.

The film follows the real life story of mob informant Henry Hill, who grew up in New York idolizing the gangsters he saw in his neighborhood. His envy grew into mutual respect as he worked his way up the criminal ladder. In the end, he chose to save his own neck and betray the only friends he ever had. The moral response is that Hill did the right thing, but *Goodfellas* does not fall for that, correctly exposing him as traitor. His downfall is predictable, because of his lack of character. It is almost distressing to witness him turning upon the family that took him in as one of their own. Henry Hill comes off as one of the most unsympathetic character in film history. He is much worse than any of the ultra violent or treacherous gangsters that are ultimately betrayed by him.

If it were based solely upon the three or four main characters, including Paul Sorvino and excluding Hill's wife, played by Lorraine Bracco, I would have no hesitation in stating that *Goodfellas* presented the finest ensemble of acting ever assembled on one film. The real star is director Martin Scorsese though. It was almost unthinkable to imagine that he could top *Raging Bull* in stylistic content and presentation, yet *Goodfellas* achieves that and much more. This movie is not just a great and interestingly told biopic. It is a cinematic event. Scorsese's unique vision goes beyond what was standard practice, into an arena that was unchartered until he chose to explore it.

For the second straight decade, exactly ten years later, Scorsese would lose to a movie directed by an actor. The first was Redford's *Ordinary People*. This time the actor who stole the Oscar away from Scorsese was Kevin Costner, actor, director and producer of *Dances With Wolves*. The Academy seems to have a problem with realistic violence, primarily when it comes from Scorsese. The Academy has never seen fit, as of yet, to finally reward Scorsese for his directorial greatness, as they finally did with Spielberg. They missed the boat in 1980, 1990 and rewarded the wrong film in 2004 over Scorsese's much better *The Aviator*. It seems that no matter what kind of movie Scorsese does he is simply not worthy of the Academy's recognition.

Often criticized as glamorizing crime and gangsters, which cost it the Academy Award for Best Picture, *Goodfellas* presented its unflinching look at the pitfalls of entering into a life of crime without asking anyone for forgiveness. If you didn't like the movie it was your fault, not Scorsese's. Most agreed with Scorsese. The story called for a harsh depiction of life, representative of what went on with these men. *Goodfellas* is Martin Scorsese's calling card. It is the best film he has ever made.

4

THE BRIDGE ON THE RIVER KWAI
1957

When does pride interfere with sanity? This is the foundation that *The Bridge on the River Kwai* is based upon. Even after a platoon of British soldiers is ordered to surrender, a rigid British Colonel is insistent upon sticking to the rules of proper conduct, at all costs. A lifetime officer, rules and codes are all he has to believe in. This directly conflicts with the sadistic warden of the prisoner camp because rules are all he has as well. Both men's lives and duties are based upon the strict adherence to orders. *The Bridge on the River Kwai* is primarily about their bizarre relationship.

The leader of the newly arrived British contingent, Colonel Nicholson, is about as stubborn as they come. Rules are what govern societies and create civilizations. After having been told that civilization does not exist here, by one of the few people who remained alive in the camp long enough to witness the new arrivals, an American named Shears, Nicholson calmly explains that it is their duty to bring civilization here. Immediately Shears knows there is something wrong with his code.

The sadistic warden, Colonel Saito, is given the task of building a bridge. He is given prisoners as laborers, but insists upon forcing the officers to work alongside the men under their command. This is a direct violation of the Geneva Convention, as pointed out by Nicholson, who refuses to allow his officers to perform manual labor. Saito punishes the officers, specifically Nicholson, almost to the point of death. Nicholson does not give in, eventually winning his freedom from a torture hut and takes over command of building of the bridge, to do a proper English job.

In a battle of wills, Nicholson inevitably wins out. But at what cost? The bridge he now takes charge of building will benefit the Japanese. This is brought up to him by a fellow officer, yet Nicholson sees the task as restoring pride in his men. Shears manages to escape early on and is forced into leading a small expedition back to the camp with the express nature of destroying this bridge. Only at the end, just before it is too late, does Nicholson recognize the error of his ways.

Upon its release in 1957. *The Bridge on the River Kwai* was one those rare films, critically acclaimed and well received by the public. It was the top grossing movie of its year. It would come to affect the theater business once again, nine years later. The film was set to be aired on television for the first time on September 25th, 1966. The TV airing was such a great success that the date was dubbed *'Black Sunday'*, due to the loss in revenue from cinemas that day. This only furthers the notion of how great a movie *The Bridge on the River Kwai* actually is. It thoroughly shatters the effete and snobbish belief that for a movie to be great it must be unappreciated in its own time.

The Bridge on the River Kwai illustrates the madness of blindly following orders beyond any interference on the part of common sense. Nicholson and Saito are completely different as men, but entirely similar as officers. It is the greatest anti-war film ever made, making a definitive statement on not only the futility of war, but also portraying two unique individuals only separated by their different cultures. If Nicholson were born in Japan, he would have been a Saito, and vice versa.

3

GONE WITH THE WIND
1939

I would never have thought it possible for anyone to glorify the South in their inhumane struggle and entry into the Civil War over the right to own and keep a race of people inferior to them. I was wrong. *Gone With The Wind* is a spectacle without rival, worthy of the title of epic. Even in its presentation of pompous cultural superiority, the look and grandeur of the film exceeds any moral objection one can muster. It is decidedly sad that the South reveled in that thinking, yet even sadder that they went to war with their own countrymen to protect what amounts to oppression.

This is a tale of the Old South. These men, and it is made clear that in the Old South it was a man's world, saw themselves as gentleman and grand old Knights. They were doing God's work by keeping ownership of human beings because of the color of their skin. One of them was different though, the blockade runner Rhett Butler. Rhett does not fight for the cause of oppression or the ability to keep an archaic way of life alive, but rather fights for profit. In a crowd of arrogant and tyrannical animals masquerading as honorable gentleman, Rhett stands out as the only person with any true character of the bunch. His demeanor often puts him at odds with the other Confederates.

Gone With The Wind is not really about the Civil War, in the same way that *Rocky* and *Raging Bull* are not about boxing. This movie is about a true heroine, Scarlett O'Hara. It is her story, or evolution that drives this grand old tale. Scarlett begins as the typical Southern belle, rich and spoiled. She gets what she wants and of course wants what she cannot have. What she cannot have is Ashley Wilkes, even though that does not stop her from trying. The movie's triumph though, is Scarlett's emotional journey. The beauty of this movie is that after Scarlett gets her comeuppance, she proclaims to go on. This displays true courage in the face of hardship, a testament to her will.

Most focus on the relationship between Scarlett and Rhett when thinking about *Gone With The Wind*, yet that is only one of many components of this majestic film. Its bigger theme is survival. That is when a true hero shines through most, evidenced by the grand finale where Scarlett declares that she will go on. It is a perfect ending for this great film. The story needed that element, one of a promise for hope, after all the carnage. Whether it was as a result of the arrogance of ignorance or not, if Scarlett can change and evolve, so can everyone. Despite the epic grandeur of the film, perhaps the grandest of them all, its basic themes are those that remain common and relatable to all.

During the original draft my editor challenged me to remove all my own personal biases of the culture displayed in the film. I obliged to a point, yet the film is based upon those biases and therefore they should be discussed. Margaret Mitchell's novel clearly was pro-South, attempting to show the struggles of what she perceived to be a proud culture. The movie did however remove the many Ku Klux Klan segments and unlike another famous movie, *The Birth of a Nation*, it refused to glorify oppression. The difference between these two films is that *Gone With the Wind* tried to be empathetic in its view of a culture that tried to break a nation apart, yet simultaneously showed the horrors of those attempts rather than promoting further hatred by praising them.

2

RAIDERS OF THE LOST ARK
1981

    I am too young to know about those Saturday afternoon serials, also called cliffhangers, which showed a hero plunging to his doom at the end. Every week, the hero would somehow get away, only to find himself in the same predicament again, leaving the audience on the edge of their seats until next weekend. Imagine if someone had the vision to take those serials and combine them into a cohesive whole? That's exactly what Steven Spielberg accomplished, in the best movie he has ever made. True, *Schindler's List* is a more mature film, but *Raiders of the Lost Ark* is simply better.

    Keeping to that cliffhanger format, the movie immediately starts out with a blast as Indiana Jones searches through a South American jungle temple for a lost relic, encountering booby traps all around him. Even when the action stops for a brief moment, it is replaced by the suspense of what will come next. The whole movie sticks to that grand style as Indiana Jones travels across the world in search of that most sought after lost relic, which for this movie is the Lost Ark of the Covenant.

    As the movie had to be expanded to include a full length story, a love interest was added. The key to that element is that it does not drag down the action, but rather compliments it. Marion Crane is led by her ability to get into situations that call for action just as Indiana Jones is. Some would say that it is in their nature. Without it, they would be empty. It was an ingenious decision to not over romanticize their relationship, creating a character that could be both docile and able to take care of herself. This is where the first sequel failed, by making the heroine too feminine. That took away from the continual danger, the element that made *Raiders of the Lost Ark* such a classic.

    Speaking of the two sequels, the magnificence of the original has been truly affected by these two movies that followed. Similar to *Rocky*, most people equate *Raiders of the Lost Ark* as part of one combined film, judging the original on the totality of the whole. This assessment is regardless of how many different movies were made. The two sequels, *Temple of Doom* and *The Last Crusade* were of such a lesser quality that companies only offer the series as a whole. It is basic economics, arriving from an understanding that no one with any taste would purchase these two sequels by themselves unless they were packaged with the original. This speaks volumes as to how great a movie *Raiders of the Lost Ark is*, that it can single handedly carry two lesser films by itself and still produce profits.

    It is imperative to see past that and judge each movie based upon its individual merits. That is what landed *Raiders of the Lost Ark* just one spot short of the best movie on this list. I understand that more than any other placement on this list, *Raiders of the Lost Ark* at the number two spot, will more than likely provide the most controversy. For anyone who has ever watched this amazing film, I challenge them to argue its ability to keep their eyes glued to screen with a masterful combination of action, adventure, mystery, suspense and intelligent unexpected bursts of humor. No other movie is like it and all attempts at duplicating it come up short. Any analysis does not do this movie proper justice. It has to be seen to be believed. Once that occurs, I am sure you will agree with its ranking.

1

CASABLANCA
1943

This is it. We have arrived at number one, after forty-nine amazing entries. You knew this movie would show up eventually and most should be satisfied that it was placed at number one, rather than the standard choice for number one, which came in at number six. Comparing these two films, one can single out the technical wonder of *Citizen Kane* or marvel at the totality of *Casablanca* when making the choice as to which is the better film. I choose totality over technical innovation.

Sooner or later, everyone goes to Rick's. There is an air of mystery about Rick though, which adds to the intrigue in this exceptional film. A long time ago Rick had his heart broken by a woman. Since then, he has become a master at cynicism, so much that it embodies him. That makes him irresistible to women and indispensable to all others around him. The traitorous Ugarte leaves stolen documents with him because Rick's loathing for Ugarte allows him to be trusted, while Capt. Renault's friendship with Rick allows him to play both sides. In Casablanca, that proves profitable.

Ilsa, the woman who broke Rick's heart, suddenly returns. She has arrived in Casablanca with her husband, a member of the French resistance and notorious escape artist. Rick takes care to keep his own neck safe in French occupied Casablanca, until she walks back into his life. Now everything must be placed on the line. Or is it possible that Rick will help her husband escape simply to get back his long lost love? It is that mystery that allows this movie to remain timeless.

Rick Blaine is one of the greatest characters in film history. The mystery that initially surrounds him, followed by the heartbreak that befalls him when he remembers Ilsa and their time together, only to be trumped by his heroic act of selflessness, is what sets Rick apart from all the rest of the lovable saps who prove their worth in the end. Bogart's acting is so superb that his only Oscar was without a doubt a makeup award, for other performances that specifically included *Casablanca*. His performance sets the tone of the movie. The supporting actors magnificently cover the rest.

Casablanca is probably the most often quoted movie ever made. There are numerous famous lines of dialogue that have taken on a life of their own. One line is generally misquoted as *"Play it again Sam"*, which was turned into a play and eventually a movie starring Woody Allen. The actual line of dialogue is *"Play it Sam. Play 'As time goes by'"*. Other great lines have been *"round up the usual suspects"*, which became the title for a fantastic movie as well and *"I think this is the beginning of a beautiful friendship"*. This last line of the film has often been called perfect, in movies that pay homage to *Casablanca* and also given birth to a novel on how the story continued.

The beauty of this film lies within its dialogue. It seems that every line is nothing short of perfect. The stories of script pages coming in as shooting went on have become that of legend. More than any other movie *Casablanca's* dialogue breathes life into its characters. Only getting better with further viewings, it is without hesitation that I say *Casablanca* is the most perfect movie ever made. Even though I rank it as number one, I still feel that I am undervaluing it, as strange as that may be.

50 BEST MOVIES

1 - CASABLANCA
2 - RAIDERS OF THE LOST ARK
3 - GONE WITH THE WIND
4 - BRIDGE ON THE RIVER KWAI
5 - GOODFELLAS
6 - CITIZEN KANE
7 - IT'S A WONDERFUL LIFE
8 - ONE FLEW OVER THE CUCKOO'S NEST
9 - THE GODFATHER
10 - THE MANCHURIAN CANDIDATE
11 - PSYCHO
12 - RAGING BULL
13 - SUNSET BOULEVARD
14 - TO KILL A MOCKINGBIRD
15 - A BEAUTIFUL MIND
16 - LORD OF THE RINGS III
17 - MIDNIGHT COWBOY
18 - BEAUTY AND THE BEAST
19 - THE GODFATHER II
20 - THE FUGITIVE
21 - THE GRAPES OF WRATH
22 - SCHINDLER'S LIST
23 - MR. SMITH GOES TO WASHINGTON
24 - THE THIRD MAN
25 - VERTIGO
26 - THE SHAWSHANK REDEMPTION
27 - THE WIZARD OF OZ
28 - REAR WINDOW
29 - THE STING
30 - FROM HERE TO ETERNITY
31 - L. A. CONFIDENTIAL
32 - TOUCH OF EVIL
33 - THE CONVERSATION
34 - THE MALTESE FALCON
35 - CHINATOWN
36 - NETWORK
37 - ON THE WATERFRONT
38 - HIGH NOON
39 - REBECCA
40 - REDS
41 - FIELD OF DREAMS
42 - TWELVE ANGRY MEN
43 - JFK
44 - THE NIGHT OF THE HUNTER
45 - ROCKY
46 - FARGO
47 - BREAKING AWAY
48 - THE PRINCESS BRIDE
49 - AIRPLANE!
50 - ALL THE PRESIDENT'S MEN

Chapter Two:

My 10 (11) Favorite Movies

First off, there must be a distinction made between favorite movies and best movies. To designate a movie as one of your favorites would mean that if it were on television, scanned as you were passing from channel to channel, the surfing ends immediately, the remote is placed down and that movie stays on. The person who considers any movie as one of their all-time favorites will watch that movie on a consistent basis especially if the movie is on television. A favorite never gets old to a viewer. If a movie does happen to grow over time into one that is not watched at any moment then it must be reclassified as something other than a favorite.

A best movie is a movie of such great value that it is generally recognized as such. The difference between a best and a favorite is that if a movie is designated as a best movie is seen the week before and suddenly passed during a channel surfing outing, it might not remain on for the duration. It was just seen, so the viewer can acknowledge that it is on and then move to the next channel, hopefully showing one of their favorites. The best film is a classic yet the viewer may not always be in the mood to watch it. That is a definitive distinction. A good rule of thumb is that the best movies can also be your favorites but it is generally rare when your favorites are the best.

Throughout this book you will see chapters that are generally block number oriented. This chapter is unique as the chapter title should have foreshadowed. Of the 10 movies that will be discussed in this chapter, over the upcoming ten pages, not one of them made the main list appearing in the previous chapter 1. For that reason, there is a second number in parentheses next to the 10. The reason is because one of my all-time favorite movies, in fact my second favorite made the main list. That film landed in the #7 spot.

I could not discuss my favorite films and pretend that *It's A Wonderful Life* was not one of them. Almost everyone who knows me knows the affinity I have for that fantastic film. However, *It's A Wonderful Life* has already been discussed in the first chapter. It would have been redundant to include that movie in this chapter so I included another movie that just barely missed my list of ten favorite films. Now that movie has.

The ten movies discussed over the next ten pages are in no particular order. *It's A Wonderful Life* is my second favorite movie and just by coincidence, the first movie discussed happens to be my favorite. That does not mean that the movie discussed on the page directly after that one is my third favorite, followed by my fourth, fifth and all the way down to my eleventh. The numbers do not go that far. I can honestly tell you that I do not know exactly what my eighth favorite movie is. Anyone who does know is a bit too anal for their own good. Therefore, the other nine movies discussed here are movies that I simply love watching and could spend an entire day going through each of them and then do it again only days later.

There are other movies like them, such as *Old School, The Zero Effect, All Through The Night, Frailty, Strange Cargo, The Hustler, Dark City, Rounders, Winchester '73, Father of the Bride II* and many more. The nine movies after my all-time favorite provided in this chapter were chosen because of my fond affection for them and my willingness to share those feelings. Perhaps after reading about them they will become favorites of yours. At the least I hope my thoughts will make you want to see them.

STALAG 17

1953

Is it more important to keep up the good fight or to merely settle in and ride out the war, after a soldier lands in a prisoner of war camp? Interesting questions arise as a result. How far does one's own country expect a solider to go to after capture for duty? Is it really obligation or an element of insanity to continue fighting despite imprisonment? During World War II, hijinks are mixed with intrigue and plots to escape for a group of prisoners who are intent upon helping the Allies in any way possible. Escape is continually tried, even if it means getting shot, as the opening scene of the films shows. This film is a comedy, yet complete with harsh dramatic undertones.

The main character, if there is one, is Sergeant J. J. Sefton. Sefton is the typical cynic. He has served his time for his country and now that he is captured, Sefton is going to sit back and take it easy, making his life as comfortable as possible in the meantime. His extreme cynicism ruminates as a result of having his property stolen upon his arrival at the camp. That quickly wised him up to the way of things. Now he runs the majority of the gambling, including mouse races and a peek-a-boo stand where the prisoners can watch the neighboring Russian women prisoners shower through a telescope, all for a price. His winnings are spent in trade with the guards, all to increase the ease of his stay. The guards are the enemy, yet only a day after they shoot two prisoners for escaping Sefton is back trading with them. This characteristic makes the rest of his barrack mates loathe him.

The movie is focused on that particular barracks. The two men who are killed for trying to escape came from that barracks, as well as the two new entries in camp that are placed there. This presents the story's main focus. Due to all the security leaks the men in the camp believe that barracks is jinxed, since the Germans seem to know everything that goes on inside. Ideas of a traitor are entertained. Immediately, all eyes become centered on Sefton. After circumstantial evidence is discovered on Sefton, the men lash out at him and beat him. He obviously knows that he's not the traitor, so now it is up to him to find the real person informing the Germans of what is going on. He soon discovers that the spy is a German planted there to gather information. Sefton is now in charge of his own safety. He must figure out a way to reveal the spy or pay the ultimate price.

Stalag 17 is one of director Billy Wilder's most enjoyable films to watch. The story mixes a unique blend of comedy and mystery to make light of a particularly troubling time in world history. There is great music and terrific acting, specifically William Holden as Sefton, who won his only Oscar for his amazing portrayal of this cynical yet tragic character. I can remember the first time I saw *Stalag 17*. I was about fifteen years old and was flipping through the channels. I saw the scene where the members of the barracks were taking turns beating Sefton in his bunk. I watched the rest of it, but I missed the first half set up. I would continually catch *Stalag 17* in the middle when it was on television, but each time I would see a little more. That still did not deter me from watching. Eventually, I saw the whole movie. I can honestly say that it is without a doubt my favorite film.

THE JERK
1979

Comedy is one of the truly subjective matters when it comes to films. Much more than dramas or thrillers, comedies are always held to a higher standard, oxymoronically because of their perceived immaturity. Whether immature or not, how can one not love a movie where a dirty white bum tells his story and starts by explaining that he was born a poor black child? This setup provides the basis for one of the most hilarious stories ever filmed. *The Jerk* is a true comedy classic.

It is a simple fact of nature that idiots are fun to watch. I am not speaking about those who are born retarded, but those who spend years of their lives cultivating their stupidity. Navin R. Johnson is one of these types of people. His exploits are of the kind of hilarity that movies do not offer anymore, at least on purpose. It is a natural style of comedy, born out of the mind of an absolute comedic genius. I cannot imagine anyone other than Steve Martin in this role. Watching his early stand up comedy, it is easy to see that this was the role he was meant to play.

Leaving his home in Mississippi to search and discover the world, Navin impacts a number of people on his meteoric rise to wealth. As he reaches new heights of stupidity in spending his newly earned money, that inevitable fall approaches. The theme of the movie is one man's idiocy and how he achieves wealth as a result. Navin does not possess the regular type of stupidity. He embodied rampant absurdity and on such a grand scale. Perhaps I am over explaining the nature of the story. There only need be one requirement for a movie such as this, heaping loads of funny material. *The Jerk* certainly does not disappoint on that basic criteria.

Moving from one situation to the next, Navin R. Johnson continues to amaze as his discoveries enlighten him and amuse us. It is hard to relay comedy from movies but one of the hysterical highlights is when Navin is stalked because his name appears in the phone book, arguing that the man shooting at him simply hates cans, I cannot help but crack up. There is also the first date where he earnestly tells Bernadette Peters that the new pizza in a cup is so great that it put the old pizza in a cup guy out of business. The first time I heard that line I actually hurt myself laughing. Other gems include when Navin insists that the waiter from a French restaurant bring some fresh wine rather than the old stuff, when he dreams of redecorating the men's bathroom at the garage so as to maximize space and not disturb the customers peeing and the legendary thermos song.

The Steve Martin movies are highly underappreciated, mainly because of their nonsensical formulas. Of all the movies he has made, *The Jerk* stands out as the absolute gem of the bunch. It is every bit as equal to those great madcap movies of the golden age, when the great comedy teams, such as the Marx Brothers and Abbott and Costello, soared above all others. The humor in this film comes off as offensive to some though. Those people need to relax. Why create humor if it will not be offensive to some, an idea that Martin fully understood? Despite what anyone thinks, Navin R. Johnson is one of the great characters in film history, if only for his utter and rampant stupidity.

GENTLEMAN JIM

1942

One of the biggest problems in distinguishing athletes from different generations is the fact that there is not enough information about the era when the old timers were at the heights of their careers. This is one of the many reasons why a movie such as *Gentleman Jim* is such a treat to watch. Clearly capturing the time when former heavyweight champion James J. Corbett arrived upon the boxing scene, this biopic details Corbett's meteoric rise, highlighting his regal entrance into boxing.

As a fan of old time boxing, I found the movie an absolute delight, specifically in its depiction of early boxing as a sideshow event rather than what the sport has been turned into today. That evolution can be traced to Corbett's influence. Errol Flynn, the swashbuckling hero of such films as *Captain Blood* and the highly underrated *The Adventures of Robin Hood*, provides the perfect amount of self confidence and arrogance in portraying one of the true early legends of prizefighting. Coming from humble working class stock, Corbett has to work his way up through the ranks the hard way.

After showing up a boxing teacher at a San Francisco Athletic Club, Corbett is then set up for what appears to be a rude awakening for the cocky but likeable guy. The members of the club have had enough of his self promotion and set up a rigged fight, yet Corbett manages to outlast and outbox their ringer. Next up are paid prizefights where Corbett begins to make a name for himself as a boxer of promise. After numerous victories Corbett finally gets a match with the first modern heavyweight champion, the legendary John L. Sullivan. There is a distinct difference between the two fighters, as proper weight classes had yet to be established. Corbett is a lean and quick moving fighter. Sullivan is a bruising brawler. Their personalities are as opposite as their fighting styles.

When the time comes for them to meet, it is billed as the greatest heavyweight match ever to have been scheduled up to that time. The boxing match lives up to its promotion, lasting twenty one rounds before Corbett's quickness and stamina finally gets to Sullivan, who goes down by way of knockout. A new era is born. It is an era of a different style of fighting ushered in by the man they would nickname Gentleman Jim. His innovative style paved the way for modern boxing.

Many biopics, specifically about boxers, often come off as flat. The general tendency is to spend too much time on the fights rather than showcasing the boxers and their stories. *Gentleman Jim* is entirely different, making a point to show Corbett's personality. It was Corbett's unique personality that was a big part of the reason why he became one of the lightest and quickest heavyweight champions ever. Flynn's performance was perfect. He translated his usual swashbuckling acting style over to the world of this self-assured pioneer. The film also showcases some fantastic supporting performances, most notable among them are Alan Hale as the father of the fighting Corbett clan and Ward Bond. Bond, who reproduces an almost perfect John L. Sullivan, steals every scene he is in. It was surprising that his performance was not recognized by the Academy for its brilliance. It may have suffered from that all too common problem, not enough screen time.

THE NATURAL
1984

Sometimes a movie can reach out and touch a person. It can be as simple as the mood a viewer is in a particular time. It can also be as simple as a great movie. *The Natural* is most definitely the latter, but not restricted to that. Set within the world of baseball, this quasi-fantasy evokes memories of supernatural heroes and tales of old. All the mythic elements are there in this magnificent story; the rising of a young hero, his downfall at the hands of what can only be deemed an evil villain, the hero's return to prominence, the struggles he must overcome and the eventual march towards victory. His defeat of those who try to keep him down becomes legendary as a result.

This story has been done before, yet for some magical reason *The Natural* seems different. It appears as fresh today as if it were an original story. An average tale told hundreds of times before, the key is that the film breathes new life into that age old tale of heroes and their mythical overcoming of all odds. There is a clear distinction between the good guys and the bad guys in stories like this, with that one special character who tips the scales one way or the other with his anticipated success or unfortunate failure. The hero is flawed, which allows his triumph to be monumental.

Middle aged rookie Roy Hobbs joins the last place New York Knights. He is the epitome of mystery, the man from nowhere. Once Hobbs is finally allowed to play, his exploits become that of legend. His monstrously long home runs help revitalize the last place Knights, another mythic reference. With fame comes the need for information about his past. A cynical sports writer, Max Mercy, remembers a young eighteen year old pitcher who once struck out the best baseball player around, the Whammer. Once Mercy places Hobbs, who knows what else he can dig up about his past? With any hero, there are always things from their past that should remain hidden.

With success comes struggle. Hobbs falls into an awful slump, continuing until one day at Wrigley Field. At this particular game he sees the childhood love of his life in the stands. Something inside him clicks as he hits a memorable home run that shatters a large clock at the top of the center field scoreboard. Now that he is back on track, his mission is to help the Knights win the pennant so the evil and corrupt judge will not be able to take the team away from the long time manager. Demons of old come back to haunt him and the team, yet the mighty hero plays in that final game. He plays through a bad injury and leads his team to the pennant, saving the day as every hero does.

The Natural is neo-mythology. It is good versus evil with all the magical trimmings in between. There is nothing to be ashamed about for liking a movie that some consider hokey. As stated earlier, there are movies that just touch your heart. Growing up playing baseball and dreaming of writing, telling stories of magic and wonder, this movie exemplified both aspects of my desired future. I consider myself lucky I was able to accomplish one of those dreams and I watch *The Natural* for the other. Whenever I wonder what might have been if my other dream came true, all I have to do is pop *The Natural* in and get whisked away to a time that has long since gone.

INHERIT THE WIND
1960

What is the correct answer to where man comes from? Is the solution to that age old riddle creationism or evolution? Despite the scientific evidence to lean modern thinkers toward evolution, there are still many, in increasing numbers, which have resumed lobbying for the teaching of creationism in the form of science in the classrooms. In 1925, a courageous Tennessee teacher named John Scopes was arrested for teaching Darwin's theory on the evolution of man. Tennessee, that bastion of educational enlightenment, had passed a law which forbade the teaching of any theory that denied the creation of man and the world as set forth in the Bible. Scientific evidence be damned, Tennessee loves the Lord. There was no way they would allow progress or evidence change that.

The 1961 movie *Inherit the Wind* chronicles the story of what took place during that time in history. Often referred to as the Scopes Monkey Trial, this legal battle took the nation by storm, remaining a trial of legendary historical value. In the actual trial, brilliant legal minds Clarence Darrow and William Jennings Bryan sat on opposing sides. In the film, these two characters were portrayed by Spencer Tracy and Frederic March. While the film spends most of its time in court, debating the points regarding that unjust law versus freedom of choice, some of the key elements to the story occur outside of the court room. The crazed religious nuts of the community are depicted feverishly marching and chanting for the teacher to be hung from *'a sour apple tree'*. It is sad to say, but when the movie was made, thirty-six years after the original trial, not all that much had changed.

The courtroom battle scenes between Tracy and March are exceptional. Their back and forth rhetoric alone is a cause for watching the film over and over again. Frederic March steals many of the scenes by passionately portraying the religious zealot who fought against those who wanted to think, believing he was instructed to lead the crusade by God himself. Tracy's character was not a disbeliever in God, but rather a believer in the power and right of freedom of speech, choice and ultimately a freedom to believe what you want. According to his character, there was no way of breaking any unjust laws because the goal was to create laws that were not of the unjust type. *Inherit the Wind* stressed philosophy versus uneducated faith, choosing thinking as the higher calling.

An additional facet to the story was the role of a cynical reporter, played by Gene Kelly. In perhaps his finest actual acting performance, Kelly's character serves as an enemy to the Bible beating inhabitants of the town and their self anointed savior who shall punish those against them and an antithesis to the lawyer who champions true justice. Kelly tells the story to the world. A story of how one backwater community is dragging the world back to the stone-age with their quest to stop the teaching of a science that they personally do not like. Although Tracy's character works toward the same goal as Kelly's, their methods are distinctly different. This eventually culminates the story with the verdict that even justice does not always triumph over the law. The differences between Tracy and Kelly shows that there is more than one way to get a message across and people who are always willing to disregard it based upon their own lack of evolved thought.

THE CINCINNATI KID
1965

Does it matter if you know that you are the best at something? It has to be proven on the battlefield. In this case, the battlefield is the poker table in Norman Jewison's stylistic gambling thriller *The Cincinnati Kid*. To be the man you have to beat the man. Nothing is going to get in the way of the head to head battle that the entire gambling underworld of New Orleans wants to see, the Cincinnati Kid versus Lancey Howard. *The Cincinnati Kid* is a tale of sacrificing everything for the achievement of notoriety. In the world of gambling, notoriety is often mistaken for immortality. There is only one rule for the poker player who wants the prestigious title of the best, to win and win with your ability. In seedy New Orleans though, that's easier said than done.

Stud poker player Eric Stoner, known as the Cincinnati Kid, is the new breed of gambler. The Kid is willing to take on anyone at anytime and at anything having to do with action. Name the stakes and he will be there. Poker is his forte though, yet the New Orleans poker scene has grown stale for him. He has beaten every game in town and holds a marker on just about every player who sits down at a table. The gambler's code is in needing that thrill of action and the town is slowly running dry. Only some great mythic challenge could peak the Kid's interest enough for him to stay in town. That's just about the time the best stud poker player in the country arrives, old time legend Lancey Howard. The Kid is calm, cool and confident. He wants Lancey, respectfully called 'The Man' because of his stature and he wants his best game. The Cincinnati Kid knows he can beat it.

Off to the side are a number of subplots. There is the rich egomaniacal gambler dead set on fixing the game between Lancey and the Kid for personal reasons, the history between the Kid and 'Shooter', a dealer who owes that gambler and the Kid's relationship with an innocent girl named Christian. She only wants to devote herself to him while asking for the slightest care in return. To take his mind off waiting for the game, the Kid visits her after she has left New Orleans for her parent's home, yet it is obvious that all that is on the Kid's mind is the upcoming game. It is his chance to prove to everybody what he already knows, that he is the best. What the Kid will learn is that it takes more than skill and talent to beat the best, a lesson he will learn the hard way.

Filled with classic scenery that evokes the time period and great music of the region, *The Cincinnati Kid* is a real treasure. There are a bevy of great performances throughout, including the final great performance of a storied career by Edward G. Robinson as Lancey and about the dirtiest type of backstabbing immoral slut the times would allow, played by the stunning Ann-Margaret. Throw in Rip Torn as the revenge driven gambler, Karl Malden as the dealer who must battle with his own demons and make a tough decision about the game, Tuesday Weld as Christian and legendary screen actress Joan Blondell as a substitute dealer with as much spunk as talent. These great actors combine to create one of the true gems of 1960's cinema. Some have called it *The Hustler* set in the world of poker. While an oversimplification, that still isn't too bad.

BEAUTIFUL GIRLS
1996

In a span of about three years there must have been close to a dozen different movies that all centered on the concept of a high school reunion. Most of these films were slowly paced and often overly formulaic. One of the really good ones that delved into this concept was the John Cusack hit man/love story *Grosse Pointe Blank*. Cusack's humorous performance helped save that movie from becoming ordinary. The only great one was a small movie that dealt with numerous characters and a diverse series of subplots, all nicely blending into one main story. The film is not based upon a single main character, yet rather based upon a solid story that perfectly functions as the main character.

From a script written by Scott Rosenberg, screenwriter of the highly stylized *Things To Do in Denver When You're Dead*, *Beautiful Girls* uses snappy dialogue and rich character depictions to relay the story of a group of guys and where they find themselves ten years after graduating from high school. The quasi-main character, played by Timothy Hutton, travels back to a fictional town in up-state New York for his ten year reunion. He is in a bit of a rut and figures on having this time help him figure things out. He finds that little has changed. Many of his friends are right where they were when he left, specifically in their maturity levels. That happens to be exactly what he needs to see to set him straight. A good dose of being away from it all does him wonders.

From old friendships to making a new friendship, Willie C. (Hutton) settles in to his new outlook on life. With a little help from his girlfriend arriving on reunion night, a visiting cousin of one of his schoolmates and an extremely intellectual thirteen year-old neighbor, Willie learns that it is sometimes better to simply enjoy what you have in life rather than searching for more of the unknown. Seeing things through an outsider perspective can often change one's opinions about life, which is just the thing that many of us need. In Willie's case, this points him back in the right direction. The thirteen year old neighbor is played to masterful perfection by Natalie Portman, in a star making performance. Portman's witty back and forth banter with Hutton is the most delightful element this film has to offer. The rhetoric among the men is what is mostly remembered about this film, with some fantastic analyses about everything from relationships to simple points of grammar.

The film boasts a fantastic soundtrack and a number of immensely clever scenes of pure dialogue, including a scene where two guys down a shot because one of them is sleeping with the other's wife and the great stream of dialogue that comes from within the bar discussing the color of a diamond. The way these friends interact with each other provides a sense of realism that many films fail to offer. Supported by a bevy of gorgeous women, including Uma Thurman, Lauren Holly, Mira Sorvino and Annabeth Gish, *Beautiful Girls* is equal parts touching and hysterical. The pacing of the film may seem a bit slow, but there are sarcastic jabs at everyone and everything to ease that along, with moments of deep clarity that should make us all think about what we have and enjoy life.

OCTOBER SKY
1999

Is it better to follow your dreams or do what is expected of you? In the mining town of Coalwood, West Virginia, there are only two types of futures, getting out of the town on a football scholarship or remaining in town to work in the coal mine. One young dreamer decided to create a third option. *October Sky* tells the true story of Homer Hickum and his driving ambition to make something more of himself. His desire and drive ultimately led Hickum to college on an academic scholarship and work in the NASA space program. His persistence gave the simple people of the town hope, a hope that if they follow their own dream it may take them wherever they want to go.

Young Homer Hickum, after seeing the lights in the sky from the historic Sputnik launch, decides to turn his attention toward rocketry. With the help of his three friends, Roy Lee, Quentin and Sherman, Homer begins building and launching rockets. With small successes and failures comes knowledge. No matter how many times their rocket fails to achieve what is intended, they push forward. In order to make something more than what is expected they have to keep trying. Their goal is to enter a successful rocket in the science fair and possibly win academic scholarships to college. The boys are dead set on figuring out an alternative way out of Coalwood, led by Homer's leadership and persistence. Their initial failures only strengthen their resolve in achieving success.

Despite the encouragement of their teacher, Miss Riley, who suffers from Hodgkin's disease, an obstacle threatens their chances. A forest fire is accidentally started, which causes major damage. The boy's rocket experiments are stopped because they are arrested. It is believed that one of their rockets started the forest fire. Forced to abandon his dream, Hickum goes to work in the coal mine, due to an explosion that almost kills his father. Seeing what life will offer him, Homer rededicates himself to his dream and proves that his rocket could not have started the fire. Armed with a new sense of hope the boys enter the local science fair. They win and are entered in the Nationals. A win means scholarships for all, but more importantly it means a way out of Coalwood.

The acting throughout is superb, yet I have to discuss one standout, Chris Cooper as Homer's dad. Cooper won the Best Supporting Actor Oscar for his performance in *Adaptation*, where he played the peculiar orchid thief John Laroche. Cooper has also appeared in the highly successful and critically acclaimed film *American Beauty*, from this same year. His performance in this movie outshines every role he has ever turned in. This role made him a star, even if he is still considered a character actor. Cooper brings such a mix of intensity and caring that when he finally comes to see the last rocket launch and is given the honor of lighting the fuse, his response is enough to break your heart. Although the entire movie is inspiring, the scene where Homer explains to his dad that he is his hero sets the movie apart from all others. Simply looking at Chris Cooper's face during this scene, portraying both a sense of pride and regret, completes the film in every way.

WITHOUT A CLUE
1988

There is only one answer to the question of who the world's greatest detective is. The masterful literary creation of Sir Arthur Conan Doyle has solved every mystery presented before him. It is a no-brainer that the great Sherlock Holmes shall solve the mystery and bring the criminals to justice. The beauty has always been in how he infers what took place based on the facts at hand, facts that he alone has the deductive power to understand and make sense out of. In this sense it is the delivery of the material rather than the basic setup of a detective solving a crime. What would happen if the true forensic genius was Sherlock Holmes' associate, Dr. John Watson?

In the brilliantly clever *Without A Clue*, the plot is such a stylish and elegant take on literary history, yet remains so simple that it works beautifully. Sherlock Holmes is nothing more than an actor playing a part, while the real mastermind behind figuring out the true nature of the crime is Dr. Watson. Watson had hoped to get appointed to the faculty of a conservative medical college, so he needed to invent a fake detective to take his place after taking his hobby one step too far by solving a case for one of his patients. Since then, the world has reveled in reading the great adventures of Sherlock Holmes, written by Dr. Watson. Holmes is the face and name, while Watson is the genius behind all the work. This is something that few people know. After taking all he could take, Dr. Watson throws Holmes out of his home due to his continual ineptitude and drinking. Watson would soon and painfully discover that it is not genius that the world wants, it is Holmes.

Watson finds Holmes in a bar and the two men work together again as a new case comes up involving counterfeiting. As they investigate the case, Holmes playing his part and Watson remaining in the shadows to unearth the truths that he will let Holmes take credit for, it becomes obvious that an old adversary is involved, the nefarious villain Moriarty. Additionally, it becomes clear to Watson that Moriarty knows their secret when a failed attempt on the life of Holmes was actually meant for Watson. Continuing the investigation, Watson is murdered, leaving Holmes to fend for himself. Knowing that he is completely outmatched Holmes somehow manages to find Moriarty's secret lair, discovering that Watson is still alive. Together, they jointly solve the crime.

Without A Clue takes one of literature's greatest teams and juxtaposes their abilities. What is created is an excellent comedy of errors. In managing to provide a touching look at what shall now become the beginning of a beautiful friendship, one must wonder why the film was not a major success, enough for there to have been at least one sequel. The first time I saw *Without A Clue* I immediately watched it again, because it was that smart and inventive a movie. That may have been its downfall, the fact that it was too smart for its own good, which usually results in box office failure. The two leads tackle their roles with brilliance, creating such believable characters that one would think Sherlock Holmes and Dr. John Watson were written in this manner from the original Doyle stories. I think that if Doyle were alive today this would have been one of his favorite stories.

THE QUIET MAN
1952

Can a return to one's home cure the memories of the past? Is it as simple as a change in location that shall alleviate those painful happenings that remain to haunt you? An American journeys back to the land of his birth, returning as one of the wealthiest men in the small fishing village. His plan is simple, to live his days out in peace and quiet. That is always easier said than done. The townsfolk want to know more about him and why he has settled here. There is a secret from his past though, one which an escape to a far off land will hopefully cure.

When he reaches the village of his childhood home, American Sean Thornton rebuys the land that once belonged to his family. On this land rests the small house where he was born. In this house Thornton attempts to make a new life for himself. With that part out of the way, a beautiful young woman catches his eye, the fiery but shy Mary Kate Danaher. As they are in the old country, complete with old ways of courtship still in use, Sean must go through the proper procedure of courting her and all the obstacles that stand in his way. To help remove those obstacles, the townsfolk devise a plan to help him out, allowing for one of the great screen romances to commence.

The secret in Thornton's past is figured out by the local Protestant reverend, who just by chance happens to be a boxing fan. Thornton was a former prizefighter under the name 'Trooper Thorn'. He accidentally killed a man in the ring, which obviously altered his outlook on life and initiated this journey to the country of his birth. The reverend agrees to keep it a secret, yet it is that secret that almost destroys his new marriage to Mary Kate. After they finally marry, Mary Kate's brother refuses to turn over her possessions and dowry. Sean, intent on never fighting again, will not battle him for it. When Sean finally gives in and fights her brother, the fight is a bare knuckle brawl the likes that cinema has never seen before, lasting for close to ten minutes and stretching from the scenic countryside to the local pub, where it is a must to pause for a pint before resuming the fight.

I was asked once why I love this movie so much. Perhaps it was the cinematography or just my testosterone acting up again, but the vision of Maureen O'Hara is beyond simple explanation. In all the movies that I have seen in my thirty three years of watching, I have never seen a woman more radiant on the screen. While her performance is fine I hate to admit that it is her stunning beauty that keeps all eyes, specifically mine, transfixed on her every move in this film.

The grand splendor of Technicolor truly displays the magnificence and beauty of the historic Irish countryside. Even though I'm not of Irish descent, it was this film that made me decide to eventually retire there one day and live the rest of my days marveling at the wonder of the land. Whenever I want to escape to that dream world I just pop this movie in and a tranquility arrives. I have *The Quiet Man* to thank, ahead of time, for setting me on the next great adventure in my life. The only possible thing that tops that beautiful region is the stunning beauty of Maureen O'Hara. I know it was said earlier but her beauty is truly an important aspect of this film experience.

Chapter Three:

Best Picture Winners

Not to state the obvious but there are only fifty entries on the main list. There have been seventy-seven years of the Academy Awards, which started in 1928. At the minimum, twenty-seven Best Picture winners have been left off the main list. That number increases as multiple entries from the same year made the main list (*Godfather II*, *The Conversation* and *Chinatown*), while the number also increases due to movies making the main list based solely on their exceptional quality (*Touch of Evil*), rather than merely the Academy of Motion Pictures presenting the historical status as Best Picture upon it. It is an understood shortcoming that the actual best picture of the year does not always win the Oscar for Best Picture. How many movie fans really think that *Dances With Wolves* is a better movie than *Goodfellas*? The answer is not many.

Working chronologically backward, I shall begin with the most recent year, 2004, to discuss the schemata for this section. As of the current writing of this particular section, the Academy Awards honoring movies released during the year 2004 is up first. I will then work down to the first year the Academy Awards were in existence, just as the main list worked down from 50 to 1, as all proper lists should do. Movies that were profiled in the main list shall not be discussed in this section, although they are mentioned next to each year for reference points. If a movie is mentioned next to a year and not discussed by name, you should understand the basic concept that it is that movie being discussed. If I explain that the Best Picture winner was not the best movie of the year and I do not name the movie that was, refer to the name next to the year if you need clarification.

2004

Two movies vied for the top honor. Politics triumphed over the grand Hollywood epic, in this case an historical drama. The two movies that battled in the press over odds on favorite to win Best Picture were Martin Scorsese's *The Aviator* and Clint Eastwood's *Million Dollar Baby*. The winner was Eastwood's fictional story of a young female boxer whose only goal in life was to become a champion and the crusty old time manager who has to make a tough decision after things do not go as planned. *Million Dollar Baby* began as a boxing film about second chances and made a complete u-turn in the final quarter of the movie to become a tense drama. It was an impressive feat to attempt and this movie did that job fine. However, it just was not enough to overcome the slow pacing and uninteresting plot to carry the movie much less deserve a Best Picture Oscar.

There are some in the industry, as well as the general public who feel the academy voters handed the award to *Million Dollar Baby* as a result of the backlash in the conservative media. The conservative media, acting with agenda over true morality, campaigned hard against the eventual winner regarding the political implications of the movie. I personally would not have placed this movie in my own Top 10 list for the year 2004, but then again I also would not have placed *The Aviator* on that list. In fact, 2004 was such an eclectic year for movies that even the most well reviewed picture of the year, Best Picture nominee *Sideways*, would not have made my Top 10 list for this particular year.

This section is not to dissect the lesser pictures of the year, but to discuss the Best Picture Winner and offer opinion as to the actual best picture that year. In this particular aspect the Academy got its nominations right, yet did not reward the true best picture of 2004, *Finding Neverland*. Based upon actual events regarding the true life story of playwright James M. Barrie, author of the timeless classic *Peter Pan*, 2004's best movie was a magical creation that one could not peel their eyes away from. The lead performance by Johnny Depp resonates with that internalized Victorian emotion that stifled some of the great writers of the time, yet also displays the ability to retain Barrie's belief in wonder. Depp pulls this off all while maintaining the facade of a proper gentleman, an unfortunate Victorian necessity. His relationship with the dying mother of four young boys, who inspire Barrie to create his masterpiece, shows the child within him. That is only until the mother's inevitable demise brings out the adult in him and tears you apart.

This movie is so pure. It is exactly what Barrie would have wanted, a revitalization of that youthful spirit within us despite the horrors and obstacles in life. The performances are amazing, with Julie Christie mysteriously passed over for a Best Supporting Actress nomination for her almost unflinching role as the elder tyrant of the family Barrie becomes involved with. Dustin Hoffman is equally good as Barrie's playhouse benefactor. Anyone seeing this movie will have their heart tugged at and enjoy a roller coaster ride into a land of wonder and a land of unfortunate reality, where sometimes the need for escapism to Neverneverland is all one's mind has.

2003

Lord of the Rings III: The Return of the King (Best Picture) - #16 on Top 50 list.

2002

Adaptation - # ??.

A lavish musical, *Chicago*, based upon the long running play created by Bob Fosse, took home top honors. While there are only two movies that would qualify as musicals on the main list, *Chicago* does not come close to either of them in quality. *Chicago* is the story of two women, Roxie Hart and Velma Kelly, who are both in jail for murder. The ladies continue to try and one up each other, as attorney Billy Flynn handles both cases looking for any opportunity to win. The movie de-evolves into a showmanship catfight between Roxie and Velma, who almost seem more involved with getting press and publicity from their case rather than attaining their freedom. This movie substitutes song for story, when the plot stalls. The meager story told in *Chicago* does not support the singing involved, which is the failure of many musicals. For a musical to leave an indelible impression upon the audience it has to have at its center a story that leaps from the page to screen and then from screen to the mind of the audience. This musical picture certainly does not do that.

2001

A Beautiful Mind (Best Picture) - #15.

2000

The lavish Roman slave epic *Gladiator* took home the top prize in 2000, with a Best Actor victory going to its star Russell Crowe. This is the kind of movie the Academy loves. It is Hollywood done on a grand scale and the type of movie that is generally rewarded. When the film was originally done in 1960, *Spartacus*, it was a much better film. The parallels are obvious, even if the story veers a bit to the left or the right from the original film it built off of. I am surprised that no one seriously challenged this film for top honors. While fun to watch with great action scenes and a tragic hero to root for, *Gladiator* is still far from the best picture of 2000.

The best picture was a small film with an all-star cast and rising director at the helm. With a cast including Michael Douglas, Frances McDormand, Tobey Maguire, Robert Downey Jr., Katie Holmes and Rip Torn, one would expect this film to have been the toast of Hollywood. It was not. Director Curtis Hanson, fresh off his critically acclaimed *L. A. Confidential*, chose to keep this film on a smaller level, focusing on both the story and the interaction between the characters as the driving force. The result, *Wonder Boys*, is an absolute gem of a movie. Although overlooked by the Academy, garnering one nomination for screenplay, this movie shines as the best picture of the year. Close behind *Wonder Boys* in quality from the same year was the wholly original *Memento*.

1999

This year contained a number of incredible movies, such as *The Green Mile, The Hurricane, The Insider* and without a doubt the weirdest of them all, *Being John Malkovich*. The Best Picture Award went to the dysfunctional suburban family picture *American Beauty*. This quasi-epic of the self-destruction within multiple families as a result of the complexities in dealing with the boredom of suburban life, where everyone is bad so therefore no one is all that bad, hit home with many viewers. The Academy Award voters got this one right. *American Beauty* happened to be the best picture of this year in a year where the overall competition was extremely fierce.

1998

There was a ferocious battle between a Spielberg war epic and an upstart British comedy, where writing actually triumphed over grandeur. *Shakespeare in Love* edged out *Saving Private Ryan* for the top honor, yet Spielberg could not be denied his second statuette for best director. Even though Spielberg's treatise on the horrors of war lost, the actual winner was more pomp than heartfelt. *Shakespeare in Love* was almost wholly a product of its witty screenplay. Its entire totality was an inside joke about attempting to over-intellectualize history. This helped turn it into an almost unwatchable exhibition of effete pretentiousness. Like so many movies that win the Best Picture, *Shakespeare in Love* was far from the best picture of the year. That honor goes to *American History X*.

Perceived by many to simply be a treatise on hate, *American History X* is actually an exploration into the creation and ultimate eradication of hate through evolving. This movie also supplies one of the defining acting performances of the decade. Hate, personified by the neo-Nazi movement that has reached out to the youth of California, is put on a visual display as the surfaced centerpiece. Using such memorable scenes as a segregated basketball game, prison indoctrinations and perhaps the most memorable, the curbing that lands the lead character into prison, the evolution of the main character's journey comes into focus. His prison sentence turns out to be the best thing for him, as he learns to shed his hate, eventually maturing and fully understanding the impetus for his original turn toward racism on a violent scale. It is not hate that is used like action to move the movie along, but rather the creation of hate. The acting performance of Edward Norton, nominated for a Best Actor Oscar, is astounding. Norton takes us through three separate periods in his life, spanning about ten years. He nails each of those three characters amazingly, not only in their age, but also in their differentiating mindset. His performance carries this movie into the status of classic, with the underlying message helping to launch it into the status as the best movie of the year.

1997

L. A. Confidential - #31.

A sprawling epic based upon an actual event took the world by storm this year. James Cameron's *Titanic* was such a movie experience that the momentum of its grandeur carried it toward Oscar history. Despite winning the Best Picture Award and tying the record for most Oscar wins, there was another movie that topped *Titanic* in excellence, even though that film only won two awards. The downfall of *Titanic* was not that it was a bad movie. On the contrary, it is pure epic on a grand scale, yet lacked the marvelously layered plot and characters of *L.A. Confidential*. The movie also suffers from a lack of identity, switching from deep-hearted love story to chase adventure to historical survival epic. The magnificence on the screen of *Titanic* definitively enhanced its charm, but many agree that the Curtis Hanson crime drama was robbed and remains as the better movie.

1996

Fargo - #46.

Another classic battle between majestic epic and upstart indie took place in 1996. The grand scale British/Hollywood epic, *The English Patient* bested the Coen Brothers' latest slice of life bizarre-o-rama for the top prize. *The English Patient*, with its sweeping historic love story and beautiful scenic backdrop swept the major picture awards. The movie however, while majestic throughout, is incredibly slow in spots. It contains definitive lags that work against its flashback structure. Watching *The English Patient* is a similar experience to reading a long book. A movie should never provide that feeling to a viewer, the feeling of slowing down time while motion is constant. The story is good though, relaying the tale of love lost from a dying man, yet its overlong pacing definitively worked against it. This is one of those movies that can be sat through once. Subsequent viewings will probably leave the viewer watching the clock and hoping for time to move faster.

1995

What is it about the epic blockbuster that the Academy loves and feels they need to constantly reward? This year, the epic biopic *Braveheart* took home top honors. Covering the life of Scottish warrior and patriot William Wallace, *Braveheart* told the amazing story of the battles between England and Scotland over sovereignty during the end of the 13th and beginning of the 14th centuries. Mel Gibson, who also took home a Best Director Oscar, was fantastic in this complex role. 1995 however, was such an amazing year for movies that there were a multitude of movies better than the one awarded top prize by the Academy.

In a year with such a tough choice one movie stands out above the rest, *Apollo 13*. Ron Howard's fantastic movie about the horror of the 1971 NASA space shuttle accident that could have left three astronauts in outer space forever, was not only wonderfully acted but also held the tense atmosphere that mirrored the actual tragedy as much as was possible. Starring Tom Hanks, coming off back to back Best Actor Oscars, his performance as the flight leader Jim Lovell guides the movie. The astronaut's continual problems reel the audience in with every new danger. When they finally make it home safely it is almost as if a weight is lifted off your shoulders. When a movie is able to do that, it performs its task to full potential. In this exceptional year, *Apollo 13* reigns supreme.

1994

The Shawshank Redemption - #26.

The 1994 Awards were a fore drawn conclusion. The magical tale of a retarded man who likes chocolates was destined to sweep the top honors. Of course, *Forrest Gump* was so much more than just that, showing how one man's simple life can affect so many others by merely interacting with them in a simple and positive manner. *Forrest Gump* is one of those purely enjoyable movies that made the viewer walk out of the theater happy, with a smile on their face as well as a tear running down from their eye. In this year however, *Forrest Gump* was not the best movie of the year, although it is not all that far from it, coming in as the fourth best movie, in my opinion, behind *The Shawshank Redemption* obviously and two other small gems, *Nobody's Fool* and *Quiz Show*.

1993

The Fugitive - #20, *Schindler's List* (Best Picture) - #22.

1992

It became time for the Academy to reward a legend in the field of cinema. Their reward was almost deserved, for the Western masterpiece *Unforgiven*. The tale of an ex-gunfighter brought back into that harsh life after a prostitute is beaten and cut up, mixes perfect pacing, great acting, an amazing storyline and a climax that leaves the viewer in awe and wanting more. *Unforgiven* is Eastwood's first masterpiece. His later films, such as *True Crime, The Bridges of Madison County, Million Dollar Baby* and perhaps his best film, 2003's *Mystic River*, have only gotten better with his age. Although I applaud the Academy for awarding Eastwood with a Best Director and Best Picture Oscar, *Unforgiven* was the third best movie of 1992, only bested by the comedic fish out of water farce *My Cousin Vinny* and the best movie of the year, *Reservoir Dogs*.

Psychologically unbalanced film auteur Quentin Tarantino's diamond caper gone awry showed the seedier side of crime. It relied upon slick, fast talking crooks who reveled in using snappy dialogue, even if it was perhaps overly abrasive and off center from the plot. *Reservoir Dogs* is even superior to the epic that cemented Tarantino's name, *Pulp Fiction*. It is better than any movie he ever acted in, better than the four-hour, two-part hot chicks fighting epic *Kill Bill* and even better than the highly underrated *Jackie Brown*. It will likely be the best movie Tarantino will ever make.

1991

Beauty and the Beast - #18, *JFK* - #43.

This was a landmark year for the Academy Awards. For only the third time in history a movie swept the top five major awards. In my opinion only two of those awards were deserved, best actress and best screenplay. *Silence of the Lambs* was the scary movie that took Hollywood by storm. Jodie Foster was brilliant as Agent Clarisse Starling and the script, from a Thomas Harris novel, was equally as fantastic. Her search for the serial killer known as "Buffalo Bill" was the glue that held the movie together. It is arguably the best female acting performance of the decade. The Best Actor prize went to Anthony Hopkins, who spent a total of less than nineteen minutes on screen in a movie that clocked in at close to two hours long. His performance was a top notch supporting performance, yet was not even the best supporting performance of the year. That honor should have gone to Joe Pesci's magnificent turn as the hyper-manic David Ferrie in *JFK*. On a side note, Pesci's performance was not even recognized by the Academy, in a movie that was actually the second best of the year.

1990

Goodfellas - #5.

For the second straight decade, which would continue for a third decade in 2004, Martin Scorsese was denied an Oscar by both an inferior picture and one directed by an actor turned director. Of the three movies that defeated Scorsese's three, the 1990 Oscar Winner for Best Picture was by far the worst of those three. Kevin Costner's wild frontier Western epic, *Dances With Wolves*, took home that honor. When compared to Scorsese's true crime thriller, considered by many as the movie of the decade, it falls short on every level. While semi-enjoyable to watch, although at over three hours and much closer to four, it gets awfully monotonous at times. Three intermissions would have been better, rather than only one. The strange part is that when the movie finally ends, there is no finale, only the opportunity for the continuation of the story. *Dances With Wolves* capitalized on the negative backlash regarding the violence in *Goodfellas* to earn its place in Oscar history. Its romanticizing of the west helped launch it to an Oscar victory, especially when comparing it to the realistic violence from *Goodfellas*. Those who know movies appreciate which was the better picture and film buffs also understand the great disparity between the two movies.

1989

Field of Dreams - #41.

There is an historical distinction regarding the year 1989, with respect to Oscar history. For the first time in fifty-seven years, the Academy awarded the Best Picture to a movie, *Driving Miss Daisy*, whose director was not even nominated for Best Director. This was only the third time in Academy Award history that distinction happened. *Driving Miss Daisy* is a sweet tale of an elderly Southern white woman who forms a bond with her black chauffeur. The performances are great, deservedly winning Jessica Tandy her only Oscar, yet Morgan Freeman lost out to another mesmerizing performance, Daniel Day-Lewis in *My Left Foot*. *Driving Miss Daisy* is just too bland of a movie to be considered the best film of the year. It does not hit the heartstrings, nor do the subtle attempts at humor match what I believe was the best movie of the year.

1988

Four of the heralded top five awards went to this year's most honored movie. The only thing that kept it from joining the other three movies to win the top five major awards, or the two at the time of this movie, was the lack of a female lead. *Rain Man* tugged at the heartstrings of America and swept the four major categories, Best Picture, Director, Actor and Screenplay. While hysterical at times, due to Hoffman's over the top performance, the best movie of the year was entirely overlooked by the Academy, perhaps due to the fact that it was a comedy.

Starring Robert DeNiro and Charles Grodin, *Midnight Run* stands alone as the finest movie made in 1988. The Academy rarely recognizes comedies as its Best Picture winner, yet I do not have to hold myself to their rigid standards. *Midnight Run* is that rare blend of drama and comedy with a chase element that spans the entirety of the movie and never gets old at any moment. Fresh with plot twists, great performances, most notably by John Ashton, and a flawless pace that most chase movies lack, *Midnight Run* is clearly better than any other movie that year, despite the fact that it was not taken as seriously as others. Once again, the rigid standards of the Academy do not apply here.

1987

The Princess Bride - #48.

1987 held another historical oddity for its Best Picture Award Winner. Bernardo Bertolucci's sprawling epic, *The Last Emperor*, won the top two awards of Best Director and Best Picture. Simultaneously, it did not receive a single nomination for acting in any of the four categories. In the long over glorified history of Hollywood epics *The Last Emperor* definitively joins that group, yet despite telling the story of the three year old child who is placed atop the throne as the last emperor of China and the sixty years of his life, it does not awe, other than perhaps with its costume design or cinematography. The movie was visually stunning, yet that is really where the hoopla ends. The story of this incredible boy turned man could have been done with greater interest, yet the movie seems content to focus on the visual elements, thereby neglecting the most vital element, the story.

1986

As was the case in the two years after it, the Academy Awards wholly ignored 1986's best movie. They chose to honor Oliver Stone's gritty Vietnam War picture *Platoon*, widely considered as one of the best movies of the 1980's. *Platoon* followed a young soldier through his indoctrination into an unrealistic war that changed and shaped the young men of America. The two main supporting characters were polar opposites, shown primarily through the way they affect the young soldier during his tour of duty. While showing the un-pleasantries of war it did not make significant strides above the late 1970's Vietnam War films, most notably *The Deer Hunter*. That aside, it does not come in as the best movie of the year, with a sci-fi fantasy movie garnering that top spot.

The intensely clever science fiction thriller *Highlander* was by far the best picture to emerge from 1986, a relatively weak year. For anyone who has seen the original version, the plot is without a single flaw. The characters are great, rich with colorful backgrounds that add to the story's gritty and unique edge. The scenery, focusing upon medieval Scotland, is a sight to marvel at that only adds to the distinctive plot structure. For those who do not know or realize, *Highlander* is actually the movie that Sean Connery earned his Best Supporting Actor Oscar, although the Academy gave it to him for a movie the following year. As in the case with two movies that made the main list, *Rocky* and *Raiders of the Lost Ark*, subsequent sequels have damaged *Highlander's* credibility and standing, for some strange or biased reason.

1985

The Hollywood epic motif of winning the Best Picture continued as Sydney Pollack's *Out of Africa* took home the top prize. *Out of Africa* was the tale of Danish female author Isak Dineson, who is taken to Nairobi after marrying a Baron and is eventually left on her own where she falls for the great white hunter, played by Robert Redford. The scenery is spectacular yet the movie is nauseatingly slow and the performances are overbearing, even when they are occasionally downplayed for the effect of the landscape. *Out of Africa* is the kind of movie that Hollywood became accustomed to rewarding in the 1980's, unassuming and way too long. This was the anti-movie, when compared to the actual best picture of the year, Terry Gilliam's Orwellian bureaucratic nightmare *Brazil*. The story behind the studio destruction of Gilliam's true vision is almost as fantastical as the movie itself. It easily prevented *Brazil* from Oscar recognition. The restored movie, a director's cut where Gilliam's vision shines through, triumphs as the best movie made during 1985.

1984

The years 1984 and 1983 are peculiarly similar. The actual movie awarded top honor by the Academy, *Terms of Endearment* and *Amadeus*, were the best films for those individual years. In the case of *Amadeus*, there were two equally brilliant performances, the backdrop of a legendary musician, his peculiar ways in spite of his genius and the musical adversary who could not come to terms with his envy regarding that pure genius in spite of his love of music above all. F. Murray Abraham won a well deserved Best Actor Oscar playing Mozart's nemesis and possible murderer Salieri. In an amazing deathbed scene at the end, the true nature of Salieri shines through, showing that even in death Mozart was more than he could ever be. By murdering him, Salieri was actually robbing himself of the one thing he truly loved, great music from an unbridled genius.

1983

Terms of Endearment also has two equally brilliant lead performances, a phenomenal group of supporting performances, led by Oscar Winner Jack Nicholson, in perhaps one of his finest acting roles as an astronaut turned pervert who is really decent at heart. Based on the book by famed Western author Larry McMurtry, it has deep heart, moments of hysterical comedy and a mother daughter bond that can not be broken by anything, including death. Even though she was a star in her own right, Shirley MacLaine's turn as Aurora Greenway made her a screen icon. The movie has been called a combination of one of the most tear producing and funniest that Hollywood has ever made.

1982

The sprawling epic of Sir Richard Attenborough's *Gandhi* was perceived as headed for an anticipated upset, with the smaller heart tugging film *E.T.: The Extra Terrestrial* and the cross dressing gender bender comedy *Tootsie* both vying for the mega upset. The voters spoke and *Gandhi* came out on top, sweeping the top 4 major awards it was nominated for, Picture, Director, Actor and Screenplay. The magnanimous biopic is a treat to see the first time, but is extremely tough to make it through a second viewing. It seems as if Attenborough wanted to include every single intricacy in

Mohandas Gandhi's storied life. At three hours and eight minutes in duration Attenborough may have succeeded. Although *E.T.* and *Tootsie* appeared as Oscar spoilers, it was another Best Picture nominee that should have disrupted *Gandhi's* Oscar night, *The Verdict*.

The tale of an alcoholic lawyer who has one last great case in him is gripping, tense and masterfully crafted by director Sidney Lumet. Newman magnificently maneuvers his way through the trials of handling a case that is out of his reach as he seems to be past his prime. Encountering flack from everyone, including the judge who takes it in his own to question a witness, Newman shrugs off all opposition to triumph in the end. Justice finally shines through for once, due to his hard fought struggle to not settle. It is widely considered as the defining acting performance in Paul Newman's storied career. While I personally disagree with that assessment, this performance is close behind only three others. *The Verdict* is a shining example of a little movie that was not allowed to topple the giant, yet for all intensive purposes outshines *Gandhi* and the rest in every way.

1981

Raiders of the Lost Ark - #2, Reds - #40.

The battle for the top prize was between Warren Beatty's Russian Revolution epic *Reds* and the tiny British upstart *Chariots of Fire*. It seems that heart won out over substance as *Chariots of Fire* upended the mighty blockbuster. Beatty was awarded top directing honors as perhaps a consolation prize for creating the better movie. It appears that it may have been too intellectual for the Oscar voters who chose a story of glory instead. *Chariots of Fire* told the story of two English runners both vying for gold in the same event at the 1924 Olympics. Due to extreme religious beliefs, both men were given the opportunity to race for gold in separate events and both men won their races. *Chariots of Fire* was a fun movie to watch. As far as a great movie it falls considerably short.

1980

Raging Bull - #12, Airplane! - #49.

The first of Martin Scorsese's three losses to actor turned directors occurred this year. Robert Redford's tale of normality taken to an extreme level, *Ordinary People*, took home top honors. Redford's classic take on suburban values and emotional restraint was a fantastic movie, yet unfortunately had the misfortune of release in the same year as the second greatest film of the decade, Scorsese's boxing biopic *Raging Bull*. The voters rewarded its non-violent approach to a relatively unnoticed problem, angst within suburban middle America, by honoring it as the Best Picture. The violence, despite the setting within the world of boxing was Scorsese's downfall. *Raging Bull*, however, remains the far better movie. It was a grittier, harder edged approach to life, versus the watered down hidden truths revealed within *Ordinary People*.

1979

Breaking Away - #47.

The Best Picture winner, *Kramer vs. Kramer*, narrowly came within a nomination of sweeping the Top five awards, which would have made them only the third picture at the time to do so. The female lead played by Meryl Streep, who took home a Best Supporting Actress Oscar, more than doubled the screen time of Anthony Hopkins in his Best Actor winning role from *Silence of the Lambs*. That aside, *Kramer vs. Kramer* was a fantastic tale of a father struggling with having to take care of his son all on his own after his wife suddenly leaves him. When she comes back just as suddenly and tries to take his son away from him, the legal battle ensues. This was another Robert Benton special, grabbing your heart until your emotions are drained. Benton also directed one of 1994's best movies *Nobody's Fool* as well as the 1984 tearjerker *Places in the Heart*. He crafted a fine movie in *Kramer vs. Kramer*, yet despite winning the Best Picture Oscar it was not the best movie of the year.

1978

The great Vietnam War movie battle encapsulated this year's Oscars. The anti-war treatise *Coming Home* swept the major acting awards, while the more hands-on depiction of the war, *The Deer Hunter*, swept the other top two awards, Picture and Director. Michael Cimino's film was labeled racist by *Coming Home's* female lead, who also thought hers was the better film while admitting she had not actually seen the other movie. The Academy did get this one correct. *The Deer Hunter* was not only a better film than *Coming Home*, but also better than any other movie produced that year.

1977

The previous year was an extremely peculiar one for movies. One nominated movie, *The Turning Point*, set perhaps the most unwanted record in Oscar history. It received eleven nominations without winning one. This is a record that would be tied eight years later by *The Color Purple*. The most successful movie of the year, *Star Wars*, took home seven Oscars. All these wins came in technical categories. In actuality, *Star Wars* is one of the worst acted movies ever to make it to the screen. In comparison to the sequel, *The Empire Strikes Back*, the two are leaps and bounds apart. *Star Wars* was technically brilliant and innovative, yet a re-release in 1997, with added scenes and an updated look, actually showed the intelligent moviegoers what they did not want to originally believe. Apart from the grand effects and innovative visual feel, *Star Wars* was actually a bad movie. The other clear-cut winner of the night was *Annie Hall*, which took home the Best Picture, Best Director and Best Actress awards.

Going against the Hollywood grand scale type the Academy chose to reward a small comedy. They missed the perfect opportunity to go further against type and reward the actual best picture of the year, a raucous sports comedy about the craziness of minor league hockey, *Slap Shot*. Although the general public will most likely never see the Academy reward a sports comedy with top honors, this was the perfect year to do so. *Slap Shot* was an amazingly witty sports comedy headlined by a top notch actor, who had been a multiple Oscar nominee in years before. Comparing *Slap Shot* to *Annie Hall* generally separates the sports lovers from those who actually loathe sports. If you can even tolerate sports a little, then *Slap Shot* is the funnier movie. By that rationale, as *Annie Hall* is basically a comedy, *Slap Shot* is the funnier comedy and therefore the better movie, in a year that was weak overall. This could be another reason why the original *Star Wars* is often mistaken as a great film, due to the lack of great films from this particular year.

1976

Network - #36, *Rocky* (Best Picture) - #45, *All The President's Men* - #50.

1975

One Flew Over the Cuckoo's Nest (Best Picture) - #8.

1974

The Godfather II (Best Picture) - #19, *The Conversation* - #33, *Chinatown* - #35.

1973

The Sting (Best Picture) - #29.

1972

The Godfather (Best Picture) - #9.

1971

The Last Picture Show - # ??.

This year displayed a wide range of interesting nominees, which included three of the four best pictures of that year. The actual Oscar winner, *The French Connection*, was not the best movie. It was however a close second to another nominee for Best Picture. Gene Hackman's coarse performance as Popeye Doyle in *The French Connection* was richly deserved as Best Actor, yet Peter Bogdonavich's landmark slice of Americana reigned supreme in this year. The events of one year in a small Texas town in the 1950's, and its effects upon the local citizens, supply the backdrop for a change in social ideals and cultural awakening. *The French Connection* was a revolutionary police thriller, highlighted by a leading character who did not act the outdated part of the honorable cop. He broke the rules when necessary and was equal parts drunk and cowboy, sometimes exerting more power than he should have. His one goal was to get the bad guys, but his means were highly questionable. That is what made his character and Hackman's performance so magnificent.

1970

The war biopic *Patton* swept the top four awards it was nominated for, Picture, Director, Actor and Screenplay. *Patton* was the classic Hollywood portrayal of an American war hero, brash and vulgar while almost superhuman in his gallantry. General George S. Patton was an old style cowboy in an era of soldiers who used bravery and forcefulness unheard of today in order to motivate and will the troops under his command to victory. These key elements of Patton's nature come through clear in this good, although a bit overlong film. For war historians it is a must see, although clearly not the best movie this year had to offer.

The true best picture however, was a small movie that was also nominated for Best Picture, which wound up putting its star on the map, *Five Easy Pieces*. Most mistakenly believe that Jack Nicholson's magnificent turn in 1969's *Easy Rider* cemented his status as a star in the making. Supporting performances do not do that however. They lead to starring performances, which can make or break a young talent. *Five Easy Pieces* was the vehicle that led Nicholson to stardom, by way of his brilliant performance as an oilrig worker/drifter who gave up pursuing his musical talent, left his wealthy upbringing and eventually returns home to deal with his dying father. After coming home he falls in love with his brother's wife, simultaneously alienating his girlfriend, beautifully played by Karen Black. That forces his quick return to that unease about his own existence, leading him to take flight once again. He is a man without the ability to live in his own skin. His choices about the inability to be happy with himself make this movie an undeniable classic.

1969

Midnight Cowboy (Best Picture) - #17.

1968

In a relatively weaker year for movies, a musical adaptation of Charles Dickens' classic novel *Oliver Twist*, called *Oliver!*, took home top honors. In any other year this movie would have been hard pressed to have been nominated for a Best Picture, let alone actually win the top award. For instance, if this movie had been released the previous year, it would not have been recognized by the Academy among the elite nominees for Best Picture. Not only were all five nominees better films, but three other films, *Cool Hand Luke, Wait Until Dark* and *The Dirty Dozen*, from 1967 were also far superior films. *Oliver!* was extremely lucky. Timing definitely played a critical part in catapulting this awful film to carve out a piece of Oscar history.

The clear-cut best picture of this year was a farcical comedy from the insane mind of Mel Brooks, *The Producers*. From the opening scene where Max Bialystock meets Leo Bloom to discuss the accounting books to the opening night of the play '*Springtime for Hitler*', a smash hit that was intended as a flop, this movie manages to sustain its hilarity. It was justifiably honored with a Best Screenplay Oscar victory, but still was overlooked when it came to the top prize. Another film from this year that came close to stealing the title away from *The Producers* was *Once Upon a Time in the West*. That film is the best of the Sergio Leone Spaghetti Westerns, yet release dates in the United States make it hard to nail down the exact time to classify it properly.

1967

In The Heat of the Night (Best Picture) - # ??.

1966

Similar to 1967, the best picture of 1966 was honored by the Academy with the Best Picture Oscar. Another similarity is that the 1966 winner, *A Man For All Seasons*, swept four of the five major awards. It swept because like *In the Heat of the Night, Patton, The French Connection, Kramer vs.*

Kramer, Gandhi, Amadeus, and *Rain Man*, it lacked a female lead that was worthy enough to be nominated. *Kramer vs. Kramer* is the exception to that group however, for the reason listed in that section.

A Man For All Seasons conveys the story of Sir Thomas More and his difficult relationship with English King Henry VIII, wholly over the King's wish to divorce his wife due to her inability to bear him a male heir. More is asked to break his ties with the Pope and grant the King a divorce so he can marry another who might bear him a son who would take over the throne of England one day. The movie is actually about a man of faith and intelligence who values the strength of his convictions over political power. More would pay the ultimate pays price for that. *A Man For All Seasons* was the fifth straight British film to take home the Best Picture Oscar and the absolute best of that lot.

1965

Doctor Zhivago - # ??.

Two musical-esque movies took home the top honors in 1964 and 1965, *My Fair Lady* and *The Sound of Music*, respectively. Of the two, the story of the young cockney girl and her uppity speech tutor loses that battle. Neither of them ranks as the best pictures of their individual year though. Musicals are an extremely tough genre to enjoy on film. It is the equivalent of watching a rock concert on television. Something gets lost in the translation. That is why within a musical movie there still should be a designated and defined plot. Luckily, *My Fair Lady* and *The Sound of Music* both have defined plots so that the singing and dancing are not the entire focus.

The Sound of Music covers the exploits of the Von Trapp family and the beautiful singing nun who enters their lives and subsequently changes it from within. The song numbers are great and actually work off the plot, rather than take away from it. *My Fair Lady* did the same. However, they are still outclassed by other films from their respective years.

1964

This is another one of those lesser quality years for movies. However, the five nominated films are more known than most years. That commercial quality does not always translate to actualized quality. As one movie, by process of elimination, has to be the best picture of the year, that picture would be Stanley Kubrick's anti-war war satire *Dr. Strangelove*. The opinion that the major decisions for the possible demise of the world are left up to a wide array of pinheads is less funny now than it was during the year of the film's release. Some of the wit is cold and the final bomb-riding scene is downright ludicrous, yet the conversations between Peter Sellers and anyone else are worth the price of admission, particularly the payphone sequence toward the end. The basic motif of almost all Kubrick movies is sacrifice. It is not a plot element, but a cinematic sacrifice where one part of the movie is great while the other part or parts are mediocre at best and can never match that one great segment. This movie is no exception, yet the great part is when Sellers takes the screen while everything else is average or less.

1963

Best Picture winner *Tom Jones*, from the Henry Fielding novel, portrays the adventures of an unrefined young man enjoying the sexual romps of his day. While an outstanding comedy it is severely flawed by camera tricks, which for some mysterious reason went unnoticed by the Academy voters. In an era of stories, a special effects extravaganza of a cinematographic nature won out. The actual best picture came from a novel also, yet from an author who has been mentioned previously, Larry McMurtry.

Hud, based on the McMurtry novel *Horseman, Pass By,* depicts three generations of cattlemen. There is the elder rancher father, the womanizing and brawling maverick son Hud and the grandson who looks up to him. In a Best Actress Oscar winning role, Patricia Neal shines as the domestic who holds the family together. Eventually, as with all good character studies, the generational battle comes to a head over a possible livestock disease that causes the demise of their long storied way of life. *Hud* is a marvelous character study told through a multi-generational approach and seen from the eyes of three separate individuals, an elder, a newcomer and the brash force whose struggles tear the family apart. Not only the best-acted picture of the year, *Hud* is also far and away the best picture 1963 had to offer.

1962

The Manchurian Candidate - #10, To Kill A Mockingbird - #14.
Lawrence of Arabia, David Lean's masterful epic, tells the story of adventurer T. E. Lawrence and his efforts to unite the Arab tribes to fight the Ottoman Turks during World War I. The problem with this film was that it was overblown and far too grandiose for a biography or its own best interest. The historical Lawrence was far from the cinematic Lawrence. The script sacrificed accuracy for extravagance and as a result something was lost in that conscious process. The movie was stunning to look at and everything Hollywood loved to honor, grand scale epics of an historical nature. Peter O'Toole was great in his earliest role, yet the difference between his performance and perhaps the best acting performance ever turned in, Gregory Peck in *To Kill A Mockingbird*, is as great as the difference between *Lawrence of Arabia* and the two movies from this year that actually made the main list.

1961

One of the drawbacks of the Academy during the 1960's was their acknowledgement of musicals as the Best Picture winner in 4 of the 10 years. Two were good films, yet the other two were absolute travesties. 1961 started this trend, with the unnecessary Latino-ized version of William Shakespeare's Romeo and Juliet, *West Side Story*. Taking one of the only original stories created by Shakespeare and re-inventing it to fit an ethnically specific story is mind boggling. Perhaps if it were done in a semi-interesting fashion it would have been a better movie. It was not. *West Side Story* is a mere recycling of a great original story, transported to a different medium for the express purposes of highlighting and showcasing some sort of ethnic stereotype. It is no wonder why stereotypes exist, because they are purported in movies such as this one, recycled for the masses and accepted as fact. In the worse year for movies this mess should not have come close to the best picture. For some reason a number of great movies such as *The Great Escape, Judgment at Nuremburg, The Man Who Shot Liberty Valence* and the actual best movie of the year, *The Hustler*, were passed over for this barrio gang songfest.

The Hustler combined the action of pocket billiards, scintillating to watch because of the money element, with a fantastic story of love, loss and redemption *The Hustler* was not just about pool. It was an innovative love story for its time, showcasing a complete collapse and final redemption when *'Fast'* Eddie Felson proves he's the best against the champion Minnesota Fats. By that time, even though he is the winner, all is lost. His career as a pool hustler has now come to an end because of his pride. *The Hustler* is so far better than *West Side Story* that there is no comparison. One is an excellent story of love, loss, redemption and realization, forcing a dynamo to come to terms with his own existence. The other is a recycled love story, told from a stereotypical mold, with not one iota of improvement. The end product shows this axiom to be true.

1960

Psycho - #11.

The first year of the weakest decade for movies decided to honor a comedy as its Best Picture. Billy Wilder's classic story of a man who lends out his apartment to the executives above him at work is poignantly funny, but a little too forced for my taste. Jack Lemmon and Shirley MacLaine coming together at the end only add to this forced feeling throughout. They settle for love with each other, making the film challenge its own stature. Is it a drama, comedy or pure unadulterated farce? It might be that stretch of comedy, taken to its farthest level that made this movie such a hit. There are better pure comedies and more heart wrenching romances, but this movie blends both in such a ludicrous manner that it launched *The Apartment* onto another level, above those movies that sacrificed comedy for romance, or vice versa. *The Apartment* does fall short of the actual title of best movie of the year. There truly is no comparison between the two.

1959

North By Northwest - # ??.

The final year of the 1950's, sometimes stated as the decade of the lavish epics, honored one of that specific variety, *Ben-Hur*. Nominated for twelve academy awards, winning a record eleven, *Ben-Hur* was the story of how Jesus Christ impacted one Jewish family during his short life. The movie focuses on the exploits of a noble Jewish man who is forced to convert to Christianity, wrongfully arrested for not backing his childhood friend's persecution of the Jews in Roman held Palestine and his long and hard fought journey back to his family.

Visually, *Ben-Hur* is fantastic and rightfully considered a masterpiece with specific regards to that medium. The chariot race is what immediately comes to mind when remembering this movie. However, it is not the best movie that was offered that year. It is often long-winded in a way that other epics, such as *Gone With the Wind* and *The Bridge on the River Kwai* are definitively not. *Ben-Hur* is the type of movie that the viewer does not think twice about getting up and walking away from for moments, to get a snack, collect thoughts or complete your taxes, because it is that long of a movie. The point – *Ben-Hur* is a really good movie, but Hollywood chose style over substance.

In 1959 there were many great movies to pick and choose from making the choice of determining the best movie difficult. Three clear cut candidates emerged. Only one of the three was nominated for Best Picture, while one of the other two had numerous nominations in major categories. The director of that movie, Billy Wilder, honored by Hollywood previously, would be redeemed the following year for *The Apartment*. The true best movie of 1959 only received three nominations from the Academy, without one win and was excluded from all major categories with the exception of Best Story and Screenplay. Its director, Alfred Hitchcock, would also be robbed the following year by not winning for creating the best movie 1960 had to offer and was robbed the previous year as well. He should have won three consecutive Best Director Oscars, rather than the zero he received.

1958

Vertigo - #25, *Touch of Evil* - #32.

The year prior to *Ben-Hur* almost single handedly swept the Academy Awards, Hollywood chose to honor a musical, *Gigi*. *Gigi* was a far cry from the two Best Pictures sandwiched around it. Telling the story of young Parisian woman groomed to follow in her grandmother's footsteps as a courtesan, her rather precocious and carefree attitude shone through during a time where presence meant more than happiness. The male lead, Gaston, has grown bored with high society and the pomp that goes along with it all. His boredom is cured as a result of spending time with the cheerful Gigi, until he inevitably realizes that he has fallen in love with her.

This movie, despite not receiving one nomination for any acting award, swept the other three major awards, Best Picture, Best Director and Best Story. It won all nine of the awards it was nominated for. *Gigi* is similar to the musicals of the 1960's, unnecessarily breaking out into song at every given chance simply to further the story. It trades rich character depictions for stylized displays of pretentiousness. The Academy was right in not awarding *Gigi* with any acting nominations, but seriously went wrong by honoring the last of the supposed great MGM musicals as the Best Picture. Most critics agree the Academy made a severe error on this year's awards.

1957

The Bridge on the River Kwai (Best Picture) - #4, *Twelve Angry Men* - #42.

1956

1976 is often viewed as the single greatest lineup of Best Picture nominees. True to form, three of those Best Picture nominees made the main list. Another opinion accepted by many is that of all the years since the Academy began honoring movies for their excellence, the composite group of Best Pictures assembled from the year 1956 is the absolute worst. Since the Academy had to anoint one as the Best Picture it chose the adaptation of the Jules Verne classic *Around the World in Eighty Days*. With this group of Best Picture nominees, only one is slightly engaging to watch, *Giant*.

Around the World in Eighty Days was one of my favorite books to read as a child, yet it should have stopped there. The movie adaptation could not capture the magic written on the page. While that alone should not indicate that it was a bad movie, it was the combination of trying to capture that unique spirit of the book and the failing to achieve it that left me empty and bored for a majority of the movie.

The actual best movie of the year was a tough choice between Stanley Kubrick's *The Killing* and a movie that came from one of the most misunderstood directors, Douglas Sirk. His satirical melodrama, *Written on the Wind*, has an independent feel to it. It was not the epic blockbuster the studios tended to pump out, nor was it the happy go lucky musicals where everyone sings and dances their trouble away. This was a pure story, one of the few of its kind. The film was both entertaining and engrossing, to the point where the viewer feels that he cannot turn away for a second.

Sirk's movies, specifically this one, were filled with subtext and hidden plot points making it necessary to keep focus upon the basic to appreciate the intricacies. This movie is considered by some to be Sirk's crowning achievement and a shining example of his method. It is easy to understand why the Academy honored the performances rather than the picture, due to the fact that many did not comprehend the underlying tone of the movie. Regardless of that fact the Academy's exclusion of *Written on the Wind*, not only as a nominee for Best Picture but also as the movie that should have won, it is still an oversight that needed to be addressed.

1955

The Night of the Hunter - #44.

The small film *Marty* took home the award of Best Picture, also winning the awards for Best Director, Best Actor and Best Screenplay. It is impossible not to empathize with this story. *Marty* told the tale of a sad nobody who eventually finds love. In finding love he begins to grow a little. The opinions of his friends and his mother do not matter anymore. Only what is in his heart counts and the movie ends with the assurance that Marty, the lovable loser that everyone wants to see get married, will be happy after all. *Marty* became the first American picture to win the top prize at the Cannes Film Festival. It remains today as one of the sweetest and purest love stories in American cinema. Although *Marty* was an extremely good film there was another that was far better.

1954

Rear Window - #28, *On The Waterfront* (Best Picture) - #37

1953

From Here To Eternity (Best Picture) - #30

1952

High Noon - #38.

Another lavish epic took home the Oscar for Best Picture this year. One of the grand old directors, Cecil B. DeMille, came out with a cinematic blockbuster of life in the circus, *The Greatest Show on Earth*. Depicting what goes on behind the scenes of a traveling circus, DeMille placed the moviegoer where they always wanted to go, but never could without actually joining up. Charlton Heston played the circus manager intent on making sure that the show must go on above everything else. There is intrigue, acrobatics, mystery and even a great train wreck that threatens to stall the opening of the circus in the next scheduled town. The combined efforts of the performers and the crew rise to the occasion, all working together to form a family and make sure the circus will open as scheduled. It is an enjoyable movie and a spectacle to watch, of the epic variety that DeMille knew.

1951

Three of the major awards, Best Picture, Best Director and Best Actor, were all awarded for different movies, similar to 1952. Different from 1952 though, where the three movies that took home those three separate awards were all high quality or amazing movies, the three that accomplished the feat in 1951 were all mediocre at best and awful at worst. The other three acting awards all went to performers from the same movie, *A Streetcar Named Desire*. This should indicate that the acting was so phenomenal in this movie, with a nomination also going to Best Actor candidate Marlon Brando that this movie could have easily taken home the Oscar statuette for Best Picture. It did not though.

The actual Best Picture winner was another musical, *An American in Paris*. The movie was also set in Paris, similar to *Gigi* and directed by the same man, Vincente Minelli. The movie told the story of a soldier who stays in Paris after the war to become an artist. I would provide a brief plot account of this movie for anyone who has not seen it, but there really is no actual plot. The movie is more of an excuse for Gene Kelly, a great dancer, and Vincente Minelli, a marvelous director of musicals, to pool their combined talents. Additionally, part of the point of the movie was to introduce a former dancer/prostitute, Leslie Caron, to the acting world. Unfortunately, this is not a live show. This is a movie. Without a true plot and not something stitched together merely to showcase musical and dancing prowess, the movie falls flat on its face. Unless you are truly into musicals turned into screen events, the seventeen-minute dance sequence at the end of the movie will make you cringe. It was nothing more than a dual showcase. As a movie, *An American in Paris* is downright awful.

A Streetcar Named Desire was a fantastic film, rich with amazing acting performances, yet Hollywood missed the actual best movie of that year, a little known British movie, *The Lavender Hill Mob*. Since the advent of videotapes, this absolute gem has garnered status as a classic, showcasing the comedic talents of what many perceive as only a serious actor, Alec Guinness. Playing a mild mannered bank clerk who plans to rob the bank he works at, Guinness provides memorable moments in this relatively short film. The comedic timing is impeccable and the problems that are created kept this viewer's undivided attention. *The Lavender Hill Mob* may be a smaller film, but in a year that Hollywood claimed to have some of its finest acting on screen this movie stands out as the best. It is not how big a movie is, but rather how big of an impact it has on you while watching.

1950

Sunset Boulevard - #13.

A tale of idolatry, betrayal and backstabbing was crowned as the Best Picture this year. *All About Eve* has been hailed as Bette Davis' finest performance and also the one that resembled her real life in the closest manner. Veteran actress Margo Channing (Davis) takes in the young adoring fan, Eve Harrington (Anne Baxter). Slowly but surely, Eve works her way up from personal valet to understudy to playing the theatrical roles once specifically written for Margo. Her manipulative abilities are spotlighted, yet it is the underlying cynical tone of the movie that rings true here. The film is driven to an extent by a theater critic, Addison DeWitt, who not only loves Eve, but also knows her true self. In perhaps the best scene of the movie, Addison harshly tells Eve that she cannot manipulate him as she has the others. Even though he deeply cares for her and wants her as his own, his hardened cynicism overpowers her ability to manipulate him.

At one time this movie was completely overrated. As a backlash to the widely growing acceptance of *Sunset Boulevard* as the better movie, *All About Eve* has suffered. It never achieves the grand status it once held, because a greater picture, one which has magnificently stood the test of time, has eclipsed it in quality to such a degree. While it should not be mistaken as the better picture of the two, it is far better than many of the other pictures from that year.

1949

The Third Man - #24.

All The King's Men chronicled the rise and eventual fall of small town lawyer Willie Stark who traded in his virtues for power, money and fame. Beginning as a champion of justice and critic of the political machine that kept poverty at a consistently high level, Stark quickly discovered that to get things done he must compromise his beliefs. Eventually those original beliefs became nothing but a memory. *All the King's Men* was a good movie, launching its star, Broderick Crawford, into A-movie status. Prior to this film Crawford was only seen as a B-movie actor, but that all changed as his terrific performance carried this compelling political drama. Unfortunately, *All the King's Men* had the bad luck to be released in this year, where a far greater film has been recognized as clearly the better of the two.

1948

Grand thespian Laurence Olivier directed and starred in perhaps the finest version of William Shakespeare's *Hamlet*. Olivier was rewarded with a Best Actor Oscar, becoming the only actor to win an acting award for a movie that he also directed. The movie also took home the top prize for Best Picture, edging out what has grown to be considered as a far better movie, *The Treasure of the Sierra Madre*. In what can only be considered as a strange year for movies *The Treasure of the Sierra Madre* ranks as the best movie of the year.

Olivier's *Hamlet* was an able retelling of the Shakespearean play, yet John Huston's slice of degradation and paranoia far exceeds the Oscar winning film. Humphrey Bogart gives perhaps his most textured performance as Fred C. Dobbs. Dobbs is an American who is down on his luck. After getting conned out his pay by a crooked boss, Dobbs and a friend catch up with their boss and beat him to a pulp. Needing to get out of town, the two men embark upon a journey into the mountains with an old timer in search of gold and fortune. Once they discover gold and become rich, the paranoia builds from within, leading toward more trouble than the gold is actually worth. Huston's film is considered by many as one of the finest ever to hit the screens. While coming in as the best movie of 1948, there were too many drawbacks that caused it to be excluded from my list.

1947

This was one of the few years where the Academy actually handed the golden statuette to the right picture. Director Elia Kazan's revelation of subtle anti-Semitism and bigotry, *Gentlemen's Agreement*, rightfully deserved to take home the Oscar from the crop of films that year. Gregory Peck plays a reporter who goes undercover by pretending to be Jewish in order to expose the hidden underbelly of bigotry. Peck gives another fascinating performance, one of his early great ones. Discovering the truth about the world, including the disclosure that his fiancé may be bigoted as well, Peck gets more than he bargained for. The movie appears tame by current standards and has grown a bit outdated, yet *Gentleman's Agreement* still resonates with a strong message that outweighs the archaic notions of subdued bigotry in middle twentieth century America, perhaps still existing today.

1946

It's A Wonderful Life - #7.

Straight off the heels of the end of World War II, 1946's Best Picture winner was a story of three soldiers returning home to the same city and struggling to adjust back to their previous lives. *The Best Years of our Lives* follows Homer, who has lost his hands, Al and Fred as they labor through their mundane existences back home. They are away from the war where their service actually meant something and it deeply wears on them. It was a powerful movie for numerous reasons, the timing of its release among them. It was this timing that may have catapulted *The Best Years of our Lives* into the multiple Oscar winning classic that it became. Another film from that year suffered from what appeared to be a morose message of despair, during a time when America needed inspiration.

1945

This was another year that the Academy got it right. Their choice of Best Picture, Billy Wilder's *The Lost Weekend*, actually was the best movie that year. The tale of four days in the life of an alcoholic, who had been sober for ten days straight, yet decides to engage in a weekend bender, was Hollywood's first gritty look at alcoholism. Prior to *The Lost Weekend*, alcoholics were portrayed as happy go lucky drunks. The subject matter was groundbreaking, opening the eyes of the world to what is considered to be one of the true problems within the world today. Although the subject of alcoholism seems tame and commonplace to the moviegoers of today, just imagine the first screen depiction of what someone suffering from this addiction goes through. Co-written by director Billy Wilder, *The Lost Weekend* is a fascinating character study and rightfully deserved top honors.

1944

Double Indemnity - # ??.

This was another of those years where a movie was chosen as Best Picture, yet another movie clearly outshines the actual winner. The Best Picture Oscar went to the pleasant music meets God movie *Going My Way*. This tale of a young priest brought in to help transform an almost bankrupt church parish, through innovation rather than holding steadfast to the ways of old, provided cinema with one of its greatest performances ever. Barry Fitzgerald as the elder priest Father Fitzgibbon, played with equal parts of humanity and divinity, is fantastic. He became the only actor to ever receive a nomination in more than one acting category. The practice of allowing a single actor multiple nominations for the same role was outlawed due to the obvious problems that could have occurred. Fitzgerald won the Oscar for Best Supporting Actor, yet if he had won both awards it would have seriously soured the process. That performance displayed that even the holy have their quirks and foibles, yet unfortunately the project was designed to be a happy vehicle for Bing Crosby, rather than what it could have been, the showcase of human emotions to those who are often and wrongly considered divine.

1943

Casablanca (Best Picture) - #1.

1942

William Wyler's best film, *Mrs. Miniver*, took home the top honor. Although some will argue that Wyler's best movie was *Ben-Hur* or *Wuthering Heights*, *Mrs. Miniver* is the movie that Wyler should be most remembered for. The movie gave courage to the allied world by showing that despite the war and all that would be lost, it was important to stand up and act in a positive and strong manner. At the time, this movie was considered as so uplifting that it became the second highest grossing movie of all time, behind 1939's *Gone With the Wind*. *Mrs. Miniver* has been grossly overlooked among the cinema elite. It does lose a little in the current era, yet for its own time it clearly impacted all who saw it. This included high ranking members of both the Allied and Axis forces, which were publicly outspoken in a positive fashion regarding the type of movie it was.

1941

Citizen Kane - #6, *The Maltese Falcon* - #34.

Similar to 1944, 1941 had a different movie win the Oscar for Best Picture that has been definitively outshined by another movie of the same year since then. In fact, 1941 inarguably holds the distinction of having the greatest disparity between Best Picture winner, *How Green Was My Valley* and the actual best movie, *Citizen Kane*.

How Green Was My Valley is the story of the disintegration of the traditional family unit as life evolves through economic constraints. It is told through the eyes of a family in South Wales entering the twentieth century. Traditionally a coal mining family, The Morgans struggle to adjust to the changes thrust upon them. They also deal with the standard human dramas that always seem to intertwine themselves when times appear to be at their worst. This movie was originally anticipated to be the next great epic. If one were to go by the Academy Awards it fit that bill to a tee, yet time has revealed a different story. Due to the timing of the film, during the crucial stages of World War II, the end product was merely a shell of what was intended, ranking it as one of the lesser Best Picture winners in quality.

1940

The Grapes of Wrath - #21, *Rebecca* (Best Picture) - #39, *The Philadelphia Story* - #??.

1939

Gone With The Wind (Best Picture) - #3, *Mr. Smith Goes To Washington* - #23, *The Wizard of Oz* - #27.

1938

A screwball comedy took home top honors this year. *You Can't Take it With You*, Frank Capra's latest, was actually a departure from the standard Capraesque movies that have come to be associated with his name. This story was more personal to Capra, showing the distinction between two families, one that focused on creating their own wealth through disproportionate capitalism, while the other found happiness in expressing their individual creativity. That creative process, of which Capra certainly used and exploited for his own benefit, won out over the excesses in attaining power and wealth. It is less screwball comedy than a drama/comedy, presenting the contrasts of the two families in a hyper manner. This method is done in order to bridge that gap between both sides through the love between one of each of the members of the separate families.

The swashbuckling pirate movies such as *Captain Blood* are generally regarded as the Errol Flynn type parts, so the title role as Robin Hood, in *The Adventures of Robin Hood*, suited him perfectly. In an interview given by actor Morgan Freeman, while discussing his role in *Robin Hood: Prince of Thieves*, he contrasts his movie with the 1938 classic. Freeman states that his movie was more realistic because one would be hard pressed to find a group of thieves frolicking around the woods in tights during the end of the twelfth century in England. Freeman's statements sum up the 1938 film perfectly. Errol Flynn and the actors that played alongside him appeared as if they were having more fun than should be allowed. That translated to a remarkably enjoyable film to watch.

While everything here is subjective, *The Adventures of Robin Hood* is the much better film, because it is pure escapism at its finest. *You Can't Take it With You* may hold more social relevance, but when it truly comes down to it, the fairy tale based movie is the one that I would prefer to watch. That makes it better than Capra's unflinching commentary on creativity versus capitalism. The latter actually forces most viewers to take time out to truly understand the precise implications, rather than allowing the viewer to strap themselves in and simply enjoy the ride.

1937

The Awful Truth - # ??.

1937 was actually the year where the screwball comedy, perhaps the ultimate screwball comedy, should have taken home Best Picture. The semi-fictitious biography, *The Life of Emile Zola*, captured that prize though. Centering on the case where the French writer Zola is accused of libelous speech regarding the conviction of an innocent man and the subsequent cover-up of the guilty party, this movie contains a slew of magnificent performances, most notable by Paul Muni in the title role. The movie as a whole, however, fails to achieve the level of greatness that one would assume a Best Picture should, especially when released in the same year as *The Awful Truth*. That film definitely and consistently outshines *The Life of Emile Zola* as the better movie.

1936

As was the case with 1937, the Academy should have recognized a screwball comedy as its Best Picture. Instead, they chose to acknowledge the biographical account of the Broadway producer F. F. Ziegfeld, *The Great Ziegfeld*. Seen as the kind of glamorous musical that Ziegfeld himself attempted to produce in order for the common man to enjoy the theater, the film interweaved numerous song and dance numbers and told the story behind the story. Ziegfeld was a man who dealt with sensitive and volatile issues regarding money and women, all blending together to form shades of the great personality that those in the industry saw on a daily basis. His life was akin to the grandeur of an elaborate musical, the theme of this biopic. The far greater movie this year though, interestingly enough, starred the same man who played the title role of Ziegfeld, William Powell.

The truly greater movie in 1936 was without a doubt the screwball comedy *My Man Godfrey*. If *The Awful Truth* is the ultimate screwball comedy, then *My Man Godfrey* is the original screwball comedy. The story would be quite shocking in today's politically correct climate, where the wealthy and semi-retarded socialite needs a homeless man to win a scavenger hunt. The title character, down on his luck, turns out to be the man of her dreams. Before that is understood Godfrey begins to piece his own life back together as a result of his dealings with the crazy woman and her even crazier family, bringing a sort of sanity to their idiotic lives.

It had to be this family that the hyper eccentric family in *You Can't Take it With You* was modeled upon, with Capra trading the great screwball comedy in for social observations. Godfrey acts as the bridge between reality and sanity for the family, just as the bringing together of the two heads of each family in Capra's 1938 film acted as a link to join the forces for Capra's vision of sanity in the form of creativity. Godfrey becomes that one link to the actual world, for the family that is so rich and so ignorant that it is almost impossible to call them bigoted or prejudiced toward others because even that would take an ounce of reality. One critique of this movie stated that it should not be dissected, yet rather just watched and enjoyed. I'm not sure why both cannot be done.

1935

The majesty and splendor of the naval thriller, *The Mutiny on the Bounty*, easily took home the top prize in 1935, despite the Best Director and Best Actor Oscars going to a different film, John Ford's *The Informer*. Known as one of the grand old MGM classics, *The Mutiny on the Bounty* is more pomp than anything else. It is an okay film, but survives as a classic because of the classic heritage of the story and the two leading actors who appeared in the film, Clark Gable, fresh off his star solidifying performance and Best Actor Oscar from the previous year and Charles Laughton, Best Actor winner in 1933. Laughton's chilling portrayal of the abusive and villainous Captain Bligh has remained as one of the classic screen bad guys. They both serve to keep the mythic status of *The Mutiny on the Bounty* alive, despite the fact that there were far better movies, including *The Informer*.

The real best movie from that year was not *The Informer* though. The Best Actor victory achieved by its star was more due to the fact that both Laughton and Gable split votes for their individual performance, allowing Victor McLagen to win his only Oscar. Laughton should have won the award for his menacing portrayal, yet Gable's performance definitively took votes away from Laughton, costing him his second Oscar. *The Informer* is also considered one of John Ford's lesser films, when compared to his masterpieces. Luckily, three nutty brothers made a classic that year.

The three brothers in question were Groucho, Harpo and Chico. The classic they created was *A Night at the Opera*. Widely considered as their best movie, the three slapstick lunatics navigate their way into trouble, out of trouble and back into trouble again. The interaction between the brothers, specifically Groucho and Chico working out the Opera contract and the legendary stateroom scene, are cinema classics. Additionally, anytime Groucho has any type of conversation with the Marx Brothers female straight-woman, Margaret Dumont, it is the stuff of legend. Their quick banter

148

highlights the film. Subjective or not, *A Night at the Opera* clearly shines as the best movie of 1935 and this chapter has not seen the last of the Marx Brothers and their insane, yet fantastic antics.

1934

It Happened One Night (Best Picture) - # ??.

1933

An epic of sorts, depicting two English families of decidedly different stock and the events that impacted their lives garnered Best Picture honors. *Cavalcade* has often been called one of the forgotten classics of cinema. It is an impressive showcase of true events spanning thirty-three years. The major events, such as the Boer War, changing of the throne, sinking of the Titanic, World War I and the upcoming struggles that could be theoretically foreseen makes this truly a generational classic. I understand the tag of forgotten classic though. *Cavalcade* is not the best movie 1933 had to offer. The best acting performance was honored with a statuette, for Charles Laughton's amazing portrayal of Henry Tudor, King Henry VIII, in *The Private Life of Henry VIII*. For the best movie of 1933, that zany set of brothers must once again be called upon.

If there is any challenge to the notion that *A Night at the Opera* is the best Marx Brothers movie, then it comes from 1933 with their satirical exploitation of government and the futility of war, *Duck Soup*. If one were to just sit back and enjoy, then this movie might have some of the funniest scenes from any movie ever made. The scenes between Groucho and Chico, once again, are downright hilarious, as well as Harpo's lemonade stand scenes, specifically the destruction of the lemonade vendor's hat over and over again. The subtext that all governments are run by egomaniacal men who only wish to serve their own purpose was seen as a direct attack against the growing economic concerns in America, as well as the rising political power of Fascism in Europe. Despite the obvious differences in political ideologies, both sides viewed the film as subversive. The way it is viewed today though is satirical and above all, hilarious. That is what's truly important. Film fans can be thankful that the rediscovery of *Duck Soup* took place during the overtly liberal 1960's in America, because it truly is a gem of a movie regardless of its message.

1932

A full blown all-star epic was produced in 1932, which holds the distinction of winning its only Academy nomination, Best Picture. *Grand Hotel* tells the story of five guests staying at an artsy Berlin hotel and how their lives intersect during a two-day stretch. It is widely considered the quintessential early MGM epic. This most likely comes from its use of star power, Greta Garbo, Joan Crawford, Wallace Beery and the Barrymores, Lionel and John, in what would now be considered supporting roles. *Grand Hotel* has also achieved mythic status for its famous one-liner spoken by Garbo, *'I want to be alone'*. In a year where there is not much to choose from, *Grand Hotel* shines as the year's best movie, with fantastic acting performances resonating throughout.

1931

The first Western to ever win Best Picture, *Cimarron*, has also been dubbed as the worst of the Best Pictures by numerous critics. The movie certainly does not date well, containing many stereotypes that evoke memories of D. W. Griffith's 1915 hate fest *The Birth of a Nation*. *Cimarron* covers forty years of Oklahoma frontier life, stressing the hardships of taming the land and trying to live in peace. Beginning with the great Oklahoma land race, a grand spectacle, the movie seems to fall flat after that. It follows the exploits of one man, which does not seem to provide that interest peak that many other main characters do. This movie is nothing but merely showcased production, rather than enjoyable. *Cimarron* trades in artistic value and substance for grandeur and scale.

1931 had two other movies that were far better than *Cimarron*. The first of which was *The Front Page*, later remade in 1940 by Howard Hawks as *His Girl Friday*. The 1931 original version does not hold a candle to the 1940 remake, perhaps due to the fantastic chemistry of stars Cary Grant and Rosiland Russell. *The Front Page* also misses the mark as the best movie of 1931, with that distinction going to one of the long-standing classics of Charlie Chaplin, *City Lights*.

Approximately three years after silent films were a thing of the past, making way for the *"talkies"*, Chaplin held firm and created what has been called his greatest masterpiece. The beautiful mix of comedy and drama displayed the positive side toward acting through body language, expressing thought and ideas without having to speak. Chaplin's impact upon two sad figures, a blind flower girl and a drunken millionaire are the crux of the film. He uses his usual blend of slapstick comedy to drive the plot and keep the story moving forward. It truly is a remarkable film, from a master who had and still has no equal.

1930

Anti-war films have become commonplace as movie audiences mature and Hollywood changes with the times. In 1930, however, that was a revolutionary stance to take. *All Quiet on the Western Front* did just that and was deservedly rewarded with a Best Picture Oscar. Showing the war from the perspective of soldiers in the trenches, *All Quiet on the Western Front* clearly displays the futility of war by portraying the soldier's plight and displaying how war truly affects the men that politicians and leaders send to fight their battles. It is perhaps one of the starkest commentaries on how the great nations fail to take the soldiers into consideration who actually have to go and engage in battles to win a war for their country.

1929

1929 saw the first musical to capture the Best Picture Award in only the second year of the award's existence. *The Broadway Melody* was the first complete musical of the talking picture era. It helped launched MGM into its iconic status as the musical studio, which they made sure to hold on to. This movie has about as basic a plot that could ever be imagined. It simply follows the multiple romances of the musical stars as they work their way through song and dance numbers. That is about it. The song and dance numbers are the real stars of the movie, yet a manufactured plot of love within the theater is artificially created in order to get from one musical number to the next. This film had a purpose, to present the musical to the new world of talking pictures. As a movie, it is dreadful and far below *Cimarron* in level of quality.

The best movie from the second year of the Academy Awards was the tense crime noir *Thunderbolt*. This unique drama has a notorious criminal searching for the man his girlfriend is in love with. The girlfriend is played by Fay Wray of *King Kong* fame. After the criminal is caught and placed in prison to be executed, he tries to stave off his execution long enough to kill the man incarcerated in the next cell, who just so happens to be the man in love with his girlfriend. There is great interaction between the prisoners and the warden, who cracks wise at every given chance. The movie has been deemed as revolutionary, giving birth to the genre of the prison drama. There are elements to the movie that are tough to watch today, yet those are more of a technical nature. As far as 1929 goes, *Thunderbolt* is the best movie out there.

1928

The first Academy Award for Best Picture went to the war drama *Wings*, telling the story of two pilots who are both in love with the same woman. It is the only silent film to win that award, yet it still remains fresh today if one can actually find a quality copy to view. The standard motifs apply: heartbreak, male bonding through the horrors of war and the longing to return home. The battlescenes in the air are spectacular and look for screen legend Gary Cooper in a small role. Unfortunately, it would take the Academy three tries to finally get it right as *Wings* was not the best movie of the year.

One of Charlie Chaplin's least known movies, *The Circus*, happens to be the best picture from the first year of the Academy Awards. His customary character, the Tramp, wanders into a circus, gets chased by the police and turns into a carnival sensation through his slapstick ability. The problem - the slapstick cannot be artificially manufactured, so the ringmaster has to devise ways for the Tramp's natural ability to present itself in order to entertain the audience. Even though it is not the prototypical Chaplin classic, it is still interesting to watch and in the earliest year of the Academy, ranks highest above all others.

As you should have noticed, only English speaking films were included in this category, as was the criteria for films included in the main list. The Best Picture from one year also does not mean it has to be better than the worst picture from another year. Year to year, movies are different. I hope it was shown that bad movies can sometimes win the Best Picture Oscar, with history fixing that wrong by examining and discussing cinema throughout the years, the true focal point of this book.

Here is a recap of the Best Picture winner from each year, followed by the corresponding best movie from that same year across from it.

BEST PICTURE AND BEST MOVIE LIST BY YEAR

BEST PICTURE WINNERS | BEST MOVIE

1928 - WINGS	THE CIRCUS
1929 – THE BROADWAY MELODY	THUNDERBOLT
1930 – ALL QUIET ON THE WESTERN FRONT	ALL QUIET ON THE WESTERN FRONT
1931 – CIMARRON	CITY LIGHTS
1932 – GRAND HOTEL	GRAND HOTEL
1933 – CAVALCADE	DUCK SOUP
1934 – IT HAPPENED ONE NIGHT	IT HAPPENED ONE NIGHT
1935 – MUTINY ON THE BOUNTY	A NIGHT AT THE OPERA
1936 – THE GREAT ZIEGFELD	MY MAN GODFREY
1937 – THE LIFE OF EMILE ZOLA	THE AWFUL TRUTH
1938 – YOU CAN'T TAKE IT WITH YOU	THE ADVENTURES OF ROBIN HOOD
1939 – GONE WITH THE WIND	GONE WITH THE WIND
1940 – REBECCA	THE GRAPES OF WRATH
1941 – HOW GREEN WAS MY VALLEY	CITIZEN KANE
1942 – MRS. MINIVER	MRS. MINIVER
1943 – CASABLANCA	CASABLANCA
1944 – GOING MY WAY	DOUBLE INDEMNITY
1945 – THE LOST WEEKEND	THE LOST WEEKEND
1946 – THE BEST YEARS OF OUR LIVES	IT'S A WONDERFUL LIFE
1947 – GENTLEMAN'S AGREEMENT	GENTLEMAN'S AGREEMENT
1948 – HAMLET	THE TREASURE OF THE SIERRA MADRE
1949 – ALL THE KING'S MEN	THE THIRD MAN
1950 – ALL ABOUT EVE	SUNSET BOULEVARD
1951 – AN AMERICAN IN PARIS	THE LAVENDER HILL MOB
1952 – THE GREATEST SHOW ON EARTH	HIGH NOON
1953 – FROM HERE TO ETERNTY	FROM HERE TO ETERNITY
1954 – ON THE WATERFRONT	REAR WINDOW

1955 – MARTY	THE NIGHT OF THE HUNTER
1956 – AROUND THE WORLD IN 80 DAYS	WRITTEN ON THE WIND
1957 – THE BRIDGE ON THE RIVER KWAI	THE BRIDGE ON THE RIVER KWAI
1958 – GIGI	VERTIGO
1959 – BEN-HUR	NORTH BY NORTHWEST
1960 – THE APARTMENT	PSYCHO
1961 – WEST SIDE STORY	THE HUSTLER
1962 – LAWRENCE OF ARABIA	THE MANCHURIAN CANDIDATE
1963 – TOM JONES	HUD
1964 – MY FAIR LADY	DR. STRANGELOVE
1965 – THE SOUND OF MUSIC	DOCTOR ZHIVAGO
1966 – A MAN FOR ALL SEASONS	A MAN FOR ALL SEASONS
1967 – IN THE HEAT OF THE NIGHT	IN THE HEAT OF THE NIGHT
1968 – OLIVER	THE PRODUCERS
1969 – MIDNIGHT COWBOY	MIDNIGHT COWBOY
1970 – PATTON	FIVE EASY PIECES
1971 – THE FRENCH CONNECTION	THE LAST PICTURE SHOW
1972 – THE GODFATHER	THE GODFATHER
1973 – THE STING	THE STING
1974 – THE GODFATHER II	THE GODFATHER II
1975 – ONE FLEW OVER THE CUCKOO'S NEST	ONE FLEW OVER THE CUCKOO'S NEST
1976 – ROCKY	NETWORK
1977 – ANNIE HALL	SLAPSHOT
1978 – THE DEER HUNTER	THE DEER HUNTER
1979 – KRAMER VS. KRAMER	BREAKING AWAY
1980 – ORDINARY PEOPLE	RAGING BULL
1981 – CHARIOTS OF FIRE	RAIDERS OF THE LOST ARK
1982 – GANDHI	THE VERDICT
1983 – TERMS OF ENDEARMENT	TERMS OF ENDEARMENT
1984 – AMADEUS	AMADEUS
1985 – OUT OF AFRICA	BRAZIL

1986 – PLATOON	HIGHLANDER
1987 – THE LAST EMPEROR	THE PRINCESS BRIDE
1988 – RAIN MAN	MIDNIGHT RUN
1989 – DRIVING MISS DAISY	FIELD OF DREAMS
1990 – DANCES WITH WOLVES	GOODFELLAS
1991 – THE SILENCE OF THE LAMBS	BEAUTY AND THE BEAST
1992 – UNFORGIVEN	RESERVOIR DOGS
1993 – SCHINDLER'S LIST	THE FUGITIVE
1994 – FORREST GUMP	THE SHAWSHANK REDEMPTION
1995 – BRAVEHEART	APOLLO 13
1996 – THE ENGLISH PATIENT	FARGO
1997 – TITANIC	L.A. CONFIDENTIAL
1998 – SHAKESPEARE IN LOVE	AMERICAN HISTORY X
1999 – AMERICAN BEAUTY	AMERICAN BEAUTY
2000 – GLADIATOR	WONDER BOYS
2001 – A BEAUTIFUL MIND	A BEAUTIFUL MIND
2002 – CHICAGO	ADAPTATION
2003 – THE LORD OF THE RINGS III	THE LORD OF THE RINGS III
2004 – MILLION DOLLAR BABY	FINDING NEVERLAND

    The next list shall be presented from best to least best. Since the main list has already been presented in the proper way, ranked in a descending order from 50 down to 1, there is no need to present this list that way. The left hand section shall rank the Best Picture winners, as is stated, yet the right hand section shall only rank the movies that were named as the best for each year. One example would be; since *The Manchurian Candidate* and *To Kill A Mockingbird* were both from the same year, 1962, only *The Manchurian Candidate* would be ranked in the right hand section. Years with multiple entries on the main list will only have the highest ranked movie from the list represented, despite the fact that *To Kill A Mockingbird* is a better movie than sixty-five of the movies placed on the right hand list.

BEST PICTURE AND MOVIE LIST
RANKED

BEST PICTURE WINNERS | ## BEST MOVIE

1 - CASABLANCA — CASABLANCA
2 – GONE WITH THE WIND — RAIDERS OF THE LOST ARK
3 – THE BRIDGE ON THE RIVER KWAI — GONE WITH THE WIND
4 – ONE FLEW OVER THE CUCKOO'S NEST — THE BRIDGE ON THE RIVER KWAI
5 – THE GODFATHER — GOODFELLAS
6 – A BEAUTIFUL MIND — CITIZEN KANE
7 – LORD OF THE RINGS III — IT'S A WONDERFULLIFE
8 – MIDNIGHT COWBOY — ONE FLEW OVER THE CUCKOO'S NEST
9 – THE GODFATHER II — THE GODFATHER
10 – SCHINDLER'S LIST — THE MANCHURIAN CANDIDATE
11 – THE STING — PSYCHO
12 – FROM HERE TO ETERNITY — RAGING BULL
13 – ON THE WATERFRONT — SUNSET BOULEVARD
14 – REBECCA — A BEAUTIFUL MIND
15 – ROCKY — LORD OF THE RINGS III
16 – IN THE HEAT OF THE NIGHT — MIDNIGHT COWBOY
17 – IT HAPPENED ONE NIGHT — BEAUTY AND THE BEAST
18 – TERMS OF ENDEARMENT — THE GODFATHER II
19 – THE FRENCH CONNECTION — THE FUGITIVE
20 – THE DEER HUNTER — THE GRAPES OF WRATH
21 – AMERICAN BEAUTY — THE THIRD MAN
22 – UNFORGIVEN — VERTIGO
23 – ALL ABOUT EVE — THE SHAWSHANK REDEMPTION
24 – AMADEUS — REAR WINDOW
25 – THE SILENCE OF THE LAMBS — THE STING

26 – A MAN FOR ALL SEASONS	FROM HERE TO ETERNITY
27 – ORDINARY PEOPLE	L. A. CONFIDENTIAL
28 – FORREST GUMP	NETWORK
29 – THE APARTMENT	HIGH NOON
30 – ALL THE KING'S MEN	FIELD OF DREAMS
31 – THE BEST YEARS OF OUR LIVES	NIGHT OF THE HUNTER
32 – ALL QUIET ON THE WESTERN FRONT	FARGO
33 – KRAMER VS. KRAMER	BREAKING AWAY
34 – LAWRENCE OF ARABIA	THE PRINCESS BRIDE
35 – THE SOUND OF MUSIC	NORTH BY NORTHWEST
36 – BRAVEHEART	THE LAST PICTURE SHOW
37 – MRS. MINIVER	IN THE HEAT OF THE NIGHT
38 – THE LOST WEKEND	DOUBLE INDEMNITY
39 – TITANIC	THE AWFUL TRUTH
40 – PLATOON	ADAPTATION
41 – MUTINY ON THE BOUNTY	IT HAPPENED ONE NIGHT
42 – PATTON	DOCTOR ZHIVAGO
43 – GENTLEMAN'S AGREEMENT	TERMS OF ENDEARMENT
44 – THE ENGLISH PATIENT	THE HUSTLER
45 – MY FAIR LADY	AMERICAN HISTORY X
46 – ANNIE HALL	THE DEER HUNTER
47 – GLADIATOR	AMERICAN BEAUTY
48 – RAIN MAN	A NIGHT AT THE OPERA
49 – BEN-HUR	THE VERDICT
50 – CHARIOTS OF FIRE	RESERVOIR DOGS
51 – MILLION DOLLAR BABY	HUD
52 – DANCES WITH WOLVES	AMADEUS
53 – CAVALCADE	MIDNIGHT RUN
54 – MARTY	FINDING NEVERLAND

55 – THE GREATEST SHOW ON EARTH	FIVE EASY PIECES
56 – YOU CAN'T TAKE IT WITH YOU	DUCK SOUP
57 – TOM JONES	APOLLO 13
58 – GRAND HOTEL	WONDER BOYS
59 – HAMLET	WRITTEN ON THE WIND
60 – SHAKESPEARE IN LOVE	MY MAN GODFREY
61 – WINGS	A MAN FOR ALL SEASONS
62 – GANDHI	DR. STRANGELOVE
63 – GOING MY WAY	THE LAVENDER HILL MOB
64 – AROUND THE WORLD IN 80 DAYS	ALL QUIET ON THE WESTERN FRONT
65 – HOW GREEN WAS MY VALLEY	THE ADVENTURES OF ROBIN HOOD
66 – THE LIFE OF EMILE ZOLA	THE TREASURE OF THE SIERRA MADRE
67 – OUT OF AFRICA	MRS. MINIVER
68 – DRIVING MISS DAISY	SLAPSHOT
69 – CHICAGO	THE LOST WEEKEND
70 – THE GREAT ZIEGFELD	CITY LIGHTS
71 – CIMARRON	BRAZIL
72 – THE LAST EMPEROR	THE PRODUCERS
73 – GIGI	HIGHLANDER
74 – OLIVER	GENTLEMAN'S AGREEMENT
75 – WEST SIDE STORY	THUNDERBOLT
76 – AN AMERICAN IN PARIS	GRAND HOTEL
77 – THE BROADWAY MELODY	THE CIRCUS

    Hopefully, the concept that movies can be great in comparison, yet less spectacular as well when compared comes through with the last list. A perfect example would be *Terms of Endearment*, which according to my list of Best Picture winners came in as the eighteenth in that category. However, the same movie came in forty-third among the best movies of each year. The distinction should be obvious and clear.

    Lists are always subjective, yet there has to be some kind of reason to these lists if they are to have any validity at all. The one thing that must be remembered when reading and analyzing the lists in this book, of which there are a number of them, is that they are all subjective yet not arbitrary. For those who cannot see the difference between subjective and arbitrary, perhaps this quick explanation will help, as I perceive the difference. Subjective is a person's opinion based upon logical conclusion, experiences and surroundings, which in this case include the history of critical opinions regarding cinema. Arbitrary, however, with regards to lists, means just placing entries wherever one feels they should go at that current time. There is no critical analysis of the pertinent factors. Subjective is more academic, although it should never be deemed scientific. Let's face it, if it were scientific there would be no debate.

Chapter Four:

Top 10 Oscar Snubs

With only five nominees per award each year someone is always going to be left out in the cold during Oscar time. It is a mathematical impossibility to include every great acting performance of every given year, regardless of whether it is supporting or lead, male or female. A committee chooses who shall be nominated for the year. Sometimes they get it right. A lot of times they do not. Sentimentality plays a big role in the selection process, as it also does when it comes time to vote.

Studios often lobby for nominations. Sometimes major campaigns are run for a movie by the studio, whether it is for a performance or for the movie itself. I have even heard about instances where a studio has spent more on the Oscar campaign than it had on the making the movie. The benefit is for the studio. Every nomination brings more free press for their movie, which turns into ticket sales and increased profits. Whether you want to believe it or not, moviemaking is a business. Anything else that comes out of it is what the audience or the individual viewer chooses to make of it.

There still remains the simple fact that great performances are often overlooked for weaker, more glamorous or even more widely lobbied for performances. I will now provide, in my opinion, the ten greatest Oscar snubs in the long span of Academy Award history. A snub is not a performer who was nominated and deserves to win, yet fails to do so. A snub is that special performance that goes unrecognized by the academy. The actor or actress does not receive a nomination for their great performance, while others, some politically and financially motivated, attend in their place. They are receiving what amounts to that snubbed performer's rightful nomination.

It should be stated that the upcoming list is simply ten performances that the Academy did not recognize with a nomination, but by no means should be considered as the top acting performances of all-time. In coming up with the chapters for this book, I toyed with the possibility of ranking that, the ten greatest acting performances, rather than the ten worst Oscar snubs. A list like that would have been something to the effect of this:

10 – Barry Fitzgerald – *Going My Way*
9 – Angela Lansbury – *The Manchurian Candidate*
8 – Jack Nicholson – *As Good As It Gets*
7 – Edward Norton – *American History X*
6 – Agnes Moorehead – *The Magnificent Ambersons*
5 – Marlon Brando – *A Streetcar Named Desire*
4 – Gloria Swanson – *Sunset Boulevard*
3 – Paul Newman – *The Hustler*
2 – Robert DeNiro – *Raging Bull*
1 – Gregory Peck – *To Kill A Mockingbird*

Those would have been some interesting write-ups, yet hopefully the following ten will be just as appealing. I feel that the Oscar snub could almost warrant a book itself, so the choice was made to highlight my opinion of the ten most overlooked performances on film.

To remain somewhat unbiased, I shall not include any performance that was snubbed from any movie I have ranked within the main list, regardless of their worth. To do so would lean toward a decline in credibility and call into question my objectiveness in assembling the main list, or any of the subsequent lists. In fact, no performance that was snubbed, despite its merit as one of the greatest snubs by the academy, that appears in any of the movies I have or will profile shall appear within the ten snubs ranked here. However, they will be discussed briefly because a number of them are extremely worthy of making this list. One of them gives such a frenetic performance that the actor not only carries every scene of the film he is in, but also mimics the actual pacing of the film with his performance. That performance would have been the top snub in Oscar history yet will be relegated to this pre-section here for credibility purposes.

It is logical to assume that the majority of the movies on the main list had one fantastic performance that was overlooked by the Academy. Some films in the main list, in addition to some of the films discussed later, have more than one great overlooked performance. It wouldn't be prudent to just pick out one performance from each of the movies from the main list and talk about that. Rather, I shall highlight those that deserve mentioning, a performance that was overlooked by the Academy and could have easily made this top ten Oscar snub list, if the conditions were not set against it. Since they are, I shall briefly discuss a few that are definitively worth mentioning. By some pre-planned coincidence I shall discuss ten of them, disregarding rankings.

Breaking Away was a fantastic tale of the loss of teenage innocence, but the true beauty of that movie is the family interaction that allows that necessary transition. While Barbara Barrie is excellent as Dave's mother, garnering an Oscar nomination for her role, the true heart of the family dynamic is in the subtle yet often outrageous performance given by the father, Paul Dooley. Starting out as the prototypical grumpy dad who does not understand his son, Dooley begins to help ease Dave's shift into understanding adulthood and all the bad times that come along for the ride. Dooley's unique presentation of a man who must rise past the expectations of keeping distance from his son supplies the basis for this movie. The Oscar went to Melvyn Douglas for *Being There*, but Dooley's job is far better and it is a complete disgrace that he was not even nominated. It is a real shame that Dooley was never able to recapture that greatness.

Almost every child has seen *The Wizard of Oz*. It is a family tradition passed down through the generations. All the bizarre creatures are magical and the journey along the yellow brick road is one that shall always stay with us. One of these creatures needed to be evil incarnate. That character was the menacing Wicked Witch of the West, played by Margaret Hamilton. For many she is the initiation of the evil character into stories. Her terrifying appearance, along with her equally over the top performance as the heinous old maid who wants to have Toto put to sleep, evoke memories of what a nightmare should be. The Oscar for Best Supporting Actress went to Hattie McDaniel, for her role as Mammy in *Gone With The Wind*. McDaniel's victory was a surprise, yet it was no greater a shock than the omission of Hamilton among the nominees, who easily could have taken home the award herself.

The Scopes monkey trial of 1925 is the backdrop for *Inherit the Wind*. Spencer Tracy starred as the lawyer who comes to the backwards town of Hillsboro to fight for the rights of a man to think. His opponent, played by Frederic March, was a Bible beating self proclaimed prophet, judge and jury of the man evil enough to question where we all came from. His performance steals the movie. March's over the top portrayal of a man who never achieved greatness in his life, other than simple notoriety and the following of those who could not lead themselves, is the best part of this excellent film. March portrays the sadness and unfortunate aspects of living with inferior thoughts and the burden of having the majority follow his every word, even after they see that he is clearly fallible. Tracy received the Oscar nomination, yet March, who was Tracy's acting superior here was really overlooked. The Oscar was won by Burt Lancaster for *Elmer Gantry*, yet March gives as equally good of a performance, if not better.

In the dialogue driven twenties-something movie *Beautiful Girls*, the best performance from the film comes from the youngest member of the cast, Natalie Portman. Playing the thirteen year old neighbor of the quasi-main character Willie C., Portman delivers the smartest dialogue of the film in by far the most realistic fashion. Her jokes work because of the way she masterfully delivers them using an intellectual innocence. Her heartbreak comes through even more realistically. It is not just the dialogue that shows off her acting, but rather her talent that highlights the fantastic dialogue. This, not *The Professional*, was the movie that made Portman a star. The award, won by Juliette Binoche for her role in *The English Patient* came as a surprise to many. The real surprise was leaving the brilliant performance by Natalie Portman off the list of nominees.

A movie that some will be probably shocked over its inclusion among the main list, *The Princess Bride*, also boasts not only the best supporting actor performance of the year but also the best acting of the year. Wallace Shawn, playing the evil Sicilian mastermind Vizzini, supplies his great rhetoric with pinpoint comedic accuracy and sets the movie in motion for a fantastical ride. Although he is a brilliant writer who made a cinematic splash with the intriguing *My Dinner With Andre*, Shawn will always be known for his one word response of incalculable puzzlement, *'inconceivable'*. That line becomes a classic because it is spoken with a perfect blend of mystifying shock and Daffy Duck like tone. The only problem with Shawn's role is that it was too short with respect to screen time. That is arbitrary however, when one remembers that Anthony Hopkins won the Best Actor Oscar in 1991 for what amounted to less than nineteen minutes of screen time, only slightly longer than Shawn's screen time. Sean Connery was awarded an Oscar for *The Untouchables*, yet most will not argue the position that the Oscar was for recognizing the body of his work. My opinion is that it was a direct make up award for his badly overlooked performance the previous year from the underrated movie *Highlander*.

You have read about the claustrophobic nightmare that was Francis Ford Coppola's highly underrated 1974 classic *The Conversation*. Perhaps more than any other element, *The Conversation* was great because of the superb acting of Gene Hackman. Hackman conveys the introverted Harry Caul, distrusting everyone and everything because of prior dealings that led to accidental fatalities. He lives his life inside himself, the only person he can trust and Hackman's acting communicates that brilliantly. Hackman has won two Oscars, three years before *The Conversation* and eighteen years afterward. This however, is the finest acting performance of his illustrious career. Of all the nominees that year, Hoffman, Pacino, Finney and Nicholson, veteran television actor Art Carney took home the Oscar. It is tough to say who should have been left off, but Hackman deserved to have been included among them.

One of the aspects about Oliver Stone's conspiracy extravaganza *JFK* is that while trying to offer mounds and mounds of information it always retains that frenetic aspect. This intimates the feeling that something shockingly revealing was to come next. Filled with great performances, specifically Kevin Costner as Jim Garrison, one performance perfectly mirrors that frenetic pacing of the movie, Joe Pesci's portrayal of the psychotic collaborator David Ferrie embodies the film. Going at top speed in the majority of his scenes, whether it is with his actions or his words, Pesci delivers one of the best performances I have ever seen, much better than his performance in *Goodfellas* the previous year, which actually won him the Oscar. Even when he is calm, in only a few scenes, there is that anticipation of him snapping. Although known for playing mob psychopaths, Pesci provides one of the most bizarre characters in cinema history. The award was given to Jack Palance, for *City*

Slickers. The award for Palance has also been theorized as covering his body of work. Palance's role in *Shane* was far better work than in *City Slickers*. Pesci deserved to win his second straight Oscar.

The 1980's was the decade for magical baseball movies. Earlier in the decade there was the brilliant and moving film *The Natural*. In the last year of the decade that movie was topped by *Field of Dreams*. Not one performance from *Field of Dreams* was nominated for an Oscar, despite a number of worthy actors, including Kevin Costner, who was robbed of a nomination the previous year for *Bull Durham* and James Earl Jones. There is another though, the minor role assumed by legendary actor Burt Lancaster as the ghost of 'Moonlight' Graham. In those few scenes Lancaster helps to explain what baseball should mean to people, while also illustrating that it is not the end all be all to life. When he makes his way out to the cornfield, looking back once more, you see greatness at work. A well deserved Best Supporting Actor Oscar went to Denzel Washington for *Glory*, yet in the true spirit of the award, Lancaster deserved to be included in the festivities.

With eight down and two to go, who can be added to this list that is left? There are so many worthwhile choices yet I believe that one man can fit the final two spots quite easily, with two fantastic performances that for some odd reason went unnoticed. Both performances could have and should have won the Oscar that year. Due to what was perceived as his inability to cater to Hollywood and the Hollywood system, Orson Welles was often passed over by the Academy for far inferior work. This time it was in relation to his acting talent. It is us, the audience, who should be thankful that Welles chose to ignore what was expected of him under the Hollywood ideal, or else he may not have made such brilliant films over the course of his career. The following two performances are the highlights of Welles' acting career.

In 1958 Welles made a small film. Once his vision was followed, the movie has become one of the best films of all time. That film was *Touch of Evil*. Not playing the main character, Welles' performance as the corrupt border sheriff is one that every actor should see. While many spend their time trying to get their face out there in the most brilliant and pleasant light possible, Welles distinctly went the other way with this character, choosing to ugly him down. Why? A horrific character was more beneficial to the story. His acting in that part however, is what truly sells the movie. Charlton Heston is okay and Janet Leigh is great to look at in everything she does, but Welles steals the movie. When Welles' character returns to drinking you want to root for his demise, although for a split second I recanted that thought because the movie needed him. The five nominees from 1958 could not hold a candle to Welles, but since he was not invited the Academy had to give the award to one of them. Burl Ives, from *The Big Country*, acted as the beneficiary of what was rightfully Welles' award.

The same holds true for his performance in *The Third Man*. When he shows up as the villainous Harry Lime at the beginning of the final third of the movie, a second wind magically arrives. We hear about Harry Lime and we see his friend Holly Martins searching for answers, but not until Welles shows up does the movie become a masterpiece of suspense. Some might say that his role was too short to be recognized, yet once again I remind those detractors of the less than nineteen minute acting job that won Anthony Hopkins a Best Lead Actor Oscar in 1991. Welles easily would have beaten out the competition from that or almost any year.

Now onto the top 10.

10

CHRISTOPHER LLOYD

BACK TO THE FUTURE - 1985

In 1985 a small movie came out that caught the eye and the heart of audiences across America. Some might say it was because of the film's star, rising television actor Michael J. Fox and his quirky way that helped make this movie such a gigantic blockbuster. Others say it was the brainchild of an ambitious up and coming writer/director who would go onto to eventually make Oscar history, which gave exceptional life to this time travel gem. Both of those are true. Additionally, one performance in the film stands out above the rest. It is as much responsible for the storied success of the film as anyone, including its designated bankable golden boy and gifted creator.

Teenager Marty McFly is accidentally sent back to 1955 when Dr. Emmett Brown is murdered after successfully inventing time travel. McFly's adventures in the past include dodging the sexual advances of his mother and realigning the cosmic forces that helped bring together both his parents in order to save his own existence. Sounds like a comedy, huh? The comedy comes from the interaction between McFly and Dr. Brown. The mix of a 1980's teenager and a mad scientist from the 1950's provides the best parts of the movie. The story of McFly saving his own life by bringing his parents together is often flat, yet Dr. Brown's keen insights and bizarre gifts help McFly realize that he not only must return home to 1985, but also save Dr. Brown in the process.

Veteran television actor Christopher Lloyd stepped into the role of the eccentric genius Dr. Emmett Brown and knocked the performance out of the park. Best known for his role on the television series *Taxi*, Lloyd brings all the crazed but downplayed enthusiasm of Reverend Jim Ignatowski, yet taken up a notch. His acting here is as if Reverend Jim got a crash course in Einsteinian physics and it drove him sane while keeping all those beautiful eccentricities. This performance is not just the same old job Lloyd did while on *Taxi*. It is the evolution of a previously played character. If this film truly is a comedy, Lloyd's is the performance that drives that home.

It is rare when a comedic performance is recognized by the Academy. It takes a number of elements for the voters to evolve their thinking and realize that a performance is a performance, regardless of what genre the film is. Unfortunately, one of those elements required is to ignore a fantastic performance, such as was done here. Christopher Lloyd deserved the nomination.

This year's crop of Best Supporting Actor nominees was an eclectic bunch. Eric Roberts got a nomination for playing opposite Jon Voight in *Runaway Train*. Klaus Maria Brandauer received one for his role in the Best Picture winner *Out Of Africa*. The creepy looking William Hickey was given a nomination for his role as the elderly Don in *Prizzi's Honor* and Robert Loggia was awarded a nomination for *Jagged Edge*. Loggia was also brilliant in *Prizzi's Honor* as well, which certainly did not hurt his chances for a nomination. The award went to legendary actor Don Ameche for *Cocoon*. Ameche's career undoubtedly played a part, yet his acting warranted the nomination and the victory. Lloyd's job however was surely as good as or better than the other four nominees.

9

JOHN C. REILLY
BOOGIE NIGHTS - 1997

When Paul Thomas Anderson released the film *Boogie Nights* in 1997 it was mainly viewed as glorifying the pornography industry. Despite the critical success it received, that assessment could not be further from the truth. Alternatively taken as a dramatic film on the trials and tribulations that the individuals go through who engage in this type of work, the true message of the film was completely lost upon those who believed the film was doing either of those, glorifying or dramatizing.

It is immaterial that the movie took elements from the real life of infamous pornographic actor John Holmes. *Boogie Nights* is a complete flat-out satire on the ridiculousness and intellectual limitations of those who perform in this field. The film poked fun at how deeply serious these people take themselves and their craft, highlighting the insanely bad choices that inevitably follow. At the heart of this movie is a performance that typifies that completely, John C. Reilly's performance in the role of Reed Rothchild and more specifically, his invented porn alter-ego Chest Rockwell.

When Reed first meets the new prodigy on the scene a verbal challenge is quickly offered. Immediately the two become friends, allowing scenes of utter hilarity to come from their on screen interaction. This introduction scene epitomizes the lack of not only intellect but also of self-confidence, in a field where that is something that normally is a pre-requisite. The audience is treated to an extreme lack of personality mixed with flashes of absolutely brilliant ignorance as we meet Reed Rothchild. Reilly plays the role to absolute perfection, hitting on all those slight nuances to make one wonder how this character has made it through the first few years of his life successfully.

As success is achieved, more is wanted. This inevitably leads the characters on the road to major problems, with Reed there for every bad decision and every great hysterical comment. The way Reilly plays this moronic buffoon focuses the entire movie on him. The movie was designed to highlight Mark Wahlberg as Dirk Diggler, the next great thing in pornography, yet all eyes should be on Reilly whenever he is on camera. He steals the scene every chance he gets. He was not duly rewarded when it came to Oscar time, despite a supporting actor nomination coming from this film.

The five nominees included Robert Forster for *Jackie Brown*, Anthony Hopkins for *Amistad*, Greg Kinnear for *As Good as it Gets*, Robin Williams for *Good Will Hunting* and Burt Reynolds for *Boogie Nights*. Williams took home the Oscar, despite the fact that Forster's performance was hands down the best of the lot. Hopkins playing former President John Quincy Adams is also of the phenomenal variety. Forster's interaction with Pam Grier, in Tarantino's second best film, provides the heart of one of the best films of that year. Reynolds received the nomination, not because of his work in this film, which was overshadowed by Reilly's comical yet realistically inept performance, but rather for his career. As I do not have to abide by the standards of the Academy, who feel the necessity to reward a body of work rather than adhering to the true scope, Reilly was by far the more deserving choice.

8

LENA OLIN

ROMEO IS BLEEDING – 1993

One of the most bizarre movies that shall be discussed in this book, *Romeo is Bleeding*, is one of those gems that not too many people know about, yet after seeing it can hardly forget. Starring Gary Oldman as a crooked cop, the plot actually heads into the obscene as the self-destruction of this wretched creature happens right before our eyes. In one way it evokes memories of an older style of moviemaking, where the main character could be shown in a darker light rather than the standard main character who everyone was supposed to root for. Combined with an insanely unique crime element, including the most dangerous and psychotic hit woman that cinema has ever seen, *Romeo is Bleeding* takes crime noir to a new level by embracing old style moviemaking with innovative tactics.

Gary Oldman is Gary Oldman. Nothing more needs to be said about him, other than he gives it his all in every acting role he undertakes. That all out job is generally the most bizarre or the focal point of every movie that he performs in. As with many movies, the distinctive quality of *Romeo Is Bleeding* comes from its supporting characters. These minor characters are put in place within the story to fill in the parts around the main character, in this case Oldman. The great minor character from this movie is the psychotic contract killer Mona Demarkov. Olin nails the role of her career in Demarkov, bringing a demented quality to her that bordered on over the top, yet was strangely centered. Her insanity was critical for the story. Lena Olin was nominated previously for her performance in *Enemies, A Love Story*. She was no newcomer to the award show scene.

As the story progresses the firsthand implosion of the Oldman character occurs. During this time, as Oldman continues down a path he cannot control, Demarkov appears regularly to torment him. Around every corner she is there. She hunts him as a killer, persecutes him as a lover, tortures him by murdering his girlfriend and in a brilliant plot twist, entraps him for the police to reveal he is corrupt. He cannot seem to escape her, even when she is knocked out cold in the back of his car. That appears to be her at her finest or most dangerous. After seeing Olin as the Russian hit woman, particularly what she does to her arm, you will never think of women as the weaker sex again.

The lineup of Best Supporting Actress nominees for 1993 was star studded. There was Winona Ryder from *The Age of Innocence*, Rosie Perez from *Fearless*, Emma Thompson for *In the Name of the Father*, Holly Hunter for *The Firm* and the second youngest girl to ever win an Oscar, Anna Paquin for *The Piano*. These five performances were all worthy of a nomination and all had enough clout and name recognition to receive one, with the exception of Paquin who actually won. Olin was as good as any one of these performers, specifically Holly Hunter whose role in *The Firm* was not as great as it was made out to be. What must have taken place was that Olin's performance was viewed as a lead performance by an actress, rather than a supporting performance. Even though both Hunter and Thompson also were nominated in the Best Actress category, Olin deserved a nomination in one of those two categories, no matter where the Academy decided to place her role.

7

DARREN MCGAVIN

A CHRISTMAS STORY - 1983

What is Christmas without *A Christmas Story*? This magnificently sweet film has become a Christmas tradition since its original release in 1983. That earnest tale of a Midwestern family and their eldest boy, Ralphie, who desperately wants a Red Ryder BB gun/air rifle for Christmas, has made a dent in all of our hearts. Although not typical of everyone's family in the days just prior to Christmas, the eccentricities of Ralphie's family remind us all of something that hits extremely close to home. We may never have wanted an air rifle to protect the family against a marauding band of black and white horizontal striped shirt wearing bad guys, but there was always something we wanted for Christmas and a secret scheme that we devised in order to get it.

As we follow Ralphie's adventures in trying to obtain this air rifle, his bizarre family dynamic mesmerizes us. His younger brother Randy only eats when he does it like a piggy and cannot get his arms down after getting dressed for school. His mother tastes the soap after Ralphie has had it in his mouth as a punishment for cursing, just to see what the hubbub is all about. The family's Christmas at a Chinese restaurant where the waiters struggle with the traditional Christmas songs and of course there is the best performance in the film, Darren McGavin as Ralphie's father. The people around Ralphie are as interesting as his plots to get a Red Ryder BB gun/air rifle, yet his father's unconventional behaviors far exceed any of Ralphie's plans to get what he wants.

From dealing with the hillbilly neighbor's dogs, to setting his own personal records for tire changing, Darren McGavin plays Mr. Parker with such flawless Midwestern ignorance that he becomes the most believable character in the film. When his great prize comes it is expected for him to think it was Italian because it is marked F-R-A-G-I-L-E. Any other analysis from him would be out of character. Portraying the typical working class father, allowing his wife to take care of the kids while he goes to work, McGavin nails this role with a perfect mixture of indifference and heart.

The key moment in the film comes when he surprises Ralphie with the Red Ryder BB air rifle, reveling in making his eldest son incredibly happy because he remembers what is was like to be a kid at Christmas. It is that same look he had upon his face when the stocking covered leg lamp was first lit up. McGavin would follow up *A Christmas Story* with another great performance as the sinister gambler in *The Natural*. McGavin would once again get no recognition from the Academy.

A fantastic list of assembled actors vying for the Best Supporting Actor award from 1983 made it easy for a performance to be overlooked. There was Rip Torn in *Cross Creek*, John Lithgow in *Terms of Endearment*, Charles Durning in *To Be Or Not To Be*, Sam Shepard in *The Right Stuff* and the eventual winner, Jack Nicholson. Nicholson walked away with the Oscar, for one of his greatest roles. Nicholson was truly deserving of his Oscar. McGavin, who played the role of his cinematic career definitely deserved to be included in that category alongside him.

6

JOSEPH BOLOGNA

MY FAVORITE YEAR - 1982

My Favorite Year is one of those precious little movies that few people know about, but is impossible to forget once you see it. Revolving around a weekly comedy cavalcade sketch show that gets disrupted by the guest starring appearance of matinee idol Alan Swann, one of Peter O'Toole's best screen roles, there are moments of flat out hilarity. Swann is a legend but also a legendary philanderer with a reputation of being more trouble than he is worth. A young freshman writer, Benjy Stone is placed in charge of him because he is a fan of his. Stone has the simple goal of making sure Swann behaves himself for the week of the show, a task easier said than done.

Although O'Toole is clearly the star and the movie is directed toward emerging a newcomer, Mark Linn-Baker, who plays Stone, the movie is single handedly stolen by the performance of Joseph Bologna as Stan 'King' Kaiser. As the star of the comedy cavalcade the King roams the set offering outrageous gifts such as steaks to a secretary who happens to look pretty that day and a set of whitewall tires to the head writer, whose monologue he completely ripped apart. The gifts are his way of dealing with the little people. It is obvious that Bologna has chosen to make the character much larger than life, resembling one of the outrageous skit characters he plays each week. It is such an over the top performance, yet also incredibly grounded in its own reality, the reality of comedy.

The King is not without his serious moments. One of his sketches, the 'Boss Hijack' sketch is a little too close to representing the local crime boss. When the real crime boss comes to visit the King with his lawyer to force them to stop the unflattering sketch, the King cannot help but put his own comedic spin on the situation. It does not matter that his life has been threatened, because his actions are funny. He throws the crime boss' cashmere coat out the window. To him that is more important than his own life. Bologna also plays the initial disgust for Swann in an incredibly realistic manner. In fact, it is perhaps the most real his characterization in the film gets. He does not hate Swann. He is actually a fan, but hates that Swann does not care for what he cares about, comedy.

The five nominees for supporting actor in 1982 were another great bunch. Charles Durning from *The Best Little Whorehouse In Texas* and John Lithgow for *The World According To Garp* were both among the bunch. This marked the first of two straight years that both Durning and Lithgow were nominated for supporting actor Oscars. Neither of them took home the Oscar for either year. Also among the nominees were James Mason for his great performance in *The Verdict*, Robert Preston for *Victor/Victoria* and the eventual winner that night, Louis Gossett Jr.

Gossett Jr. was brilliant as the drill sergeant in the tearjerker *An Officer and a Gentleman*, taking home a deserved Oscar among these five nominees. All five actors were worthy, yet the best supporting performance of the year was completely overlooked. There was too much emphasis placed on Peter O'Toole creating a comedic impersonation of his classic roles and a fantastic performance was missed in the process. Bologna would never achieve such greatness again.

5

TOM HANKS

NOTHING IN COMMON - 1986

How would you react if your parents suddenly split up after thirty six years of marriage and both of them began individually depending on you? It is one thing to help your parents out when they need you, but when living alone is a mystery to them their reliance on you can wear you down, especially when you are kicking your career into high gear. The quaint drama/comedy *Nothing In Common* examines the reinventing process from all angles, the parents and the children. In this case the child is all grown up and in his mid thirties, who has now been placed in charge of his parents.

Recently promoted advertising executive David Basner returns from vacation to find his mother has left his father. On top of that, his new promotion comes with added responsibilities, such as obtaining new clients. The new major client in question comes in the form of an airline looking for new representation. It does not help that the owner of the airlines comes with as many bizarre traits and requests as both his parents combined. It also does not help that Basner is becoming romantically involved with the client's daughter. The pressure of the job is something that Basner has always been able to handle. Dealing with his parents gives him the trouble. As they come to depend on him, needing him for every single thing, the world begins to come crashing down around him. His newfound reliability strengthens him, causing him to readjust his priorities for the better.

In the early scenes of the movie and during the processes of creating the ad campaign the great comedic talent of Tom Hanks shines through. It is the same talent that is seen in early Hanks' movies such as *Bachelor Party*, *Volunteers* and *Splash*, as well as his star making turn in the classic television show *Bosom Buddies*. What had not been seen before was the dramatic side of the young Tom Hanks. For all the great roles that would come, his performance in *Nothing In Common* set the tone. Hanks is easily considered one of the finest, if not the finest actor of his generation. This was the movie that first showcased that ability. Most people consider *Big* to be his breakthrough role. That is a misnomer, because without this performance, *Big* probably goes to another actor.

In 1986, the five nominees for Best Actor were Dexter Gordon for *'Round Midnight*, Bob Hoskins for *Mona Lisa*, William Hurt for *Children of a Lesser God*, James Woods for *Salvador* and Paul Newman as 'Fast' Eddie Felson in *The Color of Money*. Gordon and Hoskins were eccentric choices, yet the Academy could no longer ignore the wide variety of newer and more eclectic movies made during the year, allowing Hoskins and Gordon to be seen by the voters and earn a nomination. Hurt had won the previous year for *Kiss of the Spider Woman* and Woods plays one of his greatest roles in one of Oliver Stone's best movies, one that helped solidify Stone's Oscar for *Platoon*.

Paul Newman's victory was long overdue though. Most agree that it was an award for his body of work rather than his performance. It is tough to argue against Newman because he should have won three Oscars prior to this one, for *The Hustler*, *Hud* and *The Verdict*, yet Tom Hanks really deserved to be included as one of the nominees on that night alongside him. Luckily, it only took a short time for the Academy to finally notice the obvious talent of Tom Hanks

4

JACK NICHOLSON
BATMAN - 1989

      The true story of the comic book hero known as Batman is a sad tale of tragedy and the deep lengths to which one will go in order to help preserve justice. Despite all the inner demons he possesses, Batman is a hero that fights for the common man. What drives him is that he cannot forgive himself or let the past go, providing that much needed fuel to accomplish his goals. When Batman first hit the scene it was in comic books, with his stories told in *Detective Comics* and the comic that later brandished his name. For any hero to exist there must be a villain or villains. No one ever discusses Batman without making mention of his all-time arch nemesis, the Joker.

      In Tim Burton's dark visionary retelling of the comic book classic, one character stands out above the rest, the Joker. The whole movie plays as dark nightmare, evoking the world that a man like Batman must live in, yet the movie's fuel stems from an over the top performance that perfectly fits the role. Jack Nicholson's Joker brings not only an evil and disturbed genius of a character to life, but also manages to include all of the comic book character's idiosyncrasies. The key to playing such a role is in never looking back. The freefall into outlandish creativity must be embraced and never before has a character gotten so out of control in perfect sync with the character's impulses.

      There have been other actors who have played insane characters and done great jobs, yet Nicholson brings an absolutely deranged sanity to a quasi-sane madman. One could see the Joker brewing within him as far back as the infamous chicken salad ordering scene in *Five Easy Pieces*, the early joke telling scene in *Chinatown* or the half the scenes from his best film *One Flew Over The Cuckoo's Nest*. In these early performances there are elements of the Joker just longing to escape, until they finally got the chance to thanks to a magnificent piece of inspired casting by Tim Burton.

      Starting out as just an average criminal psychopath, Nicholson becomes what he has originally created, an outcast. Eventually, the Joker turns out to be the man that killed Batman's parents, in effect creating the hero that would eventually foil him at every turn, a great piece of irony. While Batman hides behind the façade of an outcast, the mask shrouding his inner demons, the Joker revels in it. It is what the Joker was destined to be, with Nicholson exuding that type of behavior once the transformation from street hood to bizarrely psychotic super villain is finally complete. It is not enough though. Nicholson's desire as the Joker to beat the bat reigns supreme.

      In 1989, the Best Actor race was between Robin Williams in *Dead Poets Society*, Kenneth Branagh in *Henry V*, Morgan Freeman in *Driving Miss Daisy*, Tom Cruise in *Born on the Fourth of July* and Daniel Day-Lewis from *My Left Foot*. Day-Lewis took home the Oscar for his tortured performance as Christy Brown, yet any one of the nominees would have been a worthy choice. In assessing this field, all the performances were worthy of an Oscar nomination, yet every single one pales in comparison to Nicholson's Joker. His performance is the core of the movie. Without it, *Batman* would have been just another basic super-hero film. The sad truth is that villains are just more interesting. Nicholson proves that truism by playing the part to complete perfection.

3

DONALD SUTHERLAND
BACKDRAFT -1991

In Ron Howard's *Backdraft*, fire is as essential a character as any actor or actress playing one of the parts. More than just a tale about a family that grew up within this type of profession, this detective mystery surrounds the world of corrupt politicians and what is going on regarding the murders of a select group of them. The brave men of the story not only fight fire but also embrace it. To destroy fire for the safety of the community, you have to hate it a little. To hate fire, you also must love it just a little in order to go after it. There is no character in *Backdraft* who loves fire more than Ronald. He is the arsonist who knows fire all too well, what he refers to as *the animal*.

The great character actor Donald Sutherland turns in one of his best and most memorable performances as the serial arsonist Ronald. Ronald's only goal is to burn the world. In his world, fire is Ronald's only friend. It is his best weapon against humanity, of which Ronald is most assuredly not a part of. Using his unique talents for manipulating fire for his own benefit, Ronald eventually lost control of his *animal* and needed rescuing from his own creation. The effects of what took place when he lost control of the fire he had set for an insurance job are present, the massive burn scars on his face. Although Sutherland only appears in two scenes they definitively impact the entire movie, as well as revealing truths about some key people that are uncomfortable to imagine.

Ronald first appears when Inspector Rimgale takes his newly appointed assistant, McCaffrey, on a mission that he terms as *'pest control'*. McCaffrey is played by William Baldwin in a mundane role that tends to drag the movie, yet Rimgale is played to perfection by Robert DeNiro, turning in a performance that also went unnoticed. Ronald is about to be paroled, convincing those who are unaware that he is ready to be set free. Rimgale knows different and is there to make sure the parole board knows as well. Just as Ronald is about to be freed, Rimgale interrupts to coax Ronald into revealing what he really wants to do, burn everything and everyone. Ronald's final scene is with McCaffrey. He supplies the key information that tells McCaffrey who is responsible.

Sutherland plays Ronald with such a calm yet crazed insanity that it is impossible to tell if he is merely a troubled genius or a psychotic madman. Ronald's scenes are the key to the entire movie, in understanding not only the mystery of what is going on, but also in understanding what it takes to fight fire. Sutherland completely convinces us of his obsession with fire. This is so key to the role, specifically during the time when he asks McCaffrey if the fire actually looked at him. When he sees that it did Ronald becomes envious for a moment, longing to be part of a world he once belonged to.

Donald Sutherland was as worthy as any of the five nominees for supporting actor during 1991. They included Tommy Lee Jones for *JFK*, Michael Lerner for *Barton Fink*, Harvey Keitel and Ben Kingsley for *Bugsy* and the winner, Jack Palance for *City Slickers*. Sutherland deserved to be nominated for his role, yet the lack of screen time severely hurt him. Ironically, the lack of screen time did not hurt Anthony Hopkins receiving and winning a Best Actor Oscar this year for *The Silence of the Lambs*. All is relative since Joe Pesci's performance in *JFK* was better than anyone.

2

HUMPHREY BOGART

THE TREASURE OF THE SIERRA MADRE - 1948

The Treasure of the Sierra Madre has often been described as a search for gold. That is inaccurate. It is a character study of how three men who start out as partners are driven to extremes by their own greed. One of the three men has seen this kind of greed before, the grizzled old timer. Rather than fight it he understands that he is unfortunately powerless to change the nature of men, so he simply goes along with the flow. The descent into greed and eventual madness is a predictable one for him and one that he cannot prevent. That journey spirals into an every man for himself methodology where the three men who start out as partners forget all the rules set forth at the onset.

Two Americans down on their luck are suckered into working a job where they are not paid after it is done. When they finally find the man who cheated them they corner him and beat him within an inch of his life, taking the money he owes them. Needing to get out of town in a hurry, the two men decide to go prospecting for gold with an old timer they met earlier who knows the land and originally came up with the idea. The three men make their hard journey up the mountains where they inevitably find gold and set up camp to mine more. The greed has not yet surfaced, but will.

Once more gold is found, more is wanted. Even though greed is their enemy other dangers occur. One of these dangers is when another American comes into camp from town wanting his unearned share of the gold. As the guys are about to deal with this stranger, bandits arrive and provide more trouble. These bandits provide one of the great misquoted lines in cinema history, regarding their need for *stinking badges*. The fight with these bandits will come back to haunt Bogart, who gets his due from the bandits after making off with all the gold.

Humphrey Bogart's portrayal of Fred C. Dobbs is of legendary cinematic status. From a man so down on his luck that he begs for a meal, to being bent on revenge against a boss that owes him, to his fall into madness, paranoia and distrust, Bogart steals every scene of the movie. An early scene shows you what type of character Bogart is conveying, after he throws water into the face of a young boy who is annoying him. Even though he stakes his claim to good intentions and a proper partnership, deep down inside that rat desires to come out. The gold is merely there to bring it out of him, masterfully displayed by Bogart. Although there are scenes where Bogart appears to be a kind and trustworthy partner, they are ultimately only segues into his true self, longing to come out.

Laurence Olivier became the first man to win an Oscar while directing himself in the same movie. Olivier won for his performance in the Shakespearean adaptation of *Hamlet*, beating out Lew Ayres for *Johnny Belinda*, Montgomery Clift for *The Search*, Clifton Webb for *Sitting Pretty* and Dan Dailey for *When My Baby Smiles At Me*. One could say that Bogart was robbed of an award that rightfully should have been his. It was arguably the finest and most complete acting performance of Bogart's career, with only *Casablanca* as a possible exception. The academy made up for it by giving Bogart the Oscar in 1951. To do so they had to deny Marlon Brando in the acting job of his career.

1

ALEC BALDWIN
GLENGARRY GLENROSS - 1992

Playwright David Mamet has a distinct knack for dialogue. His characters bring alive the often standard setting with their use of amazingly clever vernacular. It is as if his characters could live in a world where nothing existed but ideas and the discussion of those ideas. Many of his stories are the sort that should be listened to rather than seen. This is regardless of what type of medium they appear in. I often wondered if David Mamet would have made a great novelist. I believe he probably would not have, because his dialogue is not about imagination but about precise delivery. It is this type of delivery that flourishes when presented by actors, rather than left up to imagination.

In Mamet's story about the up and down times of real estate sales, one character stands out above all others, thanks to the spot on delivery of his one and only speech. Known only as Blake, Alec Baldwin steps out of the back office and delivers the performance of the movie. His job is simple, re-instruct the salesmen on what it takes to sell real estate. This is not a time for encouragement, but rather a time for strength. With the new leads of potential buyers coming in a real closer must be brought in to straighten things out. Without holding any punches or caring for anyone's feelings, he tells the salesmen what is what and then walks off, leaving a lasting impression

How does one make such an indelible impression in only seven minutes and forty-five seconds of screen time? That is simple. Delivery. Baldwin exudes confidence in this small yet noteworthy and critical role. His words setup the rest of the film, which show the audience what has been going on in the lives of these salesmen. They, Ed Harris, Alan Arkin and Jack Lemmon take it from there, but without Baldwin's memorable speech the rest of the movie would be empty. It is not only the highlight of the film but its essence and its basis for continuing. The speech made by Baldwin was specifically written for the film. Without that speech, the story somehow loses its luster.

In 1992, another member of the exceptional *Glengarry Glen Ross* cast was nominated for an Oscar, Al Pacino. Pacino was also nominated for his starring role in the movie that would win him his only Oscar to date *Scent of a Woman*. He would not take home two Oscars on this night. That feat has still yet to happen. Along with Al Pacino from *Glengarry Glen Ross*, David Paymer from *Mr. Saturday Night*, Jaye Davidson from *The Crying Game* and two powerhouse actors, Gene Hackman from *Unforgiven* and Jack Nicholson from *A Few Good Men* were also nominated.

The Oscar race was clearly between Hackman and Nicholson, with Hackman edging him out in the end. Paymer was great in a small movie, while Davidson received a nomination for showing something that shocked all audiences. Pacino's defeat in this category was a foregone conclusion. Perhaps the voters knew they were heading Pacino toward a Best Actor Oscar victory, his only one to date. With the exception of Hackman and possibly Nicholson's, Alec Baldwin's performance outshines the other three by leaps and bounds. It is confusing how Pacino was nominated while Baldwin was not, yet in assessing Pacino's victory from that night it appears body of work became the deciding factor this year. Baldwin was awarded a nomination in 2003, but failed to win.

Chapter Five:

AFI's
Top 100 List

The American Film Institute (AFI) decided to commemorate the first one hundred years of film. Their goal was a lofty one. They wanted to rank the Top 100 American films of the first one hundred years. Their purpose was to celebrate the best of American cinema over the last century. The association met in 1998 to attempt this grand endeavor, yet movies from the years 1997 and 1998 were not extended consideration within the list. Establishing 1897 as the first year for American cinema, the association was holding firm to the first hundred years, setting the cutoff point at 1996.

Now that the end year was established as 1996 the task was undertaken of who would choose these movies? To only include a small number of the AFI members would be improper because there would not be an accurate representation. The movies that were chosen would merely be a small sample of individual's favorite movies, rather than a broader spectrum of films, which tends to provide a much better interpretation and ranking.

We all should realize that any list of movies resulting from the individual lists of only a few select members of the AFI would have no credibility. As a result, fifteen hundred film industry members, including actors, directors, writers, producers, critics, historians and studio executives were specifically chosen by the AFI to participate. The hope in compiling such a large sample was to generate a universal account of what the film community believed were the one hundred greatest American films of the last century.

Another problem that existed was that AFI could not simply ask the fifteen hundred selected contributors to randomly choose what they considered were the hundred greatest films. The AFI would have received fifteen hundred ballots with one hundred films on each ballot. It would have been close to impossible to tally those correctly. There would be no guideline as to what films were to be chosen for this specific list, so the choices would be way too arbitrary and in turn possibly hurt the actual credibility of the list to an extent.

In actuality, although it would have been a logistical nightmare, this manner would have been the far superior way to handle an endeavor such as this. However, to keep things from getting out of hand, a panel of members from the AFI chose four hundred specific movies for the fifteen hundred member selection committee to choose from. The panel members chosen were then to provide their opinion of the one hundred greatest films out of the four hundred selected. The total composite of those fifteen hundred ballots would be deemed as the one hundred greatest American films of the century. The voters were specifically instructed to choose their list of one hundred from these four hundred films, although write in votes were allowed.

Let's be honest though. When collating fifteen hundred individual Top 100 movie lists, any and all write in votes would be discarded. From a strictly mathematical perspective, the write in votes would not have come anywhere close to amassing enough points to dent the final Top 100 list. As a result, all write in votes were really throwaways. The actual list of the 100 Greatest American movies is below as AFI tallied the ballots they received and ranked them accordingly.

AFI'S TOP 100 MOVIES

1 - CITIZEN KANE
2 - CASABLANCA
3 - THE GODFATHER
4 - GONE WITH THE WIND
5 - LAWRENCE OF ARABIA
6 - THE WIZARD OF OZ
7 - THE GRADUATE
8 - ON THE WATERFRONT
9 - SCHINDLER'S LIST
10 - SINGIN' IN THE RAIN
11 - IT'S A WONDERFUL LIFE
12 - SUNSET BOULEVARD
13 - THE BRIDGE ON THE RIVER KWAI
14 - SOME LIKE IT HOT
15 - STAR WARS
16 - ALL ABOUT EVE
17 - THE AFRICAN QUEEN
18 - PSYCHO
19 - CHINATOWN
20 - ONE FLEW OVER THE CUCKOO'S NEST
21 - THE GRAPES OF WRATH
22 - 2001: A SPACE ODYSSEY
23 - THE MALTESE FALCON
24 - RAGING BULL
25 - E.T. - THE EXTRA TERRESTRIAL

26 - DR. STRANGELOVE
27 - BONNIE AND CLYDE
28 - APOCALYPSE NOW
29 - MR. SMITH GOES TO WASHINGTON
30 - THE TREASURE OF THE SIERRA MADRE
31 - ANNIE HALL
32 - THE GODFATHER II
33 - HIGH NOON
34 - TO KILL A MOCKING BIRD
35 - IT HAPPENED ONE NIGHT
36 - MIDNIGHT COWBOY
37 - THE BEST YEARS OF OUR LIVES
38 - DOUBLE INDEMNITY
39 - DOCTOR ZHIVAGO
40 - NORTH BY NORTHWEST
41 - WEST SIDE STORY
42 - REAR WINDOW
43 - KING KONG
44 - BIRTH OF A NATION
45 - A STREETCAR NAMED DESIRE
46 - A CLOCKWORK ORANGE
47 - TAXI DRIVER
48 - JAWS
49 - SNOW WHITE AND THE SEVEN DWARVES
50 - BUTCH CASSIDY & THE SUNDANCE KID

51 - THE PHILADELPHIA STORY	76 - CITY LIGHTS
52 - FROM HERE TO ETERNITY	77 - AMERICAN GRAFFITI
53 - AMADEUS	78 - ROCKY
54 - ALL QUIET ON THE WESTERN FRONT	79 - THE DEER HUNTER
55 - THE SOUND OF MUSIC	80 - THE WILD BUNCH
56 - M.A.S.H.	81 - MODERN TIMES
57 - THE THIRD MAN	82 - GIANT
58 - FANTASIA	83 - PLATOON
59 - REBEL WITHOUT A CAUSE	84 - FARGO
60 - RAIDERS OF THE LOST ARK	85 - DUCK SOUP
61 - VERTIGO	86 - MUTINY ON THE BOUNTY
62 - TOOTSIE	87 - FRANKENSTEIN
63 - STAGECOACH	88 - EASY RIDER
64 - CLOSE ENCOUNTERS OF THE THIRD KIND	89 - PATTON
65 - THE SILENCE OF THE LAMBS	90 - THE JAZZ SINGER
66 - NETWORK	91 - MY FAIR LADY
67 - THE MANCHURIAN CANDIDATE	92 - A PLACE IN THE SUN
68 - AN AMERICAN IN PARIS	93 - THE APARTMENT
69 - SHANE	94 - PULP FICTION
70 - THE FRENCH CONNECTION	95 - GOODFELLAS
71 - FORREST GUMP	96 - THE SEARCHERS
72 - BEN-HUR	97 - BRINGING UP BABY
73 - WUTHERING HEIGHTS	98 - UNFORGIVEN
74 - THE GOLD RUSH	99 - GUESS WHO'S COMING TO DINNER
75 - DANCES WITH WOLVES	100 - YANKEE DOODLE DANDY

On June 16th, 1998, the American Film Institute revealed this list on CBS, which hosted a three hour prime time special dedicated to this compilation. While AFI admits that the list is subjective, as almost all lists are, their inclusion of fifteen hundred ballots in order to arrive at the final list gave them credibility past the pure nature of the list's subjectivity.

I shall critique the AFI top 100 list, which has become somewhat of a standard in the film community since its release to the public during that night in the middle of 1998. If a movie appears on the main list, already critiqued in chapter 1, then I will simply acknowledge that film by stating where they appeared upon the main list. Those films total thirty-one of the 100 that made the AFI list. That number, thirty-one, does not include the four additional movies found on this list, which shall be discussed later in this book. The easiest way to begin is to start at #1 and work up to #100. The first or highest ranked movie from the AFI list that did not make my main list is their #5 selection, *Lawrence of Arabia*. The critiquing shall start there.

#1 - *Citizen Kane* – #6 on my Top 50 list

#2 – *Casablanca* – #1

#3 – *The Godfather* – #9

#4 – *Gone With The Wind* – #3

#5 – *Lawrence of Arabia*

How is it possible that the grand 1962 Academy Award winning epic *Lawrence of Arabia* was left off the list, in favor of movies such as *Airplane!* and *The Princess Bride*? That is an easy question to answer, although one that most critics would disagree as *Lawrence of Arabia* has become one of the storied films in cinema history, obvious from its ranking of #5 among all the ballots.

David Lean, the director of all out grand epics had a stunning vision with this tale of a British soldier sent to the Arab bureau and given the daunting task of uniting the individual Arab tribes together to enlist them in aiding the British in their fight against the marauding Turks. Based upon the life of adventurer, diplomat and explorer T. E. Lawrence, Lean's film suffers from an extensive level of its own self-worth. Lawrence is one of the more intriguing characters in history. He is supremely flawed, yet this film glorifies his triumphs rather than including all his negative personality traits. The great biopics take great pleasure in offering both.

At almost four hours in length, it seems that more time could have been spent on his defects as opposed to celebrating Lean's grandiose style of filmmaking. It is sometime tough to distinguish whether this is a film about Lawrence or a film to glorify David Lean's ideas. Brilliant filmmaking is where the two can combine without sacrificing one for the other, which seems to be what happened here. The scene where a speck eventually, after a while, becomes a man crossing the desert was beyond overblown. Many critics mysteriously seem to revel in its majesty though. This scene clearly shows that the audience is watching a Lean movie rather than a movie about T. E. Lawrence or what would have been perfect, a combination of the two.

This is one of the many films that I simply do not get. I believe it to be a good film and would have placed it among the top one hundred if I were asked to provide a ballot, yet it would have wound up on the total opposite end of my list. There were two much greater films from that same year. Both films made the list although they came in twenty-nine and sixty-two spots lower than *Lawrence of Arabia* ranked. Just as the Academy voters are taken in by grandeur over substance, the AFI voters have followed in that ideal by placing this movie as high as they collectively have.

#6 – *The Wizard of Oz* – #27

#7 – *The Graduate*

Chosen as the benchmark movie for the 60's generation, Mike Nichols' film hit at exactly the right time, when counter culture was exploding onto the scene. The satirical look at relationships and sexual angst made a star out of Dustin Hoffman, who flourished in his first role. Unfortunately, this is not a 1960's revival list where movies that helped shape and influence culture are rewarded for their impact. That is one of the major problems that exists regarding the status of *The Graduate* as one of the great American films of all time. While a great piece of Americana, the movie itself is flawed by its own transformation. It starts out as a stark satire and quickly moves to a pure romance. Either one would have been sufficient and even a simultaneous blending of the two would have worked. A distinct and clear cut separation of the two, almost creating two entirely different movies, definitively hurts the flow of this film.

It ranks as the greatest American movie from 1967, if one were to strictly adhere to this list. There appears to be inconsistent symmetry here, when analyzing *The Graduate* against the other films placed upon the list. There are times when the Best Picture from specific years is ranked higher than other pictures that are viewed as greater films, while alternatively there are times when film excellence is rewarded. The Best Picture from 1967, *In the Heat of the Night*, failed to make this list, while *The Graduate* placed at least ninety four spots ahead of it. That, by itself is a monumental disparity. When analyzing the other movies from 1967 that made the list, the omission of the Best Picture winner from 1967, which in my opinion was the best movie that year as well, highlights that great disparity. I could argue that *The Graduate* placed so high on this list merely because that was the opinions of the voters. That would not be an unjustifiable or undeveloped assessment. However, it is impossible to argue that the impact this movie had upon counter culture did not strongly influence not only its inclusion on this list, but its absurdly high ranking.

#8 – *On The Waterfront* – #37

#9 – *Schindler's List* – #22

#10 – *Singin' in the Rain*

This has become one of the all-time most popular films, due primarily to the catchy song and dance numbers, most notable among them are *'Good Mornin'* and the title song *'Singin' in the Rain'*. The actual dance number where star and choreographer Gene Kelly sings while dancing in a rainstorm, attempting to show the carefree nature of a man who has recently found love, is one of cinema's most revered moments. The movie however, from a purely watchable standpoint, is at numerous times unbearable to get through because it totally breaks from any quasi-reality of the story to engage in unnecessary self promotion of talent.

The rampant self-indulgence that comes across not only in the dance scenes, specifically the extended dance scene toward the end of the film, deeply flaws the entire movie. These scenes go way past people simply acting out their happiness over into a bizarre world of *'look at me and how great I am'*. Compared to another Gene Kelly dance-travaganza, appearing later on the list, *Singin' in the Rain* has at least the semblance of a workable plot. That plot comes to a dead stop in order to promote and highlight musical talent rather than cohesive storytelling.

Once again, in comparison to the other Gene Kelly dance-apalooza that made the AFI list, *Singin' in the Rain* was much less self-indulgent, yet slightly more indulgent than a man staring at himself in the mirror exalting his own beauty. *Singin' in the Rain* therefore falls somewhere in the middle, perhaps due to the facade of some effort in character development. As far as its relation to other movies on the list, it is an indictment of the sentimentality of the voters that it ranked as high as it did. With respect to the movies from the same year, such as *High Noon*, *The Quiet Man* and *The Greatest Show on Earth*, the three pictures that took home the major awards from 1952, *Singin' in the Rain* is beneath each of them in quality. More importantly, all three of those films have a much more watchable characteristic, unless you are in an ultra overtly happy mood, which may possibly border upon necessary institutionalization. It is a travesty *Singin' in the Rain* ranked as high as #10.

#11 – *It's A Wonderful Life* – #7

#12 – *Sunset Boulevard* – #13

#13 – *The Bridge on the River Kwai* – #4

#14 – *Some Like It Hot*

Billy Wilder's cross dressing charade, where two male musicians dress up as women to escape being sought out after witnessing a gang style murder, is one of the true comedic masterpieces ever put on film. The two main characters board a Florida bound bus as female musicians, whereupon the hilarity is set. Tony Curtis' Cary Grant impersonation is dead on, while Jack Lemmon hamming it up with retired playboy Joe E. Brown masterfully captures the essence of the entire film. Brown delivers the classic ending line, *'Well, nobody's perfect'*, upon learning that Lemmon is really a man. Throw in Marilyn Monroe in her best role and Wilder has crafted a gem with multiple layers and themes, paying homage to the greats of comedy past.

When one understands how great a movie should be for it to be ranked as high as #14, then an argument immediately arises as to the overrating of this film. There is a far better movie from the same year that placed twenty six spots below it. There is no reasonable explanation that could explain that disparity, especially since the lesser of the two films is so much farther ahead in the rankings than the actual better film. Not only did Wilder erroneously topple Hitchcock on this list with *Some Like It Hot*, the Academy saw fit to honor Wilder's next film, *The Apartment*, with Best Picture and Best Director Oscars, over perhaps the all-time Hitchcock classic and one of the single best movies ever made, *Psycho*. Some small consideration exists as the AFI panel fixed, to an extent, that wrong by ranking *Psycho* well ahead of *The Apartment*. It is not at all surprising that uniformity in judgment was not used throughout, with fifteen hundred people offering their opinions.

#15 – *Star Wars*

Sequels that come after the first film generally hurt the status of the original because they are viewed as part of a franchise rather than as films of their own individual merit. In this case however, the sequel to this film, *The Empire Strikes Back*, so far exceeds the original that re-watching *Star Wars* leaves one flat and makes the thinking movie watcher wonder why all the hoopla surrounds *Star Wars* in the first place? There are reasons for that though.

There are a couple of certainties surrounding *Star Wars*. It was a commercial success in the way that no film up to its time could match, holding the box office record for years and then regaining it upon its re-release in 1997. *Star Wars* was also a major marketing success, to the tune of billions of dollars in merchandising sales, which millions upon millions of children collected and associated with the movie. Most importantly, the film was a technological breakthrough in advanced special effects, making it a movie unlike anything seen before. The problem - that's all it really was, smoke and mirrors. The acting was horrific and the writing was even worse. The story suffered immensely from the over reliance on cinematic tricks, albeit of an extraordinary nature. Once you have seen these tricks once or twice, the story must stand on its own and this story thoroughly disappoints. Is it any wonder that of all the Oscars won by *Star Wars*, six in total, they were all from technical categories?

Whatever minor veneer of a story presented behind the special effects and magic tricks was meant to set-up the rest of the story. This move was episode four of a serial where the first three episodes had not been filmed yet. It was to be followed by two more episodes and then three future episodes that also had not been filmed. To this date they still have not. In attempting to craft some kind of magic and light show, George Lucas neglected to realize that he was thrusting characters on the audience directly in the middle of a much bigger story. His focus on presenting effects, while only offering a minor allusion to a back story, was not strong enough to pull off the trick.

Star Wars is often perceived as the three movies as a whole. This could account for its bloated ranking. The sequel to the 1977 movie, *The Empire Strikes Back*, was so much better because it introduced the emotion into the story that Lucas was attempting to allude to in the first movie. The action scenes are also better, although they are merely an advancement of Lucas' own special effects design. The key to understanding this is that no one watches *Star Wars* anymore. They watch *The Empire Strikes Back* and remember what happened in the first film. Audiences and film fans know the story, but it still does not keep them from watching the sequel over and over again, because the first is just too awful to get through outside of the innovative special effects.

AFI voters ignored the above, choosing instead to reward technical design over actual movie-making and movie greatness. The sequel was one of the movies that was in the running for the main list of this book. Not once did the original *Star Wars* ever once enter the discussion of making that list. I thought about it, yet remembered how bad it was when I saw it during the re-release, even with the advanced effects and extras. They only served to highlight the acting and the story, both dreadful and unfulfilling. A far better choice for the AFI voters would have been the sequel, which was among the four hundred nominated films. They chose prestige and gloss over substance, in such a profound way as to land *Star Wars* at #15. I could not disagree more.

#16 – *All About Eve*

Soap operas have nothing on this film, although the story still remains fresh today. This is primarily due to fantastic writing. If not for soap opera acting of such an over stylized display this movie would have easily made the main list. It is true that all of the people involved are theater performers, over acting at every given turn, yet at over two hours it can wear a bit heavy on the eyes and ears. Once again, if not for a top notch story and snappy dialogue, mostly of the cynical variety, which perfectly blends with the pretentious nature of the theater, this movie would have fallen into obscurity long ago. The characters are rich and their struggles and desires are real, yet the symmetrical ending lands on the extremely hokey side. *All About Eve* is a fine film and one that will be around for a long time to come, even if it is way way over the top.

Although #16 is a bit too high for this melodramatic soap opera, the better movie from 1950, *Sunset Boulevard*, was correctly ranked ahead of it. The mix of cynicism, realism, obsession and complacency has landed this movie among the Hollywood elite. It is one of the grand old films that everyone swears by, yet critics readily admit that *Sunset Boulevard* is the better movie. *All About Eve* generally lands on most lists of the greatest films. There was just something about it that warranted its exclusion from the final list. Perhaps it was the acting that just wore me down too much. In comparison to the overacting of Gloria Swanson, specifically done for the role of Norma Desmond, the acting of ninety-nine percent of the performers in *All About Eve* seem to be over acting to one up each other. If that was planned then it was a brilliant stroke, yet for some reason it does not come across on the screen that way. It appears as if the actors were trying to hard to outdo their fellow cast members rather than work with them within the framework of the story.

#17 – *The African Queen*

What can one say about a boat trip down the river? First, it is the stars that make this movie with their acting. Their only on screen pairing has been deemed as some of the finest acting ever produced. Second, it is the stars that actually hurt this movie. Let me explain. Two iconic figures in acting, Katherine Hepburn and Humphrey Bogart, were placed together for the first time. It should have been a tour de force. Most think it was. Both screen legends had earned their chops playing a particular type of character by this time in their career.

The characters they play in *The African Queen*, however, are total opposites of what they were normally known for. Bogart begins as a hard drinking and smoking ship captain but quickly turned into a henpecked wuss within a heartbeat to satiate Hepburn's character, who was a spinster missionary, again a radical departure from her normal roles. In fact, her normal role type would have loved Bogart's original personality type before he turned into Captain no-testicles. I understand that departure from accustomed character types is what makes an actor or actress mature in their craft, yet for this type of material, a basic and altogether bland tale of opposites attracting to overcome their differences, it seems the wrong vehicle for such a change.

The magical year of 1951 where an overtly self-indulgent musical film took home top honors, saw four movies make this list. *The African Queen* ranked well above the other three. While I can honestly say that this movie is far and away better than the movie that took home the Oscar statuette, the other two movies were superior, specifically the far better acting tour de force of 1951, *A Streetcar Named Desire*. I would have placed *The African Queen* at the almost exact opposite end of the ranking spectrum among this top one hundred. There were not three hundred and one movies that were worse than it among the four hundred nominees. I can only imagine that this is a case of history and stature triumphing over true movie quality. A good movie, specifically for the acting range, yet not good enough to warrant inclusion among this list, let alone among the top twenty.

#18 – *Psycho* – #11

#19 – *Chinatown* – #35

#20 – *One Flew Over The Cuckoo's Nest* – #8

#21 – *The Grapes of Wrath* – #21

#22 – *2001: A Space Odyssey*

The term overrated perfectly fits this Stanley Kubrick movie. I understand that many reviewers and critics call it an extraordinary film, one that changed the genre of science fiction from purely voyeuristic to analytical, challenging the viewers to think rather than presenting them with the answers. I find that breakdown a thorough travesty.

In reading a famous critic's review of this movie, he remembers attending the 1968 screening and seeing screen legend Rock Hudson walk out of the theater midway through wondering what the hell this movie was about. I could not agree more. In over two and a quarter hours, I still do not get the point. If Kubrick's goal was to tell the world that he was God and that he could do no wrong, then I get it. If Kubrick wanted to tell everyone that he was above plot and story structure, then I get it. If Kubrick wanted to present an allegory to his own alleged greatness, then I get it. However, if Kubrick wanted to present a thinking man's science fiction movie to provoke thought, then he did so. The problem is that the thoughts are generally of the 'what the hell is going on in this story' variety. Why not just present a documentary instead?

As with almost all Stanley Kubrick movies there are distinctly separate stories that are attempted to be interwoven into one cohesive tale. In this particular film there are four different stories, all of which are linked in some extent by a giant black monolith, which no one ever cares to explain the true nature of. It is left up to us to figure out what this item actually is. After two and a quarter hours, with two incredibly interesting stories that could have lead somewhere but did not, I found myself not even caring anymore.

That discovery came just after the twenty minute long color extravaganza that has been said to mimic travel through a wormhole, which wound up in some bedroom where the bland astronaut was able to view his own demise. There was of course a mysterious appearance by *"Johnny"* Monolith to explain it all, or rather leave the viewer even more stumped. The final scene, known as the *"Star Child"*, continues the unexplainable. Some will get more out of this movie. Many will feel like me that Kubrick is great or at least he tried his hardest to make us all believe he was.

As far as ranking, you can see from the above diatribe that I would not have placed this movie among the top one hundred, let alone the top quarter. Of these particular movies, it would have been the opposite, placed among the bottom quarter, with complete and utter exclusion using the four hundred nominees. Style and self-indulgence only goes so far. This movie has too much of both of them and way too little organization to masquerade itself as a great film. Much like *Star Wars*, revolutionary special effects transfixed many into believing that this movie is better than it actually is. What those critics began to realize, with such special effects garbage delivery systems such as *The Fifth Element* and the three new installments of the *Star Wars* family is that technical effects are visually great but there has to be more than just that. *Citizen Kane* proved that. It remains a mystery as to why critics have forgotten that with *Star Wars* and *2001: A Space Odyssey*.

#23 – *The Maltese Falcon* – #34

#24 – *Raging Bull* – #12

#25 – *E.T. – The Extra Terrestrial*

    Told through the eyes of a child's point of view, *E.T.* has become one of the all-time classics of what is termed children's cinema. It was one of the highest grossing films during its initial release and has gone on to influence a generation. Although most have seen the film, probably as a child or with their children, few understand its meaning. It deals with escaping loneliness through the discovery of true friendship. This was Spielberg's most honest story, telling a variant of how he viewed life after the separation of his parents, yet the movie comes off more as a parable of the isolation of childhood, inescapable until one matures into adulthood.

    There were actually seven movies nominated for inclusion from 1982. My own choice for the best movie of that year, Best Picture nominee *The Verdict*, was mysteriously left off the list of four hundred nominees. In contrast, both *Missing* and *Fast Times At Ridgemont High* were offered as choices to the panel of voters. Once again, the voter's heart strings were tugged as an over emotional movie landed on the edge of the first quarter of the best American films of the last hundred years.

    Of the two that made the AFI list from 1982, they were perhaps the fifth and sixth best movies of that particular group of seven. Ignoring what has become known as a science fiction classic, *Blade Runner*, in favor of this science fiction children's fable, the voters chose to reward ultimate fantasy rather than ultra-reality and the worse of the two movies. I can only imagine what would have happened if the voters were given the opportunity to choose *The Verdict*. More than likely they would have placed that in the bottom one hundred, because it is thought provoking rather than emotion producing. It is obvious that these collective voters felt better with emotion versus thought. That is purely an assessment of the list as it ranked out.

#26 – *Dr. Strangelove*

    Often called the greatest comedic non-comedy ever made, Kubrick's satirical look at nuclear politics leaves one in amazement. The over embellished script, with its heightened satirical commentaries, does at times leave the viewer cold though. It is a great idea and wonderful lampoon of how one thing can go wrong and cause the end of the world, yet it is way too overplayed in spots, specifically the bomb riding scene and the rampant use of names with sexual connotations. Satire needs to have some basis in reality in order to expose the ironic nature and foolishness of it all. This movie, while still extremely good, tends to go way too overboard in its set-up, simply to prove a basic point that war is bad.

    I stated earlier that this was the best movie from 1964. Therefore, I have no challenge to the fact that it was the highest ranking movie included on this list from that year. While #26 is extremely high though, it is one of those movies that has become so popular, not just on how satirically funny it is, but rather due to a fantastic three character performance by one of the geniuses of comedic acting and timing, Peter Sellers. *Dr. Strangelove* would have landed much closer to the middle of the pack among these one hundred films for me. From the list of four hundred nominees it still deserves a place among the top one hundred, even if it is too far fetched for certain tastes.

#27 – *Bonnie and Clyde*

It is tough to take a movie that is supposed to be based on real life characters and not judge it for its numerous historical mistakes regarding those characters. I understand that this is cinema and not history class, yet the rampant errors in Arthur Penn's 1967 movie do detract from its appeal. Perhaps it is just me, but when watching a movie based on real people, I tend to lean toward historical realism rather than extensive artistic embellishment.

That having been said, the movie has been hailed as a cultural masterpiece, providing a cinematic realism where extreme violence both shocked moviegoers and changed the face of cinematic storytelling. *Bonnie and Clyde* is a piece of Americana and did change the way violence was depicted upon the screen. The acting was worth the price of admission, although it is tough to distinguish the actor and actresses take on these characters versus what they were like in real life.

A movie that was not eligible for this list, *A Beautiful Mind*, ranking somewhat high upon the main list, can serve as a benchmark for deciphering this issue. While *A Beautiful Mind* did not reveal certain aspects of John Nash's real life, the lead actor, Russell Crowe, delivers a dead on performance. Crowe captures all of Nash's quirks down to a tee, from what history reveals about this troubled genius. Because there is so much difference in what Clyde Barrow and Bonnie Parker were in real life versus how they were portrayed by Beatty and Dunaway on the screen, the end result suffers in some minute way. A movie is not simply one element, yet rather a combination of all elements working in conjunction. While *Bonnie and Clyde* is rather enjoyable to watch, even interesting to sit through today, there are some major problems with the overall work.

1967 was one of the banner years on the AFI list. Three out of a total of nine nominated films cracked the top one hundred. Of the three films that made the cut, *Bonnie and Clyde* is the best of the lot, although it ranks second in actual placement among those three. Among my own personal list, derived from the four hundred nominees, Best Picture *In the Heat of the Night* would have landed among the middle of the pack. The only other choice from 1967 to make the list was this movie, although definitively toward the bottom of the top one hundred as opposed to the #27 ranking it received here.

#28 – *Apocalypse Now*

To say that this is a peculiar film would be an understatement, but not entirely correct. In my first viewing of the movie I saw no purpose to the final segment. In watching that final section of the film, which I at first thought stopped the entire flow of the film, now acts as the most important element of the film. There are other problems as a result.

With the newfound understanding of the final scene, where Brando explains what has taken place and how he got to where he is in his evolution as a soldier, revealing what Martin Sheen's character is going through and heading towards. The culmination involving Brando's death is not simply for Sheen to carry out his mission, but moreover for him to eliminate the possibility of going down that same road. The powerful subtext of the final section now causes the opposite to take place.

The scenes leading up to that now pale in comparison. They do not fully serve the arc of the story. I always knew there was something missing and began by thinking it was the final section, believed by many as unnecessary and where the movie heads down the wrong path. That was wrong. It is most decidedly the other way around. The surfing, the playboy bunnies and the fishing boat sequence where a family is gunned down, all do not jibe with the deep message found in the ending. There is just something missing when connecting the entirety of the movie. A natural cohesion just does not exist and as a result, the magnificent and powerful ending swallows the rest of the movie whole. This may account for why some feel it takes away from the movie, albeit for the opposite reason.

For *Apocalypse Now* to be ranked as high upon this list as it is one thing seems for certain; the story behind it all definitively had an impact upon voting placement. Some view it as an untarnished masterpiece, perceiving total cohesion throughout. Others who notice the flow issues seemingly disregarded that problem in favor of the history behind it. There are many better movies from 1979, three of which were available for nomination on this list, yet *Apocalypse Now* was the only film from that year to make this list. Due to its over-indulgent excesses and patchwork storytelling, I would have left it off this list completely.

#29 – *Mr. Smith Goes To Washington* – #23

#30 – *The Treasure of the Sierra Madre*

Humphrey Bogart won the Academy Award for Best Actor in 1951 for his performance in *The African Queen*. It is generally acknowledged that his award was a make-up Oscar for the performance he gave in this film. Playing a vindictive and ultra paranoid gold prospector, Bogart masterfully creates a character that cannot escape his own inner demons. Bogart often stated that Fred C. Dobbs was one of his favorite characters because of the utter wretchedness within him.

The Treasure of the Sierra Madre was a fine film acting as both a quasi-Western and adventure film, yet the paranoia runs a bit too amuck and the group that searches for gold are as opposite as they come. While rich in acting the movie comes off as a touch formulaic prior to the discovery of the gold, when it finally kicks into high gear and provides the best moments of the story.

Only three movies were selected as nominees from the year 1948. *The Treasure of the Sierra Madre* was the only entry within the top one hundred. There are some that would say Howard Hawks' *Red River*, starring Montgomery Clift and John Wayne was a better film. The Best Picture winner, *Hamlet*, was not available as a nominee. That is a complete shock when other Best Picture winners such as *The Broadway Melody* and *Cimarron* were included among the four hundred nominees. I can only assume that its exclusion was because *Hamlet* was considered a British film, although all three of David Lean's epics that made the list could have the same said for them as well as the film that made Olivier a star, *Wuthering Heights*.

#31 – *Annie Hall*.

Woody Allen's diatribe on his own unique neuroses mixed with his style of Borscht-belt one liners is considered a modern day classic. The numerous issues that Allen deals with, through his usual New York type character, are highlighted here. These neuroses specifically deal with his troubles with women and his on and off romance with the one that got away, Annie Hall. His unique delivery method and destruction of the fourth wall to speak to the audience, as well as bringing in total strangers to the storyline for added effect became revolutionary for cinema. The comedy seems a bit forced at times though and the drama is really not that dramatic. The over intellectual aspects of both are just plain annoying. It is not hard to see why the two characters did not remain together, despite the efforts of narrator Allen continuing to intellectualize the reason why.

Of the three movies that made the list from 1977, *Annie Hall* is the best of them. Not one of the three would have made the first three quarters of my list, from the group of one hundred already chosen. From the four hundred nominees, not one of them would have made the list of one hundred, with *Annie Hall* as the movie closest to making it. Another movie from that year that was also nominated, *Saturday Night Fever*, came the closest to cracking my top one hundred. While there are memorable scenes in *Annie Hall*, the overall package is far less than the hype surrounding it. That should not be a consideration, yet happens to be one regardless.

#32 – *The Godfather II* – #19

#33 – *High Noon* – #38

#34 – *To Kill A Mockingbird* – #14

#35 – *It Happened One Night* – # ??

#36 – *Midnight Cowboy* – #17

#37 – *The Best Years of our Lives*

The futility of war was explored in the 1930 Best Picture winner, but this was something different. It tackled the subject of the treatment of veterans on the home front. For three returning soldiers, all of whom had meaningful existences during their military service, the unsympathetic reality that they are no longer perceived as important causes internal struggles and a myriad of additional problems. The goal was to create awareness to this issue going on in rural America more than could ever be imagined. *The Best Years of our Lives*, with great acting performances, two of which won Academy awards for actor and supporting actor, struck a nerve in the hearts of the people with its unabashed realism.

With only two of the seven nominated films from 1946 making the list, the ranking is correct. There is a better movie from that year, *The Big Sleep*, which remained off the top one hundred list. That film should have overshadowed *The Best Years of our Lives*, but it did not. Academy Award winning movies were stressed during the voting process, whether the voters were instructed to do so or not. *The Big Sleep* is the far better movie, as most critics would agree, yet this movie warrants that sentimental vote. As is the case with ninety percent of the films, ranking depends on a balance between high and low votes. I can only assume that there were panel members who ranked this movie way too high on their list, when it should have been closer to the bottom.

#38 – *Double Indemnity* – # ??

#39 – *Doctor Zhivago* – # ??

#40 – *North By Northwest* – # ??

#41 – *West Side Story*

What else can be said about this movie that has not been said in the previous chapter? It is unoriginal. It is overtly stereotypical. That is about as good as this review will get. *West Side Story* is simply nothing more than a stereotypical spin on a classic love story. Music is added as a substitute to fill in the enormous gap in character development. New characters are merely introduced into pre-existing roles within a plot that has been done before, rather than what would amount to creating an original story. It is nothing more than ripping off an age old tale by introducing new characters into the story. The equivalent would be making a movie from the Melville tale *Moby Dick*, but replacing the main characters with Eskimos and calling it *Igloo Cock*.

Why people love this movie is beyond me, yet there is no denying that it is one of the more revered films ever. As far as greatness, I just do not see it. How *The Hustler* was overlooked and overshadowed by this movie, not only for the Academy Award but also on this list is a complete mystery. Even if one can make the argument that *West Side Story* evokes a pleasant feeling upon watching, a placement of #41 is ridiculously high, especially when comparing it to the movie right below it at #42. There is not a rational critic in the world with any integrity that will argue *West Side Story* is a better movie than *Rear Window*. Let me restate that. There is no way any critic could argue that point and actually win that argument. *Rear Window* is only one movie below it, but in comparison with the one hundred movies on this list, I wish there was a way I could have left it off. Forced to place it on a list among the one hundred films of this list, I would most certainly rank among the bottom five, if not the bottom one. I also find it particularly ironic and enormously hypocritical that most groups continue to play the prejudice card when it suits their purpose, yet this overtly ethnic barrio gang fest, with all its negative stereotypes, is considered a classic among the Latino community. If it was the other way around and an original Latino work of fiction were Caucasianized, there would be hell to pay. No one has a mirror when it is truly needed.

#42 – *Rear Window* – #28

#43 – *King Kong*

This is an absolute icon of a movie as well as an absolute stinker. Creating the new *'big monster'* movie genre on the heels of the *'normal monster'* genre, *King Kong* blended fantasy, horror, adventure, flying battles, chase scenes and that unique quality, giant monsters. I wholeheartedly understand that special effects were almost non-existent in the early 1930's, yet that did not stop monster movies such as *Frankenstein* and *Dracula*, perhaps the best of the whole lot with respect to horror, from creating fright upon the screen. *King Kong* neither scares nor threatens to scare the viewer. It is viewed today primarily as campy, which in terms of movies is not a tribute. The introduction of the different monsters is hilariously bad, the monster fight scenes are ridiculous and the monkey face close-ups are absurd. If it was supposed to be campy then it worked, but that was not the case. *King Kong* was played as a serious horror film, but failed on every level. An absolutely ludicrous monster island exists and all that was taken back to civilization was a gigantic monkey?

The inclusion of this movie is nothing more than sentimentality. *King Kong* represents an icon of cinema, specifically with the final battle scene, famous and known to anyone who has ever lived. There has to be more to a movie than flash and status. The style, unplanned camp of an extreme level, makes one understand why it has been remade twice. There is no chance that the new remake by Peter Jackson could be any worse than the original. If by some scarce chance Jackson's remake is not as good as the original though, then all moviegoers should start a campaign that Jackson should not only give back the money he earned for making the new *King Kong*, but also all the money he made for the billion dollar trilogy that made him a mega-director. Even if it were a no-brainer to include this movie based on sentimentality, which it should not be, #43 is illogically high.

#44 – *The Birth of a Nation*

The same critics who rave over *Citizen Kane* for its technical creativity equate this movie with greatness under those same circumstances. The only film selected prior to 1925, *The Birth of a Nation* is pure racial propaganda. It glorifies racism by highlighting and exalting the emergence of the Ku Klux Klan after the end of the Civil War, in response to a failed culture's resistance toward the evolution of thought. Originally titled *The Clansman*, it is by far one of the worst message oriented films and one of the reasons why the country was fractured in the first place. It emphasizes the worst beliefs of the worst types of people, the section of the country who refused to treat people as equals unless they looked like them and believed what they believed.

Not a documentary, displaying the obvious erroneous beliefs that other races are inferior, *The Birth of a Nation* chose to praise the disgusting development of this cowardly, hood wearing hate group. The director, D. W. Griffith, claimed he was not a racist. Funny how we do not see Steven Spielberg making movies about Ping Pong or Tim Burton make movies about normalcy. It is because those types of stories do not interest them as filmmakers. Despite Griffith's claims, he chose material that was blatantly and openly glorifying racism. Why would that topic interest him if he did not believe in the subject matter? Shortly after its release, this movie was used as a recruitment video for the Ku Klux Klan.

Forget the material for just one moment. *The Birth of a Nation* is a bad movie. The storyline is weak, yet that is because it is almost caricaturist in its treatment of African Americans. However, the style and cinematic technologies that were used have transformed *The Birth of a Nation* into an incredibly impactful film, influencing a generation of filmmakers to come. Luckily the message contained within did not have that same effect. The use of color in a final scene and its movement of film toward a more artistic endeavor have made this awful film stand the test of time, impacting almost every film made since. You cannot ignore the story of a film, solely in favor of its technical innovations. As far as movies that changed film, this one is right up there, perhaps second only to *Citizen Kane*. As a movie, which includes the full gamut, it is almost impossible to watch unless you are studying the craft. That is not the same as considering a movie as great, yet it is that kind of thinking that got this dreadful and appalling film not only on this list, but on the top half of this list.

#45 – *A Streetcar Named Desire*

It has long been said that the seventeenth ranked movie on this list, *The African Queen*, held some of the strongest acting ever registered in cinema. Whoever ascribed to that either did not see this movie or would have agreed that *A Streetcar Named Desire* was far and away a better acted movie. One can make the argument that it is perhaps the best acted movie of all time. That however, does not always translate into great film.

The perfect example is the 1995 movie *Dead Man Walking*. The two leads, Sean Penn and Susan Sarandon absolutely blow the doors off their characters. The movie itself is almost never considered or recognized as a classic or a masterpiece, yet always thought of as an acting tour de force. The same can be said about this movie. The acting is so strong, from both the two leads and the two supporting actors that it came extremely close to achieving the only sweep of the acting categories in Oscar history. For that reason it is sometimes viewed as a greater movie than it truly is.

A Streetcar Named Desire was originally a play. That is not to say that a play cannot be transformed to the medium of film without success. The opposite is true. This film achieved major success, making Marlon Brando a star, proving Vivien Leigh could act past a foolproof character such as Scarlett O'Hara and made the plays of Tennessee Williams more visible to a greater number of viewers. Williams' rich, character filled stories are a sight to see, yet this enclosed setting highlights the great acting rather than displaying the greatness of it as a movie.

A Streetcar Named Desire is the second of four movies from 1951 to make this list. It is far better than the movie ranked ahead of it and far greater than the two movies ranked behind it. Those three movies, other than the movie discussed here did not deserve to make the top one hundred from the four hundred nominees. The top two movies on this list from 1951 were chosen strictly for acting performances rather than having been complete films. A number of movies that fall under that same criteria were left off the list because they were not complete movies as well.

#46 – *A Clockwork Orange*

Stanley Kubrick's take on Anthony Burgess' futuristic novel is at times brilliant. As with most Kubrick movies, there are two distinctly different storylines though. Once again, it is as if there are almost two separate movies in this futuristic nightmare/thriller. After betrayal that gets the main character Alex placed in jail, he is subjected to a program that intends to curtail what is perceived as his natural hatred. It is a psychological experiment into the deconditioning of pre-programmed rage, using techniques that torture their subjects as much as it cures them. Once the reconditioning works, the subject is placed back into society. The problem is that his newfound tame demeanor lands him in worse trouble.

Apparently some form of parable on behavior and the dehumanization of people, *A Clockwork Orange* shocks more than it makes people think. If shock value is what the focus of the movie was intended for, then it succeeds on every level. I do believe there is a point or lesson to be learned underneath all the nightmarish brutality presented here. The message intended does not come through by displaying the graphic scenes of rape, violence, desensitizing, vomit inducing restraint and assault. These and many other scenes like them seem to be included for their own sake.

The above review may imply that I did not like *A Clockwork Orange*. That is not the case. However, there are plenty of movies that I really enjoyed which did not make the main list and also would not have ranked as high as #46 on a list such as this. Two much better movies from the same year, *The Last Picture Show* and *The French Connection*, were both in lower spots than *A Clockwork Orange*. Of those two, only *The French Connection* made this list of one hundred, although twenty-four spots lower than *A Clockwork Orange*. Interestingly enough, I would have ranked this movie in just about the identical spot, if only given these one hundred movies to choose from. Based upon the four hundred nominees though, this movie falls much farther down the list. It still has enough of a quality to keep it among the top one hundred though.

#47 – *Taxi Driver*

This was Scorsese's signature movie early on in his career. There are those who cite *Mean Streets* as Scorsese's great early classic, which also starred Robert DeNiro and Harvey Keitel, yet *Taxi Driver* is by far the better movie. Until *Raging Bull*, only topped later by *Goodfellas*, this was Scorsese's best cinematic effort and the movie that made Robert DeNiro a megastar. His performance as the deranged yet lonely Travis Bickle created one of cinema's all time strangest characters and one of the quintessential trademark characters of DeNiro's career.

As Travis navigates his way through the city, a city where he despises everything around him, he begins to view himself as a modern day knight on a mission to save the world. The world, for Travis, takes the form of two women, one an underage prostitute and the other a campaign worker. When he cannot have them, acting inappropriately with both, his next move is to violently go after the men that he perceives as controlling these two women. His actions are a hidden message underlying the theme that Travis is relationship dysfunctional. *Taxi Driver* is an exploration into the mind of a man who does not fit in. No matter what he does, it is the wrong move. The famous tagline from the movie comes when Travis is most comfortable, when he is talking to himself.

1976 was an extraordinary year for moviemaking, with three movies making this list. That was the same amount that made my main list. *Taxi Driver* obviously was not one of them. I chose instead to reward the great newspaper/journalism drama *All The President's Men*. As far as placement, it is obvious that this movie is fourth out of those four movies for me, yet placed above the other two movies from 1976 that made this list. There are elements that worked in its favor versus the other two, which happen to be better movies. *Taxi Driver* made stars out of both DeNiro and Scorsese. Those two have not slowed at all, taking their newly acquired star power and running with it. The pairing that made that possible, *Taxi Driver*, holds a deep significance in cinematic history.

#48 – *Jaws*

They should have had a bigger boat. More prophetic words might never have been spoken. That was part of the allure of this blockbuster. Spoken as *"I think we're gonna' need a bigger boat"*, that line presents one of the biggest understatements in cinematic history. The trio of hunters, mismatched and as different from each other as they are from the rest of the world, attempt to save more than just the summer tourist spot. They are really saving themselves.

Police Chief Brody needs to eliminate the menace to save not only his job but save his conscience. He still feels that he allowed an unnecessary death to happen. Marine biologist Hooper needs to save the shark by capturing it rather than destroying it. He is saving what he believes in, his ideology so to speak. Shark hunter Quint, the third of the trio, only desires to kill the shark. That is what he does. What Quint is saving is a time honored code, something that the viewer gets the distinction that it is all he lives by. Quint believes in the rules of the sea, a world of man versus beast. That was what he needed to save, the tradition that was challenged by the elusive destructive force, the shark. All three men were different, yet the classic scene of comparing scars, between Hooper and Quint, reveals so much more than male bonding. Despite their ideological differences, they are two halves of the same coin. The beauty of the story is that the odd man out, the one not really supposed to be there, saves the day by killing the shark.

Jaws served as an homage to prior Hitchcock thrillers. It teased the audience by keeping their eyes glued to the screen in amazement. Finally, after they could wait no more, the prize was finally revealed. For this movie, it was the first time the shark rears his head above water and tries to swallow Brody whole, simultaneously frightening, shocking and finally alleviating the audience.

This blockbuster put Spielberg on the map. *Jaws* did for swimming what *Psycho* did for showers. It was unfortunate luck that *Jaws* was made in the same year as the best movie of the decade, *One Flew Over the Cuckoo's Nest*. Those are the only two movies from 1975 to make this list. The placement of *Jaws* at #48 is a perfect balance of where it should be, in comparison to the actual list of one hundred, and where it should have placed it among the four hundred nominees.

#49 – *Snow White and the Seven Dwarfs*

There should not be a person alive who has not heard this story, or at least the basics of this story. Coming from the Brothers Grimm and their fairy tales of horror, the story was basically a slight variant of an ongoing theme that is seen throughout the two writer's works. There is an unfortunate person, underprivileged, yet who is painstakingly beautiful. That person must deal with the hardships and labors of life. Somewhere in the background there is a person who is evil in nature and hates the female heroine because of her sweetness. It was the basic set-up, with this time an inclusion of seven dwarfs who take in the heroine as she tries to escape from her evil wicked stepmother. The classic themes of fleeing one's home in fear, capture, an evil demise and then a rebirth at the hands of a fair prince all exist in this film, which was Walt Disney's first full length animated movie.

It is the last description above that settled in the minds of the voters. The landmark film that paved the way for future and better animated productions was included based on history and precedence, rather than actual cinematic excellence. It is an extremely good movie, yet two other animated features, *Pinocchio* and *Beauty and the Beast*, both nominated, are far superior in quality. Even the 1994 blockbuster, *The Lion King*, is a far more popular Disney movie. It was simply that *Snow White and the Seven Dwarfs* was the one that started it all. It is no greater a movie than *Cinderella* or *Sleeping Beauty*. In fact, it is almost exactly similar in theme, which leads me to wonder why those were not nominated as well. The answer is because this was the first and therefore the Disney flagship film. That explains why this particular movie landed so high on the list.

#50 – *Butch Cassidy and the Sundance Kid*

One of the great buddy pictures of all-time. This movie however, suffers from not knowing what it really wants to be. At times it is a buddy picture, other times a grand adventure. At times it is a comedy, other times it is a musical/nostalgia work. *Butch Cassidy and the Sundance Kid* tries to be all of these things, yet achieves only minimal success as a buddy movie because of its two forceful stars, Paul Newman and Robert Redford. The two of them together are great, yet the material is just not enough to support their immense talent. Four years later, a movie would be made starring Redford and Newman that had enough material to finally support the weight of these powerhouse actors. It is somewhat of a mystery as to why *Butch Cassidy and the Sundance Kid* is generally perceived as the better movie of the two.

Of the four movies from 1969 that made this list, this film ranked second among them. This movie is not as good as the movie ranked ahead of it or the two movies ranked below it from the same year. Comparisons to the other movie that starred both Newman and Redford, 1973's *The Sting*, are inevitable. Obviously, since *The Sting* was present on my main list, I find it the much better movie. I believe that it is the myriad of elements that have helped *Butch Cassidy and the Sundance Kid* achieve a somewhat more glorified status than their other movie.

#51 – *The Philadelphia Story* – # ??

#52 – *From Here To Eternity* – #30

#53 – *Amadeus*

Most have heard of the greatness of legendary musician Wolfgang Amadeus Mozart, the child prodigy that could create symphony masterpieces at will. Director Milos Forman's account shows the side of Mozart that few knew. Mozart was a rambunctious, loud, excessive drinking roustabout who made people revel in his comic lampooning, specifically his patron, the Emperor of Austria. His true genius could only be seen or heard by his rival, the under talented composer Antonio Salieri. This is the crux of the film, as the focus is not upon Mozart's greatness or even his buffoonery, but Salieri's treachery over realizing that despite all of Mozart's quirks, his music far exceeds his own. The deathbed scene, where dramatic license allows Salieri to believe he murdered Mozart in order to steal his newly created symphony, shows two troubled figures. One is a musical genius lay dying and the other is a petty and inferior man who is selfishly extracting more from Mozart's mind. This scene clearly displays the difference between genius and mediocrity.

No other movies made the list from 1984. Upon seeing the list of nominated films from that year it is not hard to see why. At least the voters got this one correct as *Amadeus* was the best film of the year and truly one of the great films of American cinema. It reveals a side of an historical person long unknown and the lengths at which some will go to try and emulate genius. In the case of Salieri, he envied it, was jealous of it and tried to claim it as his own. The internal battle of Salieri is what actually makes this film so great rather than the buffoonery of Mozart. Unfortunately, the crazy antics of the more renowned figure is what many choose to remember. Luckily the Academy got their awards right for this year when they chose F. Murray Abraham as Best Actor for playing the troubled Salieri over Tom Hulce who played the ribald genius Mozart.

#54 – *All Quiet on the Western Front*

The term revolutionary gets thrown around a lot and I must admit that at times I use the term more than I should. If that term was ever perfect for describing a film than this is the film it should be used for. *All Quiet on the Western Front* was the first of its kind to show the hardships of war rather than the thrill of battles and the excitation of victory. Following a company of German recruits during the beginning of the first World War, this amazing film emphasizes the horrors and dread that soldiers go through during their time on the front.

From the opening scene where the school kids of a young class are rallied into joining the battle for their country, to the return of one of those children who has matured and become jaded to blind thoughts of patriotism as a result of the battles he has seen, this movie stands for how a war changes people. This was a radical departure from the prior descriptions of war as glory filled and honor driven crusades. When the main character realizes that nothing has changed throughout his tour, he finally understands the futility of war. Something inside him dies at that moment. It is perhaps one of the greatest statements on the senselessness of war between nations.

Despite the fact that the movie seems somewhat outdated by today's standards, its message still rings true today. Perhaps even more so. Not only the Best Picture winner from 1930, *All Quiet on the Western Front* is by far the best movie from that year. In comparison to another early picture depicting war, *The Birth of a Nation*, the message of the former decisively outweighs the message of the latter in every single aspect. The acting is far superior, although the advent of sound may have contributed to the emotional effect. In every aspect of moviemaking however, except for the purely technical areas, *All Quiet on the Western Front* is a much better movie. If I was chosen to hand in a ballot for this list I surely would have placed this movie among my top 100.

#55 – The Sound of Music

This was one of the last of the one hundred movies on this list that I saw. It was the ninety-sixth in fact. I was pleasantly surprised when I first saw the film. Naturally I knew about this film because I am a movie buff, but I gathered my own perceptions of what it actually was. I could not have been more wrong. It is the direct opposite of other awful musical movies in the fact that this film is plot driven and not created simply to exhibit dancing, singing or choreography from that latest star of those mediums. True, Julie Andrews was considered a triple threat; a singer, dancer and an actress, but the movie was not created to simply display her natural abilities. It was more of a cohesive fit between all three, rather than a manufactured attempt to satisfy the first two criteria with a substandard or non-existent story behind it.

Make no mistake, *Doctor Zhivago* was the better movie of 1965. Even the AFI panel of voters recognized that. However, *The Sound of Music* combined an interesting story, well developed characters and an enjoyable quality that is missing from most movies. There are plot twists that develop naturally as opposed to having them forced to suit a foregone intended belief of happiness and some nicely timed intrigue and suspense, which always seems to balance a story. The singing numbers are extremely well done and never supplant the plot. In fact, the singing numbers actually enhance it. I would disagree with classifying *The Sound of Music* as a musical. It is a fine movie that uses a clever inclusion of song and dance to complement the story. The important notion here is that the musical numbers *complement*, rather than take away from the actual story.

I wholeheartedly agree with the inclusion of *The Sound of Music* on this Top 100 list. With only three movies from 1965 nominated for inclusion on this list, *The Sound of Music* fits in perfectly with its Top 100 placement. It has been correctly placed behind *Doctor Zhivago* and in front of *Cat Ballou*, which did not make the final list of one hundred. As you have seen before there was another movie that I enjoyed more from 1965 than *The Sound of Music*. There is also and another movie from that year, *The Ipcress File*, that in my opinion is better. Neither *The Ipcress File* nor that other movie, one of my favorites, were nominated by AFI for inclusion. Therefore placement, with specific regards to 1965, remains perfect.

#56 – M.A.S.H.

Most people do not even know that famous television situation comedy was based on a 1970 movie. The pranks and hijinks began in a Robert Altman film, where the staff of a Korean War surgical hospital passed the monotony of the day by performing imperative operations, getting drunk and playing practical jokes on all of those who would be the most offended by them. In spite of their medical expertise, the horrors of war are dealt with through a series of unconnected occurrences, such as a football game with more riding on it than just camp pride and harassing the head nurse to see if she is a natural blond. The movie was brazen, especially for its time. *M.A.S.H* focused on the way men and women get through their time during the war, rather than the war itself.

Two movies from 1970 made this list. A glaring omission was the actual best movie of the year, *Five Easy Pieces*, despite having been nominated among the four hundred. In its stead, the voters chose to acclaim this Robert Altman film, widely considered as one of his lesser films and the only selection from his body of work that made the list. A paper thin plot, episodic humor and an innovative end credit sequence has helped *M.A.S.H* become as revered as it is. The situation comedy of the same name did little to hurt the movie's stature though. The television show's popularity certainly helped the movie's stature among those that knew the two were connected.

#57 – *The Third Man* – #24

#58 – *Fantasia*

Mickey Mouse meets Tchiakovsky. This highly ambitious yet absolutely insane blending of animation and music was welcomed with open arms. The goal of Walt Disney here was to revive and popularize classical music to the masses. It is not technically a movie, yet rather a cinematic operetta with eight different animated sequences accompanying eight specifically selected musical compositions. Not one of the eight work in conjunction with the other and most are independent of anything remotely connected to any semblance of a story. This movie was done simply for the sake of doing it. As a result of the financial failure of *Fantasia*, the next Disney feature had to be made on a shoestring budget.

In the world of self-indulgent this movie appeared to be Disney's way of ingratiating his own likes and dislikes onto a medium that he made his fortune in. There is simply no reason to have made this film other than a self serving one. The experience of sitting through this, for this book, evoked what it would be like going to an opera or a musical while on acid. This is one of the reasons why *Fantasia* has become such a success in the last thirty years. The movie itself has not garnered respect for its visionary blending of classical music and animation. A cult following has grown because of the surreal and psychedelic images that appear on the screen. It is not used for Walt Disney's intended purpose, but rather for a bastardized purpose of aiding a hallucinogenic drug trip. No judgments regarding what people choose to do, but in a comprehensive analysis of the movie, that should be discussed.

Fantasia came out in 1940, the year after what has been called the finest year in cinema. Five movies actually made this list of nominees from that year. Three movies from 1940 made the final list including *Fantasia*, while three movies from 1940 made the main list of this book. Therein lies the disparity. The Best Picture winner from 1940, Alfred Hitchcock's *Rebecca*, made my list but did not make this list. Hitchcock's only Best Picture winner, *Rebecca*, is such a far greater movie than *Fantasia* that on the basis of its inclusion and the exclusion of *Rebecca*, the validity issues of this list should immediately be called into question. I totally understand that these choices are subjective, yet if you are going to assemble a panel of fifteen hundred knowledgeable members of the cinematic community to rank the one hundred best films, one should expect better choices from their list for the final list to have any true credibility. Little things, such as *Fantasia's* medium high ranking on the list and

Rebecca's omission, while other Best Picture winners that were not as good making the final list are some of the inconsistencies that help create validity and credibility issues.

#59 – *Rebel Without A Cause*

This unflinching, yet sympathetic tale of rebellious teen adolescence made its young star, James Dean, not only a household name but also a legend. Starring in only three films and nominated for Best Actor Academy Awards for the other two films, Dean perfectly captures the angst of 1950's teen life. Dean's character moves into a new environment where nobody, specifically his parents, seems to understand him. The film is really about finding one's own identity in a conformist society, including the specter of closet homosexuality of one of the film's supporting characters, adding to the confusion of teenage identity seeking and discovery. *Rebel Without a Cause* was a powerful film for its time, yet in the modern world, only the powerful acting of James Dean keeps the film alive as an unabashed classic.

Of the nine films that were nominated in 1955 for inclusion on this list, it is not difficult to see that *Rebel Without a Cause* made the list when analyzing the list as a whole. It is precisely the type of film that would be rewarded by those voters who chose to reward film history over film excellence. That is proven by the incredibly high ranking of such movies as *Star Wars, 2001: A Space Odyssey, King Kong* and *The Birth of a Nation*, which all ranked above this film. The specific placement of those films displays a distinct methodology of the voting panel. From 1955 alone, where is the Charles Laughton directed classic *The Night of the Hunter* or the other great film from that year, the character piece that won the Best Picture award, *Marty?* While an important film for its time, this movie has dated poorly. It has dated much worse than *All Quiet on the Western Front*, a movie twenty-five years older. That is an indication to me that it is not worthy of consideration as a great film.

#60 – *Raiders of the Lost Ark* – #2

#61 – *Vertigo* – #25

#62 – *Tootsie*

This quintessential cross-dressing comedy struck a nerve of hilarity with audiences. Failing and self-indulgent actor, played by Dustin Hoffman, must take acting work as a woman on a soap opera due to the industry's unwillingness to hire him. The basic fish out of water theme exists, albeit of an extreme nature. Masquerading as a woman, Hoffman encounters numerous problems, including newfound fame attached to the character he plays on the soap opera, courted by an older man and falling in love with one of the female leads of the soap opera. Things become even more tense and problematic when he develops a serious friendship with her under the false pretense of being a woman she can relate to. The dilemmas placed upon the main character are extremely formulaic and have been done before. The key to the success of this movie is the placement of Dustin Hoffman in the title role. It is that extreme of extremes that worked so well for both the financial and critical success of *Tootsie*.

Another movie from the year 1982, along with *E.T. - The Extra Terrestrial*, makes the AFI top one hundred list. As stated earlier, these two were the fifth and sixth best movies out of the seven nominated from 1982 for potential inclusion. *Tootsie* was definitely worse than the movie that landed at the #25 spot, yet only slightly better than the worst of the seven, *Sophie's Choice*, which was an absolute tearjerker that had a one moment payoff and only magnificent acting by the female lead to keep it from falling into obscurity. Once again, where was *The Verdict*? More importantly, how does this movie achieve such success simply by placing Hoffman in a dress? There should be more to great film than merely that. *Tootsie* disproves that, although I strongly disagree with the majority.

#63 – *Stagecoach*

After seeing this movie for the first time one word came to mind, ordinary. Every scene, every character and every acting performance with the possible exception of the drunken doctor is plain ordinary. In the finest year that moviemaking has yet to offer this movie should have been compared to others from the same year and deemed as nothing more than bland. If not for the first major starring role of John Wayne this altogether boring and slow paced movie would have made its way into the field of obscurity. I wish it had.

The culminating scene is led up to from the first scene that introduces John Wayne's character and done so in an incredibly formulaic manner. Wayne's character, The Ringo Kid, must shoot it out with the villain who wants to kill him. The scene is over in a flash, with nothing great at all to come from it. The intended plot point that was meant to awe, Wanye's character surviving the gunfight, was designed to be an epic moment of the story. Unfortunately, it falls flat due to the anti-climactic nature of what is actually shown. It has become the stuff of cinematic legend primarily because it displays the courage and triumphs of one of the greet screen icons of cinema.

This is most definitely not one of 1939's greatest film ambassadors. There are so many better movies starring John Wayne that the panel could have chosen from, among them *Red River*, *Rio Bravo* and *The Quiet Man*. Due to obvious sentimentality issues, a reward for his first starring role has been granted to this mediocre film. *Stagecoach* has been helped in its stature because it is one of John Ford's first major Westerns, a genre that he is closely associated with. I must reiterate that the decision making process during this endeavor is highly questionable. Everyone is allowed to have their say as to their preferred choice of what is better than another. I cannot understand how a movie as uneventful as *Stagecoach* seriously made this list of the one hundred greatest American movies of the last century. Once again, the validity of this list has to be called into question.

#64 – *Close Encounters of the Third Kind*

Stephen Spielberg's first take on happy aliens who visit Earth to make contact hit screens the same year as the mega-hit *Star Wars*. This film used some of the same innovative special effects, albeit a different variety, to mimic and substitute for lack of story and plot. Similar to the other famous science fiction movie, *Close Encounters of the Third Kind* used dazzling effects and cinematic style to win over audiences. They had never seen the likes of these two films before. Additionally, in this movie's favor, was the fact that audiences were used to seeing vicious and harmful aliens who visited the Earth with plans of attacking and taking over. Spielberg now showed another kind, yet he made sure to interweave governmental paranoia as a part of the thin storyline, evoking the possibility that the visitors may be enemies rather than simply making contact.

After reading my comments about *Star Wars* you might find it hard to believe that I find that better and a more enjoyable movie than this one. *Close Encounters of the Third Kind* was part *Star*

Wars and part *2001: A Space Odyssey*, and only the bad parts of each of those movies. The characters are dull and the scenes of first and second contact are merely inspiring from a technical standpoint only, not from a story standpoint. Once again, glitz and flash are exchanged for substance and plot. In my opinion, that is not the proper sacrifice to make when constructing a movie. You may enjoy this film the first time you see it, but watching it a second, third and fourth time is where a movie moves over into the status of classic. I have watched it three times. The second and third times were a struggle, as was the first. Better movies deserved to be on this list ahead of and instead of this one.

#65 – *The Silence of the Lambs*

The third of the three movies to sweep the five major Academy Awards at the Oscars is one of the most terror filled movies on this list. While technically a sequel, *Silence of the Lambs* set itself apart its weaker predecessor, *Manhunter*. Focusing on the exploits of a young FBI trainee taking part in investigating a serial murder case, the film audience was introduced to perhaps one of the creepiest characters ever placed on film, Dr. Hannibal Lector. Dr. Lector's back and forth scenes with Jodie Foster's FBI-in-training agent Clarisse Starling set the tone of the movie. Their relationship is that emotional center that makes the film such a treat to watch.

The serial murder case is used as backdrop to present that mutual cathartic relationship between the two lead characters, which turned out to be a gripping symmetrical drama as a result of their interaction. The serial killer, known as 'Buffalo Bill', is one of the more peculiar screen villains, yet the movie suffers a bit from a lack of his presence. This is one of the few instances where twenty or so more minutes of movie, devoted to really getting into the mindset of this bizarre character, would have made *Silence of the Lambs* almost perfect. The focus is definitively on Starling and Lector, yet that does not need to be sacrificed by developing the 'Buffalo Bill' character further and more completely. That movie would have made the main list of this book.

The AFI placement of *Silence of the Lambs* is pretty close to where I would have had it. Using the list of nominated films available I would have assigned a somewhat lower spot to it, yet when analyzing these particular films chosen, it would be considerably higher than #65 on my list. Compared to the other nominated films from 1991, only *Beauty and the Beast* is a better film. *JFK*, from the same year, is not even nominated for consideration on this list. The voters remembered the Oscar sweep of *Silence of the Lambs*. That assured the number of votes required to land it at #65.

#66 – *Network* – #36

#67 – *The Manchurian Candidate* – #10

#68 – *An American In Paris*

What else can I say about this movie that has not been said in the chapter dedicated to the Best Picture winners? The plot is non-existent. The musical numbers are extremely self-serving. The dance sequence at the end is not only ridiculous but serves only as another self-indulgent mechanism for the star of the movie and the opening scene sets the entire stage for this awful movie. That scene shows Gene Kelly as a struggling painter, yet after waking up in his loft, he moves around the small room using his foot to open and close everything. The scene has no place within a story other than to highlight his dancing talent. It's amazing that someone with such obvious talent felt the insecure need to showcase it as Kelly has done in this movie. Great stars do not do that. It's what makes them better than those who do.

What does the footwork display in that opening scene have to do with painting or showing the angst of a struggling painter? The answer is nothing at all. Every single scene that highlights musical or dancing ability is similar. Even the simple introduction of the young Parisian woman that Gene Kelly falls for, in what amounts to this movie's only basic facade of a story, is done in a dance format and for no reason whatsoever other than to showcase their talent. *An American in Paris* would have been a good musical on Broadway, where it belonged. It would not have been a good play, where a plot is required to keep audiences involved. As a movie, it is absolutely wretched.

Of the four hundred movies that the fifteen hundred member panel could have chosen from, it was a no-brainer that the Best Picture from 1951 was included in that list. Immediately the notion exists that because *An American In Paris* won Best Picture, beating out such movies as *A Place In The Sun*, *The African Queen*, *Strangers On A Train* and the great acting exhibition *A Streetcar Named Desire*, all of which were nominated for inclusion on this list, it has to be included on a list of the Top 100 Greatest American films. It is that kind of backwards logic that allowed *An American In Paris* to make this list. Rather than repair a wrong that occurred in 1951, awarding a Best Picture Oscar to this farce of a movie that should have been a Broadway musical, compounding that wrong occurred when this travesty was placed on the same list as some of the greats of American cinema.

#69 – *Shane*

The ex-gunfighter trying to make good becomes one of the greatest westerns ever made. The title character shows up at the ranch of a farmer, his wife and his son, offering to lend a hand. Nothing is known about him except that he carries guns. In this era and genre, that means only one thing, trouble. Told almost as a parable, Shane comes off as a sympathetic hero, with elements from his past that he obviously wants to put behind him. Unfortunately, in the profession he chose early on in life, there is no getting away or making a clean break. There are only brief respites where hope shines bright for a moment, eventually fluttering out. When Shane realizes that he must fight, it leads to the final battle where he masterfully takes care of the enemies that threaten his new friends. *Shane* is most definitely a Western yet is told with a charm and delight that is absent from the standard Westerns of the time. That is a main characteristic that raises *Shane* above the rest.

Up against the powerhouse *From Here To Eternity*, *Shane* got lost in the Oscar shuffle, as did most other movies of that year. My favorite movie comes from this year, with a performance that nabbed the Best Actor Oscar for its star, yet I can state that *Shane* is the better movie. It is rare when AFI voters got their placement correct, yet when assessing the movies from 1953 on this list, they were ranked in the proper order. I would have placed both films higher on my own list, derived from the four hundred nominees. By the way, for those who have seen the film and wonder about the ending allow me to clear that up for you. Shane does in fact die at the end of the film, even though that debate still rages on today.

#70 – *The French Connection*

Up until this film, policemen were portrayed as characters that followed the book under every circumstance, acted only within the limits of the law and engaged in proper police procedure.

The real world knows that is a fairy tale, which is not the same as saying that all policeman break the rules. This is cinema however, where artistic license can not only take place but is often essential in presenting a compelling and original storyline, specifically when based upon characters that relate to people who exist within society.

In 1970, director William Friedkin presented a rough police drama where the main character was as close to breaking the law as he was in protecting it. *The French Connection* was radical for its time, with the performance of the main policeman cementing star status on relative newcomer Gene Hackman. Although nominated previously for two supporting actor Oscars, in 1967 for *Bonnie and Clyde* and in 1970 for the highly underrated *I Never Sang For My Father*, the role of *'Popeye'* Doyle made Hackman not only a lead actor but also a star. Hackman would bring home a much deserved Best Actor Oscar in the process.

Two of the five nominees from 1971 made the top one hundred. Neither of them were the best movie. Comparing the two that did make it however, *The French Connection* is better than *A Clockwork Orange*. Both movies are good, yet the panel of voters forgot about the richly layered saga of a small Texas town. The reason? In the two movies that were selected for this list, they both stick out in the minds of viewers. *A Clockwork Orange* is a movie event, renowned for its graphic displays of bizarre violence. For *The French Connection*, it is the documentary style chase sequence that most remember. It was the first of its kind where a camera placed the audience in that kind of action. The performance of Hackman is also a sight to see, one that had to have stuck out in the minds of the panel. *The Last Picture Show* was a slower paced story, yet the film specifically called for that. The pace actually complimented the story. Flash over substance is what everyone publicly mocks yet secretly desires and rewards.

#71 – *Forrest Gump*

Besides its christening as *the* feel-good movie for the ages, *Forrest Gump* echoes an age old literary and cinematic theme, the life of one man, no matter how unimportant they seem to be, affects so many around them. Covering the beginning of his life up until watching his own son go off to school, the audience is treated to a bevy of interaction with a variety of individuals and groups who made their mark on history. This was an advancement of that theme, where even the smallest of men can influence and impact those who have or will achieve greatness. Elements of that concept leans toward coming off as hokey, yet a top notch and Oscar winning performance by Tom Hanks brings the character and the story back down to Earth. Hanks' acting saves this film from having been any one of a hundred movies that try too hard to make a point with that overly used theme. The movie is grounded and magical because of Hanks.

Of the four movies from 1994 nominated by AFI for consideration, *Forrest Gump* ranks the highest here. While it is deserving of the higher ranking between the two movies from 1994 that made their way on to this list, the better movie from that year was forgotten. *The Shawshank Redemption*, another inspiring movie, was far superior to *Forrest Gump* though. Time has shown that. Strictly judging from the two movies included from 1994, the AFI voters got the order right, despite leaving the truly better movie off the list. With regards to list placement, among the movies that actually made the list, *Forrest Gump* could have ranked higher, yet among the four hundred nominated films it should have ranked farther down the list. *Forrest Gump* would have remained on my list of one hundred from the four hundred nominees, so its placement at #70 is a close to perfect blend of where it should have been when compiling both lists, my analysis of these one hundred films and my ballot from the four hundred nominees.

#72 – *Ben-Hur*

One of the all-time great scenes in cinema history occurs during the chariot race from *Ben-Hur*. It is the tale of a wealthy Jewish family during the time of Jesus, specifically his last few years. This movie however, focused on one man who was a noble Jew. This man chose not to support the persecution of the Jews in Roman held Judea and suffered extreme loss and hardship as a result. It is his long journey back that the movie centers on, although it is the parallels between the main character and Jesus that underlies this movie. The two scenes between Jesus and Ben-Hur show how they are unavoidably linked, supplying that necessary symmetry of the story.

Ben-Hur will always be known for its great chariot race, influencing movie making for generations to come. The central theme in the 2000 Best Picture winner, *Gladiator*, is linked to *Ben-Hur* as closely as the title character was linked to Christ. Grand scale moviemaking received a serious revitalization, rescuing it from what had become the laborious efforts of Cecil B. DeMille to present everything that ever happened in grand epic fashion, with continuously diminishing success. As far as its placement upon the top one hundred, the grand scale and history behind *Ben-Hur* played a pivotal role in securing it a spot on this list. There are far greater movies from that year, including what has been called the defining pictures of both Alfred Hitchcock and Billy Wilder, both ranking way above *Ben-Hur* on this list.

Once again, the logic of the voters, with respect to their choices baffles me. There are times when I can applaud their judgment, placing those two movies above *Ben-Hur*, yet including *Ben-Hur* on their overall list, simply because of a Best Picture Oscar and a famous chariot race is baffling to me. It can only be explained by a randomization of ballots, where some voters had a specific idea in their head, the idea that a Best Picture winner had to be better than any other movie from that same year. Additionally, there were probably voters who felt that epics deserved a higher status than smaller films. This is where extreme subjectivity of an arbitrary nature creeps into this list. Perhaps they should have extended their panel to fifteen thousand voters. I guarantee they would have ended up with a much better list.

#73 – *Wuthering Heights*

First off, holy hell Batman, the English can be melodramatic. The pomposity of this movie is enough to make one cringe, although the acting is just as overplayed. I could not tell if it was the material or simply the delivery of the material that was so tough to get through. It is almost impossible to describe the story, because it is all over the road and the film portrays that up and down sideways craziness. For all intensive purposes, a lot of stuff happens and then more stuff happens and of course then there is more. All of it so overbearing and pretentious that it was increasingly difficult to continue through the first and second watching.

This classic tale of love and loss, from the historically revered novel by Emily Bronte, was completely lost on me. There are just times when certain people do not get things that are considered classics. This one must be mine. Despite that, I will not deny that *Wuthering Heights* is considered one of the most romantic movies ever made. I can see why some would think that, because of the complex storyline specifically relating to the final scene. The entire story leading up to that doesn't support the ending sequences enough for me to rationalize *Wuthering Heights* as agreeing with that romantic label. It was as if the ending was so innovative, for the time, that a mystique surrounded the story and this ultra-romantic tab grew out of that. I found the movie boring and the acting, for the most part, was supremely pretentious.

Fighting it out for the worst of the five 1939 movies with *Stagecoach*, they are both at a definitive disadvantage. The other three films to make this list from 1939 have all been hailed as great in every sense of the word. All three of them made the main list, with one coming extremely close to landing in the top spot. *Wuthering Heights'* inclusion on this list is due to that perceived notion of a masterful romance that has deemed this overwrought tale as legendary. Laurence Olivier's quirky, yet multi layered performance is all that kept me the least bit interested, perhaps registering a note upon the minds of the voting panel. The fact that the 1939 *Wuthering Heights* is considered the definitive version of the Bronte classic could only have helped its stature among the voters.

#74 – *The Gold Rush*

Of the three Charlie Chaplin movies that made this list, out of only four nominated films of his, *The Gold Rush* is the best of the lot. The tramp, Chaplin's silent film persona, travels to the Yukon in Alaska in search of fortune. The famous scenes, from Chaplin's own favorite film, include the tramp boiling and trying to eat his own shoe, using the shoelaces as spaghetti, starvation and delirium resulting in the thinking that the tramp is a giant chicken, the famous teetering cabin scene on the edge of a cliff that sways with every movement and the heartwarming imagined dinner party. There are more important Chaplin films and there are scenes from other Chaplin films that may be funnier, yet as a complete film this one remains the best.

No Academy Awards were given in 1925, when *The Gold Rush* was released. The Oscars did not exist until the years 1927-1928. The legendary classic silent film *Greed* was released during the same year, although edited and chopped to all hell from its original intended version by a distrusting studio. It is tough to speculate which film would have taken home the statuette, although one could even lean toward the classic horror/love story *The Phantom of the Opera*. That was specifically the type of movie the Academy, even in its early stages, was fond of honoring. Only *The Gold Rush* made this particular list, from a group of four movies from that year. *Greed*, in its fully envisioned version might have been far greater than *The Gold Rush*, but that is something that we most likely will never know. Until then, the little tramp will more than suffice here in a comedic/pantomime masterpiece.

#75 – *Dances With Wolves*

The first Western to win a Best Picture Oscar in sixty years, Kevin Costner's nineteenth century epic of the life of one man sent to the untamed frontier, a last outpost at the time of the Civil War, took audiences by storm. *Dances With Wolves* struck a sentimental chord with audiences regardless of its close to four hour running time. Focusing on the relationship that a soldier, played by Costner, develops with the Indians that inhabit the immediate area, remains the essential core of the movie. Even during the beginning scene, where Costner attempts to give up his own life rather than get his leg amputated, he has reached a point of no return in his own existence. His friendship and brotherhood among the Indian tribe revitalizes his spirit.

The hardships of life are seen from the point of view of the Indians, as Costner's character merges himself into their way of life. He ultimately rejects his previous existence when discovered by troops who come to the outpost Costner was originally stationed at. By this time, Costner is one of them and the movie relays the impression that he is not only better off, but that the brutality of life existing among the Indian tribes is a far more evolved violence than the Union and Rebel soldiers have developed. It is not just a film about a man who changes from interaction with his new environment, but a commentary on cultural and societal values.

As stated in a previous chapter, the Academy robbed one of the truly great pictures of a deserved Oscar in 1990, instead choosing to reward this Western epic. Still, *Goodfellas* is ten times the movie that this was. That is not an insult against *Dances With Wolves*, yet rather a glowing compliment to Scorsese's crime masterpiece. AFI voters committed the same mistake that the Academy made by giving more credence to *Dances With Wolves* over *Goodfellas* as the better picture. I personally would not have placed this film among the top one hundred, given the choice from the films that were nominated.

#76 – *City Lights*

Probably the most well-known of all the Chaplin films involving the little tramp, *City Lights* contains a grouping of scenes that have become legendary. These scenes employ a perfect blend of not only comedy but also compassion and heart. Despite the widespread changeover to talking motion pictures, Chaplin held firm to the belief that his character's pantomiming ability would get the cinematic points across in a far more artistic manner. Most critics cite this movie as Chaplin's finest for its capacity to incorporate all of Chaplin's true cinematic qualities. The boxing scene is laugh out loud funny, while the scene where the flower girl gets her sight back and accepts the tramp for who he is will truly break your heart. While *The Gold Rush* is the better film, *City Lights* is extremely close to just as good. Chaplin should be applauded for sticking to his beliefs, a belief that the tramp should communicate through his actions, not his words.

There was not much to choose from in the year 1931. The Best Picture, *Cimarron*, was a complete dog of a film. It was exalted nonetheless. *City Lights* is far and away the better movie, yet it flew right in the industry's face, refusing to get with the times and change over to sound. This was simply Chaplin being Chaplin. He would suffer for sticking to his artistic intentions, only redeemed with an honorary Oscar much later in life.

The Front Page might have taken the top prize away for 1931 as it was a pretty good comedy, yet could have lost out as a result of *City Lights*, far superior to *The Front Page* as well. It was tough to leave this movie off my top one hundred, from the four hundred nominees, yet tough decisions have to be made. I do however rank it higher than it is now, among these specific one hundred. With the new medium of sound, the message sometimes gets lost when audiences stay away and the award presenting bodies ignore you. I do not think it is right and Chaplin showed true bravery in making this movie, which I highly recommend to anyone who has not seen it.

#77 – *American Graffiti*

This is an interesting selection. The hype behind this film is based purely upon nostalgia. Watching this movie evokes memories of the television show *Happy Days*, yet without the continual content of fun that the television show brought. It was kind of a fun movie, yet simply moved back and forth between scenes just at the time when the individual stories were hitting stride. The movie stops at right angles every few moments, in essence stalling all its possible momentum. It is not hard to see that there appears to be a building up to something, an intended culmination of all the individual stories, yet that eventual payoff comes nowhere close to fitting the buildup. Particularly good are Harrison Ford as the cowboy car racer and perhaps the best of the lot, Mackenzie Phillips, as the annoying young girl who eventually wins over the cool gear head hero. That story, also the best of the movie, never reaches true culmination. Through a semi-innovative final sequence the audience is left with the fact that it probably never will.

Only one movie from 1973 made the top one hundred list. Five other films from that year were nominated, all of which were far better. Two of them should have made the list, obviously best Picture winner *The Sting* and the fright fest *The Exorcist*. Once again, nostalgia fueled this choice. This movie, on its own merit, falls short of doing anything but provoking two types of feelings, nostalgia and emptiness. It was interesting to see all the young actors before they became stars, which included Ron Howard, Richard Dreyfus, Harrison Ford, Mackenzie Phillips, Cindy Williams and Suzanne Somers. That alone should not warrant its inclusion on this list, supplanting either of the other two better movies from 1973 or better movies that were nominated from any other year.

#78 – *Rocky* – #45

#79 – *The Deer Hunter*

This film was one of the more unique war movies made, covering the lives of a group of friends before a number of them are sent off to war. It displays an area rarely seen in a war film before, the time of those who were preparing to go, where the turmoil and apprehension of heading off to war was discussed and explored. Backlash from the movie came from those who wanted to push their own agenda and their own movie, an anti-war movie where performances shone best. For the best movie of 1978, one need look no further than this amazing film right here, which not only explored aspects unseen prior to this, but also examined anti-war themes. *The Deer Hunter* covered the complete gamut.

Of the five movies nominated from this year, only one cracked the top one hundred of this list. This is consistent with my opinion that *The Deer Hunter* is by far the best movie of the year. The ranking however, comparable to this particular group, is incredibly lower than it should be. However, the actual rank of where I would have placed it among the four hundred nominees is pretty similar to its actual ranking on this list. I can only imagine that that fluke had more to do with coincidence than actual intellectual decision making among those chosen as voters.

#80 – *The Wild Bunch*

Originally seen as a movie that glorified violence for the sake of violence, the restored version, although viewed as too long for the movie to be profitable, now helps to explain the plot of the film in a more cohesive manner. Violence is not the plot, yet rather the mechanism that these old and worn down criminals know. It is the only mechanism they truly know. It is a radical film showing how violence will always exist, changing over from the old guard to the new guard, regardless of the technologies that will come. Visionary filmmaker Sam Peckinpah showed that violence was in the heart of men who lived by a certain mythic code. Even though times change, the code and the violence will always remain.

Of the four movies that made this list from 1969, *The Wild Bunch* ranked third among them. I would have placed it second, behind the Best Picture Winner and actual best movie from that year, *Midnight Cowboy*. *The Wild Bunch* would have placed ahead of the movie that took the fiftieth spot on this list, which was more a choice due to chemistry rather than excellence. The original negative feedback against *The Wild Bunch* has given it newfound appreciation, since the restored footage was edited in. That may have given it enough momentum to crack this list. The issue of whether it should or not is irrelevant. I believe, on its own merit, it should have placed much higher among this group, yet around the same ranking that it occupies now among the four hundred nominees.

#81 – *Modern Times*

There must be a time when all great things come to an end. In the film *Modern Times*, the time had come to lay one of the greatest cinematic characters to rest, Chaplin's alter ego, the little tramp. He made the world cry, think and most of all laugh for many years through the character that everyone knew by sight. In this final film of the little tramp, Chaplin decided to keep his grand character silent, keeping his pantomiming actions as the true basis of his nature. Chaplin hated talking films, viewing them as simplistic. He attempted one last stab at critiquing the medium of talking films with this cinematic tale.

Modern Times was not made simply to protest the advent of talking motion pictures. It intended to draw attention to the country as a whole, displaying the effects the Great Depression had upon everyone through the eyes and actions of his alter ego. There was also an underlying message of rejecting the business establishment, specifically the industrialized working world and technological advancements. It was a subtle jab at the advancements in cinema, using the emerging and evolving industrialized world as a metaphor. The classic scene of the film involves the little tramp fed through the cogs of one machine into another machine. That is the scene that is most recognizable, yet there is a section where Chaplin emphasizes a factory boss and environment that eerily foreshadowed George Orwell's *1984*, years prior to that wonderful novel having been written.

Modern Times was the only movie from 1936 to have made this list. There were better movies, including *My Man Godfrey*, the original screwball comedy that still sets the stage for romantic comedy and *Dodsworth*, the story of an industrialist who travels to Europe only becoming truly alive after his wife runs off with another man. Chaplin's last ditch effort to attack talking movies is a fine film, yet not one of his best. His reliance upon making cinematic commentary takes away from the social commentary of the story. If this were a talking motion picture, made almost a full decade after pictures had primarily gone all *'talkie'*, it might have been better. The little tramp was laid to rest. It would have been nice for him to have said goodbye to us all.

#82 – *Giant*

An epic if there ever was one, told in the grand scale of the lengthy David Lean and Cecil B. DeMille pictures, except for the fact that the material was unimaginably boring. One of the major themes showcases the ignorance, bigotry and prejudices of Texans versus an enlightened view of humanity in the form of the Easterner who is brought into their lives. I am not particularly sure if that was one of the goals of the Edna Furber novel, on which the movie is based. The film captures those distinct differences in intelligent and evolved thought, yet takes forever to finally reconcile them with the culmination of understanding. For a movie of this length, close to four hours, character development is sacrificed for basic chronology, cinematography and locations.

Considered one of the worst years in cinema history, 1956 was famous for one specific item, the final film of James Dean. That was this film. By the time the movie had premiered, Dean had already passed away in a car crash. Dean's image and acting, receiving his second consecutive Best Actor nomination for his role, helped *Giant* grow into legendary cinematic status. It is an almost incomplete film, even though it covers nearly twenty-five years of a Texas family's life together. *Giant* was not the only movie from 1956 to make the top one hundred, yet it ranks as the higher of those two entries. The great success of *Giant*, both financial and commercial, the Oscar accolades, including a Best Director Oscar victory for George Stevens and the iconic status the film was accorded as a result of the short lived but highly impactful life of one of its co-stars helped land *Giant* on this list, even though it really does not deserve to be here.

#83 – *Platoon*

Called the most realistic film covering the war in Vietnam, Oliver Stone's *Platoon* hit with unmistakable force, bringing new understanding to what young soldiers go through during their time in country. Eight years earlier, *The Deer Hunter* showed a stark realism to the Vietnam War. *Platoon* advanced that theme. Describing distinctly different aspects of the Vietnam War, the two movies were as dissimilar as they were unique. *Platoon*, however, basically stuck with telling the story of a young main character and how his time was affected by the two officers his group was under, both formulaic opposites. His emotional maturity centers the movie, stemming from Stone's own experiences during the war. Growing from raw idealism to rational belief, the main character develops a sense of belonging during an incredibly difficult time.

In comparison with other Vietnam War movies, *The Deer Hunter* is far better. Comparisons to other movies, specifically of the same genre, tend to bias opinions though. *Platoon*, in and of itself, is simply nothing more than the new Vietnam War movie on the block. It does not separate itself from the rest, which in terms of greatness indicates that it is indeed lacking. The character development is extremely weak and the lack of a clearly defined plot is plain to see. What made *Platoon* a critical success was its use of amazingly stark realism, rather than focusing on a strongly defined story.

Of the six nominated films from 1986, *Platoon* may just be the best. Consideration should go to the David Lynch weird-o-rama *Blue Velvet* though. None of the six films deserved inclusion on this list, yet the Best Picture of that year was the choice for those who felt that since it won Best Picture and it was highly regarded, excluding it would be wrong. The exact opposite should have been the case. There were far better movies that deserved to make this list over *Platoon*, not to mention ten of the seventeen movies that were ranked behind it that should have been ranked well ahead of *Platoon* on this list.

#84 – *Fargo* – #46

#85 – *Duck Soup*

I am of the opinion that the best Marx Brothers movie comes from 1935, *A Night at the Opera*. The key to understanding how this affects *Duck Soup* lies in understanding that the two best movies from 1971, *The French Connection*, #70 on this list and *The Last Picture Show*, unranked, are both far better than any movie from 1970, 1977 or 1978. What that indicates, in relation to the two Marx Brothers' movies, is that despite the fact that one is better than the other, a mathematical certainty, both films can individually be better than the best movies from a number of years in the last century. And they are.

Stated earlier, my opinion is that *Duck Soup* was easily the best picture of 1933, way ahead of the actual winner, *Cavalcade*. The subversive nature of the movie hurt not only its box office appeal, but also its critical success. While *A Night at the Opera* had both critical and commercial success, *Duck Soup*, with its underlying indictments on the senselessness of war, achieved none of the successes afforded to the better movie of the two. There are those who have overcompensated regarding *Duck Soup*, because of the backlash it received. This could be how *Duck Soup* landed on this list ahead of the better film, *A Night at the Opera*. I would have placed both films on the list.

As far as the actual list is concerned, the 1971 example holds firm. #85 is an extremely low placement for a film that happens to be this good. For the nominees from 1933, only one movie ranked higher than *Duck Soup*, *King Kong*, despite the nomination of six movies from that year. My opinion regarding that movie has been stated. Comparing these two movies is an exercise in futility. There should be no reasonable comparison. The voting, that same voting that landed *Duck Soup* on this list over *A Night at the Opera*, actually worked against it with regards to its specific ranking.

#86 – *Mutiny on the Bounty*

The classic tale of betrayal along the high seas had one of the greatest leading casts, Clark Gable as Fletcher Christian and Charles Laughton as Captain William Bligh. Bligh is one of the greatest screen villains of all time. The two characters were total opposites who inevitably conflicted so significantly that Fetcher had to take over the ship. The true drama was not aboard the boat, where scenes of pure horror were shown, such as Laughton's character forcing the flogging of a corpse.

The real excitement came from the fact that mutiny was an offense that would result in hanging, with the possibility that the mutineers would be hunted and executed. The choice of allowing the deposed Captain to live and fend for himself and those members of the crew loyal to him was within Fletcher's sympathetic nature. That distinction clearly distinguished the two men. That drama alluded to above presented itself in the fact that if the Captain made it home to England, which he eventually did, he would not allow such a mutiny to stand even though Fletcher showed the kind of mercy on Bligh that Bligh actually lacked as a human being.

Despite the success and accolades of *Mutiny on the Bounty*, the film is flawed due to the amount of time it spends with the mutineers on Tahiti, the island they remain on. This really slows down the tense structure that was created by the mutiny and the doubt on whether or not Bligh and his men were going to make it home. While the mutiny is the centerpiece, it is truly a character driven story of a cruel madman versus those who would not stand for his tyranny any longer. Once that part of the story was left for dead, in favor of highlighting the frolicking around Tahiti, the movie began to lose its edge.

Mutiny on the Bounty was another of the old cinematic guard that made its way onto this list as a result of name and star recognition rather than deserving to on the basis of having been a great movie. It is one of those films that would rather be discussed than viewed, despite what most film critics and historians might claim in order to preserve the classic stature of this movie. There must be some who truly love this film, just as there are some who feel *Porky's II: The Next Day* was better than the original. I tend to believe that my opinion that this film has dated itself enough to where the luster has worn off is shared by many.

#87 – *Frankenstein*

Considered the scariest movie ever made, *Frankenstein* came one year off the heels of *Dracula*. Both films helped establish a new genre, already present in German cinema, albeit of a more natural realistic type of horror. Known as *'The Monster'*, the creature has come to be recognized as both the color green and Frankenstein. The name originates from the actual creator of the monster, Dr. Victor Frankenstein, although that man is referred to as Dr. Henry Frankenstein in the film. However, audiences saw that the movie was taken over by the lumbering performance of Boris Karloff and naturally, if not erroneously, attached the legendary name of Frankenstein to the monster itself. He was what truly grabbed their full attention.

The images still play in a frightening way, but the techniques used during the time of its release have come and gone. They have been replaced because they acted merely as parlor tricks, switched over to craftier and more successful special effects. Seeing the movie today still evokes an eerie feeling inside, yet not close to the variety that has been described as occurring to audiences of the 1930's. In that respect, the horror of this movie has severely diminished. If the basis for its ranking and stature has monstrously diminished then why is it still so highly regarded? The image of a number of films from that time has not changed as much as *Frankenstein* or even *King Kong*. *Dracula* would have been a much better choice, yet the AFI voters were not allowed to make that choice because the horror classic *Dracula* was not included among the four hundred nominees.

As far as monster movies go, this one is an all-time classic. It should go down in history as fostering a new genre within American cinema, helping to create the sequel, of which there were many *Frankenstein* movies to follow. The absolute best of that lot was 1935's *The Bride of Frankenstein*. It is interesting to note that almost all critics and movie fans say that particular sequel far outshines the 1931 original. If *The Bride of Frankenstein* is universally accepted as a better movie, why was it not included as a nominee? That technically should not have any effect upon *Frankenstein*, as each movie should be judged on its own excellence. However, that is clearly the point. *Frankenstein* was not judged on that specific criteria, based instead upon its lasting influence on culture and movies. That is not what a list such as this was designated to reveal.

#88 – *Easy Rider*

Known as the biker movie by those who do not ride bikes, *Easy Rider* came along at just the right time in American history, when the culture felt alienated and needed a getaway. That attempt at freedom was presented in this ultra sleek tale of living life on the carefree edge. A generation was influenced by this movie, where two drug dealers traveled across the country to celebrate at Mardi Gras. What they uncover are more people like themselves, but also those who live their life by a code of hatred and bigotry. The two main characters are different. That is enough to promote hatred and incite violence from idiots. The end scene shows that no matter how hard we all try, there will always be people out there who live their lives in fear of change and who are willing to cling to that fear and hatred, striking out against it in whatever uneducated manner they decide.

Believed to be the coming out party of the actor playing the key supporting role in the film, Jack Nicholson, *Easy Rider* made an immediate impact. It garnered two Oscar nominations and was not only a major financial success, but also somewhat of a critical success. Today, it is viewed as one of the films that shaped the next generation and as such has developed an overblown fullness. It came from a year where *Midnight Cowboy* was king and rightfully deserved that title. *Easy Rider* was deserving of the recognition it got though. A fantastic film, yet among the four hundred nominees, I had it just outside the top one hundred. Contrarily, I also had it much higher than #88 among the one hundred that made this list. I always enjoy the film when it is on television. I must admit that I am a fan.

#89 – *Patton*

This immensely successful biopic about the late General George S. Patton showed not only the iron will of a captivating leader, but also the tragic flaws that come with the whole package. The brilliant military mind for battle was haunted by the lack of authority and the desire to control others. That more than anything cemented Patton's legend. This all comes across the screen perfectly in a multi-layered performance by George C. Scott. Patton's slapping of a soldier after a battle because he was deeply affected by what had just taken place is the centerpiece, used to explain why he was equally great and flawed. In the minds of winners, certain sacrifices have to be made for the greater good. In Patton's mind, his control and leadership was the greater good. What he said was the law. All were to follow him or suffer his self imposed consequences. This is what came across on the screen, but the movie has alternatively been dubbed an anti-war film. A somewhat correct assessment of this film that definitely hurts the movie's overall greatness. It is its inability to separate itself out as one or the other that drags it down below the status of a cinematic classic.

Patton was not the best movie from 1970, yet it is the only movie from that year to make the top one hundred. *Five Easy Pieces*, the movie that made Jack Nicholson a star, was a much deeper and more complex film. The AFI voters reflected upon that opening scene in *Patton*, where George C. Scott stood on a platform with a giant American flag in the background and gave the speech that makes this movie famous. It is what the Academy Award voters remembered. Why should the AFI voters have show any advanced thought on the matter by placing *Five Easy Pieces* ahead of this good, but not great movie?

#90 – *The Jazz Singer*

If ever there were a sentimental choice on this list, where quality was directly ignored in favor of cinema history, then the placement of *The Jazz Singer* fits that criteria. The story of … well … a jazz singer, is an absolutely awful, disturbingly overacted and flat out boring movie to watch. I understand that this was the first *"talkie"*, yet that is also a misnomer as there are almost no talking scenes, but rather mainly singing scenes that use the then new craft of sound mixing. *The Jazz Singer* was innovative in technical craft only. It deserves its due as one of the true influential and pioneering films that began that talking motion pictures era.

However, this list was created to celebrate excellent cinema, not cinema influence. Once again, I would love to see the instructions handed out to the panel of AFI voters. There is absolutely no way anyone can tell me that *The Jazz Singer* is a better movie than over two hundred and fifty of the three hundred films left off the list, among the four hundred nominees. They say, all it takes is a few rotten apples to spoil the whole bunch. Never before has a proverb rang truer than in this case. I think it would be interesting to see the actual ballots and who cast this movie as one of their one hundred greatest American movies of the past hundred years. It could have been as few as fifty voters, one thirtieth of the total voters, who helped inch *The Jazz Singer* onto the list at the #90 spot. The inclusion of *The Jazz Singer* shows that many of the voter's list were purely arbitrary. The belief that this film must be included, due to its overall influence, negatively affects their credibility as rational thinkers.

#91 – *My Fair Lady*

Audiences fell in love with Audrey Hepburn, once again. Playing Eliza Doolittle, the cockney girl who speaks as if she were a fifteenth century retarded and deaf sailor, Hepburn illuminates the screen with her brilliant performance. Rex Harrison shines as the effete snob who tries to mold her into what he feels everyone should sound like. The magic is not in the transformation, but in the warming over of both parties to each other. Starting out as merely teacher and student, almost bitter rivals to an extent, the two of them gradually notice the softer sides of each other's personalities. Eventually they realize that they are better off together.

The better film from this year was rewarded with the higher placement, albeit perhaps a bit too high a placement for its actual worth. *My Fair Lady* made the cut as one of the last movies on this list due to, once again, the sentimentality surrounding the film. Hepburn playing language impaired and Harrison seeing more in her than meets the eye and the ears created a warm place in many moviegoers' hearts for this classic of love beyond culture and background. As far as a great film, it sorely misses the mark. People may watch it if it comes on television, yet to actually make a conscious choice of going out to rent it, or reaching into the DVD or VHS cabinet to get it and place it in the mechanism of your choice, is generally something that is rarely done. I do not know anyone who has ever said they watch *My Fair Lady* on any regular sort of basis and that goes for people who say they love the movie. What they mean is that they love the idea, the characters and the feeling it once gave them, not the actual movie itself. *My Fair Lady* is a cute movie, but far from great and less deserving as an entry on this list than many films that were left off.

#92 – *A Place in the Sun*

If *All About Eve* is pure soap opera, then George Stevens' richly layered mixing of the ultra rich and the poor is pure Hollywood drama at its highest level. The story, based upon Theodore Dreiser's wonderful novel, focuses on the social climbing of a working class man, Montgomery Clift, who becomes involved with a beautiful rich woman, played by a stunning eighteen year old Elizabeth Taylor. As the romance moves forward, Clift sees his situation improve. As in any drama there are major obstacles set in the main character's way. A past encounter with a coworker that Clift has impregnated sets about the downfall of his goal of improving himself socially and financially. This story, intended to evokes a spectrum of emotions, left this movie fan believing that the plot was too formulaic and easy to be considered a drama of any true merit. The keys with this movie are the performances by Taylor and Montgomery Clift, as well as some of the most romantic individual scenes ever filmed. That is not enough.

Sentimentality and handkerchiefs unleashed with the placement of this movie among the top one hundred. The fourth of the films from 1951 to have made the list, it is only exceeded in its inferior quality by the awful and rampantly self-indulgent *An American in Paris* and to a much lesser extent, the Bogart/Hepburn river travesty. In that aspect, this movie should rank second among the four 1951 movies, yet placed fourth. None of the four movies from 1951, as stated earlier, deserved to make this list. Although, of the one hundred movies listed here, *A Place in the Sun* would rank somewhere around the three quarter mark, fifteen or so spots above its current ranking.

#93 – *The Apartment*

Sometimes, the greatest comedies are not merely ones that evoke continual laughter. A comedy can promote laughter and thought through ironic situations that reveal more than is upon the surface. Billy Wilder's 1960 comedy is such a movie. The main character, a prototypical lonely guy, is robbed of his own freedom to be alone. He lends out his apartment to executives at work in return for job considerations that never come. That furthers his internal dilemma. This is a comedy however, evident through the performance by Jack Lemmon, who internally struggles for both isolation and companionship at the same time.

Comedies rarely take home the golden statuette. That is a sad fact of the industry. They tend to suffer because the material seems childish, almost immature. Those few comedic pictures that have won the top prize all possess the backing of dramatic subtext within them, as *The Apartment* clearly does. Strong performances almost never hurt and this picture had two of them, in Lemmon and Shirley MacLaine. Both of these performers had begun to make a name for themselves, garnering prior Oscar nominations, with Lemmon actually winning the Best Supporting Actor Oscar for his role in 1955's *Mister Roberts*. These two both emerged as stars after this film, allowing them to develop their acting skills by using *The Apartment* as that comedic bridge into more dramatic and what is often perceived as more mature work.

Four movies from 1960 were nominated for inclusion among this list. Rarely does the ranking turn out correctly, yet with regards to 1960 it actually worked nicely. The far better picture, *Psycho*, ranked much higher upon this list and deservedly so. The gap between *Psycho* and *The Apartment* seems way too far for this list of films. In comparison to another comedy along the lines of *The Apartment*, *Annie Hall*, which also won Best Picture, the writing and story of this film is much crisper. The material must have suffered in the minds of the voters who may have been unsure on how to accurately classify this movie, as a comedy or drama. Anyone who wishes to believe that that specific distinction did not affect any of the fifteen hundred member panel of voters then that swampland you bought might actually be worth something. *Annie Hall* is definitively a comedy, albeit with heart and of course deep seeded neuroses played for laughs. *The Apartment* is more though, yet that concept was missed by the voters who chose to rank *Annie Hall* as the better movie, in about as close as a gap that they also separated *The Apartment* from *Psycho*. In looking back at that one does not need to analyze too much to see it is erroneous.

#94 – *Pulp Fiction*

'Royale with cheese' and other fantastically snappy dialogue helped raise this B-movie in style, with A-list actors, to iconic status. It is a perfect use of dialogue that raises *Pulp Fiction* that particular notch above other films. It is viewed by many as the most influential film in the last twenty years. Another key to the movie's critical and commercial success was its unique scheme of storytelling, editing the movie out of chronological sequence and allowing the different stories to run into each other. The final scene, chronologically somewhere in the middle, links the whole movie together. This scene comes directly after a brief beginning that leads directly into what winds up as the cinematic finale. In a masterful blending of out of chronologically synched storytelling, the entirety of the movie makes perfect sense. Another element in *Pulp Fiction's* favor was the brilliant acting of the ensemble cast, led by John Travolta and Samuel L. Jackson. This movie revived Travolta's career and set Jackson on the road to super stardom.

Two of the four films nominated from 1994 made the top one hundred. Of those four, *Pulp Fiction* ranks as the actual third best. The voters could not ignore this highly influential and extremely entertaining movie. The massive critical acclaim surrounding the film definitively worked in its favor. If the public had access to all fifteen hundred ballots, there would be a clear differentiation between the ones who ranked *Pulp Fiction* extremely high and those who ranked it lower if including it among their ballot at all. *Pulp Fiction* is one of the few films that could actually serve as a measuring guide to assess the credibility of a voter's list. For example, if a voter ranked *Pulp Fiction* in their top ten, then the validity of that panel member's list should be seriously called into question. Additionally, the voters who completely left this film off their list are suspect as well.

I have the distinct feeling that it was way over ranked by a quarter of the voters while simultaneously having been completely left off the list by two-thirds of the voters. Unfortunately, it is that middle portion that might have provided the better and more accurate list of the top one hundred films. If a voter started his list like this; #1 – *Singin' in the Rain*, #2 – *West Side Story*, #3 – *The Sound of Music*, #4 – *An American in Paris* and #5 – *My Fair Lady*, shouldn't that voter's entire list be called into question? A much better methodology would have been for AFI to insist that the entire fifteen hundred member panel rank all four hundred nominees from one to four hundred. These people were invited to take part in an historical event and it seems apparent from this list that some put no thought into it past saying "oooohhhh I love this film", or what's even worse, saying that a movie had to be on the list because of its iconic status or because it won a Best Picture Oscar. *King Kong* and *The Birth of a Nation* immediately come to mind in this last scenario.

#95 – *Goodfellas* – #5

#96 – *The Searchers*

This is one of the few movies that has actually gotten better with age. During the year of its release *The Searchers* was widely misunderstood. It was believed that the film stood for an *'us'* versus *'them'* mentality. There is far greater depth to the story, although there are decidedly racist undertones throughout. Along with *High Noon* and *Shane*, *The Searchers* was one of the movies that helped revive the Western and is often singled out as John Wayne's best acting performance. Wayne embarks on a six year quest to find his niece who had been kidnapped by a group of Indians. These

Indians murdered the rest of her family. Wayne's heart hardens as he learns more about the group, his niece and what has transpired between the two. His mission now becomes clear. Wayne is not seeking her out to save her, but to murder her for her own sake.

This is a theme that has caused much debate. It is inarguable that Wayne's character is a racist. That quality comes through clear and is a deep and pertinent element to the story. It is the fact that he makes the decision to murder her rather than rescue her, initially, which causes the most confusion. Most say it is because he hates the Indians and that he must kill his own niece because she has become one of them. However, it makes much more sense that he feels he must kill her to save her from becoming more like them, the savages that murdered what was left of his and her family. This is why I believe the quest continues after Wayne discovers she has ingratiated herself among them. The ending, of course, shows a side to his character that one does not expect. It is not the fact that he fails, but that he chooses not to succeed. That shows growth, which is one of the true tenets of the story. It is the story's way of reconciling Wayne's character's own hatred for Indians.

In a recent poll of the leading film magazine *Sight and Sound*, *The Searchers* was recorded as the third best American movie ever made, behind *Vertigo* and *Citizen Kane*. To rank it this low among this particular group of one hundred clearly shows the sentimentality toward tearjerkers, musicals and particular actors and actresses that is evident by analyzing this list. Among the movies chosen for nomination from 1956 it is clearly the best of the five available. The actual best picture was not nominated, but has begun to grow in favor with age. *The Searchers*, however, has gotten more fanfare and a wider audience of viewers than *Written on the Wind*. It could be due to the subject matter or the fact that both films contain cinematic and plot themes that are not for the common everyday moviegoer. *The Searchers* has grown to be the better film, at least to most people.

#97 – *Bringing Up Baby*

Hailed as one of the pioneering screwball comedies, Katherine Hepburn and Cary Grant played distinctly against their standard type while navigating their way through a bevy of madcap situations that only seem to get worse. These situations include searching for a lost dinosaur bone and the animal who took it, a pet leopard named Baby. From one circumstance to the next, the hilarity comes in droves as Hepburn's character tries to woo the absent minded man of science whose only interest is to retrieve the museum's property. The cross dressing scene with Cary Grant remains one of Hollywood's most treasured moments, more than likely helping *Bringing Up Baby* land a spot upon this list.

There were better films in 1938, including the widely overlooked *The Adventures of Robin Hood* with Errol Flynn frolicking around Sherwood Forest alongside his merry band of men. That film, along with *Boys Town* and the Best Picture winner *You Can't Take it With You,* were available for placement upon the voter's lists, yet they chose to remember that particular scene with Grant, as well as Grant and Hepburn playing off each other so well, as they had done in *The Philadelphia Story*. It's obvious that all five movies from 1938 should not have made the list, yet for the voters to have chosen this one over any of the other three, specifically *The Adventures of Robin Hood*, it shows that the panel of voters chosen definitely had a preset notion of the types of movies that were good. That thoroughly indicates that theirs was a biased and arbitrary list. The bigger question emerges of how many voters fell into this category?

#98 – *Unforgiven*

There comes a time to reward greatness merely for the sake of greatness. This however, is not one of those cases. Film fans will know that Clint Eastwood got his movie career rolling by playing the man with no name in the infamous spaghetti Westerns. They launched Eastwood to the status of screen star. Along the way, which included a number of stints behind the camera and a couple of Westerns that, while somewhat enjoyable to watch, were not of the caliber of *Unforgiven*, Eastwood carved out a name for himself as a screen legend. *Unforgiven* was special, telling a fantastic tale of a retired gunfighter's last salvation. Brought out of retirement to avenge the brutal attack of a prostitute, Eastwood, his former partner, played magnificently by Morgan Freeman and a young gunfighter looking to make a name for himself, make their way toward town. Each of them has their own specific agenda.

Only two movies were nominated for inclusion from 1992, *Unforgiven* and the Robert Altman indictment of the business behind representing Hollywood stars, *The Player*. The two better movies than *Unforgiven* were not offered up for the voters to choose upon their own list, yet understanding the mechanics of what took place those two movies would have languished in obscurity with the other three hundred that did not make the final list. The fact that only two movies were nominated from this year also played an important role in ranking. *Unforgiven* is far superior to most of the films that found their way onto the final list, yet wound up as the third worst of the top one hundred. The mindset of the voters, because of the specific guidelines set definitely hurt the overall ranking of *Unforgiven*. This extraordinarily emotional tale should have found a home near the middle of this list rather than at the bottom.

#99 – *Guess Who's Coming To Dinner*

1967 appeared to be the magical year for movies that were trying to examine and initiate change. This became the third movie from that year to make the top one hundred, as it investigated the issue of interracial marriage and race relations. The classic pairing of Katherine Hepburn and Spencer Tracy, their final screen pairing, emerged as a fine film that juxtaposed an intelligent and upstanding black man who was asking for the hand of Tracy's daughter in marriage. Immediately, the minds of all participants began to wildly race in an effort to stop the happy event, until finally Tracy, the grandmaster of the film, stepped in and realized that only love matters, not the color of a person's skin.

Once again, this was the third movie from 1967 to make this list. The true best movie and Oscar winner was left off, even though it examines similar issues and does so in a more convincing manner. Stated many times before in this chapter, each film should have been weighed as independent from every other film ever made. The case with *Guess Who's Coming to Dinner* appears to obviously be that the voters were split in their opinion as to which Hepburn/Tracy film had to be included among their own list. 1949's *Adam's Rib* is far funnier and might just be their best overall film together. The ranking of this movie is an indictment of how the fifteen hundred member panel was indecisive about which of this screen legend's many pairings to include. It would not surprise me at all if *Adam's Rib* or 1942's *Woman of the Year* were ranked somewhere between the 101 and 150 region. Let's all hope that a book such as this prompts the AFI to release the full list.

#100 – *Yankee Doodle Dandy*

    Telling the life story of the great Broadway wunderkind, singer/dancer/writer/producer and all-time American patriot George M. Cohan, James Cagney turns in an Oscar winning performance in this musical tribute. Displaying the upbringing of the young Cohan in the theater to his troubles with finding work and his eventual big break and artistic maturity, *Yankee Doodle Dandy* is an altogether watchable film, yet has no real greatness to it. It is interesting as an historical biopic, yet extremely tedious in its presentation of one of the pioneers of musical comedy. The songs are fun and known by many, perhaps allowing the viewer to feel more of a part of the movie. Even despite that, this movie came off as flat. Subsequent watchings do nothing to alleviate that feeling.

    Yankee Doodle Dandy garnered the final spot on this list primarily because of two distinctions; American patriotism for its content due to the fact that this was a list celebrating American cinema and the fact that this is considered the finest and only Oscar winning performance of one of the true screen legends, James Cagney. Of the one hundred that made the list, I would rate this movie about ten or fifteen spots higher, yet among the four hundred nominated films, it did not come close to making my final one hundred. Four other movies from that same year were far better, including Best Picture winner *Mrs. Miniver*, the actual best movie of that year.

    As you hopefully have read though my analyses of AFI's 100 Greatest American Movies, the time has come for me to rank them for you. Only movies placed on AFI's list will make this particular ranking. I will place them in my own precise order, as if I were given a ballot with only these specific one hundred to choose from. It is a rearrangement of the list according to my own belief of how these movies deserve to be ranked. There is the remote chance that possibly one or even more than one list, out of the fifteen hundred separate lists, perfectly correlates to the following ranking. If that happens to be the case, you will see afterwards that I do not endorse such a list.

MY RANKING OF AFI'S TOP 100 AMERICAN MOVIE LIST

1 - CASABLANCA
2 - RAIDERS OF THE LOST ARK
3 - GONE WITH THE WIND
4 - THE BRIDGE ON THE RIVER KWAI
5 - GOODFELLAS
6 - CITIZEN KANE
7 - IT'S A WONDERFUL LIFE
8 - ONE FLEW OVER THE CUCKOO'S NEST
9 - THE GODFATHER
10 - THE MANCHURIAN CANDIDATE
11 - PSYCHO
12 - RAGING BULL
13 - SUNSET BOULEVARD
14 - TO KILL A MOCKINGBIRD
15 - MIDNIGHT COWBOY
16 - THE GODFATHER II
17 - THE GRAPES OF WRATH
18 - SCHINDLER'S LIST
19 - MR. SMITH GOES TO WASHINGTON
20 - THE THIRD MAN
21 - VERTIGO
22 - THE WIZARD OF OZ
23 - REAR WINDOW
24 - FROM HERE TO ETERNITY
25 - THE MALTESE FALCON

26 - CHINATOWN
27 - NETWORK
28 - ON THE WATERFRONT
29 - HIGH NOON
30 - ROCKY
31 - FARGO
32 - NORTH BY NORTHWEST
33 - DOUBLE INDEMNITY
34 - THE PHILADELPHIA STORY
35 - IT HAPPENED ONE NIGHT
36 - DOCTOR ZHIVAGO
37 - TAXI DRIVER
38 - THE FRENCH CONNECTION
39 - JAWS
40 - SOME LIKE IT HOT
41 - THE DEER HUNTER
42 - SHANE
43 - UNFORGIVEN
44 - ALL ABOUT EVE
45 - THE WILD BUNCH
46 - AMADEUS
47 - DUCK SOUP
48 - THE SILENCE OF THE LAMBS
49 - DR. STRANGELOVE
50 - A CLOCKWORK ORANGE

51 - FORREST GUMP
52 - THE GOLD RUSH
53 - PULP FICTION
54 - THE APARTMENT
55 - THE BEST YEARS OF OUR LIVES
56 - BONNIE AND CLYDE
57 - ALL QUIET ON THE WESTERN FRONT
58 - LAWRENCE OF ARABIA
59 - TREASURE OF THE SIERRA MADRE
60 - THE SEARCHERS
61 - THE SOUND OF MUSIC
62 - EASY RIDER
63 - CITY LIGHTS
64 - BRINGING UP BABY
65 - A STREETCAR NAMED DESIRE
66 - E.T. - THE EXTRA TERRESTRIAL
67 - MODERN TIMES
68 - PLATOON
69 - GUESS WHO'S COMING TO DINNER
70 - MUTINY ON THE BOUNTY
71 - M.A.S.H.
72 - PATTON
73 - BUTCH CASSIDY & THE SUNDANCE KID
74 - SNOW WHITE & THE SEVEN DWARFS
75 - MY FAIR LADY

76 - ANNIE HALL
77 - BEN-HUR
78 - A PLACE IN THE SUN
79 - SINGIN' IN THE RAIN
80 - DANCES WITH WOLVES
81 - APOCALYPSE NOW
82 - THE GRADUATE
83 - REBEL WITHOUT A CAUSE
84 - 2001: A SPACE ODYSSEY
85 - THE AFRICAN QUEEN
86 - GIANT
87 - YANKEE DOODLE DANDY
88 - WUTHERING HEIGHTS
89 - FRANKENSTEIN
90 - TOOTSIE
91 - STAGECOACH
92 - STAR WARS
93 - AMERICAN GRAFITTI
94 - KING KONG
95 - CLOSE ENOUNTERS
96 - FANTASIA
97 - WEST SIDE STORY
98 - THE BIRTH OF A NATION
99 - THE JAZZ SINGER
100 - AN AMERICAN IN PARIS

Immediately, there will be those who will argue with the above rearrangement. The first movie that will more than likely be challenged will be *The Birth of a Nation*. How could I ignore the grand technical breakthroughs made by D. W. Griffith, which definitively altered the scope of cinema history? Simple. It is an awful movie from every single standpoint except a technical one. The film belongs in two types of classes, filmmaking and a class on how to hate your fellow man. It most certainly does not belong in the class or list of the top one hundred films that this project was designed to offer.

Once again, a film should be an experience. It is a way to get away from your own life for a couple of hours. This film presents the horrors of extreme racism, yet decides to praise them rather than condemn them. It is such a deplorable film and more critics, with much more clout than myself, should make a stand against it. *The Birth of a Nation* should be relegated to technical study of cinematic technique or what is was used for in the early twentieth century after its release, a recruitment video for hate groups. Hopefully one day they will watch a toxic printing as their hatred is most assuredly toxic itself.

I shall not get into all the obvious differences between my precise ranking of AFI's top one hundred movies as the critiques of the movies should speak for themselves. The AFI committee provided each member of the panel with a list of four hundred movies to choose from. Write in votes were allowed, but in all reality these votes were meaningless. A write in vote for one particular movie would not be a mathematical factor when tallying points. Even if it were placed among one voter's top one hundred list, it would have to had appeared on enough of the fifteen hundred voter's ballots and in a high enough spot to actually gather enough points to crack the top one hundred. From analyzing the one hundred that made the list and comparing them to the four hundred nominated movies, it does not take a degree in rocket science to understand that all of the one hundred were among the four hundred nominees. Therefore, no write-in movies made any dent. So what were some of the prominent movies that the AFI excluded from their list?

Starting from my main list, three of the movies from that list were not even provided for the voting panel. 1991 had five nominees for this list, yet *JFK* was a mysterious omission. Among the five, another powerful movie from that year was missing as well, *Boyz N The Hood*. I have already discussed *JFK* during the first section and will not delve into it again to make a further point. There was however, one movie from that year among the five nominees that the AFI committee apparently believed was a far greater American movie than both *JFK* and *Boyz N the Hood*. That movie was *Rambling Rose*. That is a logical assessment based on what is presented. If *JFK* and *Boyz N The Hood* were not good enough to warrant consideration, while *Rambling Rose* was, then it is reasonable to assume that the AFI believed *Rambling Rose* was a better film. To even attempt a comparison between *Rambling Rose* and those other two films would be according more esteem to *Rambling Rose* than is deserved. It is not that *Rambling Rose* was a bad film, yet it is not even close to as good as the other two.

Six movies were chosen as nominees from 1987, yet missing among them was *The Princess Bride*. It is one of the most beloved and greatest comedic fantasies ever made. All six movies from 1987 were fine films, with perhaps the only exception being the Best Picture winner, *The Last Emperor*. I understand that movie's inclusion on the list, yet a movie from one year earlier was included that is so far below *The Princess Bride* in actual quality. *Ferris Bueller's Day Off* is a fun movie, but to claim that it belongs among the greatest American movies ever made is preposterous.

It was an absolute waste of a spot among the four hundred nominees, where a great film such as *The Princess Bride* could have and should have easily taken its place. It had a far greater shot of cracking the top one hundred. I'll wager that by mathematical standards, where the one hundredth ranked film on each ballot gets one point toward the final list, *Ferris Bueller's Day Off* only beat *The Princess Bride* by less than ten points. Considering that one eighty-ninth place finish on anyone of the fifteen hundred ballots would have garnered it eleven points, then it is a severe indictment on the decision making of the AFI panel for placing this movie among its four hundred nominees if I were correct. Unless they release the full list, complete with point totals, the world will never know.

Six movies from 1980 were given to the panel. Not one of them was the movie considered not only the funniest movie ever made, but also the movie that changed the face of comedy, *Airplane! Melvin and Howard* was chosen for inclusion, as was *Return of the Secaucus 7*, yet not *Airplane!* Do I even need to go into how wrong that decision was?

Other such movies that stand out as missing from the four hundred nominees are *Written on the Wind*, *The Lavender Hill Mob*, *The Man Who Shot Liberty Valence*, *Midnight Run*, *Searching For Bobby Fischer*, *The American President*, *The Ice Storm* and *Big Night*. These are just some of the notable omissions from the AFI list of four hundred, which the voting panel were forced to choose from. As rules are rules, I have compiled a list of the top one hundred, based upon their specific instructions.

MY RANKING OF THE TOP ONE HUNDRED FROM THE NOMINATED FILMS

1 - CASABLANCA
2 - RAIDERS OF THE LOST ARK
3 - GONE WITH THE WIND
4 - THE BRIDGE ON THE RIVER KWAI
5 - GOODFELLAS
6 - CITIZEN KANE
7 - IT'S A WONDERFUL LIFE
8 - ONE FLEW OVER THE CUCKOO'S NEST
9 - THE GODFATHER
10 - THE MANCHURIAN CANDIDATE
11 - PSYCHO
12 - RAGING BULL
13 - SUNSET BOULEVARD
14 - TO KILL A MOCKINGBIRD
15 - MIDNIGHT COWBOY
16 - BEAUTY AND THE BEAST
17 - THE GODFATHER II
18 - THE FUGITIVE
19 - THE GRAPES OF WRATH
20 - SCHINDLER'S LIST
21 - MR. SMITH GOES TO WASHINGTON
22 - THE THIRD MAN
23 - VERTIGO
24 - THE SHAWSHANK REDEMPTION
25 - THE WIZARD OF OZ
26 - REAR WINDOW
27 - THE STING
28 - FROM HERE TO ETERNITY
29 - TOUCH OF EVIL
30 - THE CONVERSATION
31 - THE MALTESE FALCON
32 - CHINATOWN
33 - NETWORK
34 - ON THE WATERFRONT
35 - HIGH NOON
36 - REBECCA
37 - REDS
38 - FIELD OF DREAMS
39 - TWELVE ANGRY MEN
40 - THE NIGHT OF THE HUNTER
41 - ROCKY
42 - FARGO
43 - BREAKING AWAY
44 - ALL THE PRESIDENT'S MEN
45 - NORTH BY NORTHWEST
46 - THE LAST PICTURE SHOW
47 - IN THE HEAT OF THE NIGHT
48 - DOUBLE INDEMNITY
49 - THE AWFUL TRUTH
50 - THE PHILADELPHIA STORY

51 - IT HAPPENED ONE NIGHT
52 - DOCTOR ZHIVAGO
53 - THE EMPIRE STRIKES BACK
54 - TERMS OF ENDEARMENT
55 - THE HUSTLER
56 - DELIVERANCE
57 - TAXI DRIVER
58 - THE FRENCH CONNECTION
59 - JAWS
60 - SOME LIKE IT HOT
61 - THE DEER HUNTER
62 - SHANE
63 - A NIGHT AT THE OPERA
64 - THE EXORCIST
65 - THE RIGHT STUFF
66 - HUD
67 - UNFORGIVEN
68 - DO THE RIGHT THING
69 - THE BIG SLEEP
70 - ALL ABOUT EVE
71 - THE WILD BUNCH
72 - AMADEUS
73 - THE THIN MAN
74 - FIVE EASY PIECES
75 - DUCK SOUP

76 - APOLLO 13
77 - THE SILENCE OF THE LAMBS
78 - DOG DAY AFTERNOON
79 - MY MAN GODFREY
80 - A MAN FOR ALL SEASONS
81 - DR. STRANGELOVE
82 - ORDINARY PEOPLE
83 - A CLOCKWORK ORANGE
84 - FORREST GUMP
85 - THE GOLD RUSH
86 - PULP FICTION
87 - BLAZING SADDLES
88 - THE DAY THE EARTH STOOD STILL
89 - THE APARTMENT
90 - STRANGERS ON A TRAIN
91 - ALL THE KING'S MEN
92 - THE BEST YEARS OF OUR LIVES
93 - BONNIE AND CLYDE
94 - ALL QUIET ON THE WESTERN FRONT
95 - TOY STORY
96 - THE ADVENTURES OF ROBIN HOOD
97 - KRAMER VS. KRAMER
98 - INTOLERANCE
99 - LAWRENCE OF ARABIA
100 - TREASURE OF THE SIERRA MADRE

Chapter Six:

The IMDB Top 250 List

Many of the lists ranking movies fail to appeal to the common fan because they are based upon too many background criteria. The everyday movie buff or even the fan of movies that tries to see everything out there for the joy of it often feels alienated by lists that are biased toward films holding deep significance or are technical marvels. The perfect example is *The Birth of a Nation*.

Ask a critic to give you their opinion of this film and you will more than likely receive some long diatribe about how this wretched movie shaped the way cinema would forever be shown. You may also get that its innovative, yet brief color sequence paved the way for everything from *The Wizard of Oz* and *Gone With the Wind* to *2001: A Space Odyssey* and the rock Opera *Tommy*. Without *The Birth of a Nation* we may still be watching black and white films, which is ludicrous to say and even more ridiculous to believe.

There are many films just like this that hold a much greater significance to the film critic than to the everyday movie fan. That is why the Internet Movie Database is such a fantastic website. Not only can anyone with access to a computer search the site and locate any movie they want but also learn what the movie is about, discuss the relevant or comparable points of the movie with others and vote on how good they think the movie is.

The Top 250 list from the Internet Movie Database, or IMDb, is different than almost any major list that ranks movies in a particular order. The specific ranking derives from website viewer's votes. If you like a film, rank it as a 10. If you think it was awful, rank it as a 1. For anything in between you have 8 selections to choose from. This process is how *The Shawshank Redemption* finally gained the notoriety it so richly deserved. What is the next film just like *The Shawshank Redemption* waiting to get a fan bump into a high ranking spot and get the word out to tens or hundreds of thousands of visitors out there to go and see it? Only time will tell.

This is why I have included the IMDb Top 250 list in this book, to not only compare it to my main list, but to also give the reader another list to discuss and debate the rankings of. This list is almost impossible to understand the specific methodology of, even though the website gives you the formula of how they arrive at a rating system. It is also an ever-changing list, based upon the voter's rankings. For this book I have used the Top 250 list from February 10th, 2006 at 8:04 PM EST.

#1 – *The Godfather*. #9 on main list. #3 on AFI list. Best Picture – 1972.

#2 – *The Shawshank Redemption*. #26 on main list.

#3 – *The Godfather II*. #19 on main list. #32 on AFI list. Best Picture – 1974.

#4 – *The Lord of the Rings: The Return of the King*. #16 on main list. Best Picture – 2003.

#5 – *The Seven Samurai* (Japan).

For some strange reason this film was one of the last of the Akira Kurosawa classics that I saw. By that time I had become a fan of his work, so it was surprising to me that I had not seen this film earlier because of its great impact on Western cinema. *The Seven Samurai* gave birth to the multiple hero movie, where a group of men stand up and fight to protect those who are less fortunate. Thinking back on it now, many of the movies I have enjoyed over the years were created as a result of the 1954 classic.

A group of marauding bandits return to one specific village to loot and steal the farmer's crops, leaving almost nothing for them to live on. The villagers hire a group of samurai warriors to protect their village from the bandits in return for food and lodging. The warriors work with the villagers and teach them how to protect themselves against the bandits that are set to return. When the final battle ensues, the entire village is now prepared to meet the bandits head on. A minor subplot, used as a means of explaining the traditional views of breaking the class system in sixteenth century Japan, is the burgeoning relationship between a farmer's daughter and one of the samurai.

Kurosawa takes great steps to develop the samurai characters so that the audience can understand their motivation. In contrast, the marauding bandits are hardly ever shown. Despite the battle scenes it is erroneous to call this an action movie. However, it could be correct to say it gave birth to the action/battle genre. Another fascinating statement that Kurosawa makes is that the samurai are actually the cause of their own troubles. One samurai who has moved up in class to this brand of warrior reflects that if it were not for the samurai, the villagers could live in peace. It is a shocking declaration that implies if things had gone differently in one way or the other these samurai may have become the bandits they now protect the villagers against. *The Seven Samurai* is one of the more touching action type movies I have ever seen, deserving of the status of classic.

#6 – *Schindler's List*. #22 on main list. #9 on AFI list. Best Picture – 1993.

#7 – *Casablanca*. #1 on main list. #2 on AFI list. Best Picture – 1943.

#8 – *Pulp Fiction*. #94 on AFI list.

#9 – *Star Wars: Episode IV – A New Hope*. #15 on AFI list.

#10 – *Star Wars: Episode V – The Empire Strikes Back*.

Better and more complete than the original in every single way, *The Empire Strikes Back* is singularly responsible for creating the legend of *Star Wars*. Advancing the half story offered in episode four, this amazing movie begins on a frozen ice world with a great battle sequence and does not stop gathering momentum. Every innovative technical breakthrough attempted in the original was duplicated and advanced upon in the sequel, yet the key to the magnificence of *The Empire Strikes Back* is that the story begins to make sense as the characters are finally developed properly. The 1977 film failed to even attempt that.

Interesting characters are a vital element to every story. In that respect, *The Empire Strikes Back* does not disappoint. Han Solo's former gambling buddy Lando Calrissian and the true evil mastermind behind the empire, the Emperor, are introduced in this installment of the trilogy, both central to the further development of the story. This film chooses to stress key plot elements over solely concentrating on wondrous special effects. There is Luke's training under the old Jedi master Yoda, another great new character, Han Solo and Leia's budding relationship, their betrayal at the hands of Lando, Han Solo frozen in liquid carbonite and taken to Jabba the Hut by the mechanistic bounty hunter Boba Fett and the battle between Luke and Vader. That final battle of the film between Luke and Vader is where the most shocking and best known cinematic secret is revealed.

The Empire Strikes Back is the perfect balance between the two films of the original trilogy. As a film on its own it has no equal when compared to any of the five other installments of the *Star Wars* double trilogy. Not one of those five movies comes close to it as *The Empire Strikes Back* combines all the technical greatness of the first film with all the necessary story and character development required to create a lasting masterpiece. If I ever get a craving to watch a movie from this series there is never any question as to which movie I reach for. If the reader of this book were so inclined to actually try and decipher what film was #60 on the main list, all educated bets might lean toward this one. I am not saying that is correct, but I am also not saying it is not.

#11 – *The Good, The Bad and The Ugly* (Italy).

Akira Kurosawa created the movie that gave birth to the Spaghetti Western. Those Sergio Leone Spaghetti Westerns gave birth to the super stardom of Clint Eastwood. In retrospect, one could argue that Hilary Swank owes her second Oscar to Akira Kurosawa. As far as the Spaghetti Westerns go though, *The Good, The Bad and the Ugly* is far and away the best of the three films in that genre that helped launch Eastwood's career.

A cash box holding $200,000 is sought after by three men. Each one of these men comes into the information that the money exists on their own, with two of them holding specific keys to where it is located. There is Tuco, a murderous villain who has committed more crimes than there are laws against. A bounty on his head brings him into a partnership with Eastwood, once again playing 'The Man With No Name', although Tuco refers to him as Blondie. Tuco is double crossed by Eastwood on their partnership and he exacts his revenge. This is how those two come into the information about the money. Then there is Angel Eyes, meaner than both of them put together. He forces Tuco to reveal what he knows. Ultimately, there is a final showdown where the money is hidden away.

Much has been made as to whether or not the three films, *The Good, The Bad and the Ugly*, *A Fistful of Dollars* and *For A Few Dollars More* are a trilogy. They are. These three films are packaged as such, were marketed as such and therefore are definitely three parts of a complete whole. That having been said, the further question arises as to whether or not Eastwood plays the same character in all three films. That is a much tougher question to answer. He is called something different in all three films, yet three different men give those names to him. Not once does he refer to himself by any one of those three names. He is simply known as *'The Man With No Name'*. That would mean that he does play the same character in all three movies, yet the character may not be the same person, if that makes any sense. The character is a symbol, not merely a recurring person.

#12 – *One Flew Over the Cuckoo's Nest.* #8 on main list. #20 on AFI list. Best Picture – 1975

#13 – *The Lord of the Rings: The Fellowship of the Ring.*

Another trilogy that made its indelible mark upon cinema began with this first installment. Although not the beginning of the story, with that distinction going to the short story *The Hobbit*, this film picks up where that cute, almost childish fairy tale left off and enters into an adult tale of magic, wonder and amazement. Once again there is the fantastic combination of technical wonder without sacrificing character and plot development, as was the case with *The Empire Strikes Back*.

It was long thought that the massive J.R.R. Tolkien fantasy novel could not be transferred over to the cinematic realm. There were far too many characters, immense battles, grand locations and nuances within the story that could not be filmed accurately enough to do it justice. That stood in the way of making a live action adaptation. An animated version of the story was tried, but failed miserably. That failure further solidified the idea that a live action version could never work. Boy was that concept flawed. This excellent movie, only bettered in quality by *A Beautiful Mind* from 2001, perfectly sets the tone for one of the greatest stories ever told.

The Fellowship of the Ring showed how a group of warriors, regardless of size, could work together for one common cause, conquering the forces of evil. Even though their strength and resolve were strong their will ultimately failed and the fellowship was broken. Peter Jackson continued that magic with the second installment and topped all expectations with the amazing third and final film to complete the trilogy. Movie fans everywhere should be immensely grateful and thankful to Jackson for even attempting such a challenging feat. His success opens the door for anything to come. That kind of influence will be felt within cinema for the next half century.

#14 – *Rear Window*. #28 on main list. #42 on AFI list.

#15 – *The Lord of the Rings: The Two Towers*.

Continuing upon the great success of the first installment *The Fellowship of the Ring*, *The Two Towers* was another fantastic spectacle of cinema. The side stories are more prevalent in this installment than in the first, which present an added dimension to the story and how it continues to develop. The hook for this movie is how the brilliant story from the first will continue. In that aspect, this middle segment of the story succeeds as more important elements to the story are introduced.

As the audience learns numerous secrets about the characters this makes their immensely difficult journey that more alluring to watch. *The Two Towers* does not repeat the success of the first film and comes nowhere close to the final effort of the trilogy. As that final installment ranked #16 on the main list of movie excellence, it is tough to match that movie's greatness. *The Two Towers* was a fine film and a nice bridge between the interesting setup of the first and the sheer magnificence of the third. I thoroughly enjoyed the movie, yet I place it as the least enjoyable of the three.

In comparison to another film that was the middle segment of a trilogy, it is not as good of a movie based upon individual merit. The problem with *The Two Towers* is that the two movies that bookend it were of such great splendor that this middle segment becomes overshadowed to a certain extent. That came nowhere close to happening with *The Empire Strikes Back*. In actuality, it is not that *The Two Towers* is so much lesser of a movie than *The Empire Strikes Back*. Their similarities shall always draw comparisons and the circumstances surrounding both trilogies decidedly lean toward *The Empire Strikes Back* greatly overshadowing *The Two Towers*. Truth be told, it is a better film than *The Two Towers* though, as almost everyone who has seen both films readily admits.

#16 – *City of God* (Brazil).

When you see a movie that is based upon actual events you immediately wonder how much of the story is embellished and how much actually took place. That doesn't change the cinematic experience. In fact, stories that are based upon real events are often more real in their depiction of life, even though that may come off as sounding strange. Of course they are more real than if it was fiction, but to know that the events you are watching took place does heighten the cinematic experience. *City of God* is one of those experiences.

Rocket lives in the slums known as the '*City of God*', a ghetto outside of Rio de Janeiro, Brazil. His brother Goose belongs to a gang called the Tender Trio, along with Shaggy and Shorty.

They allow a younger hood to hang around with them because he is brave. His name is Lil Dice and he will grow up to become one of the biggest lords in the slums, taking the name Lil Ze. The Tender Trio split up after a major crime, where Lil Dice stands as lookout. That leads to two of their deaths. Rocket grows up he wants to be a photographer, yet lives in a slum that is torn apart by two rival gangs run by Lil Ze and Carrot. More characters are brought in including Knockout Ned and the Runts to finish the perfect arc of the story in dynamic style. Only photography will get Rocket out.

City of God is one of the bravest and moving films I've seen. It is unique when a story flows so well throughout and winds up finishing perfectly. The scenery of the harsh slums of Rio de Janeiro serves as a fantastic backdrop for this story of poverty, crime and hope. The movie has that Tarantino feel to it mixed together with a moving emotional drama. The action is crisp and the acting is even better. Each of the characters are unique in their own way and the director takes the requisite time to develop them rather than use them as a plot sacrifice when other stories would normally come to a complete stop. The filmmakers did a fantastic job of showing us how basic human themes exist everywhere.

#17 – *The Usual Suspects*.

Pulp Fiction helped reinvent the crime drama. It also gave birth to the appeal for the gang caper, where a group of interesting criminals were put on display for the audience to root for. One year after *Pulp Fiction* hit the screens and created a mega-buzz in the industry a small film came out and put the stakes up a notch. Most people will say I am insane to say that *The Usual Suspects* is a better film than its obvious predecessor, but that is why I discuss film, because everyone's opinion is valid in its own way. I enjoy this movie much more than *Pulp Fiction*.

Following a group of five criminals who band together to pull a few jobs, the story is truly the star of the film. It is told in a non-linear style, similar to every Tarantino film, yet one ups that by creating two separate stories at the same time. What many people miss about the movie is that there is the actual tale of events as the police unfold them and there are the series of events as relayed by the character of Verbal Kint. Once you know the true secret of the film, which many know by now, you should understand that Kint's entire story is filled with half-truths and manipulations. After he is released the movie shows that Kint is lying, but he is doing so much more than that. That is the beauty of the film, how amazing Kint is in doing what he just did. His actions show that the evil villain Keyser Soze is truly unstoppable.

When I first saw this film I was amazed at the finale. The action and the development of the story throughout were fantastic, but it is that ending that hooks you in. The last five minutes of the film, the twist, perfectly works within the entire scope of the film. It is beyond unpredictable, but also provides an added dimension to an already great movie. Strictly as a caper film it is incredibly stylistic and enjoyable, yet that brilliant twist allows *The Usual Suspects* to reach another level. It is one of those films that you wish you could go back and see for the first time all over again. That always indicates how great of a cinematic experience this film was.

#18 – *Dr. Strangelove*. #26 on AFI list. Best movie - 1964

#19 – *Raiders of the Lost Ark*. #2 on main list. #60 on AFI list.

#20 – *Twelve Angry Men*. #42 on main list.

#21 – *Citizen Kane*. #6 on main list. #1 on AFI list.

#22 – *Memento*.

Everything that could be done within cinema had already been done by the time this movie hit the screens. There were no new idea concepts waiting to be unleashed upon the audience so the majority of material was merely old stuff given a new look. That is perhaps one of the reasons why classics of cinema have been remade in recent years, because filmmakers are giving up any attempt at originality. Someone forgot to tell that to the creator of *Memento*.

Memento follows the story of a man who suffers from short-term memory loss. He is actively seeking out the man or men who have murdered his wife. Along the way there are a couple of characters who know his situation and help him, for their own benefit as is eventually revealed. What makes this story so original is that it is told entirely backwards. The beginning of the film is actually the end of what we have seen. The beauty is that it will now be a new beginning. The more the story goes forward, or backward, the more is explained. That invariably leads to further questions. It is a mystery, yet told in such a manner that even though information is revealed the method of how this information is useful becomes the mystery. When the film finally ends, a revelation of what took place and why explains the entirety of this mysterious story.

The beauty of this film is in the way it is depicted upon screen. The staging of a backward story such as this has never been attempted before, to my knowledge. A system such as this could have imploded in the face of the filmmakers, yet the story kept it all in place. Too often movies like this have major plot holes, but this movie works on every level and kept me focused throughout. The first time I saw it in the theater there was a standing ovation. I don't give standing ovations because the actors can't hear me, but this movie came as close as any other before it to deserving one.

#23 – *Once Upon a Time in the West* (Italy).

There is a word to describe this film. It is only one word but it perfectly sums up the whole movie. That word is anticipation. Few movies today have that effect upon the viewer. They are generally in a rush to get to that ultimate showdown of good versus evil. Often times the movie becomes somewhat forced as a result. This movie typifies that difference. The story develops almost as a whodunit, leading up to that final showdown that the entire movie is based upon.

The expansion of the West serves as backdrop for this amazing story. The railroad is continuing westward. One rancher, McBain, has bought property in the hopes of building a town for his new bride and family. The man in black, Frank, has different plans. Frank viciously murders McBain and his family so he can take the land. The land will be worth millions once the railroad moves through it. The deed is signed over to McBain's new bride though, who now becomes sought after by Frank, a gunman named Cheyenne and a mysterious stranger called Harmonica. The woman's charms work on Frank and Cheyenne, although Frank is smart enough to find out who she really is, or was. Harmonica is different. Everything he does has a purpose. His goal is to setup a showdown with Frank to settle an old score that not even Frank understands the significance of until it is too late.

Once Upon a Time in the West is the best of the four Leone Spaghetti Westerns. This is the only one not to star Clint Eastwood, yet that theme of a villain dressed in black and a mysterious man with no name is present in this tale as well. In comparison, Charles Bronson's anti-hero is much more textured than the general character played by Eastwood. Both men have intriguing and dark pasts, yet the perfect pacing of this film makes Bronson's character the more dangerous and more interesting one. Leone has exceeded the quality of what were definitively three great films, culminated by the best of that lot. This film is a monumental epic and one of the best Westerns ever.

#24 – *Psycho*. #11 on main list. #18 on AFI list.

#25 – *Goodfellas*. #5 on main list. #95 on AFI list.

#26 – *North by Northwest*. #?? on main list. #40 on AFI list.

#27 – *Amelie* (France).

When I first saw this film, I was immediately reminded of Audrey Hepburn in *Roman Holiday*, yet with a touch of her in *Breakfast at Tiffany's* as well. The lead actress, Audrey Tautou, handles the material with such style and grace that barring any unforeseen circumstances I see her becoming a major star, even one that can crossover into English language films. Usually I remark that the story and material define a movie, yet Tautou steals the show here.

Amelie is a young woman living in Paris. She is particularly attentive to those around her, trying to help out as much as possible. The trick is that she helps in a subtle and unique way so as not to get noticed or thanked for what she is doing. She feels the necessity to help people to make herself feel better as a person, yet realizes she will likely end up alone. Her excursions around town include fantastic intrigue regarding a picture booth, taking pictures with a gnome and finding love.

Amelie is such a sweet and funny movie that I try to watch it every month or so. It is one of those films that can liven up your day no matter how bad or even how good the day is. My favorite part of this film was her work with the gnome. The look on her father's face as he keeps receiving pictures of his gnome visiting far out exotic locales is priceless. It is by far the best part of the movie and perfectly sums up her unselfish nature. When she finally finds happiness you know that it is deserved. Far too often in films people get together and it is anti-climactic. That does not happen in this great film. *Amelie* is a magical film that is guaranteed to bring a smile to your face.

#28 – *The Silence of the Lambs*. #65 on AFI list. Best Picture – 1991

#29 – *Lawrence of Arabia*. #5 on AFI list. Best Picture – 1962

#30 – *It's A Wonderful Life*. #7 on main list. #11 on AFI list.

#31 – *Sunset Boulevard*. #13 on main list. #12 on AFI list.

#32 – *American Beauty*. Best Picture – 1999

#33 – *Fight Club*.

Who wouldn't love a movie about soap? The director of such bizarrely claustrophobic films such as *The Game* and *Se7en*, David Fincher, creates another fantastic piece of cinema with *Fight Club*. One could even describe this film as *The Game* meets *Se7en*, with all the necessary paranoiac elements from the former and all the brutality and discovery of the latter combined. Based upon the Chuck Palahnuik novel, Fincher's directorial vision sets this movie apart from almost anything previously seen. It is at times overly masculine in its depiction, yet also incredibly sensitive or almost feminine when dealing with issues of personality.

An ordinary employee from a car company has trouble with insomnia. His life is meaningless until he finds an outlet that allows him to sleep, attending group meetings where people share their feelings about their problems. As time goes by the meeting are not enough. With the help of a new friend, Tyler Durden, this man is finally able to properly unleash his inner demons by bare knuckle fighting with other men who have the similar issues and are looking for something more. Soon, the fighting is not enough. All that is left are acts of anarchy and terrorism, that next step in allowing emotions to run wild and handle your problems. The narrator sees the problem with this and attempts to stop Tyler and the legion of followers that he has formed. There is only one problem with trying to stop Tyler Durden. Those who don't know the problem should see this movie.

Fight Club is often seen as a movie that only men would enjoy. The barbaric fights that are exhibited within have drawn negative criticism and are viewed as a plot element trying to distinguish itself from movies that generally have a more balanced tone. That could not be further from the truth. The macho aspects in *Fight Club* are essential to the arc of the story, while they are extremely enjoyable to watch, they serve a purpose that goes beyond chauvinism. The people who ascribe to *Fight Club* as too violent for their tastes simply do not understand the story. Life is violent and the fighting within this movie is used as a metaphor for that, showing how it is often cathartic to release one's anger yet that is never enough. I love this film and it is not merely because of the fighting or the violence, but because it uses those aspects properly within the framework of a great story.

#34 – *The Matrix*.

Keanu Reeves knows Kung Fu. Immediately the movie became somewhat of an inside joke. Most saw that tagline or heard that declaration from the commercials promoting the upcoming film and thought the worst. I was definitely in that category. A *Bill and Ted's Excellent Adventure – Kung Fu Style* was not out of the realm of possibility. No one really knew what to expect. After audiences flocked to see *The Matrix*, no one could deny the force that it struck with. I was also in that category, watching with eyes glued to the screen wondering what was to come next.

Although the film is obviously an homage to Jesus and his followers as laid out in the New Testament, *The Matrix* is more about the amazingly innovative fight scenes. The hand to hand combat battles were enough of a spectacle to fully ignore the nonsensical attempts at allegorical implications and simply sit back and enjoy the film for what it was, an astonishing array of action thrusted at the audience. The development of an amazing technical effect, what has been deemed *'bullet time'*, adds to the splendor of the film, providing images that have never been seen anywhere before. The visual aspect of the film is one of its greatest traits, yet their interesting take on an overly used mythological theme helps the film along during the intervals between amazing fights.

Easily one of the most awe-inspiring cinematic experiences I have ever been witness to, *The Matrix* succeeded where many films similar to it have failed. It perfectly blended a unique story and visionary cinematic technology to create a complete film. It comes nowhere close to the literary prowess of the Biblical allegory it works out from, yet this movie should be enjoyed for what it truly is, plain cinematic fun. The failure of the two sequels that followed was as a result of taking itself too seriously. There are moments however, most notably the thirty minute fight/highway chase sequence in the second installment, *The Matrix Reloaded*, which outdoes any single sequence from the original.

#35 – *Eternal Sunshine of the Spotless Mind*.

Charlie Kaufman is at it once again. The brilliantly creative mind of writer Charlie Kaufman created another wholly original story, one that has never been done or seen before. He succeeds with this amazing story. One has to wonder if the well is ever going to run dry for Kaufman. As a writer myself I believe the answer to that is absolutely not, because there are always more stories out there waiting to be told. I sincerely hope that Kaufman does not corner the market on them all until I get my chance.

Describing this movie is almost futile, but there are a couple of basics that can be offered. A woman decides to have her memory erased. A company has developed a special procedure where they can isolate and erase specific unwanted memories. This company promotes itself as having the ability to erase a bad relationship from a person's mind. The woman, Clementine, has already had the procedure done. Once her ex-boyfriend finds out about it he decides to do the same. Nothing is ever easy, as the story encompasses flashbacks of their relationship, to the two of them strangely meeting and falling for each other again after both procedures have been done. Once they are back together both discover that they were together before and had these procedures done. The question now arises of whether they should part or is their love strong enough to withstand the erasure.

Eternal Sunshine of the Spotless Mind is the most insane and unique love story I have ever seen on film. Once again I am not sure how Charlie Kaufman comes up with this material but I applaud him and sincerely hope he continues striving for even more original material. Walking out of the theater after seeing this film I believed that this film would gather an audience of followers one day and become a major classic. As it is ranked so highly on this list by voters I see that has already started. *Adaptation* is a better film, yet this film is not far behind it. I cannot wait to see what Kaufman has in store for us next.

#36 – *Vertigo*. #25 on main list. #61 on AFI list.

#37 – *Apocalypse Now*. #28 on AFI list.

#38 – *Paths of Glory*.

Anti-war films got their start with the great picture from 1930, *All Quiet on the Western Front*. The way war could be depicted was forever changed after that daring film, which paved the way for movies such as *Paths of Glory*. Co-written and directed by Stanley Kubrick, this film has that unique Kubrick signature. It plays as if there are two separate movies going on, one in the beginning, where the actual horrors of battle and futility of war is showcased and the story the film ends with, a mockery of justice due to politics rather than integrity.

A tyrannical General is given command of a group of French soldiers during World War I. He visits the trenches where the battle rages and the effects are present upon the faces of the soldiers under his command. The General does not care for weakness, instructing the leader of the troops, a Colonel played by Kirk Douglas, to advance out of the trenches and capture a region currently held by the enemy. It is a suicide mission, yet the Colonel is forced to try. When his soldiers refuse to advance against a barrage of fire the General, watching the battle safely inside a covered area from their original position, orders his own men to be fired upon for not advancing and capturing the intended target. When they refuse to fire on their own men the General threatens to court martial everyone involved for cowardice. This is where the trenches are left and a pseudo-courtroom battle ensues, with the Colonel defending his troops on the charge of mutiny and cowardice. Examples are made and they are executed by firing squad. The film ends with Douglas' character taking over for the General, who does not understand the erroneous nature of his actions.

Called the greatest anti-war film ever made, I must disagree with that statement. If it were known as a shining example of pomposity and regality of those placed in high command then I would wholeheartedly agree. This movie shows the difference between theory and practice, highlighting the insanity of leaders who use war as an excuse for glory rather than actively using their intellect to understand and examine the horrors of the battlefield. Once again, Kubrick chooses to tell two stories and attempts to blend them into one cohesive whole. To be honest, this is as close as he has ever come to unified success. Still, this movie is a touch overrated. Those who disagree should watch *All Quiet on the Western Front* again or even the 1978 film *Coming Home*, both of which are superior.

#39 – *Taxi Driver*. #47 on AFI list.

#40 – *To Kill A Mockingbird*. #14 on main list. #34 on AFI list.

#41 – *Spirited Away* (Japan).

Japanese anime became somewhat of an art form, stemming from the cult status of the 1988 blockbuster *Akira*. With the success and fanfare of that film, the envelope continued to be pushed as to what could be done. The problem – the story here is absolutely ridiculous. It is as if Akira Kurosawa brainstormed the story on an acid trip and the Brothers Grimm met an unfrozen and pissed off Walt Disney and Tim Burton for lunch at a Mexican restaurant serving only beans and ecstasy. What I am getting at is that there is no point here at all.

Chihiro is a ten-year-old girl who is unhappy about moving to the suburbs. On the drive to the new house her parents are diverted to what they believe is an abandoned amusement park. They enter through a tunnel, with an apprehensive Chihiro behind them. As the parents sit to eat Chihiro looks around. She returns to find that her parents have transformed into giant pigs and that she is in some mystical other world. Chihiro must work at a bathhouse for spirits run by an evil troll/woman creature to prove her worth. The little girl surprises everyone with her bravery eventually winning back the freedom of her parents and herself, with a lot of nonsensical imagery shown on the screen.

The point of the *Spirited Away* is that children are ill mannered and spoiled as a result of the evolution of culture, I guess. The writer/director, Hayao Miyazaki, is a legend in Japanese animated cinema. This film however, which some consider his crowning achievement in film, is all over the road. I have read the message boards regarding this film and do not understand how this movie can be considered great. I could see where someone might think it was good, maybe, but nowhere near great. The equivalent of saying this movie was great is like saying Hitler did some good things. If you search hard enough you can find greatness in anything. I thought the movie, as far as movies go, was utterly awful. That is regardless of the social commentary *Spirited Away* attempts to make.

#42 – *The Pianist*.

My opinions regarding Roman Polanski were made known during my analysis of *Chinatown*. Whether your opinions regarding Polanski's personal life affects your own attitude of his work then that is something you have to rationalize for yourself. I abhor the man as a human, if one could call a man of forty whom sexually preys upon a teenager a human, but I cannot deny the quality of his work. *The Pianist* is among Roman Polanski's best work.

Wladyslaw Szpilman is the greatest pianist in Poland, perhaps in Europe and perhaps even the world. He is a Jew though and the Germans are coming to invade. Szpilman and his family struggle to stay together as the Germans move them from their house into assigned Jewish ghettos, indiscriminately slapping, spitting on and shooting any Jews they see fit. Szpilman is lucky enough to have a reputation as a brilliant pianist, which saves him from going to the concentration camps through the intervention of a Jewish police officer. Now the story turns to one of extreme survival for Szpilman, where he goes days at a time without eating. Only through the last minute help of a sympathetic German officer is Szpilman able to survive and later return to his career as a pianist.

The Pianist is a remarkable story of courage and survival in the face of tremendous adversity. Polanski does not hold back in depicting the carnage that was the German occupation of Poland during the second World War. Incredibly emotional scenes are on display, including a full screen view with a panning back of the destroyed buildings reduced to rubble that was the Polish Jewish ghetto. Adrien Brody is amazing in his nuanced performance and was rewarded with a well-deserved Oscar for Best Actor. Polanski won for Best Director but was unable to attend for obvious reasons. How this film lost the Best Picture Oscar to *Chicago* is beyond me. This year will go down as one of the all-time great Oscar disparities, with both *Adaptation* and *The Pianist* as far better films than the actual winner.

#43 – *Se7en*.

David Fincher made a name for himself with this stylish murder mystery. Coming off the deplorable *Alien 3*, Fincher was given an amazing script by first time screenwriter Andrew Kevin Walker and crafted a fine film adaptation of Walker's dark story. It was a cross between mystery, suspense and horror, although only classified as a horror film because of some of the gruesome images depicted on screen. The film plays on many levels, including adding a new twist to the buddy cop movie. In retrospect *Se7en* defies any genre classification. It is merely a fantastic film that kept getting better the further it delved into the unique story.

Two police officers, the soon to be retiring Sommerset and the newcomer taking over his spot, Mills, begin investigating a series of murders. When they discover that the murders are not only connected, but also committed with a purpose in mind, they form an unlikely bond of pseudo-friendship while working the case. Sommerset is the aged veteran, weary to the awful ways of the world, while Mills is the wide eyed and hardnosed field cop, always looking to jump in to battle. They are perfect opposites, yet work together for the benefit of the case. The murders keep coming, evocative of the seven deadly sins, which are planned that way by the murderer for what he believes will be his masterwork. As they get closer to the end it becomes clear that the two detectives, specifically Mills, are an integral part of the murderer's plan.

The movie is set in an unnamed city. The locale is gloomy and for the most part there is continuous rain. That atmosphere perfectly landscapes the story as a whole. Sommerset and Mills are a major part of this world, as is the killer. When his masterwork is completed it is evocative of the world with which he lives in. Although some do not like the surprise ending, I believe that *Se7en* is one of the most perfectly crafted thrillers I have seen. There are almost no wasted moments in the film. The minor upbeat segments are quickly disintegrated by the return of an ominously planned murder or an even worse revelation. I do not watch this movie as often as I should, because of the depressed outlook, yet even the simple writing of this paragraph has made me want to see it again. It is that good of a movie.

#44 – *The Professional.*

French director Luc Besson earned his cinematic standing with the 1990 assassin film *La Femme Nikita*. That movie had a distinctive brilliance that made it unique. As with almost everything that is original Hollywood saw an opportunity to mass market it and Besson was paid to write an Americanized version of what is often considered his classic masterpiece. The end product was the film *Point of No Return*. That film lacked all originality and only made viewers long for *La Femme Nikita*. The only interesting material in that film was the introduction of the character known as 'the Cleaner'. That character is what *The Professional* is based upon.

Leon is a hit man. He is one of the best. The problem is that he lives his work. That aspect of his life never bothered him until crooked policemen murder his neighbors. He acts quickly enough to save the neighbor's twelve-year-old girl from suffering the same fate. The two of them, both children in a way, develop a bond of friendship. Besson attempts to move their relationship toward love. It is a subtle subplot yet one that fully explains why Roman Polanski fled to France after he was arrested in America for what he did. That element of the story did not transfer from French culture well, yet the awesome action and assassination scenes are what make this movie such a treat to watch.

Jean Reno, as Leon, provides an exceptional reserved performance, realizing there is something more to life than simply his work. The style with which he operates highlights this extraordinarily enjoyable film. Gary Oldman as the crooked DEA officer creates another character out of the realm of the ordinary into a world of the unbelievable, while Natalie Portman would have to wait until 1996 to give her star making performance. She is merely used as perverted and felonious window dressing to try and show that love is blind to age. People who enjoy this movie are those who love it for the ultra cool and fast assassinations. The attempt at a cohesive story is not enough to support Besson's ability to create highly stylistic action elements, so the story merely and clumsily gets in the way of those scenes. *The Fifth Element* is similar in its specific failure.

#45 – *The Third Man.* #24 on main list. #57 on AFI list.

#46 – *Downfall* (Germany).

There have been numerous stories about what happened to Adolph Hitler at the end of World War II. There was actually a document offered to the public in 1983, but that proved to be a hoax soon afterward. The legend lived on. What actually happened during Hitler's last days in an underground bunker after the war was coming to an end? What if someone who was in the bunker during the last days decided to reveal the events that transpired?

Based on the book by Traudl Junge, Hitler's personal secretary from 1942 until the final days of the war, *Downfall* begins with Junge's introduction to Hitler as she is chosen to be his new secretary out of five women. The film quickly cuts to April of 1945 when the war has turned against the Germans. Hitler has retreated to the underground bunker to prepare for what must be done, surrounded by men who have pledged their lives to his cause. They are beginning to see that he has lost his mind to a degree. While many of them can accept that the war is over, Hitler still believes there is hope. There are some who refuse to go on living and decide to take the coward's way out. Without a full victory, these men and women believe that life is not worth living, including Hitler.

Downfall is an amazing tale of what went on in the mind of a madman as his plans failed and were coming apart around him. The kind of maniacal insanity possessed by Hitler and many of his loyal followers provides an example of how people of weak minds can be recruited and brainwashed for any cause, if the leader is proficient enough to rally them around his ideas. The film is slow paced but perfect for this type of story. These were the final moments of an evil beast and as such needed this precise kind of presentation. The subject matter is not pleasant but is historical. *Downfall* is a film that is definitely worth seeing, if only to realize how events like this could have happened.

#47 – *Chinatown*. #35 on main list. #19 on AFI list.

#48 – *The Boat* (West Germany).

Director Wolfgang Peterson is more known for his films *In the Line of Fire*, *Air Force One*, *Troy* and the highly underrated *Outbreak*. Peterson had directed a number of films, mostly on television, before he finally got noticed as a director of merit. *Das Boot* is the film that introduced him to the world. Peterson plans to come full circle in 2006 with the upcoming release of the remake of *The Poseidon Adventure*, cleverly titled *Poseidon*.

Life aboard a German u-boat is at times monotonous. The beginning of the story spends its time getting to know the crew while they are waiting for their orders. There is also the element of how they feel about each other and their mission. When the action starts the film takes on a whole new level, yet never sacrifices the characters for submarine thriller clichés. These characters have the same worries that have been presented in other submarine films, with *Crimson Tide* and *Run Silent, Run Deep* coming to mind. The visual style of the film is what separates *Das Boot* from the rest. The underwater battle is a fantastic sight to see, although it takes awhile to finally get going.

Das Boot is a cinematic epic in every way. It never gets boring even when it delves into the depths of a character. That to me is part of its charm and allure. The temptation to make the film an all out action thriller was there, yet that would have made it like all the others. In Perterson's Hollywood films he generally focuses on the action as the focal point of the film. From those few that I mentioned in the first paragraph I would recommend *Outbreak* above the others, simply because it is the one that most closely resembles *Das Boot*. I would watch *Das Boot* over *Outbreak*.

#49 – *Hotel Rwanda*.

The African civil wars have been going on for centuries. Every single country of that continent has had some version of a civil war, whether it be tribal or recently through the advent of modernized weaponry and colonization. Where there are differing cultures in close proximity there will always be struggles and conflict. The lack of education does not help. What went on in Rwanda in 1994 between those loyal to the original colonizing European country and those who were not, drove wedge between families and caused the death of over one million people. The true story of one brave man stands out as a bastion of hope, flying directly in the face of utter despair surrounding that uncivilized country and the unspeakable actions committed.

Hotel manager Paul Rusesabagina is excellent at his job. He knows the ins and outs of the hotel industry, how to manipulate the system for the betterment of the hotel. In war torn Rwanda, life becomes endangered as the civil war escalates beyond control. Paul remains at the hotel with his wife, his family and hundreds of refugees that he has saved from execution using whatever favors and goods he possesses to keep them alive until help finally arrives. Forced to leave the hotel for necessary supplies, Paul sees the horrific carnage on the streets, littered with bodies from the massacres that are happening. Paul must stay strong for his family, but in a private moment breaks down at the horror. Finally he is able to get his family to safety. In the process he saved hundreds of fellow countrymen from execution in the process. Despite saving his own neck he is every bit a hero.

Hotel Rwanda is an amazing movie. The fact that it is based upon true events makes it that tougher to watch. Jamie Foxx took home a Best Actor Oscar for his performance in the admirable biopic *Ray*, yet the scene where Don Cheadle, who plays Paul, breaks down from what he has seen in the streets should have warranted the Oscar on that scene alone. His performance is the beauty of the movie, which is a story clouded in horror. Not the kind of movie that can be watched over and over again, yet Cheadle's performance is something that should be witnessed by every fan of cinema. It was what got me through the dreadful nature of the events depicted within this film.

#50 – *Requiem for a Dream.*

The first film from writer/director Darren Aronofsky was such a brilliant piece of material examining the mental condition as it borders on the insanity of brilliance. Can someone be too brilliant for his or her own good? That is how I viewed his first feature, *Pi*. His next effort is another exploration, although extremely different than *Pi*. *Requiem for a Dream* is an exploration into drug addiction and the lengths at which one will go to feed that beast.

The story follows the lives of four people who become addicted to drugs for a variety of reasons. They are all connected in some manner, yet the story does not go through that painstaking process of creating an epic mosaic in order to relate a common bond between these characters. Harry and Marion are a happy couple. They are even happier when they get their heroin fix. To complicate matters they devise a plan, with Harry's friend Tyrone, to start selling heroin in order to start a legitimate business. The drug abuse takes over their lives though. All three of them will do almost anything for that next fix, including a scene with Jennifer Connelly that borders on pornographic. Harry's mother becomes addicted to speed in order to lose weight and the audience is shown that addiction, specifically drug addiction, can take hold of anyone regardless of their age.

I saw this film for two reasons. I thought *Pi* was an outstanding story and one of the bravest most ingenuous films I have ever seen, and Connelly is about the hottest woman on the planet. I was disappointed in the fact that *Requiem for a Dream* could not capture the brilliance of *Pi*, yet for anyone who thinks the same of Connelly as I do then I highly recommend it. This film is more about individual performances than about story cohesion or entertainment. Ellen Burstyn earned a well-deserved Oscar nomination for playing a mother who becomes addicted to diet pills, yet the rest of the cast seems to be going through the motions. Perhaps that is just in comparison to the magnificent performance of Burstyn. I half-heartedly recommend this film, yet I strongly urge everyone to see *Pi*.

#51 – *American History X*. Best movie - 1998

#52 – *Monty Python and the Holy Grail*.

One of the beautiful things about religious mythology is that the stories are so far out there that they are perfect fodder for parody. The famous British comedy troupe Monty Python knew that and created what is considered their classic film farce. Taking the most basic of Christian themes to that utmost level of comedy has garnered this film as one of the funniest ever made. Their take on the events of history are a sight to behold.

King Arthur and his Knights of the round table set out on a quest to discover the holy grail. What ensues after that is an exercise in both futility and hilarity. Each of the Knights encounter strange creatures that have become synonymous with the legend of this film, including horny nuns, a killer rabbit, the Knights that say *"Ni"* and the fearsome yet thoroughly inept Black Knight. I was not a huge fan of Monty Python, yet this movie is pretty funny. If you are not into British humor, you can still get some enjoyment out of this movie, yet be prepared for a sketch style of comedy taken to the cinematic level, which does not always work as well as it should. In this case it did.

#53 – *Million Dollar Baby*. Best Picture - 2004

#54 – *The Maltese Falcon*. #34 on main list. #23 on AFI list.

#55 – *M* (German).

Known as the 'Düsseldorf Vampire', serial killer Peter Kurten was caught during the middle of 1930, sentenced to death and executed for his crimes in 1931. That same year, director Fritz Lang released *M*, a story loosely based upon the exploits of Kurten. This was Lang's first talking picture. A master of German expressionism, Lang reveals a city held in terror where even the criminals cannot function properly due to the rash of child murders. In crafting this story, Lang reveals a dualistic nature of crime unseen in cinema today.

Once a number of young girls go missing and are found dead, a city turns to chaos as a child murderer is hunted. Due to the massive police search for the child killer Beckert, the regular criminal activity of the underworld cannot go on as normal. The criminals band together to hunt for the killer as a result. One of them finds him walking with a child, marking his back with a white chalk M so he can be followed. Beckert discovers this and flees from the young girl, knowing that he has been found out. He escapes into a gated building where he finds himself trapped. He is cornered, found and taken down into an abandoned basement by the criminals to stand trial.

The entire finale in the basement is absolutely brilliant where the criminal syndicate and the townsfolk confront Beckert. The syndicate commits their crimes because they are selfish, yet Beckert kills because of impulses he cannot control. It is an amazing treatise on criminality, with two distinctly different types of criminals to counter balance. Lang's use of sound and editing was extremely visionary. Rather than show the actual murders of the children, he set the background theme to music so the audience would equate that music with another murder. That final scene actually produces pity for Beckert, because he reveals that these acts are beyond his control. It was an incredibly creative decision to produce that type of emotional reaction for a horrific creature such as Hans Beckert, but one that makes *M* stand out as an absolute cinematic classic.

#56 – *L. A. Confidential*. #31 on main list.

#57 – *Rashomon* (Japan).

The movie everyone recalls when discussing Kurosawa is *The Seven Samurai*. Most critics will state that it is not his masterwork, just his most popular film. From my own opinion, two of Kurosawa's works stand out above all others, *Ikiru*, where a dying man who never accomplished or even tried anything in his life decides to find meaning in his own life and the magnificent film to be discussed here, *Rashomon*.

The story is simple, or is it? The murder of a man, after his woman is raped, is told from four perspectives. All four perspectives are different from each other. As the stories of how the man was killed are revealed, the mystery grows deeper. Who really killed the man? As the story unfolds, we believe the answer will come. When it does not, or more to the point, when we are confused by the fact that three different people confess to the murder, it is not so much of a betrayal as it is an enlightening. Revealing the actual murderer was not Kurosawa's intention.

The first line of dialogue is that the woodcutter does not understand what he has been told. That is the point of the story. The murder is not to be understood, only that each person is retelling what they want to believe happened. The truth is now only a matter of what they have turned it into. Because they are all different, Kurosawa makes a unique commentary on the way we see ourselves, deriving that from what takes place around us. All four stories end with a different outlook on the murder, yet those claims are far more important than who actually committed the murder. It is not a detective story, but rather a voyage into our hearts and minds, arriving at the assessment that each person in unique in their own way.

Rashomon is great not just for its impressive visual and unique literary style, but also for introducing the Western world to the genius of Akira Kurosawa. Unappreciated by its producer, *Rashomon* would go on to garner critical success and has become one of the most copied movies. Those who followed it, using the innovative style of revealing flashbacks of a story told from differing viewpoints, could not come close to matching its genius. More than any other film this is a complete work of art. From every single solitary aspect of the film you can see Kurosawa's brilliance.

#58 – *The Bridge on the River Kwai*. #4 on main list. #13 on AFI list. Best Picture – 1957

#59 – *Modern Times*. #81 on AFI list.

#60 – *Singin' in the Rain*. #10 on AFI list.

#61 – *The Treasure of the Sierra Madre*. #30 on AFI list.

#62 – *Alien*.

In space, no one can hear you scream. Well everyone in Manhattan heard me scream the first time I saw this movie. After numerous invasion movies where aliens land and try to take over the

Earth, it was time to criss-cross that concept by sending a crew of humans into deep space and have them deal with an alien defending itself and attacking the holy hell out of them. This is one of the most frightening movies I have ever seen, not in the way that a movie like *A Nightmare on Elm Street* or *Friday the 13th* was scary, but in a much more realistic manner.

    A mining crew heading back to earth intercepts an SOS signal and is forced to investigate. The crew is awoken from their hyperspace slumber and lands on the planet the stress signal originated from. While on the planet, one of the crew investigates the surface and discovers hundreds of strange eggs. Looking further, one of the alien eggs attacks him and attaches itself to his face. He is returned to the ship, and the ship heads back for Earth with the alien still attached to his face. It is thought that the alien dies, yet during a routine meal it emerges from the host body's stomach and flees into an unknown area of the ship. One by one the crew members are killed by this creature, which is growing by the minute. All the while the ship is still on course back to Earth.

    Even though the movie is science fiction the manner in which it was presented on film struck a deep chord of realism. The infamous meal scene where the creature first emerges is of legendary cinematic stature, yet the real fright comes from this monster killing off the crew. That fright comes from the anticipation, because the alien is hardly shown yet its presence is surely felt. At any moment the alien might come after them. The crew tries to protect itself in the only sensible manner, by hunting after it. One of the true screen classics of horror, *Alien* will always be remembered for that creature that lurks around the corner, just waiting to come after you and Earth as well.

#63 – *All About Eve*. #16 on AFI list. Best Picture – 1950

#64 – *A Clockwork Orange*. #46 on AFI list.

#65 – *Saving Private Ryan*.

    It took the Academy a number of years to finally reward Steven Spielberg, which they did in 1993 for *Schindler's List*. By my account their reward was twelve years overdue and should have been rightfully given to him for *Raiders of the Lost Ark*. After they gave him his first, the monkey was finally off his back. That did not mean he was going to stop creating quality pictures. In 1998 he nabbed his second Best Director Oscar for this amazing film.

    The first thirty minutes of the film are almost impossible to watch. They depict the horrors of storming the beach in such a grisly and realistic style that I turn away during most of my viewings. Once that episode is completed, the story centers on a battalion led by Captain John Miller. He has been given a special mission to locate a Private James Ryan. Pvt. Ryan is one of four brothers who were in service during this war. His other three brothers were killed in battle, so the brass wants the remaining Ryan removed from the battlefield and sent home to his mother. Tom Hanks, who plays Capt. Miller, leads his group in search of Ryan, trying to evade trouble along the way. When they finally find him, it is his courage and bravery that reaffirms why the soldiers are here to begin with.

    I recently saw Spielberg's 2005 film *Munich*, for which he was once again nominated for Best Director. The reason why I'm telling you this is because after seeing *Saving Private Ryan* a few times I thought that Spielberg could not top himself once again. He did. I also thought the same after seeing *Schindler's List*, *Raiders of the Lost Ark* and *Jaws*. While *Schindler's List* and *Raiders of the Lost Ark* were both on the main list, Spielberg continually challenges himself to create better and more amazing movies. *Saving Private Ryan* is a film of that variety.

#66 – *Crash*.

Movies that attempt to blend numerous stories together often have a hard time pinpointing the accuracy necessary to achieve the feat correctly. When that is done, the end result often becomes a movie that succeeds on numerous levels. The story however, is a key element to the cohesion of many side stories into one complete whole. *Crash* accomplishes the feat that others have tried, yet primarily failed. It is not the only movie to succeed, yet the story, where prejudices of every possible manner are explored, separates this film out as anything but standard.

Beginning with a car crash that culminates the story, a group of diverse characters of different backgrounds, ethnicities and races come together during a short period of time. There are way too many characters to reveal all the elements of their individual side stories, yet that is not the main focus here. Prejudices and racial stereotypes are put on trial, from every angle. Each character has them and each character must come to terms with those beliefs. Situations arise where everyone is tested. How that person evolves in their ideology affects their particular outlook on life.

At the time of final writing of this book *Crash* is nominated as one of the five movies vying for Best Picture of 2005. I thought the movie was good enough to be noticed but truth be told, it was the material that got this film the nomination. The great cast of actors, specifically Terence Howard and Matt Dillon highlight a wonderful ensemble performance that really drives the point of the movie home. I personally believe that *Crash* does not deserve to win the Oscar, but I think it will. Of the five nominees it is third best, yet struck a chord with the public like few films have.

#67 – *Double Indemnity*. #?? on main list. #38 on AFI list.

#68 – *Raging Bull*. #12 on main list. #24 on AFI list.

#69 – *Some Like it Hot*. #14 on AFI list.

#70 – *Reservoir Dogs*. Best movie - 1992

#71 – *Sin City*.

Graphic artist and author Frank Miller has been working in the comic book arena since the 1970's. His first mainstream success came from the creation of the female assassin character Elecktra, a foe/love interest of the super hero Daredevil. After resuscitating that comic franchise Miller moved onto the caped crusader, Batman. His anthology, *The Dark Knight Returns*, reestablished that grim brooding tone of the character who had turned too peppy for his own character's good. That major success led to more freedom. With this freedom Miller began infusing more noir styled stories into comic books. *Sin City* is Miller's first solo excursion into that field.

The story contained within *Sin City* combines an amalgam of bizarre characters all living in and or around a city that is devoid of proper justice. Most of the characters are crooked in the story, even though some are merely trying to protect themselves and their specific area of the city. Although there is no main character, Marv, the giant jawed behemoth would come as close to one as there was. He meets the love of his life, yet she is killed after he falls for her. The rest of his part in the story is spent searching for her killer, coming across one of the coolest characters on film, played by Elijah Wood. Told in a non-linear style, the movie moves back to the initial story of Hartigan, a cop who rescues a young kidnapped girl from a psycho who turns into something that has to be seen to be believed. Hartigan's return only happens after another story involving Dwight, a crooked cop with a talking decapitated head named Jackie Boy and the Old Towne girls, who police their region of the city with assassin like speed and tendencies, takes place to round out the tale.

The film includes an interweaving tale of three separate stories by Frank Miller, although elements from others may also be included as well. There is so much action and background material going in this film that it becomes hard to follow the literary history and more important to sit back and enjoy what is placed on the screen. The look of the movie is absolutely amazing and the stories merge together nicely. It is a fluid blending of visual effects and interesting storytelling. My only wish was that they developed the Elijah Wood character more as he seemed to be the most intriguing character the story had to offer. That said, I still highly recommend the movie to all.

#72 – *The Manchurian Candidate*. #10 on main list. #67 on AFI list.

#73 – *Life is Beautiful* (Italy).

Roberto Benigni is one crazy guy. To quote the hysterically funny sequel to *Ocean's Eleven*, *Ocean's Twelve*, Benigni is *'Italian television crazy'*. That's okay because he is Italian. Everyone should know by now that most foreign films possess a bizarre mix of their own country's cultural style, which may come off as extremely weird to Americans. The ability to look past the silly cultural quirks and focus on the bigger picture is what it takes to realize that this movie is such an astounding treat to watch. Frank Capra could not have done this any better.

Guido Orefice and his friend Ferrucio want to open a bookshop. One day, while in the country, Guido runs into a vision of beauty, Dora. He runs into her later on in the city of Venice while on a bicycle and begins to make a habit out of surprising her until she finally falls in love with him, after some magical moments that include a red carpet walk down stairs on a rainy night and a ride out of a ball on a horse that happens to be painted green. The film begins this segment in 1939 and then moves to 1945, where the couple has a five year old son. Guido is Jewish and on the son's fifth birthday Guido and his son are taken by German troops. Dora catches up to them and insists on going with them on their train ride to who knows where. While at the labor camp, Guido pretends that it is all a game for the benefit of his son, saving his life in the process more than once.

Life is Beautiful is such a sweet and tender film. It is extremely hard to trivialize the events in Europe during World War II, much less create comedic fodder out of them. Using a charming romance as the starting point and his deep love and affection for his son as the mechanism to create this game, Benigni succeeds where other have primarily failed. His acting is a bit overstated and the Academy Award for Best Actor was a major stretch. His performance easily could have and should have come in fifth among the five nominees. The picture however was clear and away the best of those five nominees. For anyone who has yet to see this movie it should be a top priority.

#74 – *Metropolis* (Germany).

Fritz Lang was the unrivaled master of German expressionism. In his 1931 film *M* it became clear that Lang was a cinematic genius. That should have occurred four years earlier with *Metropolis*. The implications of this film were more than likely not loved or embraced by those in charge at the time. That is probably because they could not understand what Lang was trying to get across. *Metro-*

polis is a more important film than even Lang could have possibly imagined, regardless of whether or not it inspired a generation of filmmakers.

There can be no understanding between the hands and the brain unless the heart acts as a mediator. That line, used throughout in the film, perfectly sums up the entire story. The world of the future is divided up into two types of people. There are the workers who live underground and only exist to work. Then there is the upper class that lives in the city and enjoys all of life's pleasures. The workers are the hands, interchangeable with one another, while the upper class is the brain of the system. They never meet, until the heart comes in, in the form of the main boss' son Freder who goes below to see what the underground is like. He gets more than he bargained for. It seems as if there should be more to this movie than described above and there is. It is the first great science fiction film and its master villain, Rotwang, is the prototype for the majority of villains to come.

This is one of the most influential movies ever made. That is not merely because of its stylized look, depicting a futuristic society. *Metropolis* was visionary in its concept of storytelling, separating the classes of people to highlight the self-appointed righteousness of the upper class and the struggles of the workers, which makes them mere followers rather than leaders. Even by today's standards *Metropolis* is one of the most ambitious films ever made. More films can trace their roots to Lang's futuristic vision than probably any other. I cannot recommend this film highly enough. *Metropolis* should be seen by everyone and is a must see for anyone planning on a career in film.

#75 – *The Shining*.

The old adage that a book is always better than the movie it is based upon has never been more accurate than in this instance. Stanley Kubrick attempted to adapt an immense book and condense it into a less than three hour film. In the process, a number of key concepts from the book were sacrificed, not to mention Kubrick installing his own take on the theme. It may be unfair to judge the movie based on the success and quality of the book, specifically since Jack Nicholson took the main character to a place that even Stephen King could not have imagined.

Jack Torrance is hired as the winter caretaker for the Overlook Hotel in the mountains of Colorado. The job lasts from the end of October to the beginning of May, where Jack will be alone in the vast hotel with only his wife and young son. Jack is a former drunkard and it is briefly intimated that he was abusive, one time dislocating his son Danny's shoulder. The hotel has demons of its own, with one former caretaker going insane from the isolation and chopping his family up before committing suicide. Jack is made aware of this at the final interview for the job, yet isolation is what he craves. It is also what he gets. The longer they are there, the more Jack begins to change. The hotel begins to exert a strange hold over him, while his psychic son is haunted by images of the hotel's past. When his wife discovers that his writing is nothing more than the same sentence over and over again, Jack loses all control. With the help of hotel spirits, Jack maniacally goes after them.

This is one of Nicholson's greatest acting performances. I stated earlier that in watching his roles during the early part of his career there were touches of the Joker just itching to come out. In *The Shining*, he may have actually shocked the Joker with his over the top psychotic behavior. An alternative title of this film is *Stanley Kubrick's The Shining*, because of the fact that it departed from the novel to such a great extent. They really could have called it *Jack Nicholson's The Shining*. Without him this film would have been awful and not memorable at all. I think that every writer should see this movie, although if you are a fan of Stephen King you might want to stay away.

#76 – *The Incredibles*.

Pixar is one of the great companies, not only for their realistic animation, but also for their ability to create remarkable stories. Every Pixar movie I have seen has taken an interesting concept and turned it into a realistic adventure, albeit of a fairy tale like nature. Obviously toys do not have a life of their own and monsters do not exist to scare children so they can power their monster world. The same holds true for super-heroes and super villains. They do not exist, but what if they did and were forced into hiding because of litigious citizens?

Mr. Incredible and all the other super heroes are forced to go underground and resume normal lives by the government after a number of lawsuits cost the government millions of dollars. Mr. Incredible, also known as Bob Parr, must adjust to regular life. Along with his wife, formerly Elastigirl, and his three children, Parr struggles through his latest job as an insurance claims handler. There is the feeling that he wants something more. On bowling night Parr and his friend Lucius, formerly Frozone, listen to the police scanners and sneak back into their alter egos. That is until Parr is offered the opportunity to become Mr. Incredible again. That turns out to be more than he bargained for, especially when his family, all with super powers, is brought into the trap.

This latest Pixar animation fest, at the time of this writing, was by far their best effort. The story is so genuine and the juxtaposition of this tale is priceless. Filled with awesome characters, specifically their infant son Jack Jack and the villains who threaten their lives, *The Incredibles* lives up to its title. Like all the previous Pixar films comedy is an important element of the story. The juxtaposition of a super hero getting sued and having to live life as a commoner is a great idea, yet the process of bringing it all together not only works magnificently well but also places their most highly developed and funniest film to date on the big screen.

#77 – *Amadeus*. #53 on AFI list. Best Picture – 1984

#78 – *The Great Escape*.

The 1950's and the 1960's had a number of fantastic movies centered on World War II. My all time favorite film is in this type of mold, *Stalag 17*. The trick was that filmmakers had to figure out a way to create more original stories than had been told before related to the war. Even though there are still movies made to this day on World War II, the influx of films during that time made most of them similar. *The Great Escape* was unique.

The story centers on a prisoner of war camp, where a large number of troublesome British and a few American soldiers are held. This camp is a new German maximum security camp, from which escape is believed impossible. That only makes the officers in charge desire escape that much more. To counter the German ideal of an inescapable prison, the prisoners devise a plan to have two hundred and fifty prisoners escape at the same time. The payoff is that they get a large number of prisoners to escape through three massive tunnels built for the plan. It was their way of defeating the Germans and showing them that no matter what they do they would not capture their spirit, even though many of them are recaptured only after they taste a bit of freedom.

The Great Escape is not a great movie in the way that *Schindler's List* is. It is pure enjoyment, the way a movie like *Stalag 17*. There are plenty of great characters, most notably Steve McQueen as the 'Cooler King'. All the prisoners are of the troublesome variety for the Germans. They are dubbed the rotten eggs of the bunch because of their willingness and success at escaping. In that vain the story has a severe plot hole. Putting even ten men together who are master escape artists will result in only one course of action; escape. Put 250 together and you get a great escape. The plot has to be thrown away for the sheer enjoyment of watching the events take place. This should be required viewing because it is what the movies are about, pure fun.

#79 – *City Lights*. #76 on AFI list.

#80 – *Aliens*.

Fresh off the heels of the science fiction classic *The Terminator*, James Cameron advanced upon the original 1979 horror classic by making the story more of a badass all out fight to the finish against the evil aliens. Advancing the genre once again, Cameron helped create the sci-fi offshoot of fighting aliens in outer space. Humans on other planets had been done before, yet Cameron's approach to the futuristic battle between man and beast has such an original feel to it.

Starting off where the first movie finished, Ripley's ship is discovered in space and she is woken from her hyperspace slumber. One problem – she had been floating in space and sleeping for fifty seven years. The world she knew is gone and so is her young daughter, dead two years before Ripley is awakened. There are other problems as well. Ripley is blamed for her part in destroying the ship and she cannot shake what took place on board with the alien that killed her crew. She is offered the opportunity to join a mission to rescue colonists from the planet where she first encountered the alien. This time, she will have more than just miners and salvage experts on her side, although she will be fighting more than one solitary alien this time.

Aliens changed the face of moviemaking. Along with *Die Hard*, these two films paved the way for those kick ass action movies of the 1990's. Even though this film is more of the horror / sci-fi genre the action contained within this film was brilliantly crafted by Cameron. What he was able to do was create a unique movie that could not be pigeonholed within one specific genre. *Aliens* is a pure adrenaline rush and also a great continuation and advancement of an already terrific storyline. It is a shame they did not stop the series here, because this one is as good as the original.

#81 – *The Sting*. #29 on main list. Best Picture – 1973

#82 – *Touch of Evil*. #32 on main list.

#83 – *Rebecca*. #39 on main list. Best Picture – 1940

#84 – *On the Waterfront*. #37 on main list. #8 on AFI list. Best Picture – 1954

#85 - *Kill Bill: Volume 1*.

Quentin Tarantino loves women. We all get it. The only person who does not understand that we all get it is Tarantino. As a result, he devised a story of a super woman assassin and created a story pieced together from a number of different genres and other movies already done before. From the signature yellow suit of the main character (an homage to the outfit worn by Bruce Lee in his final film) whom he never names (similar to Eastwood's character in the spaghetti Westerns) to the use of ridiculous Japanese anime and his standard technique of non-linear storytelling, everything about this movie reminds me of other movies made previously.

A woman is shot by a group of assassins and remains in a coma for four years. Once she finally awakens she plans to exact her revenge upon those who tried to assassinate her. There is the first battle, an indoor knife fight with one of her would be assassins, who has miraculously turned into a PTA mom. Once she is defeated, the next assassin up is the current ruler of the Chinese underworld, O-Ren Ishii. Before battling O-Ren, the woman must fight all of her kung-fu fighting soldiers. Once she defeats all of them, there is O-Ren's personal bodyguard, Gogo. Their battle is the best of the film because it is the one that offers the least amount of unrealistic behavior. Once Gogo is defeated, O-Ren is next. The battle between O-Ren and the woman, later identified as *'the Bride'*, should have been the epic finale of this film. It falls short in every possible way.

Of course, there was never the intention to create two separate films, yet the self-indulgent Tarantino made a movie that ran over four hours in length. The logical conclusion made by the studios was to break it up into separate volumes and release them individually. That was purely a monetary decision. The correct decision would have been to cut out all the unnecessary garbage and fashion a three hour film that would have been more complete than either of these two individual parts and could have lived up to what Tarantino wanted, epic status. Watching each one of these movies, specifically this one, left me unfulfilled. This movie never should have been broken into two parts and that fracture completely destroyed it as a great film, creating two awful movies in its place.

#86 – *2001: A Space Odyssey*. #22 on AFI list.

#87 – *Mr. Smith Goes To Washington*. #23 on main list. #29 on AFI list.

#88 – *Ran* (Japan).

Kurosawa has a number of his films spread out on this list. Of all those films *Ran* is easily the most visually stunning and beautiful to watch. He is considered the most Western of the well-known Japanese directors, something that surely tainted his image for a time in his own homeland. Kurosawa went beyond anything he had ever done before here by adapting Shakespeare (King Lear) into a traditional tale that still emphasized historical Japanese values.

Lord Ichimonji divides up his kingdom between his three sons. The leadership of the land will be given to his eldest son Taro, along with the grand castle. Ichimonji tries to instill in them the knowledge that if they remain together they shall stay strong. Even though he has made his wishes known the three sons battle for supremacy of the kingdom, thus tearing it apart. Ichimonji is attacked and cast out of the kingdom by one of his sons. He begins to wander the countryside with a psychotic yet philosophical jester and a loyal follower. Ichimonji is headed toward insanity, while the kingdom he spent fifty years building falls apart, resulting in no small part from his own vanity. One of the more compelling aspects of the film is the supporting character Lady Keade, who craves power so badly that she manipulates anyone she can to achieve it, or so it merely seems at first.

Kurosawa loved the history of his country and loved regaling in stories about the unique characters that helped shape the history of Japan. *Ran* was truly a labor of love for Kurosawa, encompassing ten years of his life and paying off in dividends as it is generally considered the masterpiece of his final years in cinema. This particular film holds deep significance, introducing a whole new audience to his movies. *The Seven Samurai* is often considered his best work by fans. *Ikiru* is generally offered when critics discuss the greatest film of Kurosawa's career. I prefer to think his best movie was *Rashomon*, because it has the finest and most intelligent story of his collection. There is no arguing the fact that *Ran* is his greatest cinematic sight to behold though.

#89 – *The Apartment*. #93 on AFI list. Best Picture – 1960

#90 – *The Seventh Seal* (Sweden).

This is the Ingmar Bergman film that everyone knows. I am sure that it is also the one that has received the most praise because of its notoriety and also the most flack against it for the same reason. Rather than seeing the film for what it was, an emotional and psychological journey into a warrior's mind and heart, there will always be those who will view it as blasphemous, which provides an ironic twist as faith is deeply explored in this film.

Antonius Block is a medieval Knight home from the Crusades with his squire Jons. While on a beach, Block is encountered by the Grim Reaper, who has a job to do like everyone else. Block challenges Death to a game of chess to keep his life and soul. Death allows this reprieve for he knows that certain things are inevitable. As long as Block can hold off Death from defeating him at chess he remains alive. During this reprieve, Block travels through the countryside and witnesses firsthand how the plague has affected his homeland. While searching for a way to stave off Death, Block also encounters numerous characters who add more puzzlement to his feelings and thoughts on the situation of God, life and the beyond. And Death keeps popping up to remind Block that it is his turn and that his time in the chess match, a metaphor for existence, is growing shorter by the moment.

In the end, no one can escape Death. This is obviously Bergman's prophecy here, using a struggle of wits against powers that cannot be defeated because they exist on a different plain than us as his guiding mechanism. The cinematography of this harrowing tale of the beyond is as haunting today as I would imagine it was back in the 1950's. The specter of Death following you at every turn, waiting for you to slip up and make the wrong move is both slightly unnerving and awe-inspiring. Block can try all the tricks he wants. Death will always triumph because we are mortal. I think Bergman knew that but wanted to pose the questions anyway, perhaps to get people to realize it.

#91 – *The Wizard of Oz*. #27 on main list. #6 on AFI list.

#92 – *Jaws*. #48 on AFI list.

#93 – *Strangers on a Train*.

Hitchcock was the unparalleled master at taking a classic or standard suspense story and creating something wholly original out of it. His movies are that of legend and he is generally considered the greatest director of his or any other generation. He had more movies on the main list (4) than any other director. There was a reason for that. He also has more than twice that number on this list here. *Strangers on a Train* is one of his lesser known classics, despite the fact that it is ranked among the top 100 here and praised by most critics.

Simple. Two strangers meet on a train. Guy is a famous tennis player. The other, Bruno, recognizes him and starts up a conversation. They get to talking and Bruno eventually describes his idea of a perfect murder to Guy. Bruno's idea is for each of them to commit a murder that would never lead back to them, Bruno murdering Guy's wife and Guy returning the favor by murdering Bruno's father. Thinking that to be a strange topic, Guy leaves the conversation and the stranger's company. He is shocked when Bruno shows up one night to tell Guy that he has finished his part of their plan, murdering Guy's wife. That is where the true suspense begins as Bruno begins to stalk Guy to get him to complete his part of their bargain. *Strangers on a Train* worked as perfectly as Bruno's scheme of murder should have, or at least should have in theory.

This film is a true treasure. It was remade to an extent in 1987, the underappreciated yet extremely decent *Throw Momma From the Train*. I saw that film prior to seeing this Hitchcock mystery. Now I understand perfectly why the 1987 remake is underappreciated. It is so far beneath the quality of the 1951 original that it could never possibly live up to it. This film is one of Hitchcock's most original efforts and helped the director reinvent himself after a string of so-so films, which included *Rope*, the bizarrely bad *Under Capricorn* and the just plain odd *Stage Fright*. Its fantastic story structure and subtle touches from the master make it a genuinely amazing film.

#94 – *The Great Dictator*.

Inevitably, all good things must come to an end. Charlie Chaplin held onto his silent film persona as long as he could, making such classics as *City Lights*, *Modern Times*, *The Kid* and *The Gold Rush*, the best of his entire collection. The audiences wanted *'talkies'* and Chaplin had to oblige. This film is his first of the talking era and perhaps his most socially relevant statement. As is usually the case, there were many who did not understand the tone of the film, thinking that Chaplin was glorifying war and belittling those who fought against tyranny.

This beautiful farce follows the story of two men. One is a lowly Jewish barber and the other is the dictator of Tomania, Adenoid Hynkel. The two men have one thing in common, they look exactly alike. That is never developed until the end of the film, used to drive home the social commentary that Chaplin intended. Throughout the film, up until that part, he portrays the evil dictator as a complete buffoon with a severe maniacal side, although one could argue that he was not far off from portraying his subject accurately. When the barber is mistaken for the dictator, Chaplin chooses to infuse his greatest message in a final speech that the dictator is delivering to his loyal followers. The whole movie is geared toward this one final moment of the film.

It might be morally dismissive to merely say that I liked this movie. Some people feel that it is important to recognize the statements it makes rather than watching it because a person likes movies. I would disagree with those people. The social proclamations are obvious and were an important stance to make at the time. It is one of only a few movies to denounce the fascist regime of Hitler prior to the involvement of America in World War II, so there is the added historical relevance. However, I approached the film from the standpoint of whether it was good or whether it was bad, how much I liked it or disliked it. Political opinions aside, I enjoyed the film immensely, yet still longed for the days of the pantomiming little tramp.

#95 – *Donnie Darko*.

Despite the fact that I consider myself an intelligent person there are just some things that I do not get. I don't understand why the French love Jerry Lewis or why Asians love Michael Jackson or why anyone likes the music of Brittney Spears. I have accepted the fact that I will never understand certain things in life, no matter how hard I try. *Donnie Darko* is something I do not understand. Let me rephrase that. The growing appreciation for *Donnie Darko* as a movie of excellent stature is something that I will never understand.

Donnie, a teenager with psychological problems, begins to be led around by a giant bunny rabbit who tells him that the world will end in less than a month. He sleepwalks, winding up in strange places. When he returns home one night he discovers that a jet engine has crashed through his bedroom. If he were sleeping he would have been killed. With his visions of this soothsaying bunny rabbit Donnie begins committing acts of vandalism in his school and other places, including setting fire to a house that reveals sordid secrets about the owner, a self help guru with issues.

Donnie Darko is a cult movie. There is a distinct following surrounding this strange film. The ending has been interpreted so many ways that to list them it would take up pages, not lines. I have seen this film three times. I have my own opinion about the ending and have been told by two people that I am wrong. I chalk this movie up to one of the few that I just don't understand, although I think it is part of the allure of the film that it can be interpreted in numerous ways. Without a doubt, watching *Donnie Darko* is a surreal experience. You may not like it. You may not understand it. One thing is for certain though, you will never forget it. I have tried and failed.

#96 – *Braveheart*. Best Picture - 1995

#97 – *Cinema Paradiso* (Italy).

Italian cinema is full of romance, regardless of whether the story is a comedy, tragedy or a flat out love story. Italian culture is based on simplicity, with love as one of its strongest characteristics. There is the love of good wine, the love of food, the love of a good woman and most importantly the unabashed love of life. *Cinema Paradiso* has captured the last quality marvelously, becoming the first Italian film in fifteen years to win the Academy Award for Best Foreign Film, achieving what Federico Fellini's *Amarcord* accomplished in 1974.

Toto loves movies. From the time he was a young boy he loved everything about cinema, watching the town's projectionist Alfredo's every move. One day Toto helps Alfredo pass his equivalency exam and becomes his young apprentice, learning everything there is to know. Later on in their relationship, Alfredo is seriously injured by a fire in the projection room, which permanently scars and blinds him. Toto is now in charge of running the projector for the new cinema, bringing joy to the simple townsfolk. Growing up, Toto struggles through the standard trials and tribulations of life, eventually leaving town only to return many years later for the funeral of his old friend Alfredo, where his reminiscences on his early life become his new friend once again.

Cinema Paradiso is a human story if there ever was one. This film is about one man's life and the decision he made that changed his life forever. It is such a beautiful and heartfelt picture, charming from the first moment it begins on the screen until the final moment of its cinematic life. I try to watch this movie every so often because it reminds me of my dreams and how to remain focused in the face of adversity. It is truly one of those films that always brings a smile to my face.

#98 – *Forrest Gump*. #73 on AFI list. Best Picture - 1994

#99 – *Finding Nemo*.

Cartoons are for kids. Never has a dumber statement been uttered since someone out there argued that Hitler was right. Originally cartoons and fairy tales were intended to present lessons about life. Then they became a means for distracting kids. Luckily that trend has ended to a degree, although there is still plenty of garbage out there currently for that explicit purpose. The animated movies created by Pixar are not only for children. They are for everyone because the stories they tell are universal in their appeal.

Nemo is a young clown fish. Marlin is his dad and extremely overprotective of Nemo. When Nemo finally is old enough to start attending school with the other fish his dad is visibly concerned. Nemo wants to be like everyone else, so he challenges his dad's authority by venturing out into open water and is captured by a human. The human is a dentist from Australia who plans on giving Nemo to his niece, the psychotic Darla. Marlin goes after Nemo, battling a group of sharks in the process of renouncing the practice of eating fish, a whale and jellyfish during his journey across the ocean blue. With the help of a fish named Dory, some sea turtles who speak in surfer language and a pelican named Nigel, Marlin is reunited with Nemo, who is helped by a unique group of aquarium dwellers.

Finding Nemo is the fifth full length animated feature from Pixar studios and their best up until that time. It is brilliant how they keep coming up with fresh new ideas and stories that push the boundaries yet always seem to provide that all-important aspect of entertainment. I do think that *The Incredibles* is a better movie than *Finding Nemo*, yet there is a sweetness about all of Pixar's films that is clearly present here. Anyone who ascribes to the notion that cartoons are for children should see anyone of the fine films from Pixar, with *Finding Nemo* close to the top of that list.

#100 – *Fargo*. #46 on main list. #84 on AFI list.

#101 – *Blade Runner*.

Coming off the heels of the major success of the science fiction/ horror classic *Alien*, Ridley Scott decided to not tread too far away from what had brought him his first real glimpse of fame. The science fiction genre that Scott helped create, moving away from the ultra campy films such as *Battlestar Galactica* and *Buck Rogers*, could be done in an even more stylistic manner. The place to start was in quality science fiction literature. The author to utilize was Philip K. Dick. Dick's work has led to numerous films with *Blade Runner* generally considered the best.

Deckard is a blade runner. A blade runner is a police officer who hunts down replicates and retires them for good. He is retired himself, although not in the way he retired the replicated androids that went astray. It is time for him to come back into the game. Six replicates return to Earth after banishment to search for their maker. A fail-safe device was installed in these replicates to prevent them from evolving past humans. These replicants will do anything in their power to survive, led by a maniacally philosophical replicate named Roy Batty. The final showdown between Batty and Deckard is a classic scene where more issues arise than are ultimately settled.

Philip K. Dick's work always has many levels to it. With this story he explored the dehumanization of man and the roles of creator versus the created. This is one of those rare movies that is both thought provoking and interesting to watch, unlike *2001: A Space Odyssey*. Scott saw the possibilities in Dick's work, capitalizing on a combination of a great ensemble cast and stunning cinematography to create the kind of film that Kubrick, Lucas and Spielberg wanted to make but failed. If

I were to recommend this movie I must state that it should be seen more than once. If you think you fully understand it after one viewing than you are either too smart or too dumb.

#102 – *Full Metal Jacket*.

The great success of *The Deer Hunter*, *Coming Home* and others made it possible for filmmakers to offer their own take on the horrific war in Vietnam. The critical and commercial success of *Platoon* the previous year returned the war into fashion. In 1987 Stanley Kubrick decided to provide his particular and peculiar take on it. Kubrick fashioned another of his dual and separate stories within one movie, which as you know is a signature of almost all his work.

A young marine recruit goes through two stages of his life in the service. The first part is the basic training under a tyrannical drill sergeant. Rather than providing training and experience dehumanizing humiliation is substituted. The main character, Private Joker, sees how the recruits around him become hardened, with one deficient recruit going over the edge into insanity. After those dramatic events during basic training the newly trained soldiers are sent off into battle, where their newly learned killer instincts are put into place on the field of battle. These men were prepared for the horrors of war instead of having been taught the horror that is war. That subtle difference makes the film an important statement against war as a whole.

Just like every other Kubrick film, the sudden right turn from the magnificent basic training segment of the film to the rigors of battle left me cold. Once again it appears that Kubrick was unsure of which of the two films he wanted to make so he simply combined them together with a cut and paste job. The first part is great yet the back end of the movie, where the themes and the core should be driven home thoroughly fails. Everyone I know who likes this film enjoys the first part immeasurably more than the finale. I couldn't agree more with their assessment.

#103 – *Princess Mononoke* (Japan).

In 1997, Japanese Anime was exploding onto just about every international scene. Ten years had passed since *Akira*, the film that more than likely started it all. What needed to be done now was continue that westward expansion of Japanese themes and culture that Anime was capitalizing on. More adventurous stories were attempted, bringing together all the mysticism of their culture. *Princess Mononoke* was quickly westernized with English language dubbing, with voices provided by big name actors. This was the big chance to break through.

Prince Ashitaka saves his village from a wild demon boar creature, yet is bitten on the arm and infected with whatever demon the boar had inside him. He has two choices, remain in the village and die or seek out the forest spirit and discover the secret cure to save his life. His journey takes him to Irontown, where he discovers that there is an ongoing war between numerous enemies, most notably Lady Hiboshi and the wolves who are led by Princess Mononoke. Ashitaka does not join sides, yet rather sees this as an opportunity to unite everyone to live in peace and harmony agreeing that will work together and save the forest. All sides believe that he is working against them though.

First and foremost, what an absolutely awful movie, regardless of the botched dubbing and horrific voice casting that turned one of the characters into a Japanese hillbilly. The story alone makes me long for those two hours of my life back. I get it already, the Japanese will believe anything you tell them, even if it includes the existence of pig demons, talking animals and mini ghosts running around the forest. Japanese animation may be visually stunning, but the story must not continuously enter into a realm of mystical insanity. There are a number of great Japanese animation films but I have to state that this is not one of them.

#104 – *Kill Bill: Volume 2.*

The conclusion of Tarantino's attempt to create a Kung-Fu epic was at least better than the first volume. Since they were released independently and the audiences were forced to see them separately, they must always be considered as two separate films, rather than one completed whole. Even though this film delves into the necessary back story of why *'the Bride'* was betrayed by Bill's group of assassins, it is too little too late. This movie is now missing the vital parts of her revenge against the first two assassins, shown in the first film.

'The Bride' turns her attention toward the third member of the group of assassins who tried to murder her on her wedding day. This one does not go as easily as the first two. He is made aware that she was not killed and is coming after them, by Bill. The third assassin, Budd, is ready for her. He takes her out using a shotgun filled with rock salt, incapacitating her and then burying her alive. This gives Tarantino the opportunity to present the back story of her training, which foreshadows how she will escape from her crypt. After escaping, she doesn't need to take care of Budd, because the fourth assassin does that for her. She quickly engages the fourth assassin in battle and easily defeats her. Next up is Bill. *'The Bride'* was in fact pregnant when Bill attempted to have her assassinated and the baby was his. Her murder of Bill is comical at best, but she now has her daughter back and has completed her mission of revenge.

Both films are incomplete, yet this film is so much better than volume 1. There is added depth to the main character, something that the first film sorely lacked. Still, this film on its own is not one of Tarantino's better efforts and he only has attempted five, counting these two as individual. Hopefully Tarantino has gotten this type of film out of the way so he can get back to creating the innovative films he made his name from. After seeing the first I promised myself I would not waste my time with the second volume, yet could not resist. After seeing it I wish I would have resisted. Maybe one day Tarantino will go into the editing room and properly combine these two films, cutting out about an hour of the superfluous garbage to make the epic he should have to begin with.

#105 – *Terminator 2: Judgment Day.*

Sequels are tough to make and get right. They should advance upon the original. What other reason would there be for making them? James Cameron knows a little something about sequels though, helming the sci-fi classic sequel *Aliens*, taking that franchise to the next level. This film was of the same variety, an amazing expansion of the original story and one that was designed to blow the doors off the first film, whose action pales in comparison.

Twelve years has elapsed since Sarah Connor was saved from a futuristic cybernetic killing machine by Reese in *The Terminator*. Sarah has changed, yet the machines in the future have become much more advanced also. They send back an updated terminator to eliminate her son, who leads the resistance in the future. Always one step ahead, the John Connor of the future reprograms a terminator to serve as his protector and sends him back in time. After explaining the scenario to the wise cracking and street savvy John, the two of them help bust Sarah out of the asylum she is confined in.

Her next move is to assassinate the man responsible for creating the machines before they can carry out judgment day. John and the protector terminator realize her plan and set about stopping her. The newer terminator is fast on their heels though and will catch up with them shortly.

From the description it would appear that this film was as in-depth of an intellectual sci-fi thriller as the first one. That would be incorrect. *The Terminator 2: Judgment Day* is the equivalent of *Aliens* in that it is a sequel that is all about the intense action, with the story merely as a minor backdrop. The story does guide the action in one direction or another but the real star of this film is the elaborate fight scenes between the two terminators and the amazing action scenes. This movie is an intense experience mixed with fantastic touches of comedy and a subtle but decent continuation of the amazing story revealed in the original. It is a shame the series did not stop here.

#106 – *The Big Sleep*.

The 20's, 30's and 40's was the time for the great American private eye story. Some of the classic characters came out of that time, written by such fantastic writers as James M. Cain and Dashiell Hammett. Included in that list must be Raymond Chandler, the author who created perhaps the best known of all the fictional American private eyes, Philip Marlowe. One of the major selling points of this film was the re-pairing of Humphrey Bogart and Lauren Bacall, married by the time of the film's release. Their first outing, 1944's *To Have and Have Not*, would leave an indelible impression, yet the Marlowe character and Bogart are the real hooks of the film.

Private detective Philip Marlowe is hired to investigate a case of blackmail. One thing leads to another and Marlowe finds himself entrenched in a case involving multiple murders, where bodies keep turning up, including the 'alleged' blackmailer's body. Paid off and warned to stop working the case, Marlowe continues because he will not stop until everything makes complete sense. To complicate matters, one of the daughters of the man who hired Marlowe is falling in love with him and consequently keeps showing up at places Marlowe is led to by his investigation, not a surprise to him at all. Just when Marlowe has it all figured out, new wrinkles pop up and the case continues.

This was the type of character that Bogart was meant to play. With the exception of his role in *Casablanca*, Bogart was at home playing the fast talking private eye more than any other type of character. Lauren Bacall is a gorgeous woman, but her acting is less than spectacular. If it were not for her beauty and Bogart's back and forth rhetoric with her, she would have been a major negative for this film. I don't even want to bring up her awful singing scene. *The Big Sleep* is a wonderful detective story, the type that glues you to the edge of your seat with anticipation of what is to come next. I know the story and still watch it that way now when I watch it.

#107 – *Batman Begins*.

There is no bigger fan of Batman than me. That is a misnomer. I am sure that there are people out there who dress up like Batman or Robin and have major issues with their own personality. Hopefully they will create a utility belt and jump off a building to see if it works. What can better describe my appreciation for the character is that there is no comic book super hero that I enjoy reading about or watching more than Batman. Although the villains are important and ultra cool, what makes me love Batman above all others is the story of his origin.

After witnessing the death of his parents as a child, a grown up Bruce Wayne travels to the

Far East in search of answers as to why criminals act the way they do. To further understand them he becomes somewhat of a criminal himself to get closer to the mindset of a person who would commit such an act. In prison, he is approached by a representative for a secret order of ninja assassins. Their goal is to protect the world from criminals, or so Wayne is told. Wayne accepts an offer to join the group and train in the ways of the Samurai, the protectors of the common man. After disagreeing with their philosophy regarding justice, Wayne returns home to Gotham and begins protecting people the only way he knows how, with the help of his alter ego.

I looked forward to this movie more than any other film coming out in 2005. I thought nothing could top Tim Burton's 1989 version, *Batman*, yet the first half of the movie did just that. After Wayne returns to Gotham City the movie slows down a bit as it tries to rev up the story of super villains taking over Gotham City and destroying it for their philosophical cause. I understand that it would not be a Batman story without a super villain, yet if the filmmakers had focused strictly on the tale of his origin, *Batman Begins* could have been the best super hero movie ever made. Even though they return to Gotham where Batman fights crime as usual, *Batman Begins* is still a fantastic movie, only topped by the original *Batman* in quality.

#108 – *High Noon*. #38 on main list. #33 on AFI list.

#109 – *Notorious*.

No one argues that Hitchcock is the master. Every poll of the world's greatest directors has Alfred at the top. Any poll that does not immediately falls under the veil of incredibility. The reason why he is on top of the list is because he continually challenged himself to do better and more interesting projects. That has its advantages and disadvantages. The projects do not always live up to his much more heralded films, but *Notorious* is considered one of his best.

Alicia is the daughter of a convicted member of the Nazi party. Her loyalty is to America though. A federal agent named Devlin approaches her with the opportunity to help her country by spying on a ring of Nazis working out of Rio, one of whom she knows well. Alicia is portrayed as an alcoholic and a whore, although that was toned down somewhat because of the era the movie was filmed in. If the movie were filmed today she might be taking on three guys at once. As Devlin prepares her for an unknown assignment he falls in love with her. The problem is that the job calls for Alicia to become intimate with a man named Sebastian, who is involved in some secret mission that threatens America. Her job is to find out what, although the movie focuses on the relationship between Devlin, played brilliantly by Cary Grant, and Alicia, played by the absolutely stunning Ingrid Bergman. The erotic tension between Alicia and Devlin helps to carry this movie.

With so many gripping thrillers among Hitchcock's films, *Notorious* is often singled out as among the top tier. I wholeheartedly disagree. With nine films alone on this list, I would rank *Notorious* among the bottom three, possibly as high as seventh best. That is not even counting the great Hitchcock films left off this list, such as *To Catch a Thief*, *The Birds* and *Dial M for Murder*, all of which are better films than *Notorious*. I believe the over hyping of this film is due to the philosophical implications of the story. The story was not the problem. The real issue I had with *Notorious* was the fact that the tension never reached its zenith despite numerous chances that the film had to produce that effect. I would have to say that this film was not one of Hitchcock's best.

#110 – *Yojimbo the Bodyguard* (Japan).

When I stated earlier that Hilary Swank owed her second Oscar to Akira Kurosawa I was being facetious. To continue along that line, one could further the argument by saying that Swank really owes her gratitude to the author Dashiell Hammett. His story, *Red Harvest*, was the impetus for the film *Yojimbo*. *Yojimbo* led to those Leone Spaghetti Westerns, which led to Eastwood's super stardom and Swank's second Oscar, although her acting had much to do with it as well. She could also just as easily thank Fred Zinneman, whose *High Noon* was a distinct influence on the stylistic content of this film.

Sanjuro is a samurai who is out of work. He wanders into a town that is controlled by two separate gangs, fighting with each other over supremacy of the town. Assessing the situation, Sanjuro decides to play both gangs against each other, for his own benefit, as well as the town's benefit. He knows that he cannot defeat the armies of men that both gangs have hired, so a scheme is required rather than a sword fight. Make no mistake, these men will all pay with their lives, yet Sanjuro understands that the thinking warrior always wins out over the one who acts hastily. Plans never seem to work out as some would imagine, no matter how intricate they are.

The Eastern philosophy of women as lesser and treacherous is a staple within Japanese culture although some would argue that it is a universal belief in all cultures, despite its deeply erroneous nature. Every character is a little bit of a villain in this film, yet the wife of the brothel keeper, Orin, is perhaps the worst. The gangs that run the gambling in town are fighting for power, yet she appears to be scheming for herself. Her plan to backstab Sanjuro sets the tone of the movie, where the samurai learns that he must play all sides against one another to achieve victory. Orin is Lady Macbeth and Catwoman rolled up into one and more than likely the impetus for Tarantino's O-Ren Ishii character from *Kill Bill*. *Yojimbo* is far better than *The Seven Samurai*, masterfully combining story, action and philosophy, while influencing Western cinema for decades to come.

#111 – *Crouching Tiger, Hidden Dragon* (China).

Eastern history is filled with ancient tales of warriors, codes of honor and epic battles. The stories of their culture reflect such traditions. *Crouching Tiger, Hidden Dragon* perfectly blends that into an absolutely stunning visual spectacle. Using a specific style of storytelling, Wu Xia, a Chinese form of fiction that mixes Eastern fighting styles with mythology and mysticism, Ang Lee creates one of the most magical films ever. The fighting lures you in, the visual scope entrances you, yet it is the story that ultimately wins you over.

The two fight scenes between Zhang Ziyi and Michelle Yeoh are by far the best, although the scene where Ziyi fights an entire restaurant is breathtaking to watch. One must suspend reality to enjoy the fighting. The visual wonder contains an acrobatic element that allows people to soar in the open air and walk on water. Once the viewer can do that, as they have before in science fiction films such as *Star Wars* and *The Matrix*, they can truly begin to enjoy the majesty of this film. Without that suspension of reality the movie does not reach its full potential. The true beauty of the film remains though, which includes the richly layered love stories. They hold the heart of the movie.

Ziyi, the daughter of a public official, has two separate love stories within the film. One is her love for a bandit called *'Dark Cloud'*. The second is an unquenched desire, one that has been building up inside her since she was ten years old, her desire to enter the world of the warrior. That elemental desire has turned her into a thief, driven her away from her husband to be, alienated her from *'Dark Cloud'* and set her on the path to self destruction. The true romance in the film is the unspoken love between the great warrior played by Chow Yun Fat and Yeoh. Their love reveals the nature of the culture within the film, that of both Chinese culture and the ancient warrior code.

Sense and Sensibility was a bit overplayed for my taste, yet director Ang Lee's follow up to that movie, 1996's *The Ice Storm*, was almost perfect in its simplicity. I firmly believed that Ang Lee had his masterpiece in *The Ice Storm* until I saw *Crouching Tiger, Hidden Dragon*. Having an affinity for those badly dubbed Kung Fu movies it was about time for a movie like this to come out, mixing all the intense fighting, a great story and great acting finally bringing those three variables together.

#112 – *The Elephant Man.*

It is always the case that truth is stranger than fiction. Never has that axiom been truer than in the sad case of Joseph John Merrick. After the small yet unforgettable film *Eraserhead* made David Lynch a director of extreme promise, albeit with an explicit darker side, *The Elephant Man* was the perfect choice for his next project. What was quickly discovered about Lynch is that his ability to present gripping material extended past the simply darker elements.

London surgeon Dr. Frederick Treves hears about a freakish man and eventually sees that he is on display at a carnival. After Treves takes a medical interest he is called to help Merrick after he is beaten by the even more hideous creature exploiting him for profit. Treves takes Merrick to the hospital where it is quickly discovered that behind all the monstrous deformities he is a sensitive and caring person. Even at the hospital where Merrick is given shelter there are those who exploit him, including Treves who often wonders if he is similar to those who once profited off Merrick. Once Merrick is returned to that carnival atmosphere, something inside him dies. He has tasted normalcy for a brief moment. Perhaps that is more cruel and painful than never tasting it at all.

The story of how a surgeon comes in contact with a man suffering from grotesque disfigurements is both part horror and one of the most heartbreaking films ever made. One can only assume that the studio intended to exploit the horror, considering their choice of director. Throughout the film however, we as the audience must ask ourselves the primary question of whether we are as bad as those who exploited Merrick for his condition, which includes Treves who used Merrick for science. *The Elephant Man* is a film of unspeakable honesty and overpowering emotion. Most will probably disagree but this is the finest film David Lynch has ever made.

#113 – *Once Upon a Time in America.*

The Spaghetti Western meets the Matzoh-Ball Mafia. Sergio Leone made four good films in the 1960's. Two of them could easily be considered great. The three films he made after 1968's *Once Upon a Time in the West* were all less than spectacular. He returned to directing with an epic story in 1984 about a group of four young boys growing up in Brooklyn and carving a name for themselves in the Prohibition era. It was an auspicious move for Leone, who had not achieved success in close to sixteen years. This would not be a glorious return.

An elder gangster returns to Brooklyn after thirty years upon receiving a mysterious invitation. He relives in his mind what took place during his childhood when he met Max, who would change his life. Noodles, as he is called, teams up with Max and their three friends. A well respected neighborhood gangster guns one of them down, so Noodles murders him. After he is released from prison more than a decade later, Noodles discovers the gang he helped found has become major players on the scene. With more power comes greed. When Prohibition finally ends Max's greed gets the better of him and a tough choice has to be made that will shape their destiny.

Once Upon a Time in America is a long movie, at close to four hours in duration. There is a genuinely slow pacing to the film that is evocative of Leone's earlier Westerns. That was a signature of his work, yet for this story it does not work as well as it did for those earlier Westerns. This is not a bad movie, yet compared to other movies of a similar nature there are far better efforts to watch. Even Robert DeNiro and James Woods could not make this bland material worth watching, which is a strong statement against the story. This is one of those cases where a movie would have been better if it were a novel. The material is simply not right for a cinematic presentation.

#114 – *Annie Hall*. #31 on AFI list. Best Picture – 1977

#115 – *The Sixth Sense*.

Writer/director M. Night Shyamalan erupted onto the cinematic scene with this blockbuster of a film. In 1999, *The Sixth Sense* became one of the top grossing films of the year and was easily the most talked about film of the year. Everyone that is a fan of movies knows the secret twist that comes in the end. That one surprise is what created the legend of this movie, yet upon a re-watching of the film recently I found it better than when originally seen.

Psychologist Dr. Malcolm Crowe only wants to help people. One of his former patients kills himself after breaking into his house, claiming that Crowe abandoned him when he needed him most. A year later, Crowe has to come to terms with failing that child. A new patient emerges for Crowe. Cole is having major trouble in school and in dealing with his problems. He has another major problem, he can see dead people. With the help of Dr. Crowe, Cole figures out how to use his gift rather than fear it. What Dr. Crowe figures out next is how the movie sets itself apart from all the rest. The ending is a twist that would be criminal to reveal, although it is probably known by all.

I knew the twist, actually figuring it out the first time I saw the movie. Although everyone says that I do mean it. There are two basic ways to figure it out, which upon multiple viewings become even clearer. The beautiful part of this film, which grew on me, is that it becomes better the more you see it. Knowing that secret in no way detracts from the quality of the story. It actually enhances it. My only negative comment about *The Sixth Sense* is that segment toward the end that brings the picture to a complete halt. Although that scene is essential to the story, if the film could have found some way for it not to drag the story down, this film could have been one of the greats.

#116 – *Star Wars: Episode III – The Return of the Jedi*.

The great successes of the first two films set the stage for the finale. By the time this movie was released the merchandising had created a worldwide phenomenon. The *Star Wars* series is the most lucrative movie series that has ever been made, including the *Lord of the Rings* trilogy. *The Return of the Jedi* may have been the most anticipated film of all time, not only from a merchandising standpoint, but after what was revealed at the end of *The Empire Strikes Back*, audiences eagerly awaited what was to come next.

Starting off at Jabba the Hutt's lair, the rebels are intent on rescuing Han Solo from the clutches of this massive monster. Luke Skywalker has come to grips with his power and enters the lair by manipulating all those around him, with the unfortunate exception of Jabba. After defeating an even more horrendous monster Jabba keeps as a pet, the rebels are set to be put to death, which includes the recently unfrozen Han Solo. Using the force, Luke and his allies are able to escape from Jabba's clutches safe and secure. Now the movie shifts over to the land of the Ewoks. In trying to capture an empire stronghold on the planet Endor, the rebels run into these fur laden koala bear creatures. The main part of the second half of the film is the return battle between Luke and Vader and even better, the saving of Luke from the Emperor by Vader, who turns from the dark side.

It was as if this film was directed by Stanley Kubrick. There are two different movies here. The entire segment with Jabba the Hut is fantastic. The story development to put everyone into place for that final miraculous escape is perfect. A combined effort is needed and given as rescuing Han Solo becomes priority number one. The problem with the film is that the second half absolutely rots. It is totally boring with the exception of Vader saving his son from the Emperor. The movie started out great and went downhill in an incredibly fast manner by introducing nothing more than a group of characters targeted for merchandising. I know a lot of people who own this film and not one of them, including me, watch it past the Jabba the Hutt part. *The Return of the Jedi* is two separate halves of a movie that do not work well together, a la Kubrick.

#117 – *Oldboy* (South Korea).

I know it may seem as if I am culture bashing but this movie was out of this world, and not in a good way. It could be nothing more than a bizarre filmmaker taking what could have been an interesting albeit out of the ordinary story and infusing his own particular take on the matter. This is nothing new. Kubrick was famous for it. So was Hitchcock. There were times when they took a story and made something more out of it than even the writer thought possible. Then there were times like this, when the director's vision destroyed a story.

Oh Dae-Su is taken prisoner by an unknown kidnapper. He is held inside an apartment that is substituted as a cell, spending fifteen years inside this apartment with no contact to the outside world other than a television. Then all of a sudden he is released and told he has five days to figure out the answer to that all important question. As Oh Dae-Su investigates, given basic clues and instructions by his captor, he finds a connection with a female chef who he becomes emotionally and physically involved with. A clue reveals a secret to his past that may hold the answer. In the end, Oh Dae-Su discovers he has found the answer for the wrong question. The real question's answer sends him through a whirlwind of pain that he wishes he never found out in the first place.

I am not sure why anyone would like this movie. From the above description it seems like a fine story and if it were not butchered by awful direction and purposeful use of sick imagery *Oldboy* could have been fantastic. It was though and as a result the movie is one of the worst I have seen. Even when the two ultimate secrets are revealed, the two hours spent watching this disgusting piece of cinema far outweigh any significant and innovative plot points. If I were to take a guess as to why this movie was rated as highly as it is, the only thing that comes to mind are those two final revelations. For me, they are nowhere near good enough to erase two hours of absolute garbage.

#118 – *The Bicycle Thief* (Italy).

How far would a man go to feed his family? The internal depths at which one man must go so as not to face the reality of what is to come lies at the heart of this beautiful and touching film. Directed by Italian auteur Vittorio De Sica, *The Bicycle Thief* is consistently ranked among the greatest films ever made. Its stark use of neo-realism gets to the heart of the awful situation, a bicycle that is stolen. You might inquire why the simple stealing of a man's bicycle is so meaningful or whether or not this is one of those foreign cultural barriers that does not reach most Americans in their specific way of thinking? It is not simply the bicycle or the fact that it is stolen, but more what the bicycle represents; food and security for his family.

After having been out of work for close to a year, a simple man named Antonio Ricci is offered a job. The catch; he needs a bicycle. To feed his family Ricci has pawned his bicycle. It is an ironic twist that is told within such a desolate style of cinematography that the pain is immediately felt. The sheets are stripped from the bed by his wife to get the bicycle out of hock. The choice seems well worth it as Ricci, intent on working hard, can now support his family with the wage he will earn. The first day on the job Ricci's bicycle is stolen.

What commences next is an all out search for the bicycle, the only true means of support for Ricci to keep his job. It was explained to him early on that without the bicycle there would be no job. With the help of a few friends and his son, Ricci sets out on finding his stolen bicycle. Going from one market to the next, Ricci eventually sees the man who has stolen his bicycle. After a chase that leads father and son to a church, a restaurant after all hope is lost, a house of ill repute after the search for hope is regained and finally toward a choice that shall destroy all integrity and pride. That choice will feed his family, yet once that choice is made there is no turning back.

The real story here is not just a man's search for his bicycle but the tender relationship between father and son. De Sica's intent was probably to show the harsh, poverty filled atmosphere of Italy after the Second World War, yet inadvertently has created a poignant story showing the unsympathetic realities of life, which Ricci is reluctant to pass along to his son. The choice of ending is consistent with the time and the overall tone of the film. In the end, society can beat down the common man. There is good reason why this movie is as heralded as it is internationally.

#119 – *Cool Hand Luke*.

Paul Newman is about as hip as they come. From a pure acting aspect, the guy can almost do no wrong. He brings that personable and easygoing quality to every movie he acts in. The film here, *Cool Hand Luke*, seemed custom made for Newman's screen persona. It was as if the story was written with him in mind. Although not one of his critical successes, this character is one of the few that has become synonymous with his name.

Luke is arrested for cutting the heads off parking meters and sent to a prison camp. Immediately he gathers a reputation for being hard nosed, pissing off the leader of the convicts who challenges Luke to a fight. Luke earns his respect by getting his ass handed to him but not giving up. After that he presents the façade that he can do almost anything, including eating fifty eggs in one hour. A natural born rebel, Luke refuses to conform to prison life and makes an enemy of the strict and slightly psychotic warden. Numerous escapes only end up with Newman back in camp as an example to anyone who will try the same. The final escape is too much for the warden to take.

There is just an atmosphere surrounding Newman's performance that makes the film one of the most fun movies I have ever seen. The men in the prison look up to Newman and his character revels in that limelight. The egg scene and of course the car washing scene are the ones most remembered and cited by fans of this film. My preference is for the final scene when Luke is taken down. That smile on his face says it all, no matter what the warden or prison can do to him he will always be one step ahead of them. I feel like watching this movie right now.

#120 – *The General*.

Two names always emerge from the silent era of films, Charlie Chaplin and Buster Keaton. For years the two of them battled each other for greatness during the golden age of cinema, prior to the advent of talking motion pictures. Recent history regarding silent era comedies has favored Chaplin over Keaton, yet that was not always the case. The classics of Keaton were much more appreciated in the 1950's and 1960's, yet Chaplin received a momentous revival after he was given an honorary Oscar in 1971, widening the number of viewers who were introduced to his films. The belief that his films are of greater quality than those of Keaton is not shared by all.

The General tells the true story of Union soldiers stealing a Confederate train, the General and the sad but possessive engineer of the train who chases after it. Keaton uses whatever means necessary to go after his beloved train; on foot, sidecar, bicycle and another train, eventually moving on to saving the woman he loves who has been taken prisoner. Although an artistic retelling of an actual event, this was one of the more expensive silent films ever made. It recreates a piece of history that has long since been forgotten, yet is focused enough to showcase the zany antics of its star Buster Keaton. His energy and flair for comedy make this film stand out as one of his best, if not the best he has made. Many noted film critics cite *The General* as the finest film of Keaton's career and will even go far enough to say that it is one of the greatest silent films ever made.

Keaton and Chaplin are equally brilliant in their own right. Neither is greater than the other and the movies they made were all a treat to watch. The first time I saw this film I realized what all the fuss was about. He was every bit Chaplin's equal in the art of silent expression. This film did get me seeing more of his work. I must state that that had its negative effect on *The General* as my favorite Keaton film has without a doubt become 1924's *Sherlock Jr*. That film is far better than *The General*, yet this film is a fine example of a brave comedian giving it all for his craft.

#121 – *The Princess Bride*. #48 on main list.

#122 – *It Happened One Night*. #?? on main list. #35 on AFI list. Best Picture – 1934

#123 – *Unforgiven*. #98 on AFI list. Best Picture – 1992

#124 – *Ben-Hur*. #72 on AFI list. Best Picture – 1959

#125 – *Duck Soup*. #85 on AFI list.

#126 – *The Deer Hunter*. #79 on AFI list. Best Picture – 1978

#127 – *The Graduate*. #7 on AFI list.

#128 – *Butch Cassidy and the Sundance Kid*. #50 on AFI list.

#129 – *Wild Strawberries* (Sweden).

Swedish cinema begins and ends with Ingmar Bergman. The film that catapulted him to the top of the international cinema scene was *Wild Strawberries*. Bergman has a knack for exploring the deeper meaning of life, whether it be as a philosophical point or if he were examining the actual history of people. Bergman films can be somewhat tough to watch, yet if they are seen the whole way through no thinking person can deny their impact.

An elderly college professor takes a trip with his daughter-in-law across country to receive an honorary doctorate from a University. Along the trip the cynical professor relives memories from his youth in flashback scenes that are gut wrenching to witness. These scenes perfectly explain his isolation and cynicism. The main flashback scene involves the cousin he was to marry, Sara, kissing his brother, who sneaks out to kiss her while she was gathering wild strawberries. The entire trip is a cathartic transformation for both the professor and his daughter-in-law, who grows a deep sense of fondness for him along the journey.

Bergman is definitely not for anyone in a depressed mood, unless they wish to remain in that mood. The desire to infuse deep emotionality within a thematic sense causes Bergman to be loved primarily by those who can sit through the art of a story rather than needing or craving the entertainment factor. The true lover of film can enjoy both, the deeply haunting images that Bergman wishes to portray to progress his cinematic themes and the guns blazing, roller coaster of an adventure comedy thriller that is prevalent in films today. I don't understand why one type of film has to be better than the other type. A film can be good regardless of whether or not you think the material is above another type. This movie was good, but definitely not one of Bergman's best.

#130 – *Love's A Bitch* (Mexico).

One of the most rewarding types of stories is when a number of different lives intersect at that one special moment. In the real world we only know what is going on directly connected to us, yet the bigger picture of the world is that one event can have an effect on so many lives. This is the foundation of *Amores Perros (Love's A Bitch)*, one of the most ambitious stories I have ever seen attempted by a Mexican filmmaker.

A devastating car crash intertwines the stories of three separate people. Octavio is in love with his sister-in-law who is mistreated by his brother. He begins entering his dog in fights to win money so they can run away together. It is his car that is involved in the crash. Valeria is a famous fashion model who is in love with a married man and suddenly has to deal with the accident resulting from Octavio's car crashing into her. El Chivo is the bum who is hired to murder a policeman's half-brother. He is at the scene when the two cars crash into each other. Each one of the three have specific love stories and each of them has a dog that plays a vital role in their lives. As the stories are told from individual perspective, the other stories move in and out of the highlighted one, culminating with the event that explains their unique connection.

First of all, I think the organization PETA consists of a bunch of psychopaths who love animals more than people, yet even I found this movie tough to watch at times. Cultural barriers aside, what goes on throughout the story with the dogs is absolutely ridiculous and horrific to witness. It was as if love was not the only connective factor between the lives of these three people, yet rather the hardship of what happens to their dogs. One could argue that they brought it all upon themselves, but that is not what the story is designed to depict. *Amores Perros* is a hard movie to sit through, especially if you are a dog person, yet the multi layered story makes the film watchable.

#131 – *The Green Mile*.

The first adaptation of a Stephen King story by filmmaker Frank Darabont was a huge success. It took this internet database to build *The Shawshank Redemption* to the status it holds today, just in time for the second adaptation of a King story by Darabont to hit the screens. The word of mouth that helped the first undoubtedly help audiences flock to *The Green Mile*, which was not as good as Darabont's first one but a marvelous film nonetheless.

Paul Edgecomb is the chief prison guard of what is referred to as the green mile, the last holding cells of prisoners sentenced to death. One day a giant of a man is brought in. His name is John Coffey. Despite his massive size, he is actually a child in intellect and emotionality. Edgecomb soon discovers that there is more than meets the eye when it comes to this monster of a man. After Coffey relieves severe pain from an infection by simply touching him, Edgecomb delves deeper into the mystery surrounding him. To make matters worse, there is a new guard who torments the prisoners. His interference can mess up the guards plans to use Coffey and his unique powers, a power so good that he can not only heal the ill but also that he can show Edgecomb that the actual murderer of the two girls he was arrested for resides along the mile. This story is an remarkable character study with a tragic culmination and a brilliant film.

Darabont tried to reclaim the magic he created with *The Shawshank Redemption*, yet few films have been able to. This movie is amazing in its own right and should not be compared to that first film. This movie tried its hardest and came up short, yet it has its own unique brilliance and a great ensemble cast of actors, most notably the underrated Sam Rockwell and David Morse. If I had never seen *The Shawshank Redemption* I may have enjoyed this film more. That is an unfortunate reality of life, yet *The Green Mile* is still one of the better films I have seen.

#132 – *Indiana Jones and the Last Crusade*.

After the abhorration that was *Indiana Jones and the Temple of Doom*, it was a complete surprise from an artistic standpoint that a third movie in the series would be made. Critical success is much different than commercial success. After *Raiders of the Lost Ark* became both a phenomenal critical and commercial success, a sequel made perfect sense. That sequel was awful. It tried to imitate the basic setup of the first and did include a couple of nice action sequences, yet completely failed when it came down to the critical element, the story. I have to give the producers credit with this third installment, because they got back to that basic and vital element that made the original so great.

Indiana Jones is back at it, fighting the Nazis and trying to discover the hidden secrets of the ancient world. This time the artifact is the Holy Grail, the cup that Christ drank from at the last supper. Mirroring the grand adventure of the first film, Indiana Jones travels across the globe for even the most remote of clues, this time with the added distraction of having to save his father who has been kidnapped. After rescuing his father and escaping the Nazis, the Jones' boys search after the Holy Grail, now needing its mythological healing properties to save the life of Indiana's father.

The teaming of Harrison Ford and Sean Connery as his father was a stroke of brilliance.

They work incredibly well together and their dynamic as father and son comes off not only as natural but gives the main character an added depth, which helps move the story along. I am glad that they decided to add to the franchise with this film. There was the belief that this would be as awful as the middle movie, yet the producers took great care to quash those thoughts by creating a thoroughly enjoyable movie that could never live up to *Raiders of the Lost Ark* but would erase the memories of *Temple of Doom*. This movie is entertaining and a treat to watch. It is worth it when Hollywood tries, even though sometimes the end product is *Temple of Doom* rather than this really good film.

#133 – *Run Lola Run* (Germany).

This hyper kinetic MTV-esque German holy what the hell is going on fest eventually won me over as it moved toward the culmination of the film. It is as unique as any film has ever been, although at times the choices shown appear out of place and overplayed. That can be said of many films such as this one that have the courage to try and shape and alter the face of cinema. Once again the culture shock is clearly evident, yet the brilliant story, needing realism to be discarded for the plot to work, makes the film work so well as a whole.

Lola receives a phone call from her boyfriend Manni. He explains that he is in deep trouble and needs her help. She has twenty minutes to get 100,000 deutschemarks and get it to him before he robs a supermarket. Thus begins her sprint across town. First she stops at her father's office in a bank to ask him for the money. He refuses and explains that he is not her real father throwing her out in the process. When she finally reaches Manni he has already begun the robbery. Not thinking, she promptly joins in. The end result is that she is shot by policeman after they are surrounded. This is not the end as she refuses to accept her death. Thus begins the second round where a little intuition about what happened before allows her to alter the future. The second go around ends badly as well, so the events must go on once again from the start.

Run Lola Run is about the way every single one of our actions affects our lives no matter how small they may seem. It has now become a common theme in movies for a character to *will* their way out of a bad situation. Two major films, *The Butterfly Effect* and *The Jacket* use this exact premise. To my knowledge *Run Lola Run* is the first to do so and the best of these three. The two films mentioned above developed stories that were different from the one presented in this film, yet the basic premise owes its originality to *Run Lola Run*. If there was a film before 1998 to use this as their hook, I have not seen or recognized it. This movie is pretty unique and awe-inspiring.

#134 – *Back to the Future*. Oscar Snubs – Christopher Lloyd

#135 – *The Best Years of our Lives*. #37 on AFI list. Best Picture – 1946

#136 – *Life of Brian*.

There are those who firmly believe that Monty Python may be the funniest comedy troupe to ever take the stage. Their skits are famous and known throughout the United Kingdom, yet that was not enough for them. They decided to make some movies as well, based upon their take on a few historical matters. The theme of religion and divinity runs through their classic films, with a great comedic idea to switch the man who Christians believe was the savior.

Three wise men visit a baby born in a manger named Brian. Even though they brought gifts they got the address wrong. Thirty-three years later and Brian has not accomplished anything. He still loves at home with his mother, who has recently told him his father was a Roman soldier, only making him a half-Jew. Brian decides to joins a local Jewish resistance and rises up one day to the level of their messiah. No matter how hard he tries to discourage them his followers listen to every word he says, craving more. Brian is crucified and martyred, the price of having been a messiah.

The Life of Brian obviously works from a principle that anyone could become a leader if there are enough followers to blindly do whatever they say. The comedic touch that the Monty Python troupe puts on makes the movie almost bearable. There are some inside jokes about Romans and Jews that border upon the hysterical and also the seriously unfunny. When comparing which of the two famous Monty Python movies are better it is certainly not this one. I wouldn't waste my time with seeing this film unless you are a serious fan of their sketch comedy. Two or three funny lines are not worth the ninety minutes of your life it will cost you.

#137 – *Toy Story 2*.

The sequel is almost never better than the original. Some will cite *The Godfather II* as the only instance in cinema history where that idea has been disproved. I have stated earlier that *The Empire Strikes Back* is so far superior to its original that a comparison between the two is comical. Even the other trilogy that made this list, the *Lord of the Rings* films, had a second segment that did not match the first, although that is somewhat misleading because the finale of the trilogy was such an amazing film that it bested both prior movies combined. In the case of the *Toy Story* franchise, the sequel actually succeeded in outdoing the original.

Sheriff Woody and space ranger Buzz Lightyear have become good friends after their struggles over jealousy and envy from the first film. Putting those problems behind them they are ready to jointly lead Andy's toys in the day to day activities that occur when Andy is not around. A slight tear in Woody's arm forces Andy to leave him home during his week long trip to cowboy camp. Accidentally, Woody winds up as part of a garage sale and is stolen by a toy store owner who knows his true value. Seeing this, Buzz leads the toys into action, embarking on a cross town adventure to save Woody and reunite their happy team.

It was tough to match the originality of the first film so I was skeptical when going to see this movie. The characters were such a pleasure to watch that I gave it a shot. What happened was something I could never expect. The sequel offered an even better story. The actual origin of Sheriff Woody is presented here, along with a great cameo appearance by Buzz Lightyear's evil nemesis, the Emperor Zurg and my new favorite cinema cartoon character, Stinky Pete. This movie was absolutely fantastic and I only hope that if they go for a third that it is half as good as this one. Anyone who was as skeptical as I was about the quality of the sequel should disregard those notions.

#138 – *The Wages of Fear* (Italy/France).

The term original gets thrown around a lot. A film has to look and feel like no other before it for it to get tabbed as original. Alfred Hitchcock was a master of originality. Looking throughout his filmography an attentive person would recognize one original film after another. Those that were not original in the Hitchcock collection have tended to fall into obscurity. The reason why I mention Hitchcock is because the director of *The Wages of Fear*, Henri-Georges Clouzot, is often likened to

Hitchcock, specifically because of films like this one.

Four men go on what can almost be termed a suicide mission for a simple paycheck. A Frenchman named Mario only wants to get out of the South American village he finds himself stranded in. Bimba is the calm one of the bunch, due to previously working in salt mines. Nothing shakes him. M. Jo is the elder member of the group who develops a severe case of the shakes along the journey. Luigi only wants to return home as well, although back to his native Italy. He sees only the future, which allows him to cope with the stress of this job. These four men are driving a truck filled with nitroglycerine three hundred miles across a road that could surely eat them alive. Every single event on the journey is magnified due to their cargo, no matter how small it may seem.

The Wages of Fear is one of the most distinctive films I have seen. I must state that it is not for everyone. The pacing is slow, but is balanced by the plight of the four men. The pacing is also necessary for the tension to exist. I have read a lot about this movie since my first viewing. Everyone has a different take on what the story means, almost in a pseudo-*Rashomon* like existence to the individual viewer. I see it as a battle against nature. The men, even Bimba, are in a fight against the elements that may result in their existence taken away from them. That makes every moment of the trip more precious and also more dangerous. I can easily recommend this film to everyone, although if you are in the mood for a fast paced adventure, choose something else that has been watered down to quickly provide what it is you need. If you want a fantastic and developed story, watch this film.

#139 – *Platoon*. #83 on AFI list. Best Picture - 1986

#140 – *The Killing*.

Stanley Kubrick is best known for his controversial movies. He had a desire to push the envelope and create movies that people would leave the theater talking about. Many of his classic and best known films are a bit off for me. I find them to be non-cohesive in their attempts to combine two totally different variant stories. This is not the case with all of Kubrick's films, specifically the movie that made his name known throughout the industry, *The Killing*.

Johnny Clay has recently been released from prison. He is masterminding a race track heist that is both incredibly complex and brilliantly simple. It requires each and every person in on the heist to pull off their jobs perfectly and at the exact moment required of them. The first half of the film is the setup for the heist, while the second half goes through the actual heist. The heist is told through the eyes of all the parties involved, going back in time to the beginning of their involvement during the day of the heist. This provides a unique perspective on all the elements necessary to pull of the perfect crime. The audience is also witness to the problems that can occur after the criminals believe they are home free. Nothing is ever easy and the end of the film is a stroke of brilliance.

When I said that I have problems with Kubrick films I was simply being honest. *A Clockwork Orange* was fantastic for the first half and when it delved into the mind control aspect of the film it became utterly awful and purposefully nauseating. *The Killing* may have been the film that gave Kubrick the idea to go from one story to another. The problem is that it only works perfectly for this movie. I can unhesitatingly state that *The Killing* is the best movie that Kubrick ever did. It is a real shame that he could never recapture the brilliance he created here.

#141 – *The African Queen*. #17 on AFI list.

#142 – *The Gold Rush*. #74 on AFI list.

#143 – *The Philadelphia Story*. #?? on main list. #51 on AFI list.

#144 – *Glory*.

The 1970's and 1980's were generally dedicated to war films that centered on the Vietnam War. At the end of the 1980's a film came along that brought us back to our soiled heritage as a country, when brother fought against brother over the desire to own men of a different race merely because they thought they were inferior and had built an economy off the backs of others. We all know the basics of the war and that the grandest epic to delve into this particular was without a doubt *Gone With the Wind*. The time had come to tell another side of the story.

Colonel Robert Shaw volunteers to lead the first black battalion of soldiers to fight for the North during the Civil War. He is a friend of a black corporal named Searles, but understands that his leadership must come before their friendship. Shaw gets more than he bargains for as he learns that prejudices and racial discriminations exist on both sides of the fight.

The movie is technically not about Shaw. He is there to act as a pseudo-protagonist for the men. The story is more about their hopes and dreams. Some of the soldiers take that for granted, specifically Private Trip, in one of Denzel Washington's greatest performances. Morgan Freeman as Sergeant Major Rawlins is the emotional center of the film. He is what could be deemed as the middle point between Shaw and Trip. He feels both of their struggles and tries to drive both toward the greater goal, even if in the end the war turns against them. What matters is that they fought.

Glory is not a movie about a specific battle or battles, but rather shows the more important injustice of the war effort. There were battles of course, yet even in attempting to free the slaves the North was hypocritically deficient in providing black soldiers equal status. There are far reaching implications within this story, based upon actual events from the war. For a moment you begin to question whether or not the North was fighting for the freedom of a race and the abolition of slavery or whether there were financial implications that drove their desires to battle. If the fight was truly for freedom and equality, then this film flawlessly showed how not everyone loyal to the North was loyal to their public cause. This film should be required viewing for all high school students, as well as anyone who blindly chooses to be patriotic rather than assessing the deeper scenarios.

#145 – *Before Sunset*.

In 1995 a quiet and sweet movie, *Before Sunrise*, hit the screens. That film told the story of an American boy and a French girl who meet on a train and make a unique connection, discussing their way into falling for each other. The movie ends with the possibility of what is to come. Nine years later, the audiences who loved that movie finally have the answers as to what happens next, whether or not these two characters wound up together.

Nine years has passed and their planned meeting in Vienna is not kept, at least by one of them. Jesse is on the final leg of his European book tour promoting the events that occurred nine years earlier. Celine shows up at the signing and the two of them agree to get coffee and catch upon old times. As they talk the day away, moving from the coffee shop to a ferry to a cab and eventually to a quiet walk up to Celine's apartment, the movie ends again with more possibilities. Will Jesse miss his plane? That is one of the beautiful elements of this film. It is left up to the viewer to hope.

No matter what anyone says, *Before Sunset* is definitely a companion piece to the original. Both films are dialogue driven and offer an innovative perspective on relationships. After reading some of the reviews it is easy to tell that this movie has deeply affected many viewers, who claim it as one of the most beautiful films they have ever seen. I can understand that rationale because there are movies that can just feel right to people. I doubt there is a person in the world who likes one and not the other. Strike that. I like the first one much better, but both are fine films. Neither of the films are beautiful, although I can see how the setting and romantic element of the film could affect people.

#146 – *Nights of Cabiria* (Italy).

Federico Fellini is one of the geniuses of Italian cinema. In consecutive years he walked away with the Oscar for Best Foreign Language film. The first was for *La Strada*, followed by this much loved picture from 1957. Despite garnering consecutive Oscars, Fellini was still not yet a recognizable name among the international scene the way Kurosawa was.

The film follows the adventures of a tiny prostitute named Cabiria as she continues to think all will be well in a harsh world. The opening scene, where Cabiria is thrown into a river by a man she has been living with, sets the tone. She is trusting beyond reason and usually pays for it. An encounter with a famous actor shows her a better side to life, which she in turn believes is now a possibility for her one day. While attending a magic show she is picked up by a man who sincerely wants to get to know her. After they meet a few times a proposal of marriage is offered. Cabiria accepts and sells everything to live with this man. As is par for the course, things are not as rosy as they seem. Even after the heartache ensues Cabiria manages to produce a smile in the end.

I believe that Fellini was trying to show a character that truly believed life was worth living, despite her request toward the end of the film that goes unfulfilled. Cabiria's unbendable optimism borders upon insanity, yet she is not unlike many who always try to find the brightness in an often dark world. At first I hated this movie. The main character annoyed the hell out of me. Then she walked face first into a plate glass door. I laughed for an hour and then realized that she is a literary example of a pure and unrealistic optimist. No matter what happens to her and a lot happens to her, she will think it can turn around for the best. The longer the movie went on the more I liked it.

#147 – *Throne of Blood* (Japan).

There was a time when few had the courage or desire to attempt a translation of Shakespeare onto the screen. It was indeed a daunting task. That is why a foreign filmmaker such as Kurosawa is on a level above most others Japanese filmmakers, because of his bravery and vision. What Kurosawa may have been aware of is that Shakespeare translates perfectly into Japanese culture, due to its profuse reliance on story elements of a mystical nature.

The Shakespearean tragedy of Macbeth meets the traditions of the Far East. It is not a word for word or moment for moment translation of Macbeth because this movie was made for Japanese audiences. However, the material translates perfectly. A samurai warrior charged with protecting a castle for his lord is told a prophecy by a mystical witch. Once he reveals this prophecy to his wife she instructs him to murder his lord and heightens his ambition about supreme rule. As the predictions become fulfilled, this samurai's ambitions increase, leading to his ultimate downfall.

With *Ran*, Kurosawa tackled the overwhelming subject of Shakespeare's *King Lear*. That film was a spectacle to behold. With *Throne of Blood*, completed almost thirty years prior to Kurosawa's crowning achievement in film, he has crafted an equally fine film. I did not understand why *Ran* was such a great film until I saw *Throne of Blood*. The acting or overacting, also called the Noh style where expressions are overplayed, is a perfect form for translating Shakespeare. I was taken away at first with the visual beauty of *Ran*, but now understand that Kurosawa was the perfect director for interpreting Shakespeare. I only wish he had made more movies like *Throne of Blood*.

#148 – *Patton*. #89 on AFI list. Best Picture – 1970

#149 – *Finding Neverland*. Best movie – 2004

#150 – *Hero* (China).

I was a big fan of Saturday afternoon Kung Fu theater. The badly dubbed films were at first awe inspiring in their visual scenery, specifically with respect to the fighting. As I matured the films become funny, usually because of the ridiculous dubbing, language barriers and cultural differences. Still, those corny and badly dubbed movies were fun to watch. It was too bad that there were never any great ones. *Hero* is the kind of film that all those cheesy Kung Fu movies should have been, mixing action, story and stunning visual detail.

A warrior known as Nameless is invited to meet the most powerful King in the land after he vanquishes the King's three most dangerous enemies. Nameless reveals to the King how he bested the invincible warrior Sky and played the two great warriors Broken Sword and Flying Snow against one another. Once Flying Snow kills Broken Sword she takes on Nameless in battle, but falls to his mighty sword. Now that the King's enemies are killed he must offer Nameless his reward. The King's reward is disclosing that he has seen through Nameless' plan to get close enough to kill him, offering his take on how Nameless got the three warriors to conspire with him so he could infiltrate the palace of the King. While Nameless admits the King is correct, there is still more to be revealed.

Hero is one of the most beautifully filmed movies I have seen, along with *Ran* and *Reds*. Cinematography is only one element to a film, yet like *Reds*, *Hero* has an absolutely magnificent story behind it. The plot is similar to Kurosawa's classic *Rashomon* in that the story is told from differing perspectives, a cinematic theme also utilized in *The Usual Suspects*. One of the most important elements of this film is its philosophical structure. I found myself amazed at the implications of the story, where the ultimate ideal of a warrior is to lay down his sword. One minor criticism is that the story depicts that Asian tradition of gender inequality within its philosophy. The deep ideal is only understood by the men in the story. The two main female characters are at complete odds with this ideal, in keeping with the bigoted cultural traditions. All in all, *Hero* is nothing short of brilliant.

#151 – *Gladiator*. Best Picture – 2000

#152 – *A Christmas Story*. Oscar Snubs – Darren McGavin

#153 – *The Night of the Hunter*. #44 on main list.

#154 – *The Grapes of Wrath*. #21 on main list. #21 on AFI list.

#155 – *The Adventures of Robin Hood*. Best movie – 1938

#156 – *Shadow of a Doubt*.

    One thing Alfred Hitchcock did better than anyone was create suspense. One could argue that his films led toward the evolution of horror, crossing over into the overtly violent and often nonsensical slasher picture. Those films were made in large part due to failed attempts at recreating the magic that the master of horror and suspense offered with a large portion of his films. Nobody did it like Hitchcock, who had a habit of reinventing himself.

    The Newtons are a normal family. Their eldest daughter Charlie invites her uncle, who is also named Charlie, to visit and bring some much needed excitement into her humdrum life. The two Charlies have always had a special bond. When Uncle Charlie arrives, young Charlie's perks right up. Uncle Charlie is a strange fellow and his oddities begin to make young Charlie wonder. When two detectives posing as interviewers begin taking pictures and asking questions, young Charlie discovers that they are searching for a serial killer. This is where the tension builds to a frenzy as every move Uncle Charlie makes arouses young Charlie's suspicions, until he finally confesses to her about committing those murders. That's when the movie really kicks into high gear.

    One word can perfectly describe this film; creepy. There is an eerie type of tension once young Charlie begins to suspect Uncle Charlie, which builds for the rest of the movie. One of Hitchcock's earlier films, this one truly is nerve racking to watch. The only drawback was that knowing about Hitchcock left me waiting for that special surprise twist. I think that if I saw this film in 1943 it would have made a better impression on me. Still the movie is enjoyable and provides those signature suspenseful moments. Not one of his best films but certainly not one of his worst.

#157 – *For a Few Dollars More* (Italy).

    The second installment of the trilogy that made Clint Eastwood a star, *For A Few Dollars More* returns one of the great characters to the cinema only a year after his introduction, the man with no name. Like all movies that are part of a trilogy, it is tough to distinguish each as separate films. The great ones have the ability to stand on their own and reveal a special quality about them even though they are always related to the trilogy as a whole.

    The legendary man with no name is back as a bounty killer (hunter) making his fortune by ridding the west of the worst of the worst. There is another bounty hunter, the man in black. They work in the same arena yet their goals are extremely different. One of the worst criminals, Indio, is broken out of jail by his gang. The bounty on his head is more than either of the two bounty hunters have ever made at one time. Their hunt for Indio brings them into each other's cross hairs. Rather than fight it out for supremacy they decide to join forces. Eastwood must infiltrate the gang while Lee Van Cleef (the man in black) will work the problem from the outside. Things, as usual, do not go as planned. Both bounty hunters prevail in the end though, with one getting the revenge he sought.

    All fans of Sergio Leone will have their favorite choices of which of his four Westerns were actally the best. I cannot understand why anyone would choose *For a Few Dollars More* as that best of Leone's four Western classics. I would definitely rank it as the worst of the four. This is Leone's most stylized film and that is where the problem occurs. Leone took the film to a self-indulgent level in stylistic quality. It is way too over-stylized and he has sacrificed story elements for the feel and look of the film. This is something he did not do in *A Fistful of Dollars* and did not repeat in *The*

Good, The Bad and The Ugly. Those films had a flow resulting from the combination of all cinematic elements, which is missing from this segment. I'd say watch it if you enjoy art more than film.

#158 – *Die Hard*.

In the 1980's the action movie got an intense revival. After the death of the true Western, where a lone gunfighter could ride into town and save the day, there was something missing from cinema that strongly needed to be resurrected. In 1987, *Lethal Weapon* burst onto the scene and created a fantastic slam bam action movie where good triumphed over evil while overcoming major obstacles. That film was a buddy movie though, so the void still existed. Enter *Die Hard*. The action movie genre would never be the same again after this film.

New York cop John McClane travels to Los Angeles to visit his wife, who has moved across the country for business. She works for a Japanese company in a downtown skyscraper. McClane meets her there as the company is having a Christmas party. McClane is not the only visitor to the skyscraper on that night. A group of thieves masquerading as terrorists take over the building. McClane is able to sneak away from them before they know who he is, although they will find out shortly that he is not only a police officer but also a major thorn in their side. The one thing that they never could have counted on was McClane seeing things through until the end.

The action movies released after 1988 all emanate from *Die Hard*. The sequels could never measure up to the original, even though the second one was decent. For that matter though, not many action films that followed could measure up to *Die Hard*. Most have tried to emulate its success with few films coming even remotely close. This blockbuster action picture reinvented the genre but also broke the mold in the process. Hollywood should have buried the mold with it, because nothing since has recreated its brilliance. This film truly revolutionized modern cinema.

#159 – *Gandhi*. Best Picture – 1982

#160 – *Gone With the Wind*. #3 on main list. #4 on AFI list. Best Picture – 1939

#161 – *Kind Hearts and Coronets*.

Although not specifically a comedy, this is the prototypical Ealing film. Ealing studios came out with a number of films in the 1940's and 1950's, the majority of them starring Alec Guiness, who was unfortunately better known for his role as Obi-Wan Kenobi from *Star Wars*. *The Lavender Hill Mob* was the funniest comedy from Ealing studios, yet *Kind Hearts and Coronets* is the better film. It is the best film that Ealing ever produced.

Louis Mazzini's mother was of the royal family D'Ascoyne. She married an Italian and was therefore forced to remove herself from her family. As Louis grew up his mother reveled in telling him stories of the D'Ascoyne family. Despite attempts to try and reconcile with them, they continually shunned her and Louis, who by her accounts was eighth in line to inherit the dukedom. After an encounter with one of the uppity D'Ascoynes in line ahead of him, which causes immediate termination from his job, Louis embarks on a diabolical plan to begin murdering the eight D'Ascoynes in line ahead of him so he can rightfully reclaim his birthright and the dukedom. Once he succeeds an ironic twist has him arrested for the murder of his lover's husband, which he did not commit. A bargain is struck with his former lover and Louis is released after a suicide note is found, although Louis leaves behind his memoirs containing vital information of his rise to the dukedom.

Kind Hearts and Coronets has been described as a dark comedy. I can see that, although it is a dark comedy in that extremely dry British humor way. The main character is thoroughly annoying in his effete pomposity, yet the film is saved by the amazing performance by Alec Guiness, who plays all eight of the D'Ascoyne family members ahead of Louis that he must take out to rise to the dukedom. I will say that this movie is one of the best of its kind, yet there aren't too many like it to compare it to. That fact adds to its quality, yet it is Guiness' performance that steals the show here.

#162 – *Shrek.*

The only thing left of fairy tales is to turn the tables and poke fun at their silly nature. I am surprised it took this long to come up with the idea to do that, yet it was well worth the wait. The signature animation feature from DreamWorks studio, *Shrek* was such a breath of fresh air that it became both a critical and commercial success. The animation is fantastic, although slightly different from Pixar. It is the story that corralled fans of all ages, as is usually the case.

Shrek is a happy ogre. He lives by himself in a swamp and that is the way he likes it. Once the masses of fairy tale creatures are forced into his private swamp, Shrek must seek out the diminutive Lord Farquad to get rid of these overly happy and bothersome creatures. Farquad agrees to give Shrek his swamp back if he rescues a fair princess from a dragon guarded castle and deliver her to Farquad. Shrek, along with his self-appointed sidekick, Donkey, rescue the princess and deliver her to Farquad. On the journey, Shrek and the princess, Fiona, begin to fall for each other. Fiona is hiding a secret that she believes will make Shrek shun her. After giving her to Farquad Shrek eventually returns to claim Fiona as his, with his fantastic comedic sidekick Donkey.

Every thing about this movie is great. The story is wholly original and the comedy is as funny as any live action movie. Mike Myers and Eddie Murphy delivering the voices of Shrek and Donkey create one of the great buddy teams in movie history. I understand that they are merely reciting words into a microphone to work with digital animation, but no one should be dissecting this movie to understand its thematic statements. It is pure unadulterated fun and a movie that everyone can enjoy. It does not matter what age you are, everyone I know enjoys this film.

#163 – *Mystic River.*

Clint Eastwood is one of Hollywood's greatest actors. Best known for his role as *'the man with no name'* in Sergio Leone's spaghetti Westerns and as policeman Dirty Harry Callahan, Eastwood has created a wealth of memorable characters. He might even be better as a director. From his directorial debut in the stalker film *Play Misty for Me*, Eastwood has slowly built a name for himself as an accomplished director, winning the Academy Award for Best Director in 1992 for the modern Western classic, *Unforgiven*. He continued making films from there, with his second best directorial effort coming in this tragic story of loss, *Mystic River*.

A young girl is murdered and the police begin investigating the case. The girl's father, former convict Jimmy Markum, decides it is in his best interest to ask around and find out what happened. One of the officers investigating the case is Markum's childhood friend Sean Devine, and one of the possible suspects is another of Markum's childhood friends, Dave Boyle. Boyle has never been the same since he was kidnapped and molested as a child, taken right in front of Markum and Devine. His actions since the death of Markum's daughter make him a suspect by both the police and by Markum's informants. Dave is hiding something, but when the investigation into Markum's daughter is finally solved, it is too late to take back what has already mistakenly happened.

Mystic River is known for the film that finally rewarded Sean Penn for his brilliant acting career. Tim Robbins as Dave Boyle also took home an Oscar for his tortured performance. If it were not for the grand finale in the *Lord of the Rings* trilogy this film could have given Eastwood his second directing Oscar, which would have made it two in a row the following year for *Million Dollar Baby*. Working from a novel, *Mystic River* is a great tale of mystery and discovery, of suspicion and redemption and one of the best films of that particular year. It is one of the more complete stories told on film and is without a doubt another in the line of Eastwood's recent string of great movies.

#164 – *Witness for the Prosecution*.

There is no arguing that Agatha Christie is one of the greatest mystery writers that ever picked up the pen. A large number of her stories have been turned into films, all introducing quirky characters and an off beat story that will always provide interesting twists and turns. Christie's stories are perfect for transfer to the big screen. One of her most revered plays, *Witness for the Prosecution*, made it there in 1957.

A lawyer, played by Charles Laughton, recently released from the hospital after recovering from a minor heart attack is approached to defend a man who will be charged with murder. Against the wishes of his crazed, overprotective nurse and his doctor's orders, the lawyer chooses to accept the case after the client passes a self created test of his to determine honesty. The majority of the intrigue unfolds within the courtroom, where Laughton shines as a stuffy and overblown but greatly knowledgeable lawyer, challenging all the minor arguments posed against his client. The more revealed about the case the more things are not what they seem. Laughton masterfully presents enough evidence and doubt to get his client off. It does not end there, as the major twist of the story is to follow, which is also followed by an even greater twist and then another one. To reveal them would be wrong. All I can say is be prepared for the insights to keep coming after the trial is over.

The placement of twist on top of twist on top of twist does not work here. It is too much at once for the concepts to be believable. Nevertheless, *Witness for the Prosecution* has become somewhat of a cinema classic. The banter between Laughton and his real life wife Elsa Lanchester as the skittish and overbearing nurse highlight the film, yet the story is dull and the ending would have worked if it were not so much all at once. Christie really went for the whole gamut yet should have pulled back a notch to create a more believable ending. I found the film an utter disappointment and do not see why it is rated as highly as it is. It is often boring and the characters are uninteresting.

#165 – *The Conversation*. #33 on main list.

#166 – *Brief Encounter*.

David Lean a masters of the epic. His three films between 1957 and 1965; *A Bridge on the River Kwai*, *Lawrence of Arabia* and *Doctor Zhivago* have all become classics in their own right. Two later films, *Ryan's Daughter* in 1970 and *A Passage to India* in 1984 continued that trend of filmmaking. Whenever you hear the name David Lean you immediately think of an epic, yet early in his career he made a fantastic small film that set the tone for his directorial prowess.

Laura Jesson is a woman of middle class. Dr. Alec Harvey is of a similar class to Jesson. They meet one day at a train station. Jesson's marriage is in a state of disarray, where she begins to feel less and less each day. In walks this man who arouses her interest. Their mutual curiosity creates the idea of a possible affair, yet the movie is not about a torrid affair, but rather about the possibility of something more. The movie is told through her perspective of what could have been, yet finishes on what has been deemed as a downbeat ending. It is a more realistic style of storytelling than the ultra happy song and dance endings pumped out regularly though, making it innovative.

Brief Encounter was a landmark film for a number of reasons. It is often described as the first *'woman's'* film due to its depictions of themes generally unseen in film before. This film was also the first British film to breakthrough at the Academy Awards, in 1946. Lean received a nomination for director and Celia Johnson a nomination for Lead Actress. The film is most definitely a tearjerker, but not a film that you will walk away from and soon forget. That raises it up a notch to a different level, one that for me is just below the status of classic.

#167 – *Talk To Her* (Spain).

Internationally acclaimed writer/director Pedro Almodovar has as unique a style to his work as any other director in history. One could attribute it to the clash in culture, yet that would be an easy over simplification. Almodovar's stories center on time honored literary and cinematic themes such as love, loss and sexual identity. *Hable con Ella* is no departure from his trademark work, yet in true visionary style this movie has its own distinct qualities. Although comparable to Almodovar's earlier films, it is most assuredly a step forward.

There are two main characters, Marco and Benigno. Benigno is a male nurse and Marco is a writer. Their paths cross at the beginning of the film as they are sat next to one another during an interpretive dance performance. Benigno is in love with a dance student named Alicia. Marco falls in love with a bullfighter named Lydia. The two men come into contact with one another again after Lydia is severely gored by a bull and falls into a vegetative coma. Benigno works in the hospital taking care of Alicia, who has been in a coma for awhile. The two men develop a friendship based upon their mutual hardships. They are similar in some ways but extremely different in others. Their differences are what eventually bring the two men closer together before the unfortunate end.

Almodovar has crafted another fantastic cinematic experience with *Talk to Her*. He has a flair for developing strange characters and maneuvering them into the paths of others who profoundly affect them. There is simply that bizarre extra element that Almodovar revels in that keeps his work from bordering upon the status of classic. There are many who believe he has achieved that level already, yet his work suffers in the same way that David Lynch's original work suffers, from an over reliance to include unnecessary characters for the mere sake of spicing up the story in an unusual way. For Almodovar, it remains the constant expansion of the theme of sexual identity. For this film it was when he had a man who had shrunk to a few inches tall actually crawl inside a vagina. Like all of his films, this one is something that should be seen, but not revered.

#168 – *Stand by Me*.

Who would have ever thought that a Stephen King novel could actually be a heartwarming tale of four friends who bond during a trip? Rob Reiner. King has had many of his novels and novellas turned into films, yet all of them were classified as horror films, sticking to the initial intent of the story. *Stand by Me* changed that. This was the first adaptation of a King story that did not have that aspect of horror or suspense in mind. This opened the door for the two later adaptations by Frank Darabont that became fantastic films of hope and courage.

Four twelve year old boys set out a trip to see a dead body. One of the boys overhears his brother and a friend talking about seeing it, but that they should not tell anyone about it. The four boys, Gordie, Teddy, Vern and Chris, spend the next two days in search of the body. Along the way they share stories and poke fun at each other, while escaping trouble in the form of a junkyard dog, an oncoming train while they are on a bridge it crosses and a pond full of leeches. Once they find what they came in search of, a group of teenagers try to muscle them out of they way and take credit for finding the dead body. Recalling this weekend after the death of one of the boys, the writer who narrates the story comes to terms with the best summer he had and the great friends from that trip.

The element of this film that makes it so endearing is the camaraderie of the four boys who work together and protect each other. Although the group fractions off after returning to school, with two of them remaining close friends, it is that special time of friendship that we all have had at one time or another that shines through. Beautifully nostalgic, the music of the movie is enough to bring a smile to your lips. This is one of those special kind of movies that is a treat to see.

#169 – *The Celebration* (Denmark).

On March 22nd, 1995, a new form of filmmaking was announced, Dogme 95. Dogme 95 is a style, or more to the point, a movement in filmmaking that rejects the new trend in cinema to create huge blockbuster films based on special effects and digital gimmicks. There are a strict set of rules, but more importantly the focus on cinema within the Dogme 95 style is to create better stories and induce finer acting to highlight those stories. Dogme 95 was started by a group of Danish filmmakers, led by Lars Von Trier, noted for his film *Breaking the Waves* and the director of this masterpiece, Thomas Vinterberg. *Breaking the Waves*, not technically a Dogme 95 film, may be more known, but *The Celebration* is one of the best foreign films ever made.

The patriarch of a Danish family, Helge, is turning sixty. Everyone is gathering at the lodge he owns for a celebration. One person not in attendance is one of Helge's daughters, who has recently committed suicide. She is part of a set of twins, with Christian, who attends with a distinct purpose in mind. Also in attendance are Helge's son Michael, who has major marital, alcohol and anger issues, Helge's daughter Helene, who invites her new boyfriend, a black American man and the rest of the family. The party turns from festive to silent to utter shock once the issues are brought to the forefront and can no longer be ignored. Nobody wins, although some clarity is finally observed.

Thomas Vinterberg's *The Celebration*, or *Festen*, is the first film to employ the Dogme 95 style of filmmaking. Generally it is tough to get a new style of filmmaking right on the first attempt, especially a style as ambitious and difficult as Dogme 95. Vinterberg did it though. His film is almost perfect cinema, the best of every pure element that a film should focus on. I was extremely skeptical when I had to see this film to analyze it for this list. Since my original viewing I have watched it three more times. I think it is one of the greatest films I have ever seen. It would have made the top ten of the main list had the rules been appended to include foreign films. I almost want to go back and change them so it can.

#170 – *The 400 Blows* (France).

In 1977 Steven Spielberg created a magic and light show. Although critically acclaimed, it was deeply overshadowed by another magic and light show from that same year. Spielberg wrote a part in his story specifically for a famous French director, Francis Truffaut. Truffaut's first full length film was *The 400 Blows*. This is the film that was responsible for the new wave of French cinema, influencing filmmakers like Spielberg for decades.

Antoine Doniel is a twelve year old boy that nobody understands. His parents do not pay attention to him other than to scold him and accuse him of lying. His teacher at school is the same way. Naturally, Antoine acts out. He is expelled from school and later arrested for breaking and entering. Rather than proper punishment he is sent to a prison camp for troubled juveniles, a reform school. What Antoine wants more than anything is freedom. He has seen what restrictions the world around him has put on him and only longs for the right to make his own choices.

The way the story is presented, an all out exploration on the disenfranchisement of youth, Antoine would be better off on his own. He has matured on the streets and would more than likely do a better job at taking proper care of himself than his adulterous mother and stepfather can. Truffaut toys with the notion that Antoine's intellect and experience will win out in the end, yet that is not the case. The famous final shot, where the camera moves into a close-up of Antoine on the beach into freeze frame is one of the classics of foreign cinema and oft-repeated. I found myself sympathizing with Antoine, as most do, yet for some reason that was simply not enough for me.

#171 – *Big Fish*.

Who hasn't told an over embellished version of what happened from some aspect of their lives? Of all the Tim Burton films that he has made over the years, this may be the one that has the least sense of the macabre. I am actually surprised that he directed this after I saw the movie for the first time. Going in to the film I was waiting for the severed head or the guy with a pair of rusty pliers for feet. That character never came. I waited, but he or she never showed up.

A man flies home because his father is stricken with terminal cancer. He attempts to learn more about the exaggerated stories he has told regarding his younger days, which are told through flashbacks of what took place during the father's life. These flashbacks detail the man, Edward Bloom, and his experiences and adventures during the times he was growing up as a teenager, meeting the love of his life, fighting in wars for his country and meeting all sorts of strange and interesting creatures. His son does not feel that he knows him at all, believing that all the stories are lies, until the funeral of his father where many of the people he spoke of arrive to pay their respects. It is a sweet moment when the son realizes maybe he did know his father all along.

I enjoy Tim Burton and his work. The original *Batman* is one of the finest films of the 80's. He followed that with a string of great movies that all bordered upon the level of extreme weirdness. Perhaps that is why I liked them so much, because I hated this film. It was way overblown and Ewan McGregor's attempts to convince us that the overblown stories are real were sorely overacted. I never thought I would say this but Burton should go back to cutting people's heads off and giving them scissors for hands. Burton should stick to what he knows, the morbid and dreary stuff.

#172 – *The Hustler*. Best movie – 1961

#173 – *The Wild Bunch*. #80 on AFI list.

#174 – *Stalag 17*. Favorite Films

#175 – *Magnolia*.

Paul Thomas Anderson has made two prior films to this one. The first was a small film with an all-star cast of actors who knew how to work together as an ensemble unit. The four stars of that film, *Hard Eight*, were Gwyneth Paltrow, John C. Reilly, Philip Baker Hall and Samuel L. Jackson. They allowed the story to be front and center rather than their individual performance. *Hard Eight* was followed by the monumental breakthrough hit *Boogie Nights*, where performances began to dominate the material rather than blending into the background. This film, Anderson's third, is nothing but performances, so much so that I had to wonder why the stories were there at all. Independent monologues could have just as easily been substituted.

The story follows nine characters and their lives during one day. All of the characters are connected to each other in some specific way and all of them are in the midst of dealing with some major emotional problem. Not one of the characters is normal, or even remotely happy. They all come to grips with loss, lies, redemption and or death as any other tragic character in any other movie usually does. The movie inter-cuts all these stories building toward a culminating finale that has to be seen to be believed and makes one wonder what the hell was Anderson thinking?

I loved *Hard Eight* and thought that *Boogie Nights* was hysterical in its presentation of the ridiculous nature of the pornographic industry. Anderson wanted to create an epic and that he did. What he did not do was create a good movie. The movie is concerned more with showcasing character driven material rather than producing material that characters can work with and combine into a cohesive whole. I can see why all the actors wanted to be involved with this piece. It is an absolute showcase for them, a way to explore their craft in monologue type scenes. I don't see why Anderson thought these individual stories could be so easily connected by one single event.

#176 – *Nosferatu* (Germany).

The first vampire film to use the historic Count Dracula was released in 1931. Bela Lugosi starred as the nefarious monster in what I believe to be the original film that created the horror genre. Nine year earlier, A German film came out based on the Bram Stoker novel that was not allowed to use the name Dracula. Director F. W. Murnau titled his film *Nosferatu* and it has become one of the all time creepiest movies ever made. The joke that Count Dracula has grown into has taken him over the realm of comedic horror, the same way Frankenstein and the Wolfman have. Count Orlok remains a dark clad figure drenched in evil.

The mysterious Count Orlok wishes to purchase land in the town of Bremen. A real estate employee named Hutter is assigned the case and travels to the Carpathian Mountains to close the deal. On his journey the people he encounters provide an eerie sense of dismay when he mentions Count Orlok, yet he must complete his job. Orlok is a strange figure, perhaps the strangest the cinema has ever known. Hutter eventually realizes there is danger and escapes, yet Count Orlok is already on his way to Bremen by boat. Hutter's wife Ellen discovers the secret of how to kill the creature, keeping out until the sun rises. It is the classic Stoker story with the names changed.

Murnau has crafted what is generally called one of the scariest movies ever made. I am of the similar opinion of most film critics that the fright has severely waned from this film. Don't get me wrong, there is still an eerie and creepy aura about the film and the one scene that most know who have heard about the movie, where Count Orlok rises from his coffin straight up, will surely provide chills. Perhaps the film has not become campy because the material was treated differently, where the realism of Count Orlok was readily apparent. A better film is 2000's *Shadow of the Vampire*, based on the making of *Nosferatu*. This film postulated that Max Schreck, who played Orlok, was an actual vampire and that Murnau made a deal with him to create a more realistic film.

#177 – *Harvey*

For those who loved the film *Donnie Darko*, for whatever reason, this should be required viewing. Both movies are similar in many ways, although the nature of this movie is far gentler and the story is far superior. The performances are also brilliant when compared to the weird performances in *Donnie Darko*. Those who have seen both movies will understand why the two films are linked. Some might say that *Harvey* is the father to that other film. If that's true than *Harvey* never should have had any kids, because they turned out disturbed and quite awful.

Elwood P. Dowd is a simple man. He likes taking walks and lives with his sister. They take care of each other. Also, Elwood has an invisible giant six foot imaginary friend named *Harvey*. One more thing. *Harvey* is a rabbit. One of the things that Elwood and *Harvey* take great pleasure in is walking down to the saloon and drinking. Elwood's sister decides to have Elwood examined by a doctor from a sanitarium. She is actually only looking out for herself because with Elwood around always talking to *Harvey* it has hampered her social activities. What is discovered by all is that *Harvey* produces no real harm and that they might be better off with a friend like him.

Beginning as a madcap comedy romp, including a case of mistaken identity where the eccentric sister is confined because of her peculiarities, *Harvey* turns into a sweet emotional tale of a simple man who is good natured at heart. Eccentric is perhaps the wrong word for Elwood's sister. I would have called her a selfish and snobby douche rocket, yet even she realizes that there is no real harm in having an imaginary friend to keep her brother happy, other than to her own interests. James Stewart continually proved after World War II that he could tackle challenging roles. This was one of his finest acting jobs, conveying the sweet yet flawed nature of a kind and helpful man.

#178 – *Manhattan*.

I read that the character Woody Allen plays in *Manhattan* is different from any other character he plays. That is such an oversimplification that it almost loses credibility as an accurate statement. Allen plays the same neurotic character he always writes for himself, a neurotic, yet intellectual and relationship impaired Manhattanite. There is a distinct depth to each of his characters yet they are all minor parts of the same troubled persona, the character that Allen chooses to base his screen image upon. One might be more selfish than the other, but when it all boils down to it every character possesses every quirk of every other character he has played.

A forty year old man is dating a seventeen year old high school student, yet struggles with the obvious problems that occur as a result. Allen slowly moves toward self-destructing his unhealthy relationship so he can engage in an even unhealthier, yet non-felonious relationship with his best friend's mistress. Brilliant one liners are included throughout to move the basic story around. The main element here is to show how one man can continue to sabotage every relationship he has and negatively affect those he gets involved with, including his former wife who has turned to lesbianism and decided to write a tell all book about their severe marriage problems.

Allen's movements as an actor are always the same though, giving the false impression that every character is the same, even though he writes them all from a comedic standpoint. On the written page I can imagine that the character is far different than Allen's impersonation of what he wants to come across upon the screen. Many have cited *Manhattan* as Allen's intellectual and cinematic masterpiece, although there are still the legions that prefer the less serious *Annie Hall*. I love neither and if I had to choose I would go with option C and watch *Sleeper* or *Bananas*. I am not a Woody Allen fan but I can appreciate his humor. For a movie of his to be enjoyable the humor needs to be the primary focus. I did enjoy this for those one liners, but found the story tedious.

#179 – *The Straight Story*.

Director David Lynch is known for his warped sense of storytelling. His films are usually of the variety that does not make sense to many who see them while simultaneously making little if any sense to almost all. *Lost Highway* is a perfect example of this. Every so often Lynch will make a film that does not rely on intricate plot points that border upon the psychologically demented. *The Straight Story* is one of those films, not usually associated with the kind that Lynch is known for. Sometimes filmmakers simply enjoy different stories.

Alvin Straight is a seventy-three year old man with numerous health problems. The story begins as he is found on the kitchen floor after falling and not having the ability to get up. A trip to the doctor reveals that Alvin is indeed in bad shape, yet as cantankerous as he is he will not be changed. News comes in that his brother has had a bad stroke. Despite the fact that they have not spoken in ten years, Alvin begins setting the foundation to go see him and mend their problem. Refusing to take public transportation and not being able to drive, Alvin sets about making the trip from Iowa to Wisconsin on his lawn mower, meeting a slew of interesting people during the almost two month trip. Along the way we also learn about Alvin and why he is the way he is.

I believe the contest is over. The search can come to an end. *The Straight Story* is the slowest movie ever made. That is not to say that the movie is bad. On the contrary, it is a fine film with an absolutely brilliant performance by Richard Farnsworth as Alvin Straight. Be prepared though. This is visual Nyquil and a surefire cure for insomnia. If you are wide awake I highly recommend this film. Along with *The Elephant Man*, this is one of David Lynch's best films. Although Alvin has a slow and archaic demeanor to him, the feeling comes across that more people should be like him, especially in the way they treat their fellow man. I believe that was one of the main points of the film.

#180 – *Bringing Up Baby*. #97 on AFI list.

#181 – *Spartacus*.

With two major hits under his belt, Kubrick decided to test the boundaries of what he would be allowed to do as a filmmaker. Those previous two hits were 1956's *The Killing* and 1957's *Paths of Glory*. Their success brought with it the ability to garner more control as a filmmaker. The tense problems between star Kirk Douglas and Kubrick over control did little to help. Their mutual rejection of the end product has definitely hurt the overall appeal of this film. Bad timing, coming only one year off the heels of *Ben-Hur*, was also one of the factors that led to this film's historical recognition, almost viewed as redundant rather than remarkable.

Spartacus was sold into slavery as a thirteen year old. Saved from death he is trained to become a gladiator, until he orchestrates a revolt against those holding him captive and the other gladiators in training. After escaping, Spartacus begins to lead the gladiators who escaped from the training camp. His mission is to gather enough slaves like him and march on Rome, a feat never tried before. There is the romantic interest between Spartacus and a slave girl named Varinia and the political battle between Crassus and Gracchus to provide a backdrop yet the epic quest of Spartacus is the primary concern here. It is not his failure that matters, but his attempt at victory.

The first time I saw this film was only a few years ago. Even on my first viewing I noticed a strange familiarity about it. Perhaps it was the sense of having seen it because I had heard so many things about the film. Then I realized. The 2000 Best Picture winner *Gladiator* is eerily reminiscent of *Spartacus*, with a more modernized and pumped up feel to it. I am not the biggest fan of Kubrick but this was one of his best films. Even at over three hours in length, with that bizarre sense of familiarity, I found myself drawn into the story and thoroughly enjoyed this film. In comparison to *Ben-Hur* or *Gladiator*, *Spartacus* is far better than both yet did suffer from ego issues. I do feel that *Spartacus* would have been a classic had it not been deliberately orchestrated as that next great epic.

#182 – *Arsenic and Old Lace*.

Cary Grant was one of the great stars of his day. It is an absolute shame that he was never properly awarded for his acting efforts. He will go down as one of the few performers who was at home in almost every style and genre of movie, possessing such a natural charisma about him that it made the audience believe what was happening upon the screen was really happening to him. That is why when Grant was in comedies, the crazier they got the more enjoyable the movie became. *Arsenic and Old Lace* may contain Cary Grant's funniest performance.

Long time bachelor Mortimer Brewster has finally met someone he is willing to marry, Elaine. Before he goes on his honeymoon with his new bride he stops in to check on his two aunts, Abby and Martha. Also living in the house is Brewster's brother. He thinks he is Teddy Roosevelt. Needless to say there is a strange aura around the house that is only calmed by his lovable aunts. Then he finds out that his aunts have poisoned twelve people and hid them in their basement. The madcap hilarity starts as Grant does whatever he can to protect them, when the police, his homicidal brother and his brother's plastic surgeon arrive at the house. The comedy of errors comes in droves.

Based on an original play and touched up for the screen by the genius writing team behind *Casablanca*, *Arsenic and Old Lace* is one of Frank Capra's greatest achievements as a director. Two of his films landed on the main list and another of Capra's classics will be discussed in the following chapter, but this deserves to be placed on a short list directly under those three in quality. One of the great things about this film is the ensemble cast, all characters in their own right. It is tough to single out anyone other than Grant, although the two aunts help give this movie that extra comedic edge.

#183 – *Dog Day Afternoon*.

From 1973 to 1975 there were two men who vied for acting supremacy, Jack Nicholson and Al Pacino. They fought it out by making fantastic movies and receiving numerous accolades, with

Nicholson eventually winning that battle. In three successive years, Nicholson and Pacino were nominated for Best Actor Oscars, all for uniquely different roles from the prior year. Of the three roles that Pacino was nominated for, this is by far his best pure acting performance. He unfortunately ran into the juggernaut of *One Flew Over the Cuckoo's Nest*.

Sonny, Sal and a third man enter a bank in broad daylight to rob it. Sonny and Sal have different reasons for the robbery. Sal is involved because Sonny is his friend and he is not too bright. The reveal of that is in a simple scene where Sonny asks Sal what country he wants to go to and Sal responds by telling him 'Wyoming'. Sonny wants the money for an extremely different reason. He needs it to pay for a sex change operation for his wife, a man named Leon. The robbery goes slower than expected, prompting the third man to flee. The next thing Sonny and Sal know is that they are surrounded by cops outside the bank and the event has turned into a media circus. All Sonny wants to do is get away from the situation and make Leon happy. All Sal wants to do is make it known that he is not a homosexual. Their unique chemistry makes the claustrophobic atmosphere work.

Director Sydney Lumet is brilliant at working within cramped settings and getting the most out of them. The bank in this film serves a similar function as the courtroom in *The Verdict*, the jury room in *Twelve Angry Men* or the news station in *Network*. The movie is dominated by Pacino though. When he eventually won the Best Actor Oscar for *Scent of a Woman* in 1992, there were a bevy of performances that many postulated it was a make-up award for. I believe that if he ever deserved an Oscar before it was for this role, as well as the highly underrated John Cazale, who is brilliant in everything. Once again, the year in question, 1975, doomed this movie from the start.

#184 – *All Quiet on the Western Front*. #54 on AFI list. Best Picture – 1930

#185 – *The Day the Earth Stood Still*.

Outer space invasion movies from the early years of cinema always came off as campy and funny, rather than what was intended. The sight of flying saucers on clearly visible strings and humans running in fear as giant aliens attacked them with lasers made these movies classics, although classical farces. The 1951 sci-fi film *The Day the Earth Stood Still* was not that type of film. To my knowledge it is the first film of its kind to introduce an alien that did not want to conquer and destroy the Earth as its goal, but rather insure peace.

A UFO lands in Washington D.C. and paranoia immediately ensues. First contact comes not with open arms but with weapons firing. The alien in charge, Klaatu, is struck by gunfire. At that moment a robot alien emerges from the spaceship and disintegrates the weaponry on the spot. The believed to be injured alien is taken to an army hospital, where he escapes in order to learn more about this planet. It is easy for him to blend in with humans since his form so closely resembles theirs. While learning about the planet he stays at a boarding house and meets with a physics professor who he reveals his secret to. In the end, Klaatu decides to leave Earth, but leaves them with a warning that if they continue their current course of war the planet will be obliterated for the safety of the galaxy.

When I first saw this film I was struck by how smart a movie it came off as. It was not the common green aliens attacking every human in sight type of alien invasion film, but rather one that attempted to offer a message of understanding and visiting by a much greater race of creature, something that the warring humans should aspire to be. Even after Klaatu is shot by paranoid soldiers who surrounded his spaceship, he reacts in an intelligent way. The movie stands out as one of the most intelligent films I have ever seen, sticking to its message at all costs rather than taking the easy way out and turning itself into a battle between humans and aliens. Because of the intellectual approach it employs, the movie does not turn campy at all or date badly. Even though it is fifty years old it is one of those films that is still extremely enjoyable to watch today.

#186 – *The Cabinet of Dr. Caligari* (Germany).

  Germans obviously have different cultural traits than Americans. This can easily be seen in their cinema. There is a morose sort of expressionism that ruminates throughout the work of German filmmaking, specifically prior to the advent of sound. *The Cabinet of Dr. Caligari* is one of those odd films that clearly has its roots in the macabre sentiment of that culture's history at the time. On an historical note, this film paved the way for *Nosferatu*, which made the vampire film a staple of horror cinema.
  Francis sits next to an old man, about to tell him a story to top the one just told to him. He begins by recalling a fair he went to in his hometown accompanied by a friend of his named Alan. One of the features of the fair was a somnambulist (sleepwalker) named Cesare, controlled by a man named Dr. Caligari. Cesare has been asleep for twenty-three years and can only be awakened by Dr. Caligari, to reveal the future. Alan asks him how long he shall live and is told that he shall be dead by dawn. After Alan is murdered that night, Francis involves the police. They discover that the story of Caligari and Cesare goes back centuries. The three mysteries at the end of the story only serve to create more suspicion as to what is going on. The film leaves off with numerous possibilities.
  Although it seems quite dated today, as many silent films often do, *The Cabinet of Dr. Caligari* is still an amazingly creepy mystery. The dawn of the slasher film has lessened the effects of the classic horror film. That is why it is such a treat to see a film such as this one. There is no camp or gore at all. The horror is conveyed brilliantly through a perfect tone of creepiness through the revelation of mystery. The interpretive element of speculating what the true nature of the story was meant to be is a stroke of brilliance that few films offer today. I was surprised at how much I liked this film the first time I saw it. Subsequent viewings have only solidified that opinion.

#187 – *His Girl Friday*.

  Director Howard Hawks was one of the few directors who could excel in a multitude of genres. He made great Westerns (*Rio Bravo* and *Red River*). He made great mysteries (*The Big Sleep* and *To Have and Have Not*). The genre that he is most associated with is comedy though. His 1938 film *Bringing Up Baby* is often cited as his finest achievement. I have spoken about that film earlier, yet this 1940 classic is along those same lines, but far better.
  Cary Grant stars as newspaper man Walter Burns. His ace reporter is Hildegaard Johnson, known as Hildy, played by Rosalind Russell. I should have said she *was* his ace reporter because Hildy is quitting the business to get married. Hildy is marrying Bruce Baldwin, a nice sweet guy who only wants to treat her well. That is where Burns steps in. He begins playing tricks on Baldwin that will unnerve him in order to keep Hildy with the paper, or more importantly him. He knows that what she loves best is the rapid fire pace of big time reporting and he needs her there with him as much as he loves her. Throwing her neck deep into a story is what might just make her realize it.

If you are a fan of quick back and forth dialogue with all the natural chemistry that is possible between actors, then *His Girl Friday* is the movie for you. This film was actually a remake of the 1931 film *The Front Page*, discussed previously. There have also been two additional remakes, one in 1976 and another in 1988 called *Switching Channels*. The last two and the original could not match the brilliance of this film, from its fantastic direction to its star chemistry to its way of treating the story as it really should be treated, one of a pace that should keep you gasping for air, and does.

#188 – *Diabolique* (France).

The story of the buying of this novel is almost as great as the book itself. After reading the book, Alfred Hitchcock picked up the phone and asked to buy the rights to make a film. He was thirty minutes late as it had already been purchased by the director who has become known as the French Hitchcock, Henri-Georges Clouzet. At least that is how I heard the story. Even if there is some embellishment, as there always is, it is still an interesting tale.

Michel Delasalle works at a school owned by his wife Christina. Michel's lover, Nicole, also works at the school. Christina and Nicole somehow get along, using their mutual dislike for Michel as a bond. They come up with a plan to murder him. Nicole is the mastermind, setting up every little aspect while Christina is the timid co-participant with a heart condition. The two women lure Michel to Nicole's apartment away from school, poison him, drown him and then dump him in a swimming pool back at the school. The problem, when the pool is drained Michel is gone. There are many tricks played on the two women regarding Michel, as if it was possible that he did not die at all, until the finale when the amazing twist is revealed, followed by an even better twist after that one.

The 1996 remake with Sharon Stone in the lead role could be one of the single greatest arguments as to why classics should not be remade. The 1955 original was an absolute masterpiece. If I had not known better I would have believed it was made by Hitchcock himself. I only learned the story of Hitchcock trying to purchase the rights after I saw it. I'm not sure if he could have made a better film than Clouzet, but I know he would have given it his all and is on record as saying that *Diaboliques, Les* was one of his favorite films. I cannot recommend this highly enough and warn to stay away from the remake. It is absolute garbage and does not hold a candle to the original.

#189 – *Trainspotting*.

In the 1990's, movies from the UK made a definitive revival. There was the hysterical *The Full Monty* from England, the touching *Waking Ned Devine* from Ireland and of course Scotland would have the last laugh, producing the best of the lot to hit the mainstream American cinemas, *Trainspotting*. This film mixed the raw feel of the streets of Scotland with the underbelly of drug addiction, making a conscious choice to show the darker and horrific side of both.

Renton is one of a group of four friends. He is also a heroin addict. Two of the other three are addicts as well, Spud and Sick Boy, yet Renton's story's is the main focus as he is having the most difficult time in dealing with his heroin addiction. He vows to quit. That only heightens his other desires, leading him back to one last hit. It seems as if he is always going back for one last hit. The fourth member of the group is the athletic and ambitious Tommy, yet heroin takes over his life after he loses his girlfriend. A psychopath named Begbie affects their lives even after Renton moves away, gets clean and starts working. The problem is, nothing ever good comes from dealing with Begbie.

Trainspotting hit with the force of a thunderbolt. It's raw images of heroin addiction and the problems that will result made it stand out. It is in the line of previous movies that dealt with the harsh world of addiction such as *The Lost Weekend*. Although the drug of choice is different it is not about taking drugs or alcohol, it is about willpower and the inability to restrain oneself. Even when you are trying your best, as the main characters in both movies are doing, the specter of those addictive juices still lives within them. I do not recommend seeing this movie after a meal, because there are some severely graphic scenes, yet if you are interested in quality film this is a must see.

#190 – *Toy Story*.

Cinematic animation has gone through many advancements over the years since the images were originally drawn on the page by hand. The latest in that line has been the digital type of animation employed by Pixar studios. The look of the characters was completely unique, adding another element toward producing a more life like cartoon. This type of more realistic animation possessed greater attention to detail. Pixar's first full length animated feature to employ this specific brand of digital animation was 1995's *Toy Story*.

What happens to a child's toys when he is not around? That is the basis of this amazingly original story presented here. A child's toys engage in lives of their own when he is not around. Led by a fast talking, ultra cool sheriff named Woody, who all the toys look up to, jealousy and envy cause issues as the new toy on the block. That new toy is a space ranger named Buzz Lightyear, who vies for the child's attention. To make matters worse for Woody, Buzz Lightyear does not realize he is a toy, further complicating things because he is starting to win over the affection of the other toys. What began as a sweet tale of innocence turns into an all out journey to return home, where the two main characters, one who still believes he is an actual space hero, must rely upon one another and break all the rules in the process.

Toy Story was brilliant because of its new technology, but even greater because of the sweetness and originality of the story. That new animation technology was beautiful to see at first, but the story is what keeps people coming back for repeated screenings. I know that when I watch the film it is because of the story, not the animation. I loved this movie and make sure I watch it every couple of months to remind how great a combination of story and visual technology it is. *Toy Story* is simply one of those movies that everyone likes and will remain a classic of minor stature for years to come. I thought it was good enough to place it on my top 100 list in the AFI chapter.

#191 – *Groundhog Day*.

What would you do if you were forced to live the same day over and over again? At first it might seem like a treat, yet the longer this treat goes on the more it becomes a burden and moves over into the realm of a curse. Harold Ramis directs his long time friend and collaborator Bill Murray in this comedy classic. Ramis and Murray working together generally equals entertaining comedy at its highest level. This partnership does not sour that notion.

A weatherman, Phil Connors, is forced to cover the emergence of the groundhog for his network. He does not hide his distaste for the situation. A snowstorm forces the crew to remain in town, where Connors begins to live the same day over and over again. He begins to have fun with the fact that no matter what he does he will wake up at 6:00 AM the day before, moving on to trying to find a good deed to do, anything that will allow him to move to the next day. Soon his efforts turn to trying to pick up his co-worker, eventually getting her to fall in love with him. That for some reason seems to break the curse and allow him to move to the next day.

Although a ridiculous concept, which is where the extreme comedy derives from, *Groundhog Day* works because of the brilliant comedic timing and antics of Bill Murray. His natural cynicism and demeanor blends together perfectly for the type of character he plays. There are some definite laugh out loud moments and the entirety of the movie is a stroke of comedic genius. Despite the tough premise, which could have easily backfired, the two principals, Murray and Ramis, pull off the job of turning this inventive screenplay into a great comedy film.

#192 – *Ikiru* (Japan).

When I mentioned that *Ikiru* was generally considered Kurosawa's finest film, yet I thought *Rashomon* was better, it was only after my first viewing of this masterpiece. I have definitely changed my mind. *Rashomon* is a great film. *Ikiru* is a far better one. This film is without a doubt the greatest achievement of Kurosawa's career. It is pure storytelling and works on every single level. There is almost nothing that does not come off as perfect about this film.

Mr. Watanabe is the head of his department at City Hall in charge of citizen complaints. He has had a perfect attendance record for nearly thirty years, never missing one day due to sickness or taking any time off for himself. In all that time at work he has never really accomplished anything. All he does is shuffle papers back and forth across his desk. Then he discovers he has gastric cancer. Coming to terms with his fatal illness, he begins to try and have some fun. The sad part is he does not know how. He befriends a former worker who seems happy, but soon discovers that he can achieve happiness in his work by getting something productive done.

The style of storytelling here is absolutely brilliant. It is even more brilliant than in *Rashomon*. Once Watanabe passes away, a quarter of the movie is spent on the other bureaucrats at his funeral, first mocking him, questioning why he suddenly changed and finally desperately wanting to be more like him at the end of his life. Watanabe is finally viewed as accomplishing something. The message is that the other bureaucrats will wind up like him before he began to take charge of his life. *Ikiru* is one of the deepest and most thought provoking films I have ever seen. It is also one of the best foreign films ever made and would have easily made the main list had it not been for the exclusion of foreign films. This movie is so good it would have challenged for the top ten.

#193 – *The Searchers*. #96 on AFI list.

#194 – *Beauty and the Beast* (France – 1946 – Live Action).

When this film came out it must have been viewed as a surrealistic nightmare. Evocative of the true nature of fairy tales, Jean Cocteau's *Beauty and the Beast* is both magical and poignantly tragic. Those who know the magnificent 1991 animated Disney version are in for a real surprise when watching this French version. The two, while possessing similar story characteristics, could not be more different.

Belle's father has financial troubles. She has a brother whose friend, a prince, wishes to marry her. She also has two wicked stepsisters. Belle refuses to marry the prince and in order to spare her father agrees to take his place as a hostage in a castle ruled over by a hideous beast. The beast continually asks her to marry him slowly winning her favor, yet she is homesick. He allows her to return home using the magic that has made him what he is. Once she is home, the prince connives to go to the Beast's castle and steal his treasure. Belle returns after learning the Beast is in trouble. She finds him dead, yet he magically transforms into a handsome prince when she reveals her true feelings with a glance. After realizing the Beast is a prince, they whisk away in each other's arms.

This version definitively suffers from self-indulgence. If I were asked to choose the better film, between the 1946 and 1991 versions, the choice would be obvious. The update by Disney is a better story with a higher emotional punch. The ending also makes more sense in the 1991 version. Cocteau has created a fine film, but it is obvious that he has tried to create a piece of unmistakable cinema rather than merely a film, over reached and something got lost in the shuffle. This film should be seen if for no other reason than to see what Cocteau has done to the original story.

#195 – *Monsters, Inc.*

I know I have said this before, probably four times in this chapter, yet Pixar studios keeps turning out great movies. They work from a basic story and create some form of a juxtapositional turnaround that enhances the story and brings it to another level. It seems like such a simple concept. Kids are afraid of monsters. Everyone knows that. Pixar was not satisfied with that notion. They had to take it further and create a story of why they were afraid of monsters.

Monsters are scary. At least they are scary to kids. There is a reason for that Monsters live on another world and are forced to scare kids so they can generate enough power to light and heat their city. The way they generate power is by harnessing the cries and screams of kids. The best scarer is Sulley, who works with his best friend Mike. A human child named Boo is let into their world. Human children are thought to be toxic and a fast acting swat team must decontaminate anyone that comes in contact with them. Sulley becomes attached to Boo after he discovers that she is not toxic, yet Mike insists that she be returned to her own world. Once a rival scarer learns what has happened, Sulley and Mike must band together to protect Boo from his evil clutches.

Monsters, Inc. works from a basic premise taken to the umpteenth level by the most intelligent studio in Hollywood today. After watching *Toy Story* and *Toy Story 2*, Pixar had me hooked. With this film they did not disappoint from their earlier classics. The story is touching and provides an inside look at the insecurities that monsters go through in their daily life. They are just like us, or would be if they weren't monsters. The film has comedy and a great deal of heart.

#196 – *Ed Wood*.

Tim Burton is definitely a strange dude. He really enjoys the weirder aspects of life, reveling in passing them off as normalcy. His movies tend to exhibit a subtle effort to show the peculiarities of people and why they should be okay with those eccentricities. Burton's forte is to showcase bizarre behaviors and create wondrous stories that are truly about people, rather than merely plot. His interest in the macabre has paid off with his best film, *Batman*. This film is easily his second greatest work.

The early career of the internationally acclaimed worst filmmaker of all time, Ed Wood, is told in this interesting tale of faith in the face of obvious lack of talent. Wood wants to make movies, but for some reason he can not see that the movies he wishes to create are downright awful. Every idea he has for a movie has been turned down by studios, yet he perseveres, gathering an eclectic group of friends and crew members along the way. His curiously uncanny lifestyle, which includes dressing in women's clothing, carries over into his work. Wood finally makes the films he wants to, although the price he pays is that his name will go down as a filmmaker of unmistakable inferiority.

I am a fan of biopics. I love the historical aspect of almost anything, specifically cinema. Burton has crafted a fantastic account of the career of Wood, focusing on all those crazy little personality traits that earmarked his work. The film comes off perfectly in black and white, evocative of the period that Wood made movies in. Wood's movies are generally considered the worst ever made, yet Burton's take on his life is one of the better biopics I have ever seen. I do hope that Burton was not trying to erase Wood's stature in cinema history, because no movie could ever accomplish such an impossible task. Even if he were, he created a great movie in trying.

#197 – *Grave of the Fireflies* (Japan).

As an American I rarely get a chance to see stories of how the actions of my country truly affect other countries we have engaged in war with. The movies that come from America generally tend to tell that American point of view. While not incorrect, it is askew from the absolute overall truth of the matter. This is the first film I have seen that shows the perspective of the individuals on the ground at the end of World War II, in Japan at least.

Fourteen year old Seita is required to take care of his four year old sister Setsuko after their mother is seriously injured during a bombing from the sky. The children's mother dies shortly thereafter, but the story is not about the dying mother or about the final days of World War II when Japan was a bombing target. This is about a brother and sister's will to live and their unfortunate failure. Food is rationed and Setsuko suffers from serious malnutrition, while Seita does whatever is necessary to provide for her. It is all for naught as she passes away from starvation and probably some form of poisoning from the multitude of bombs reigning down upon their village. Seita passes away shortly thereafter, bringing the story full circle from its opening line of voice over dialogue.

It is tough to create such a moving piece of cinema using animated characters, yet *Grave of the Fireflies* ably does that. While it is an anti-war movie it is much more about the human spirit. There are times when no matter what you do the end result is futile. When their spirits are reunited after death, the horror of their situation becomes almost cathartic. *Grave of the Fireflies* is an emotional journey that is sure to touch your heart and make you wonder about the innocent victims of wars that have been unfortunately affected by situations beyond their control.

#198 – *Young Frankenstein*.

Of the two films that Mel Brooks directed and had a part in writing the screenplay for during 1974, it is surprising to me that this one is rated higher than *Blazing Saddles*. That film is perhaps one of the three funniest movies to ever grace the big screen, yet this monster movie farce is not that far behind. One of most underrated comedic actor/writers, Gene Wilder, came up with the idea for this film and it is a shame that his other comedic ideas turned into film, such as *The Adventures of Sherlock Holmes' Smarter Brother*, aren't as revered.

The grandson of the legendary scientist Victor Frankenstein is a college professor who is trying to live down the name of his family. He inherits the ancestral castle and one night finds a secret passageway leading to a basement laboratory where he discovers his grandfather's material regarding the legendary work he conducted. The impulse to correct the mistakes made is too great so Victor begins researching the possibility of actually reanimating dead flesh. Of course, the story is filled with comedic touches that border upon the hysterical, specifically the monster's singing duet with Victor and the tea party with the blind man, played in an uncredited cameo by Gene Hackman.

If I had to choose between this film and *Blazing Saddles* I would choose *Blazing Saddles* every time. It is a question of who the better painter was, Picasso or Da Vinci? *Young Frankenstein* is a high concept comedy with just enough low brow humor to keep it balanced. The movie plays exactly as it should, a farce that is paying a great homage and poking immense fun at the revered monster movies from the golden era of Hollywood. When I said I would watch *Blazing Saddles* over *Young Frankenstein*, I never meant that I do not watch this extraordinary comedy on a regular basis.

#199 – *Sling Blade*.

Southerners talk funny. That is not a bigoted statement so much as it is a truthful one. There is a simple reason for why they do, because of a different take on the importance of education. The main character in Billy Bob Thornton's great film has what some would call a speech impediment. They would be wrong. He simply was never taught how to pronounce words properly and develop the characteristics and traits of normal speech. This character would have additional problems as well, as they usually go hand in hand with each other.

Karl Childers is about to be released from a mental facility/prison after spending the bulk of his entire life inside for murdering his mother and her lover. The state feels that he is rehabilitated enough to send him out into the world, even if he may not be ready to adjust to such a different way of life. He is provided with a job as a mechanic and his ability to deal with mechanical issues rather than emotional ones allows him to succeed. He makes a friend though, a twelve year old named Frank with problems of his own. His step father is an abusive alcoholic who mistreats him and his mother. In developing a close friendship with Frank, Karl does all he knows how to do, eliminate the problem in his own way, which lands him back to the only world he knows, the asylum.

Sling Blade is hysterical in an unintentional way, primarily in the voice used for the character by Billy Bob Thornton. That is not the full merit of the film though. It is a touching tale of friendship and the issues that arise due to a lack of education stemming from a particular way of life. When Karl confronts his father and challenges what he did to Karl and his brother, you begin to see how a person like Karl became the way he was. He was not evil in the way that those who murder are. He simply did not know any better. That is because the parental figures in his life were either the same way or into their own selves. Anyone who sees this film should not feel bad about laughing. The movie is layered in that it also evokes sadness for a person who deserved better.

#200 – *Twelve Monkeys*.

Former Monty Python cast member Terry Gilliam is another filmmaker who enjoys creating bizarre fantastical stories. He ascribes to the ideology that standard storytelling is boring. I believe he is right. There are times when his unique vision actually hurts the project. In the case of *Twelve Monkeys* though, Gilliam's interesting and almost hallucinogenic interpretation of the short French film *La Jetee* works perfectly in conjunction within the context of this altogether strange tale of time travel and probable perpetual insanity.

A convict is sent back in time to discover facts about a devastating plague that sent the sole survivors underground. Initially, he is sent back to the wrong period, where he is incarcerated in a mental facility. While there he meets an even stranger man who turns out to be the son of a well known virologist and the eventual leader of the army of the twelve monkeys. Going back and forth from one reality to the other, which includes multiple trips back in time, begins to wear on the convict to the point that he believes he is insane and has made the entire thing up in his mind. The problem with that is his former psychologist, who was previously kidnapped by him, discovers that he is telling the truth and must help him save the planet from what the army of the twelve monkeys will do. In the end, everything finally comes full circle to explain the bizarre happenings of the story.

Twelve Monkeys is definitely one of the strangest movies I have ever seen. Bruce Willis plays a character that has never been done before, a sort of anti-criminal rather than an anti-hero. This film should have solidified his status as an actor who could perform ably in challenging roles. Brad Pitt steals the movie though, who plays Jeffrey, the schizoid who befriends Willis in the psychiatric institution in 1990 and later leads the army of the twelve monkeys into history. Pitt earned a well-deserved Oscar nomination for his performance, although he lost to Kevin Spacey who gave an equally great performance in *The Usual Suspects*. Pitt's acting is the highlight of the film, yet Gilliam's eccentric vision of storytelling makes the film a wonder to marvel at.

#201 – *Grand Illusion* (France).

One of the great anti-war films ever made was 1930's Best Picture *All Quiet on the Western Front*. It set the tone for films to be told in a more humanistic style versus merely exploiting the glorifications of war. The great French director Jean Renoir, son of the famous Impressionist painter Pierre Auguste Renoir, told stories such as this. The humanization of the characters was of far greater importance than the exaltation of war. *Grand Illusion* is his cinematic triumph. His 1939 film *The Rules of the Game* may be better received yet *Grand Illusion* is the much better film, one of stark honesty while depicting a time of terrible turmoil.

Grand Illusion takes place in a German prisoner of war camp. The first camp is numbered seventeen, which Billy Wilder must have paid a silent yet obvious homage to in his 1953 classic. In fact, throughout *Stalag 17*, you see elements of *Grand Illusion*; the prankster/jokester prisoners, the attempts at taking their minds of their imprisonment, the officers dealing with the serious nature of the war and the planning for escape, as some believed was their duty. There are differences, most notably taking place during different wars, yet numerous films to come after *Stalag 17* would also borrow from *Grand Illusion*, indicating that it was considered a work of brilliance.

The key to the film is in the relationship between the two officers on opposing sides. Meeting early on in the movie and then again at the second prisoner of war camp, the German commandant treats the captured officers with trust and respect. It is his way of showing his nobility as a gentleman and he expects them to honor his hospitality. To him, gentleman must remain gentleman above all regardless of the horrors of war. Countries shall always advance and prosper because of the upper class, therefore it becomes his duty to honor a code that barbarians would ignore.

Differing from *All Quiet on the Western Front* in that it did not show the horrendously realistic scenes of battle, *Grand Illusion* chose to humanize those involved on both sides. Renoir makes a point to show that there are truly no evil men in war, just products of their country doing what they are told, which in some case meant performing acts of a horrific nature. One might call it a plea for the upcoming battle to be fought in such a manner, where gentleman could treat each other as equals despite their origins. That was precisely one of the reasons the Nazis attempted to destroy it.

#202 – *Roman Holiday*.

Audrey Hepburn is generally considered as the princess of Hollywood. Over the course of her career she has made such great films that she probably has a larger percentage of her films as classics than any other major actress in history. That is not the only reason why she is considered Hollywood's princess. Some of it has to do with the character she played in *Sabrina*. I am sure they incorporated elements from *Breakfast at Tiffany's* and I am positive certain traits were taken from *My Fair Lady*. However, *Roman Holiday* is where it all began.

Hepburn plays Princess Anne, who winds up in the care of a reporter named Joe Bradley, although she cannot remember how she got there. There is the beautiful scene where the naïve princess presents the shock upon her face that she has spent the night in a strange man's room, with Bradley wittily stating that nothing actually happened. He knows who she is, yet presents a façade for the interests of writing a story on her. Her motives are different. For the first time she is in the company of someone who does not know who she is, even though he does. This affords her the opportunity to be someone other than the princess. Bradley becomes torn between writing his story and protecting her, because they begin to fall for one another. In the end, she must return to her life.

Written by the blacklisted writer Dalton Trumbo, *Roman Holiday* is one of those special films. It is okay but as far from great as a film can get. To sum it up in one word I would have to use sweet. It is a nice story. It was nothing more and nothing less. Hepburn was wonderful in her first role and Peck is equally good, although he is amazing in almost every movie he ever played in. The chemistry between them is nothing special. Since we can see the fun on Hepburn's face as she has her one day holiday it lends more credence to the possibility that their relationship could have worked in another time and place. I liked the film, but have not thought about it once until now.

#203 – *The Exorcist*.

The pea soup spitting out of Linda Blair's mouth or her head spinning all the way around are what most remember about this film, similar to the shower scene in *Psycho* or when the shark finally rears his head above the water in *Jaws*. Those who do either have never seen the whole film or have forgotten what a fantastic story the movie offers. I would not disagree that this might well be the scariest movie ever made yet there are moments in other films that are scarier than the top moments here. As a whole, *The Exorcist* is definitely the scariest film ever.

There are technically three main characters here. There is Chris MacNeil, the mother of the young girl, Regan, who becomes possessed. There are also the two priests, Father Karras and father Merrin. Each of the three has a unique story of their own, with of course Regan MacNeil coming into the story as its main focus after she is possessed. Chris is having trouble with her husband, Regan's father. He has not called for Regan's birthday and the feeling is that he continually lets them down. Chris actually states it within earshot of Regan. Father Karras is dealing with his own guilt over entering the priesthood, questioning his faith in the process. Father Merrin has his history as well. Father Merrin has faced Satan before, so the fact that Chris and Father Karras may not believe in what is being done is no matter to him. He remains the steady force of the group.

The beauty of the story is that the exorcism is not just thrown right into your face, it is allowed to develop as we learn a bit about these characters. More than likely, that came from having the novelist, William Peter Blatty, write the screenplay. So often when a novelist writes a screenplay for his own book he makes sure to include the subtle yet important intricacies of his characters. The plot develops but the characters must be a part of the plot. That is where their development becomes key. While definitely a horror film, *The Exorcist* is an emotional tale about three people struggling with life and hoping that their role in what is taking place will somehow help them move forward.

#204 – *The Man Who Shot Liberty Valence.*

Director John Ford is primarily known for his Westerns. That is strange because some of his other movies in various genres have been hailed as classics, most notably *The Grapes of Wrath*. Of all the Westerns that Ford made, including movies that are viewed as classics such as *Stagecoach, The Searchers* and *Fort Apache*, the best Western Ford ever made was *The Man Who Shot Liberty Valance*. This was also the first time two legendary screen icons of cinema, James Stewart and John Wayne, were brought together for a film.

The story begins with Senator Ransom Stoddard returning to the town of Shinbone for the funeral of an old friend. On his way he remembers the story that has become a legend. Stoddard (Stewart) is brought to Shinbone after he is attacked by the lethal criminal Liberty Valance and his gang. While recovering, Stoddard decides to remain and set up a law practice to bring some order to the West. Liberty Valance will not stand for it. There is someone on Stoddard's side though, Tom Doniphan (Wayne). Doniphan lives by the code of the west like Valance, yet far different than him. Valance challenges Stoddard to a duel, which Stoddard reluctantly accepts. What transpires in the duel raises Stoddard's courage to the level of legend. The truth is not always what it seems.

The old adage mentioned in the film, *'When the legend becomes fact, print the legend'*, perfectly sums up this monumental film. Things are almost never as they seem, yet with enough people telling the story the line between fact and fiction or even fiction and embellishment moves farther and farther apart. The story is about friendship but it is more about living with a lie for the better good. Stoddard knows that his whole career is based upon a lie, but the work he did because of that is the greater good, which is what his old friend would have wanted. I was shocked when I found out this movie was not even offered as a choice for the AFI list. See this film and compare it to some of the awful films they put on that list. Perhaps you will agree with me that their list is flawed.

#205 – *The Big Lebowski.*

Leave it to the Coen Brothers to create a fantasy movie where the hero is a stoner bowler who drinks White Russians. As with every other movie they make, the characters are individually showcased for their extreme weirdness. Every single character, including the minor ones, all have something about them that makes them watchable. The actual story serves only as a backdrop because the true genius of the film is in allowing the characters to interact and naturally develop bigger and better problems as they go along.

'The Dude' has his carpet pissed on by one of two henchmen for a pornographic film producer. It is a case of mistaken identity, because his name is the same as the person they really meant to collect money from. Not being able to take what happened and move on, *'the Dude'* visits the

intended target and explains what happened. Needless to say he is not sympathetic, yet later contacts *'the Dude'* about helping trade a bag of money for his kidnapped wife. Of course *'the Dude'* and his friend Walter screw up the drop and are now hunted after by the kidnappers, who never kidnapped anyone in the first place. That doesn't matter because the bag never had any money in it to begin with. All *'the Dude'* wanted was a new rug. It really held the room together.

These are just some of the major problems that occur within this awesomely hysterical movie. The characters are enough to make the movie enjoyable in that aspect, yet how they continually manage to weave their way into and out of trouble makes it that much more fun of a movie to watch. If it were not for a few awful fantasy dream bowling sequences that are extraordinarily out of place this movie would be almost perfect. The acting and writing are flawless, with that one exception. It is the characters that makes repeated viewings worthwhile though.

#206 – *Brazil*. Best movie – 1985

#207 – *Three Colors: Red* (Poland).

The genius behind the critically acclaimed ten one hour films known as *The Decalogue*, Krzysztof Kieslowski, finished his flag color trilogy with this last installment. The first film of the trilogy was simply called *Blue*. The second was called *White*. This installment finishes the trilogy, although the three stories are not interrelated other than all three films deal with particular aspects of contemporary French society.

Red centers on a fashion model who accidentally runs over a German shepherd. She gathers the wounded dog up and returns it to the house of the owner. The owner acts indifferent to the news so the woman takes the dog to the vet and keeps it as a pet once she is fixed up. One day the dog runs away. She follows the dog back to the house of the original owner where she learns that the elderly man listens to other people's phone conversations as a means to fuel his cynicism. The man is a retired judge and even though she despises what he does she feels some type of connection to him. Intercut with her and the retired judge getting to know each other is a brief story of a man who discovers that his girlfriend is cheating on him. At the end of the film there is a shocking revelation that brings everything into perspective.

This was the third film of the trilogy that I saw. *White* was a decent film and *Blue* was brilliant. This film however, left me cold. It is more about the metaphysical aspects of existence and destiny rather than focusing on telling a good story. I understand that this type of meta-realism is a trademark of Kieslowski, yet for this film the end result did not work for me. There are reviews calling this film brilliant, going so far as to call it a masterpiece. This goes to show that a film can touch different people on many levels, yet for me, *Red* was an overall disappointment.

#208 – *Snatch*.

British director Guy Ritchie hit the big time with this story of a number of stories simultaneously going on around one another. It is the old classic theme that eventually your path will cross with everyone else's. Ritchie's take on that involves boxing corruption, numerous robberies, searches for missing diamonds, missing thieves and missing dogs. There are so many strange characters in this film that it almost feels weird to break down the story.

Frankie Four Fingers robs a diamond shop in Antwerp. He plans to go to London to sell the diamond. One of his crew says he can buy a gun from his cousin, Boris the bullet dodger. Boris knows that Frankie has a massive diamond on him, but cannot kill him so he hires Vinny and Sol to steal the briefcase that carries the diamond in it. Vinny and Sol rob the bookie joint where Frankie is supposed to be. The bookie joint belongs to Brick Top, who is fond of feeding his enemies to giant pigs. Brick Top also runs fixed fights, which brings Tommy and Turkish into the mix. Turkish has a fighter, Gorgeous George, who he sends with Tommy to a gypsy, or pikey camp to buy a trailer. George is knocked out flat by Mickey, who then is forced to fight in his place. Avi flies in from America to find Frankie, so he hires Bullet Tooth Tony. And those are just the basics of the story.

Snatch is in the vain of the new version of *Romeo and Juliet.* They all are ultra frenetic stories going at one hundred miles per hour. The difference between the two is that *Snatch* is both original and incredibly interesting. It is great when a filmmaker can bring a story full circle the way that Guy Ritchie has done here. Brad Pitt as Mickey steals the show, specifically in his pitch perfect Pikey accent that can barely be understood, on purpose. This is one of the few movies that I can watch over and over again without any fear of getting bored. I try to watch it every week or so.

#209 – *The Lady Vanishes.*

Every person who loves movies knows the name Alfred Hitchcock. There was a time when his name was not known within the business. Then he made a couple of British films to bolster his name as a director of importance. Some of those early films were *The 39 Steps*, *Sabotage* and his original version of *The Man Who Knew Too Much.* Even in those early films his trademarks were present. *The Lady Vanishes* made Hitchcock a directorial force.

Miss Froy is a governess who makes the acquaintance of an English woman, Iris, as their train is delayed due to an avalanche. Right before they board the train the following morning, Iris is accidentally struck on the head by a falling flowerpot. She spends a brief time on the train in the company of Miss Froy, who reveals a few minor details about herself. All of a sudden Miss Froy is gone and Iris begins the search for her. She runs into a young music student named Gilbert during her search, who she had a run-in with the previous night at the hotel. After convincing Gilbert that Miss Froy has been kidnapped, they search for the nutty old broad, uncovering a secret plot that leads toward the true identities of numerous passengers and Miss Froy herself.

The Lady Vanishes is one of Hitchcock's better early efforts, but among the films he has on this list it definitely settles in the lower third. The opening scene is hilarious from a special effects standpoint, where a miniature train set is meant to intimate an Alpine mountain resort. Even though this early part of the film provides some background for the characters it is awfully slow and the movie does not pick up until they board the train and then only after Miss Froy disappears. For the better part of the first thirty minutes the movie is at a standstill. Only the mystery saves this film. Once all is discovered, *The Lady Vanishes* reverts back to a mostly boring film. The last twenty minutes are absolutely ludicrous, specifically when a passenger is shot and he calmly walks it off.

#210 – *A Streetcar Named Desire*. #45 on AFI list.

#211 – *The Terminator*.

The Terminator was the film that started it all, launching the careers of action megastar Arnold Schwarzenegger and Oscar winning director James Cameron. This film went on to achieve cult status, prior to 1991 when the sequel exploded the franchise into movie stardom. Cameron revived the original he created by expanding and further developing the story in the sequel, although the second one has that distinct *Aliens* bad ass feel to it. The original, as a result, received renewed praise for its originality and was finally recognized for its innovative vision.

In the year 2029, the machines rule the world. A few surviving humans have taken up the fight. The machines have devised the ultimate plan to eliminate the rebels who have challenged and are defeating them with their will. They send a killing machine back in time to kill the mother of the leader of the resistance, thus changing the future. The resistance captures their defense system and uncovers the plot. Their move is to send a human back to protect her and destroy the time travel mechanism so they cannot send more machines back. This is merely the back story of the film, told in bits and pieces throughout. While running away from the stalking machine killer, Sarah Connor learns about her destiny, falling in love with her protector and quickly maturing in the process.

The Terminator is not merely a science fiction movie. It is a futuristic adventure, but also has many other elements within it, including a poignantly moving love story and an amazingly crafted time travel script that uses the present as its primary setting. The problem with most movies that rely on time travel is that there is usually that one plot hole that crashes down upon it to destroy its validity. If one were to spend hours upon hours dissecting the intricate possibilities then I am sure one could be found. The problem with that scenario is that this is a movie, to be enjoyed. The plot hole does not jump out anywhere within the film, specifically from watching only the original. *The Terminator* is a brilliant movie and one that also makes you think about the possibility of a future.

#212 – *Lock, Stock and Two Smoking Barrels*.

This is the movie that got the directing career of Guy Ritchie on the road to stardom. At least his career was headed that way after this film and *Snatch*, until he hit a major roadblock with the awful *Swept Away*, starring his wife Madonna. As he had done in *Snatch*, this film focuses on a number of stories, yet within this one there is a fuller main story than there is in *Snatch*. That is not to say it is a better film, because it is not.

Four friends invest an equal sum of money for their friend to gamble in a high stakes poker game. The game is rigged, yet that does not matter because now all four of them have to come up with the extra money that is owed. While coming up with solutions to their problem that will not work, they overhear their next door neighbors planning a robbery of a group of pot dealers. Their new plan is to rob the robbers and pay back what they owe. The problem that exists after they pull off the job is that the drug dealers work for the same gambler they originally owed the money to. Now they are in even deeper, until they are sent a piece of information that may change their luck.

Lock, Stock and Two Smoking Barrels was sort of a pre-*Snatch*. It is a good film but it is obvious that Ritchie was using this film to springboard to a much better and far more multi-layered story. A number of the actors in this film also appeared in *Snatch*, yet this film lacked something that *Snatch* had, a great story arc. The first time I saw this film I enjoyed it. The more I see it nowadays the more I wish I had chosen to watch *Snatch*. Even in watching *Lock, Stock and Two Smoking Barrels* for this book, I consistently thought how things were done better in that other film.

#213 – *Charade*.

Audrey Hepburn is considered Hollywood royalty. She only appeared in twenty-seven films but many of them have become memorable classics. *Roman Holiday* has already been spoken about and the light hearted comedies *Sabrina*, *My Fair Lady* and *Breakfast at Tiffany's* all helped to cement her image. *Charade* fit that mold perfectly. Although the multi-layered story is perhaps the greatest element of this film, Hepburn's playful demeanor helps make this movie great.

Hepburn plays an American living in Paris who is married to someone named Charlie. When she returns from vacation she finds out that Charlie has been murdered. After speaking to a police commissioner and a bureaucrat working for the CIA, Hepburn learns that her husband was a thief and that she is in terrible danger. Three men who knew her husband are all looking for the money Charlie stole, as well as another man who pretends to be helping her. One by one the three men are murdered until it is finally revealed what they were after and who is killing everyone.

Charade is one of the most fun and entertaining mysteries ever put on film. It has a unique blend of the two that many films try but fail to accomplish. It never hurts that Cary Grant was a member of the cast, acting as one of the great mysterious characters in cinema. The film also included Walter Matthau, James Coburn and George Kennedy, just to name a few. Hepburn steals the show however. Her humorous revelations and sly flirting with Grant add depth to this brilliant story. The ending does not disappoint, matching the pace and tone of the film perfectly. From the way it was going there was the feeling that the ending would be something spectacular and it was.

#214 – *Almost Famous*.

Writer Cameron Crowe became known for his in depth look at a California high school, which was turned into the movie *Fast Times at Ridgemont High*. That movie produced some of the great teen moments in cinema and introduced numerous young actors who would go on to brilliant careers, most notably Sean Penn and Nicholas Cage. Prior to masquerading around a high school Crowe invaded the world of rock and roll, when he was a teenager himself. His material was so good that he was featured in *Rolling Stone* magazine. This is that story.

Teenager William Miller is given the opportunity of a lifetime, to go on tour with the rock band Stillwater and write about the band for the best rock and roll magazine at the time, *Rolling Stone*. Still in high school, his psychotically overprotective mother leaves messages for him at the hotels they stay at, freaks out members of the band he is covering and embarrasses William at every turn. That does not stop him from forming a bond with the band, specifically the lead guitarist Russell Hammond. He also develops a crush on one of the band's groupies, who happens to be in love with Russell. The two relationships that William develops are the heart of the film.

I am not a huge rock and roll fan, but I enjoyed this movie completely. It was one of the best from the year 2000 and was largely overshadowed by the epic film *Gladiator*. Although not an independent film *Almost Famous* has that independent feel to it. Maybe it is because of the great character development, perfect blending in of music to the story and comedic moments that ground the film in reality. Although Frances McDormand as William's mother and Kate Hudson as the main groupie Penny Lane both received Oscar nominations, the best performance of the film comes from Billy Crudup as Russell Hammond. It seems apparent that Crudup is quickly taking his place as the next great underrated actor of this generation.

#215 – *King Kong* (1933). #43 on AFI list.

#216 – *The Road* (Italy).

This was the first film of back to back foreign film Oscars for Federico Fellini, with *Nights of Calibria* as the follow up. Many critics divide Fellini's career into two separate stages, with his early films called his poetic or artistic phase. *La Strada*, or *The Road*, is the film that has been called his most poetic attempt at cinematic art. The themes running throughout the picture evoked memories of the Italy of yesteryear, yet the ideas within were not far removed.

Zampano is a strongmen and a strolling performer. He buys the half-retarded yet more probably child-like Gelsomina from her mother to be his companion on the road. Zampano is a typical brute, complete with all the trimmings that stereotypically go with that. He is emotionally and physically cruel to her and leaves her wherever he pleases while he goes off to do whatever he chooses. She learns her job and excels at performing, yet Zampano's temper gets the better of him. He chases after a clown, called *'the Fool'*, and is arrested. This respite from Zampano shows Gelsomina that they need each other and that love can sprout from their differences. Zampano finds *'the Fool'* on the side of the road and beats him to death. This fractures something inside Gelsomina, whom Zampano leaves on the side of the road never to see again. When he finds out what became of her he finally realizes what he lost and learns the lesson Fellini wanted us all to know.

The lesson is about change. Gelsomina is a simple girl but is able to change Zampano with her inner beauty. Zampano is the dumb abusive brute that breaks down in the end because of his memories of Gelsomina. If these two people can change everyone can. It is a simple yet profound lesson and one that more people should try to understand. As a movie it is okay, but nothing spectacular. The simple lesson seems more prophetic and therefore poetic because of the extremes Fellini uses to showcase the ability to change. I truly find this one of the lesser of his great films.

#217 – *Sideways*.

The one independent type movie that impacted cinema in 2004 was *Sideways*. A small budget film from the director of the highly underrated *Citizen Ruth* and *Election*, as well as the recent hit *About Schmidt*, this movie captured the world of wine and wine tasting perfectly. Paced masterfully for the material it presents, *Sideways* was consistently the best reviewed film of 2004, garnering plenty of accolades and breaking into the Oscar party generally reserved for epics and highly marketable studio films.

Miles and Jack are heading up to wine country for one last week of freedom before Jack is to be married. Miles is waiting to hear about the publishing of his novel, while Jack is only interested in one thing, a last fling before he ties the knot. While visiting a couple of the local wineries, Jack turns on his charm to one of the wine pourers and sets up a dinner date for the two of them with her and a waitress named Maya that Miles knows. That leads to an affair that ends up with Jack getting his nose broken for not revealing he is getting married. Another hookup between Jack and a waitress ends up bad as well, which Miles has to fix. They return home and everything is good for Jack, although Miles begins a downslide. The only happy time he can remember is the brief time he spent with Maya, who he drives to see as the movie fades to black.

Part of the beauty of this film is that the future is unknown. Jack's marriage will more than likely fail because of who he is and Maya will probably reject Miles for his part in the lie that was told. It is that last possibility of hope that the movie tries to ingratiate upon the audience when it knows the future will end up bleak that makes it a great film. There are touches of comedy throughout and watching a character as self destructive as Miles, perfectly played by underrated actor Paul Giamatti, provides that spark needed to get through a movie that is generally slow in nature. The characters are the gem of the movie, even though wine is meant to be the highlight.

#218 – *Heat*.

Michael Mann is a stylish director. That can never be seriously argued. He has a knack for visually setting the tone of a film and simply allowing his characters to play around within that field. That is not to say that the characters within a Michael Mann film are merely backdrop. They are not. They are vibrant, intelligent and most importantly they all possess a human quality about them, whether they are criminals or whether they are charged with taking criminals down. In *Heat*, the only thing that distinguishes the characters are what side they are on.

Neil McCauley runs a crew made up of people he knew while he was in prison. He can trust them. The fact that they are so good will bring them into the sightline of Lt. Vincent Hanna. His job is to take down major crews. He has done it before and the job runs his life. Hanna and McCauley are going to run into each other eventually and so we arrive at the beginning of the movie. An armored car heist goes wrong when an extra man on McCauley's crew guns down a guard for looking at him. Hanna is brought in and through his multitude of snitches learns about McCauley and his crew. There is so much more that goes on, yet to include all the minor characters and the roles they play could take up an entire book itself. I will say that every performance is great.

Heat was the film that finally brought Al Pacino and Robert DeNiro together. The two had worked on *The Godfather II*, yet had no scenes together. This film almost took that same path. Pacino and DeNiro only appear on screen together twice, once at the end and once for a fantastic scene in a coffee shop to get to know each other. Mann wisely refused to go in an ultra action style with this film, preferring to develop the characters, which in turn would lead toward a number of quality action scenes. The coffee shop scene is one of many where you feel like you are having a great novel read to you, filled with many interesting characters. Those are the kinds of movies that you can walk away from and feel like you took part in something. I wish they made more like them.

#219 – *The Bride of Frankenstein*.

Movies that are campy get a bad rap at times. So often they are campy for the wrong reasons, which is why they suffer in the eyes of critics and audiences. When a movie is planned that way, to deliver a nuance to an emerging genre, the end result can turn out to be a stroke of genius. *The Bride of Frankenstein*, arguably one of the greatest sequels ever made, was intended by director James Whale to have that specific purpose in mind. Whale helmed the original *Frankenstein* in 1931 and saw the genre explode as a result. Now he envisioned moving the genre forward with a tale of love on numerous levels, yet with a sneaky twist, poking fun at itself.

The story begins with Lord Byron and Percy Shelley prompting author Mary Shelley to reveal the rest of her infamous story. Starting from where the story/original movie left off, the monster was assumed destroyed in the fire. The monster lived and is now in search of a friend, eventually finding a blind hermit who does not fear him. The monster is hunted by the frightened townsfolk who eventually capture him. In the meantime, Dr. Frankenstein is visited by Dr. Pretorius who was conducting similar experiments into restoring life from dead tissue. After manipulating Dr. Frankenstein to help him create a mate for the monster, his appearance scares the hell out of her, causing the monster to destroy the castle from his disappointment. Did they all survive again?

The fantastic 1998 biopic of Whale, *Gods and Monsters*, briefly describes the tone of this film while also showing a select few shots from the filming of this 1935 classic. In the film, Whale explains that the movie was intended to be a funny. That was the only way he could slip in the homosexual undertones of the relationship between Dr. Pretorius and Dr. Frankenstein. Colin Clive, who played Frankenstein, played the role unaware of it. Despite Whale's agenda, the movie still came off as horrific and is viewed today as a horror masterpiece. I see it both ways. It is a great work of old style horror and an interesting job at presenting the genre with a kick in its own balls.

#220 – *8 ½* (Italy).

Internationally acclaimed Italian filmmaker Federico Fellini created the ultimate movie about the process of getting a movie made. His two earlier Oscar winning films, *La Strada* and *The Nights of Cabiria* did not bring him the grand success that *La Dolce Vita* and this picture finally did. *8 ½* plays like a surrealistic comic nightmare, where the exhaustive processes a director goes through causes him to revert back to his memories in order to save his future.

Noted filmmaker Guido Anselmi is planning to shoot his next picture. The film deals with harrowing images of a religious nature so he must get counsel, or more to the point, permission from a Cardinal. In trying to relax as well, Guido is constantly bothered by the many women in his life. They include his mistress, an aging actress, ingénues and his wife. When reality closes in, Guido escapes into a world of fantasy that incorporates his memories of past events. In the end, Guido finds that he has located what his next masterpiece will be, incorporating everyone he knows into it.

8 ½ has been called Fellini's autobiographical film. If it truly is then more power to him. I wouldn't mind having those dilemmas, although I can see where the constant issues thrown at him from every angle can get tiresome. This is definitely a film that should be seen more than once. The initial viewing had me asking what all the fuss was about. I enjoyed it but did not buy the hype about it being the quintessential film about filmmaking. Upon subsequent viewings I have discovered an affinity for this movie. It is a man going through the process of going through a process. Once I finally began to understand that the film took on new meaning for me, becoming one of my favorites.

#221 – *The Insider*.

The old adage that truth is stranger than fiction was never more powerful than in this story of a *60 Minutes* episode where a tobacco scientist decided to become a whistle blower. Despite the amazing performances by Al Pacino and Russell Crowe, who received his first of three straight Oscar nominations, it is the story that steals the show here. There is more to doing the right thing than meets the eye. It is not as simple as acting on one's conscious because there are always deep and painful ramifications waiting around the corner.

Dr. Jeffrey Wigand is fired from his research and development job at one of the country's most profitable tobacco companies. His mistake was challenging the company's policy of including a specific carcinogen meant to increase the addictive properties of their cigarettes. It was all about the profits for them. Wigand is contacted by a producer for *60 Minutes* in regards to giving an explanation of specific documents, yet the producer who contacts him can smell a deeper story. After Wigand is threatened and stalked by his former company he agrees to give the interview and release his information into a public forum. This begins to take its toll on Wigand, who develops marital problems and becomes paranoid, although that is presented equally as his paranoia and a warranted response from Wigand regarding the truth about the situation.

Crowe's performance is a treat to watch. Along with Denzel Washington in *The Hurricane* from that same year, 1999, they provide some of the finest acting ever put on film. Neither of these two actors won, losing to Kevin Spacey from *American Beauty*. In typical Hollywood style, both men would have their performances rewarded in the following two years, although for far lesser performances. The first time I saw this film I was shocked at the back story that in this day and age a news show as reputable as *60 Minutes* actually caved into corporate pressures from their parent company and shelved the show. This film goes to show you that the truth is not enough. One of the exceptionally great films of the 1990's, delivering both a great message and great entertainment.

#222 – *Cinderella Man.*

Like I stated earlier, I am a fan of historical biopics, specifically ones that deal with the history of boxing. In my favorite films chapter I included *Gentleman Jim* and probably liked Michael Mann's *Ali* a little more than I should have. After *Batman Begins*, this was the movie that I looked most forward to during 2005, especially when I discovered that it would reunite actor Russell Crowe and director Ron Howard, both of whom took part in *A Beautiful Mind*.

Up and coming boxer James J. Braddock has a run of bad luck with some minor injuries that affect his career. That is nothing compared to what happens to him and his family during the Great Depression. Losing all his money in the stock market and not able to compete enough to continue earning money as a boxer, Braddock and his family go through the same hardships that affected the entire country of working class people. That is until he is given that one last chance to earn a few dollars by stepping back into the ring. With one victory comes another and another and finally a shot at the Heavyweight Championship of the world. The champion is the ruthless Max Baer who has already killed two people in the ring with his vicious brutality, but Braddock's hope is stronger than Baer's sheer force and power. Braddock is fighting for everyone.

Cinderella Man is one of the truest stories about hope I have ever been lucky enough to see. Crowe magnificently pulls off this tough role of Braddock, a decent man with a string of bad luck who used his opportunities to bring hope and dreams to a long suffering nation. The stunning cinematography not only shines during the boxing scenes, but also evokes a period of real sorrow in American history. For some reason it was not the critical success that it should have been. After the Spielberg film *Munich*, this is the best movie from the entire crop of films released in 2005.

#223 – *A Night at the Opera*. Best movie – 1935

#224 – *Battleship Potemkin* (Russia).

For a long time after its 1925 release, *Battleship Potemkin* was widely considered as the best film ever made. Times change as they often do, one of the themes of the film. *Citizen Kane* holds that distinction now from a universally viewed standpoint. However, Sergei Eisenstein's retelling of an historic 1905 naval mutiny was viewed as so authentic that a later fictional scene developed a mystery surrounding whether it actually took place or not.

The naval crew of a battleship during the Russo-Japanese War is at their wits end. They long for home even though there are work strikes and mother Russia appears to be in chaos because of their involvement in the war. Once they are served maggot infested meat, the crew can take it no longer and conduct a mutiny. The citizens, upon hearing of the mutiny, send basic supplies out to the ship. This leads to the legendary scene at the Odessa steps where armed troops march down the steps and unemotionally begin firing into the crowd of civilians, massacring them. This is the legendary scene that was believed to have occurred due to the extreme realism of the film.

Battleship Potemkin is not an easy film to watch. I personally prefer the other films that Eisenstein is noted for, *Alexander Nevsky* and *Ivan the Terrible*. The frequent cutting, perhaps close to fifteen hundred cuts in total of a film that did not span eighty minutes in length takes away from the story. The mistake that most critics make when assessing film is to overestimate films that have deep historical significance in the field of technical achievement. *Battleship Potemkin* is one of those films. Its images are startling and it is a great historical drama, even if part of it is fictitious. The problem remains that Eisenstein wanted great film achievements rather than to make a great film.

#225 – *Lost in Translation*.

The 1990 film *The Godfather III* proved a couple of things. First, they should have stopped after *The Godfather II*, but more important, Sofia Coppola was not meant to be in front of the camera. All by herself she turned that movie into a laughing stock, yet as a director, where she does not have to act a part, she appears to be a natural like her father. Her first full length feature film as a writer-director was the critical success *The Virgin Suicides*. This film would outdo all expectations.

Bob Harris is an American movie actor who is paid a large sum of money to appear in a whiskey commercial in Tokyo. He meets a young woman who is staying at the same hotel. She is recently married to a photographer on assignment and is bored in her new environment. The two of them eventually strike up a friendship to alleviate their loneliness. There is an immediate connection between the two, which involves hanging out and coming a little too close to acting on romantic impulses. The film ends with a touching display of emotion coming from two people who genuinely enjoyed each other's company and knew that is as far as it could ever go.

Lost in Translation exploded onto the scene in 2003 and became one of the most critically acclaimed movies of the year, if not the top one. Carrying an independent feel to it, this movie cornered the market on those awards shows and broke into the mainstream award ceremonies. I have heard dozens of different reasons for why this movie was liked so well, ranging from its perfectly underplayed comedic tone to its heartfelt sentiment of two opposites who are closer than meets the eye to the farcical depiction of a different culture. I enjoyed the movie for all those reasons yet I cannot echo the sentiment that it is a work of genius. Good film, but not close to great.

#226 – *All The President's Men*. #50 on main list.

#227 – *In the Heat of the Night*. #?? on main list. Best Picture – 1967

#228 – *Scarface*.

When people speak about films and they go over into the category of cult films they undoubtedly discuss *Scarface*. Its unabashed brutality and violence for violence's sake has made it a staple in every man's collection. This movie has become the quintessential movie to promote that macho outlook on life, where all that matters is money, chicks and guns. I suppose that guys want to emulate the lifestyle of the main character, yet always forget to remember what happens to him as a result. That existence has its drawbacks. In this case, it was a hail of bullets.

In 1980 a Cuban refugee named Tony Montana comes to Miami and slowly makes his way into the drug trade, working from the bottom up, murdering another criminal for a green card. You get the feeling that he will do anything for anyone to get ahead. Soon his ambition gets the better of him and he longs for what he sees is possessed by the top drug bosses. Utilizing his violent nature, Montana murders the crime boss and takes over his operation. Even all the wealth that comes with that is not enough, because a person as greedy as him will always want more. What he loves is more and that is all. That, along with the jealousy that comes with it, leads to his downfall.

The 1932 original *Scarface* by Howard Hawks on the life of gangster Al Capone is a far better film, although by today's standards may seem outdated. Brian DePalma's 1983 version, written by Oliver Stone, is way to over the top for my tastes. I understand that Tony Montana is the anti Michael Corleone, all action and no thought, which is why Pacino probably took the role, but the character seemed too hokey for me. From a personal standpoint I do not particularly like this film. There seems to be no justification for anything going on. Even if one were to say that the justification was merely greed the movie still would not work for me. I just don't find it interesting.

#229 – *Mulholland Dr.*

David Lynch is a great director. He is also a great writer. He enjoys telling stories that are not the straightforward type the country is used to. They require intellect and imagination rather than merely popcorn and a movie stub. The problem is that every time he directs something he writes, the end product turns out to be monumental crapola. This movie could have easily been called *Lost Highway II: I'm Trying This Again*. It did not work again Mr. Lynch.

The film begins with a bang in the form of a car crash on Mulholland Drive. A woman walks away from the crash dazed and in a half conscious state, suffering from amnesia. She stumbles into an apartment complex and into an open apartment to rest. An innocent woman named Betty arrives in Los Angeles with dreams of becoming the next big star in movies. The apartment the unnamed woman wandered into is where Betty will be staying, her aunt's place. After quickly becoming friends the two of them embark on an adventure of discovering who the unnamed woman really is and why she has a bag full of money and a strange blue key. The mystery unfolds as the plot thickens until ultimately nothing is what it seems, even if you think you might understand what is taking place.

Mulholland Dr. is a brave movie. This screenplay would have been an almost perfect and visionary novel. As a film it is utter garbage. Lynch simply does not understand the fact that his stories do not translate well to a cinematic medium. They have a missing element to them that Lynch feels is an important part of the storytelling process. For *Mulholland Dr.*, there are a number of plot elements that do not make any sense within the context of the story, yet within a fiction setting of a novel would have worked perfectly to enhance the story. The reader wonders when those minor side stories will interact with the main plot, yet if they do not that is fine also. On screen, those moments seem wasteful and actually detract from the story, specifically from the types of stories Lynch likes to tell, incredibly complex mysteries. I would recommend reading this, but can not recommend this movie, outside of the amazingly hot lesbian scenes.

#230 – *Pirates of the Caribbean: Curse of the Black Pearl.*

Everyone loves a pirate movie. There is that element of action and adventure on the high seas and the possibility of finding a buried treasure of gold or jewels that intrigues most people. Pirate movies are tricky to pull off though because reality must be suspended, therefore the story must be good enough to keep the audiences interested. When no one really cares what happens in a story, why should anyone concentrate on what is depicted upon the screen? The answer is they will not.

Pirate captain Jack Sparrow was overrun by the men of his ship. They left him for dead on an unchartered island. Sparrow survived and made his way to the sea town of Port Royal. His former crew attacks the town in search of a gold medallion, which is in the possession of Elizabeth Swann, the daughter of the governor. Swann is taken to the boat and kidnapped by the crew, led by their new leader Captain Barbossa. The medallion holds special significance for the crew of the ship, who have been turned into some form of living zombies that must find all the gold they stole from a cursed treasure before they can become whole again. Sparrow and a young man named Will Turner go after Swann and the ship, for different reasons. When the movie reaches one of its finales, a trick is played on the mutineer cursed pirates that can be seen coming a mile away.

I was extremely glad that Johnny Depp was finally recognized by the Academy Awards committee for his acting talents, yet this movie as a whole was utter garbage. I love a swashbuckling pirate adventure as much as the next reader, but this movie reeked of crap from start to finish. The story was dull and the bad pirates were not close to as scary or terrifying as they were intended to be. The ending with the crew is predictable and the true finale is even more so. They are both setup perfectly for a sequel rather than written to complete a story. The purpose here was franchising, not storytelling. I left the theater absolutely hating this film, even though Depp was great as usual.

#231 – *Bonnie and Clyde.* #27 on AFI list.

#232 – *Sleuth.*

This may come off as bigoted but there is something about the uppity and pompous nature of the Brits that annoys me. Their historical melodramas are tough to watch at times, and their humor is way too dry for my tastes. This film is different. When a movie is this clever it transcends any pre-conceived notions of cultural bias I may have picked up while sitting through boring films such as *Wuthering Heights* or *Remains of the Day* that put me to sleep.

Based on Anthony Shaffer's enormously successful play, Laurence Olivier stars as Andrew Wyke, a famous and wealthy author. He is visited by Milo Tindle, played magnificently by Michael Caine. Milo informs Andrew that he has plans of marrying Andrew's estranged wife, whom Andrew despises. Milo wants his blessing, yet even though Andrew hates her he is still hurt by the fact that she left him. Andrew decides that this will not stand and decides to take matters into his own hands, devising a game for Milo to play that will humiliate him. Things get turned upside down as the twists and turns keep coming in this magnificently devised story.

I know it sounds like I did not explain a thing in the above paragraph but if you ever see the movie you will understand why that is about all I could say. To reveal more would be putting the reader at a disadvantage upon seeing this film for the first time. The first time I saw it I remarked at how brilliant it was, since I am a fan of mystery. Even though I know what will happen I am still a big fan of the film, primarily because of the amazing acting of the two leads, Olivier and Caine. If you do wish to see it after this write-up then I am glad and you will be also. I do not know anyone who has seen it and not thought it was a fantastic film.

#233 – *Rosemary's Baby*.

I have been somewhat cruel to director Roman Polanski in my criticism of his nefarious activities. This book should focus on movies and movies alone, yet I felt that what was said needed to be a matter of record. That still does not make Polanski any less of a brilliant filmmaker. Everyone knows what a great job he did with *Chinatown* and the 2002 hit *The Pianist*, but few know that in 1968 he directed one of the creepiest psychological horror films ever.

Rosemary and Guy Woodhouse are moving into a new apartment building. They have been told by a friend named Hutch, a writer, that the apartment building was once a coven for secret satanic rituals. They move in anyway, dismissing the information. Rosemary befriends a young woman staying with her neighbors, but discovers one night that she has committed suicide. As a result those neighbors take a liking to her. The wife, Minnie, is always dropping by and trying to find out information about what is going on. She is played as if she were the prototypical nosy neighbor. Guy takes a liking to her husband Roman, who regales Guy with his great stories. Once Rosemary gets pregnant, her world is turned upside down as she fears she is part of a sinister plot to give birth to a baby that will be consumed as part of a ritual by the neighbors, who she thinks are witches. The paranoia continues as she thinks her husband and her doctor are both involved.

Rosemary's Baby is unlike any other horror movie I have seen. First off, there are no jumps and no gore. It is truly a psychological film as we see the deterioration of Rosemary's body along with her mind. The pacing of the film is perfect, all leading up to the grand finale where Rosemary discovers the real truth of what was going on the whole time. More than just a horror film, *Rosemary's Baby* is also in part a great mystery. There are red herrings and little plot points that enhance the suspense of the film with a killer ending that must be seen to be believed.

#234 – *Laura*.

In 1944 there was a severe discrepancy in the Academy Awards process. I am not referring to the double nomination of actor Barry Fitzgerald in the Lead Actor and Supporting Actor categories for the same role. What I am speaking about is the film Fitzgerald acted in, *Going My Way*, taking home the top awards of Best Actor, Director and Picture. In that year there was the amazing film *Double Indemnity*, which has gone down in history as the far better film than the movie that actually won the award. Mistakes are made all the time, yet *Laura* was also nominated for Best Picture, also passed over and also a much better film than *Going My Way*.

Detective Mark McPherson is brought in to investigate the death of Laura Hunt. There are a few prime suspects in her murder. One is her friend Waldo Lydecker. Another is her fiancé Shelby Carpenter. There is also her Aunt Ann who may have some relationship with Carpenter. While McPherson is investigating the murder and interrogating the suspects he begins to fall in love with Laura. This goes in keeping with the theme of the movie as Laura meant something extremely different to each of the suspects and people who knew her. The finale is one that I will not reveal. To do so would destroy the mystery, yet there is more than simply the mystery going on.

In reading the last sentence you are probably confused as to what I am referring to. Those who have seen the movie are not. Otto Preminger's *Laura* is not just a murder mystery. It has deep psychological layers and richly developed characters. *Laura* is a uniquely different brand of film noir, yet definitely falls under that category. The buildup to the climax is tense and the brilliant plot had me on the edge of my seat. I would recommend watching this film with no distractions, because it reminded me of reading a book that I couldn't put down. *Laura* is that engrossing of a movie.

#235 – *Frankenstein*. #87 on AFI list.

#236 – *This is Spinal Tap*.

Rob Reiner has made a number of great films since becoming a director. They include *The Princess Bride*, *The American President* and *When Harry Met Sally*. There is a sly wit to his work that he developed during his years as an actor on the classic show *All in the Family*. His first film delved into the insane world of an English rock band, which became the ultimate mockumentary that all others would forever be judged on.

Director Marty DiBergi, played by Reiner in the film, records the day to day activities of the English rock band *Spinal Tap* on their United States tour. The journey is filled with in depth interviews of each member of the band, with the exception of the drummers because they keep dying. Every interview reveals a unique idiosyncrasy of hilarity, most notably when Nigel explains that he has an amplifier that goes up to eleven. When DiBergi asks him why they don't just make ten louder, his only response is because eleven is one more than ten. He cannot fathom the mathematical possibilities of a stereo only going up to ten being louder than his, which goes to eleven. It is the scene that everyone knows, along with the sausage metal detector scene at the airport.

This is Spinal Tap was written by Reiner and the three actors who play the members of the band, Christopher Guest, Michael McKeon and Harry Shearer. All three have gone onto decent careers in the industry, reuniting again for a short and for the great mockumentary written by Eugene Levy and Guest, *A Mighty Wind*. The appeal of this film is in its great comedy, but it is not the standard type of comedy, because the filmmakers actually make you believe that there are people and bands like *Spinal Tap* out there. If DiBergi were a real person I'm sure that he could find his actual *Spinal Tap*, but for now I am more than satisfied with this wonderful and hilarious creation.

#237 – *Rain Man*. Best Picture – 1988

#238 – *Star Wars: Episode III – Revenge of the Sith*.

Once again, this was the part of the second trilogy that was the most highly anticipated. I guess that is an obvious fact of cinema, that the final installment of a trilogy is always the most eagerly awaited one. This was different though, because of the implications of where the story was going. Everyone knows what happens to the characters after this film is over, but the sole impetus for creating this second trilogy was to explain how they got there. This was the part of the trilogy that was supposed to most completely answer those questions. It does and it really does not.

This film focused on the destruction of the Jedi council, the continued transformation of Anakin to the dark side and highlighted the anticipated battle between mentor and apprentice that everyone knew was coming. Slowly moving toward that encounter, the film continues to delve into the clones as an enemy of the republic, while the Emperor plots his next move, turning Anakin into his next Sith Lord and apprentice. That scene where Anakin is outfitted in the black tomb he must wear until his redemption comes in *The Return of the Jedi* is as mechanistic as Hayden Christopher's acting throughout the whole film. The opportunity existed for so much more to be told.

Revenge of the Sith had the opportunity to bridge the gap between the original set of stories and the original story started in 1977 with *Star Wars: Episode IV – A New Hope*. This movie failed miserably, leaving enough of a hole in the connection to make three more movies that could fill in the gaps. The basics are there, specifically how and why Anakin turns to the dark side and becomes Darth Vader, but that is not all that the original story is about. Vader is such a minor entity in the first movie, outside of having been the most ominous villain ever, yet that is only backed by his thorough and complete villainy in *The Empire Strikes Back* and his redemption in *The Return of the Jedi*. Lucas chose to over emphasize the turning of Anakin into Vader. Where is Chewbacca meeting Han Solo? Why can't Vader feel that the two children or Obi-Wan survived? This last installment was a total failure in my opinion, creating more questions than it answers.

#239 – *The Thing* (1982).

John Carpenter has a knack for creating interesting material. It is not always new material, but whatever Carpenter seems to show on screen there are always interesting and tense moments throughout the story. *The Thing* is a reworking of the 1951 sci-fi classic *The Thing from Another World*. Comparing the two films, you can see why Carpenter felt the need to rework the original. With modern effects, this story takes on a whole new relevance. The 1951 version is eerie, yet this modern attempt is frightening as hell.

A group of American scientists at an Arctic research station are alerted to the presence of a helicopter that appears to be chasing after a dog. After the helicopter crashes, killing all the passengers, the dog is let into the camp. The helicopter pilot for the Americans travels to the nearby base that the helicopter and the crew aboard belonged to. He discovers the camp in ruins and sees a mangled body, which he brings back to his camp for further investigation. The dog turns out to be an alien, who can take the form of its host. Immediately, that is when the paranoia sets in. The alien, or thing, could be anyone of the humans in the camp. Figuring out who the creature has morphed into becomes priority number one with everyone beginning to distrust each other.

Carpenter's version is much better than the original version, but one could almost say that they were two entirely different films. They had similar stories and derived from the same original story, but each chooses to inspire a different emotion from the audience. I prefer the Carpenter version, although I can sit back and enjoy both. Both are creepy, yet only the newer version is scary. It is almost a matter of philosophy versus experience, where both films were meant to be horror films yet one tried to represent that it should be scary while the other one actually succeeded.

#240 – *Miller's Crossing*.

The Coen Brothers are nothing if not stylistic. They have a definitive idea of what type of story they want to tell, filled with memorable characters within the framework of a specific setting. One of the beautiful aspects of their work is that, despite getting the feeling that a movie is a Coen Brothers film or not, there is always that special hint of originality. From their early work, no film is more original than *Miller's Crossing*.

A consultant for a Prohibition era crime boos gets caught in the middle of warring crime families and his own self destructive nature as he falls for his boss' woman. Tom Reagan only wants to keep the peace and his job. There is enough money for everyone, but each crime boss wants more than his fair share. Circumstances arise forcing Tom into playing both sides. There are always people who want to use him, such as the boss' girlfriend's brother who blackmails him after he shows mercy by not killing him, the signature scene of the film that occurs with a begging John Turturro in the woods with Gabriel Byrne stalking him. Byrne's mercy eventually brings more trouble than it was worth, yet that in and of itself helps things work their way out in the end.

The style and feel of the movie itself plays as one of the characters. The hardcore violence, reminiscent of the era, plays as a secondary character as well. The Coen Brothers have fashioned one of the better films that sets itself in the Prohibition era, with great characters and snappy dialogue to add to the overall flavor. This is the movie that made me a fan of the Coen Brothers work, even though I enjoyed their prior film *Raising Arizona*. It is one of their stylistic masterpieces.

#241 – *Being John Malkovich*.

The #35 movie on this list is only the latest from the brilliant yet strange mind of writer Charlie Kaufman. His originality knows no bounds and it all began with this deranged yet exceptional story. Thinking about the possibility of stepping into someone else's shoes could have been that simple impetus needed in order to create and develop the distinctive idea presented here. Of course, this film is so much more than stepping into someone else's shoes.

An out of work puppeteer is given a job on the seven and one half floor of a building that contains a secret portal into the mind of actor John Malkovich. Having feelings for one of his co-workers, this man tells her that he actually entered the portal and was for a brief period of time inside the mind of the noted actor. Immediately she does not believe him, yet ultimately sees the financial opportunities. Once they setup a business where the general public can enter the portal and the mind of Malkovich for a price, things start going downhill, with Malkovich learning of what is going on and entering the portal himself. The scene with Malkovich inside his own mind is absolute insanity and the highlight of the film. The puppeteer develops the ability to manipulate Malkovich and takes over his body, quitting acting and taking up stage puppeteering. The portal is a secret that holds greater significance than even the puppeteer can possibly imagine.

This is one of the films that I saw with my father. When we left the theater we had mixed reviews of the film. He believed the movie was *"fucking retarded"*, while I thought it was the most original story concept I had ever seen on film. Of course it is a strange movie, yet that is part of the delight of the film. Standard has been done a million times over and has gotten stale. The time had come for a great new idea in storytelling. *Being John Malkovich* was that story. Even though *Adaptation* is a better film, I cannot deny the highly innovative structure of this insane film.

#242 – *Doctor Zhivago*. #?? on main list. #39 on AFI list.

#243 – *Planet of the Apes* (1968).

One of the all time great lines comes from this movie. Everyone knows it, because it has been parodied over and over again. That is a testament to the film's popularity. When Charlton Heston finally says that classic line, there is the immediate sense of relief. It was as if the audience was trapped alongside the humans, with their only hope coming in the form of Heston who could not muster the words to put those filthy apes in their place, until he finally said it. After that, the movie took on a new life with that major secret waiting to be revealed.

A crew of astronauts leave Earth in search of something better than what the world has become. The pilot, Taylor, hates what mankind has turned into enough for him to search for a better way of life on a distant planet. The three survivors begin looking for any form of life, eventually finding humans, who appear to be mute, yet that is not all that strange compared to what comes next. The humans are hunted by apes on horseback that speak English. Something is terribly wrong, but there is no time to rationalize the problem, only time to run. Taylor is captured and his throat is injured so he cannot speak for a short time. When he finally does the apes that are sympathetic to humans see the error of their ways in keeping humans captive and experimenting on them. When they help Taylor escape he gets more than he bargained for upon discovering the secret of the planet.

Based upon a novel by French author Pierre Boulle, the story was originally meant to act as a satire on the folly of the over important sense of self worth of humans, specifically in their belief that the planet was theirs. It was Americanized to an extent by *Twilight Zone* creator Rod Serling, yet the basic themes remain the same, albeit in a ironically juxtaposed manner. Moving past the implicit themes of the film, it is pure unadulterated enjoyment. The numerous sequels were primarily weaker although they always prompted me to watch when they were on. The original is still amazing and as far as sci-fi movies go, *The Planet of the Apes* is one of the all time best.

#244 – *The Sea Inside* (Spain).

Biography films always seem to have that extra element of emotion to them. I suppose it is because the events depicted on film transpired in real life, making them easier to relate to. Since the events actually happened the viewer becomes emotionally attached and this film is no exception to that rule. The true story of Spaniard Ramon Sampedro will make you question your values and break your heart. His courage regarding personal freedom and the right to die is a battle that spanned over twenty-eight years. Even in defeat he emerged victorious.

Ramon Sampedro loved the sea. When he was a young man he traveled the world, working as a ship's mechanic. One unfortunate day, Ramon suffers an accident while diving. The tide pulls back at the wrong time while Ramon dives in, crashing his head and neck into the shallow end of the ocean floor. He is saved from drowning but is a quadriplegic. With his mind still intact, Ramon wages a close to thirty year campaign in order to be given the right to commit euthanasia. Toward the end he comes in contact with two women who fall in love with him, both wanting to talk him out of it yet come around to see his way of thinking in the end. His case is turned down by the courts, yet Ramon's will to die with dignity outweighs the law's improper upholding of an unjust law.

I have only seen *The Sea Inside* twice. The first time I saw it I was incredibly moved at how important a statement it makes regarding personal freedoms. The second time I saw it I was able to see the other side, how so many people felt so much for Ramon and how they would be affected after he took his own life, needing help of course. There are two sides to most issues. This happens to be one of them. The best scene in the film was between Ramon and a quadriplegic priest battling wits. The priest was no match for Ramon, who explained that he was a flat out hypocrite in his beliefs on this issue. Whether I believe in his choice or not, I absolutely back his right to make that choice. This film presents his position in a clear manner and is an altogether fantastic piece of cinema.

#245 – *Network*. #36 on main list. #66 on AFI list.

#246 – *Who's Afraid of Virginia Woolf*.

The first on screen teaming of Richard Burton and Elizabeth Taylor was planned to be a magnanimous spectacle. That movie, *Cleopatra*, fell flat on its face. It was a nice film and visually stunning, but *Cleopatra* could never live up to the hype surrounding it. Their second and third pairings, *The V.I.P.'s* and *The Sandpiper* were silly and forgettable, yet the fourth time out this Hollywood power couple finally got it right.

A married couple, Martha and George, invite over a younger married couple, Nick and Honey, for drinks after a party attended by the four of them. Martha's father is in charge of the university where George and Nick teach, so inviting them over is a welcoming to the neighborhood that quickly turns askew. The liquor flows and the psychological games begin as Martha and George reveal more than the other will like and new information is divulged about Nick and Honey, eventually used against them. Both couples learn more than they bargained for on that long night.

Who's Afraid of Virginia Woolf has nothing to do with the author of the same name, but rather is a mere comical play on words from a haunting fairy tale line of dialogue to set the tone of the film. Upon first viewing I thought it was way too talky and believed the characters were of the type that I personally could not stand, always trying to one up each other with intellectual banter. On subsequent viewings I discovered that that was one of the primary points. The elder couple was so unhappy with each other that they needed to engage in these twisted games of one-upmanship in order to stand each other. Once I realized that I was able to see how ingenious and unfortunately realistic a story this actually was, taking on a whole new depth for me as a viewer.

#247 – *Barry Lyndon*.

The ninth and final Kubrick film on this top 250 list is the adaptation of the epic novel by William Makepeace Thackeray. There are many who cite this film as Kubrick's best, with even more exclaiming that *Barry Lyndon* is not only his best but one of the most beautiful pictures ever filmed. It is pure Kubrick, although strictly of that customary self-indulgent style he molded into after his first great film *The Killing*. In this case it works because of the material. The Thackeray novel was the ideal vehicle for Kubrick's self-important demeanor.

An 18th century Irishman, Redmond Barry, must leave his home after he believes he has killed an English officer in a duel. Starting off his new life, Barry is robbed and then joins the British Army, involved in the Seven Years War. On the battlefield, an old friend is shot and killed before his eyes. This is all that Barry needs to solidify his plans of desertion. Impersonating an officer delivering an important message, he is determined to be an imposter and forced to join the Prussian Army, where he receives an award for bravery in saving an officer's life and assigned to a new position. In this new position Barry is allowed to escape his service and enter a life of gambling, eventually settling down with Lady Lyndon and takes the name Barry Lyndon. Marrying into nobility is thought to be enough, yet Barry finds out that life, in all circles, comes with challenges.

Some fans cite *Barry Lyndon* as amazingly beautiful to watch while others find it dull and uninteresting. I can see both points of view. Kubrick takes great pleasure in showing all the minor nuances of the story, the incredibly minor plot points and the added minutiae that a novel set in 18th century England usually offers. On film, these images come across as either visually stunning or enormously boring. I experienced both of these reactions after watching this film. A second viewing did not change that opinion. *Barry Lyndon* is a movie for those who enjoy reading novels where pomposity is a character itself. If you cannot sit through a novel like that you will not like this movie.

#248 – *Fanny and Alexander* (Sweden).

Toward the end of his career, Ingmar Bergman began delving into more autobiographical subjects. That did not change his desire to search for answers to the questions he felt haunted us. Bergman was fascinated with death. That is not an understatement. However, he challenged the audience to ask itself questions about the beyond, where death was the natural progression to the other side. He wanted to take the audience on the journey that he was in the process of discovering so everyone could share the expedition with him.

Fanny and Alexander follows the story of one family, the Ekdahls. The parents are Oscar and Emilie. Oscar runs the local theater company and Emilie is the star of its productions. Fanny and Alexander are the children. Oscar become ill and passes away, whereby Emilie seeks consoling from the Bishop, Edvard. Through helping her Emilie believes she has fallen in love with him and they marry. This deeply affects the children who are forced to leave their spacious home for the lifeless dwellings of Bishop Edvard, who becomes not the guiding force that Emile wished for her children but rather a dominating figure to them. There are numerous subplots in the film, yet this is the main story. The full-length version runs at over three hundred minutes, so pack a lunch.

Bergman has created a great story about the hardships that a single family must go through during their lifetime. The characters in the film are definitely at a crossroads in their lives, struggling with everything including guilt, hate, honor, shame, love and of course Bergman's favorite theme death. Bergman has had such a storied career as a director that I am forced to say that this was one of his lesser efforts. In comparison to some of his other great films, I would rate *Fanny and Alexander* well below them, of which I include *Cries and Whispers*, *Persona* and *Winter Light*. *Fanny and Alexander* is a good film, but nowhere close to his cinematic masterpieces.

#249 – *Garden State*.

Every year there are a few treasures in cinema that get overlooked. That is a natural yet unfortunate part of the process as more and more films are made each year. Only so many films can be properly recognized, although that is the primary job of the award nominating bodies and organizations. As has been stated in an earlier chapter, great films are often missed, passed over in favor of films that possess any number of qualities that the Academy and other groups tend to focus their attention on. Still, gems are made and find their way into cinemas across the country, gathering a following through word of mouth rather than major marketing campaigns. *Garden State* is that type of film and the cream of that crop for smaller films from 2004.

Actor Andrew Largeman returns home to New Jersey for the funeral of his mother. While back home he must settle a few things with his father and figure out what his life is all about. Through the help of a new friend, played by Natalie Portman, and some friends from high school, Andrew's sense of reality begins to become clearer. He makes peace with his responsibility regarding an accident that left his mother in a wheelchair and leaves the mass of medications he has been on for years behind him. With newfound love and a clearer, less medicated outlook on life, Andrew must decide to return to his old life in California or remain with the person he has fallen in love with.

Written, directed by and starring Zach Braff from the hit television show *Scrubs*, *Garden State* is one of those movies where as a fan of movies you will walk into the theater and give it a shot and walk out with a giant smile on your face. Totally different from the show that made him a star, Braff creates a great comedic story with perfect touches of heart and reality blended in. Natalie Portman gives an amazing performance as the bizarre woman Braff falls for. Her Oscar nomination for the movie *Closer* was really for both movies. Portman is actually much better in this film. A total surprise that wound up paying off large dividends, *Garden State* has gathered a reputation from fans that allowed it to be talked about and seen by more people than it was originally intended for.

#250 – *The Passion of Joan of Arc* (France).

This is another of those stories where the events surrounding the film are almost as interesting as the film itself. Danish filmmaker Carl Dreyer made the film in 1927-1928 and it was immediately censored and eventually feared lost. A number of the negatives were destroyed so Dreyer had to piece the film together from a second negative. The original version that Dreyer envisioned has probably never been seen other than by him and his crew. The version audiences can see today was from a print found in a Norwegian insane asylum in 1981. The belief is that this print, long though lost or non-existent, was sent to a Danish film festival.

The famous French teenager, crusader and martyr Joan of Arc is put on trial. The notes for the screenplay are said to have been taken from the actual transcripts of the trial. Stranger things have happened. What the audience is treated to is Joan facing her accusers who blatantly charge her with blasphemy for believing that God spoke to her. No matter how hard they try to get her to admit it is a lie Joan remains steadfast in her beliefs. Even their tricks do not make Joan admit what they want her to. Eventually she will pay for her beliefs with her life as she is burned at the stake.

This is a fantastic film. It is not the flashy type of film that the world has gotten accustomed to but rather a thinking person's film. The implications of what is portrayed on the screen may have even escaped Dreyer at the time he was making the film. When the judges demand that Joan was spoken to by the devil rather than God, the clear cut consequences of this are why could they not have been spoken to by the devil also. It is an archaic approach to a chauvinistic belief in divinity that Joan challenges with her thoughts, yet once again, I am not sure that even Dreyer knew the far reaching connotations of his masterwork.

Additionally, the acting of Maria Falconetti has been singled out as some of the best ever. I equate her performance as equal in an extent to that of Max Shreck from *Nosferatu*. Both performances border on the bizarre, with her continuous weird gaze past the camera quite disturbing. All she does is stare with her eyes wide open and cry at every moment she is on film. I am not sure how the hell she got so many tears to flow. It is as strange a performance as they come.

Chapter Seven:

Movies 60 - 51

60

????

    In my first book that focused around a list, the most frequently asked question was who filled the number fifty-one slot? The readers I spoke to all wanted to know who the person was that had just missed the cut for that particular list. It was that element of the unknown that people seemed to want told to them. Fifty was not good enough. Even adding a section on those not included but historically famous was not enough. The people wanted to know who #51 was. Natural curiosity I guess. There is nothing wrong with that and actually one of the main points of that book was to discuss who the next couple of individuals could have been and why they were left off the list in favor of the last few who were included. That same principle should hold with this list book. As an added bonus therefore, I have included this extra chapter to hopefully fill the reader's curiosity.
    Here is the problem with revealing what movie number sixty is, everyone will want to know what movie sixty-one is. I have offered you, the reader, numbers fifty-nine through fifty-one for that same reason. After reading the main list, I assure you that ninety percent of the readers immediately wanted to know what number fifty-one was. I am offering that to you in this final chapter. That still will not quench your thirst. That's good though. Giving you number sixty will only make you want to know what sixty-one is that much more. As a result I have concealed sixty from you as well. Either you can speculate on what movie number sixty is, not care in the least or do what I would do, speculate on what numbers sixty and sixty-one would be and discuss that with your friends who love movies. That seems more interesting and thought provoking than just dealing with the speculative idea of the identity of sixty-one.
    Simply put, maybe the number sixty film has already been given to you and maybe it has not. Part of the beauty of a book such as this, I would hope, is that your imagination can play an integral part. Just like the movies, I truly hope this books has taken you on a ride away from reality, if only for a moment, bringing with it an impetus for further discussion and debate. Now as a bonus for you I present numbers fifty-nine through fifty-one. Enjoy.

59

DOCTOR ZHIVAGO
1965

How can a movie adaptation live up to what has been called one of the greatest love stories ever written? Making this film would be a daunting task, one which only a true master of cinema would choose to undertake. David Lean was that type of director, simply a man who thrived on creating cinematic epics. At the time, no one was more perfectly suited than Lean to transfer this epic love story onto the screen. Fresh off his most renowned epic, *Lawrence of Arabia*, and only eight years removed from his best film, *The Bridge on the River Kwai*, both Best Picture winners, as well as uncredited work on another epic in 1965, *The Greatest Story Ever Told*, Lean was not satisfied with remaining stagnant within film. His goal was to continually challenge himself and those cinematic boundaries. If there was an epic to be made Lean made it a point to be involved with the production.

The love story between Yuri Zhivago and Lara Antipova has become an immortal one. The film, however, is not about their romance. Their tragic romance occurs solely within the framework of the film. Although they meet a number of times prior to ultimately acting upon their love for one another, it takes a long while to see their romance come to fruition. That is a double edged sword, because those who know of the romance prior to seeing the film eagerly wait in anticipation for the two star crossed lovers to finally embrace. Those who do not know of the story's more famous theme will notice the signs when the two are together early on, hoping that it shall lead somewhere and sensing that it must. Of course by now it is common knowledge that their love is doomed, but it is the magical journey toward the two of them finally coming together that still amazes today.

The true greatness of *Doctor Zhivago*, not arguing against the love story between Yuri and Lara, lies in its grandest theme, survival. Throughout the movie, the audience is treated to the evolving ideology of a common yet extraordinary man. Zhivago is not only a doctor who cares more about healing the wounded than about taking a hardened stance on the turbulent times but also a poet. One of the lesser known gems of the story is how his poetry is viewed as inventive early on, yet due to the harsh politics of revolutionary war torn Russia, those same ideas evolve into anarchistic. It is a brilliant mechanism to display the change from totalitarianism to communism and how things only seem better on the surface. It is Zhivago's will to survive, as well as the will of all the characters that sets the movie apart from mere love story during a time when personal feelings were sacrificed.

As stated earlier, David Lean was coming off two Best Picture winners in eight years, as well as two Best Director Oscars for Lean with each of those films. *Doctor Zhivago* offered the chance for Lean to make history and become the first director to achieve that feat three times in an eight year span. History proved that task impossible as the Academy chose to go with the much sunnier and more uplifting tale *The Sound of Music*. History has corrected that mistake to a certain degree, with *Doctor Zhivago* perceived as the better film, ranking higher on the AFI list than the film that took home the award. That would be no consolation for Lean, who always sought after higher and greater challenges, which a third Oscar victory in both categories might have provided.

58

IT HAPPENED ONE NIGHT

1934

There are a couple of essentials in making a movie that will stand the test of time. First and foremost there must be a solid story. In the current state of cinema the films that truly transcend era are the ones that have solid stories as their backdrop. A solid story can transcend generations, appearing as if what was happening to the characters of the film could happen to anyone at any moment. The direct opposite is also true that those events could not happen to anyone, ever. That, in and of itself, creates a continual attraction toward this film. *It Happened One Night* starts with that, a basic story. It is that grand old theme of opposites attracting while placed in a situation together. Naturally, obstacles and pitfalls are placed in their way on a road that inevitably leads toward love.

A rich heiress escapes from her father's boat to meet up with the wealthy playboy she has married. The man does not meet her father's approval, causing him great dismay in the process. Along her journey, she meets a man with a distinctly opposite type personality, the typical working man who comes complete with a rough exterior and fast talking ways. Their initial meeting is not the most pleasant and it takes awhile for them to realize that they are in a mess. This becomes the obstacle, which they must work through together. Out of that grows mutual reliance, which in turn breeds mutual affection and love. There are subtle moments that reveal it to the intelligent film audience, without having to say the words, until that grand cinematic moment finally arrives.

Unfortunately, those obstacles continue to remain despite the revelation of love for one another. In a story such as this that is where the true magic occurs. In the face of all the barriers and surviving one last necessary conflict to reinforce their mutual feelings, they can ultimately openly share what has been going on in secret through their masterful use of subtle glances, innuendo and shared yearnings. The two of them, as different as oil and water, want the same thing when it all comes down to it. It is truly bizarre that this movie dates better than most today that employ the same cinematic theme. One such movie was *Forces of Nature*, which dated after its weekend release.

Both stars, Clark Gable and Claudette Colbert, came from an era where studios held the rights to actors. It was part of their studio contracts. The two stars however, were both loaned out to make this movie by their respective studios. Colbert initially thought this slapstick type material was beneath her, yet Gable jumped at the chance to play against his established type. He was known for playing the mean spirited guy that the audience rooted against, so this role was a definite departure. Neither of the two stars were happy with the final cut of the movie, yet middle America fell for their irresistible charm and chemistry, as well as flawless directing and a fantastic script. The film's sweep of the five major Academy awards, Picture, Director, Actor, Actress and Screenplay is often viewed as the single greatest Oscar achievement. That feat would remain untied until forty-one years later when *One Flew Over the Cuckoo's Nest* did it as well, followed by *The Silence of the Lambs* in 1991. The Academy voters are way off at times. This was not one of those times.

57

ADAPTATION
2002

     Who would have thought it possible for a movie to have been written more uniquely than 1999's *Being John Malkovich*? That story was so innovative that one would think there could never be another to come as close to it. Charlie Kaufman did, with the help of his brother Donald. Any work not as original as the first would be viewed as inferior, specifically since that was that movie's calling card. It would not be easy to construct something even more bizarre than that story, yet the Kaufman brothers succeeded. Even that fact alone, that it was a joint effort on their part is part of the distinctiveness of this movie. It is a movie working within the framework of creative insanity.

     The first thing to do when reaching past the brink of insanity is to head back into one's own mind. Therein lies the originality. The co-writers infuse themselves as characters in the story. That in and of itself is not unique, yet the fashion with which it is done fits that bill. They created a story about trying to adapt an unadaptable book. Rather than merely telling the story contained within the book, an actual book on the beauty of orchids, the Kaufman brothers chose to reveal the story of what was going on during the adapting process. It was sort of the pre-story showing what took place before the work on the adaptation was finally complete and the problems with actually completing that work. The blending of both aspects provides one of the more creative story concepts ever told.

     The movie is truly a story about many different types of characters. The two characters from the book, the writer Susan Orlean and the orchid thief John Laroche, as well as the two characters that transport themselves into the story, Charlie and Donald Kaufman are all highlighted as main characters. In that unique Kaufman style, each and every character has its own rareness. That is one of the major story components with what has come to be known as Kaufman's work. Orlean becomes sexually involved with Laroche, who is actually running drugs through his flower cultivating, while also creating internet pornography. Charlie depicts himself as a fat, balding man with no self confidence and writer's block, while Donald is almost the exact opposite. Donald is killed in the end after discovering information about Orlean that leads them to the Florida everglades. It would be too much of a spoiler to reveal anymore about the story, other than stating it must be seen.

     The beautiful part of the character development is that it is all a farce. Charlie Kaufman is nothing like he represents himself in the film, according to what is known about him. Orlean is real, but never got sexually involved with Laroche, who was not running drugs so far as is known. These are all literary creations of Charlie and Donald Kaufman in presenting an original story. One other thing that should be known, Donald does not exist. He was made up by Charlie to enhance the story. Tough to understand at first, yet brilliant when finally realized. Charlie Kaufman has done it again, continuing to present written material in such a unique way that it simply amazes. Too early to judge, yet I believe this will become one of the classics, specifically in its steadfast desire to stick to its originality. When historians go back and examine cinema, they shall use *Adaptation* as a guide.

56

THE PHILADELPHIA STORY
1940

What would a movie about high society look like if it were made by high society? All the air and pomposity is present, told in a style of self defense for their own livelihoods. High society defending their rights to privacy and their own specific brand of lunacy shines on screen here. More than simply an excuse for a screwball romp, *The Philadelphia Story* presents a number of interesting concepts, including class values, those specific rights to privacy and the understanding of the simpler pleasures in life. Although it is easy to see that the characters are extremely privileged, the journey of discovery that each character goes through is told in a masterfully comedic and extremely stylized format. If the rich did make this film, they were poking fun at themselves. They had a definitive purpose in mind, the idea that they are people too even though they act as they are above the rest.

Rich and spoiled heiress Tracy Lord is getting married over the weekend. This is her second marriage. Her first marriage to C. K. Dexter Haven failed shortly after its inception. The couple was too much alike in their stubbornness for the marriage to have worked out. Due to the public philandering of her father, two reporters are allowed to infiltrate the inner world of the soon to be married Lord. Their infiltration is set up by Haven, who presents them as friends of Lord's brother, not attending the wedding. A fine piece of subterfuge, all for the inside story of the wedding event of the year, except for the fact that Haven alerts the Lords as to who the two reporters are. For the reporters benefit, as well as the father's, whose neck they are saving by allowing the reporters access, a performance of extraordinary flamboyance is put on for them as a rouse to protect their privacy.

As the weekend unfolds and the wedding draws near, the rich and the working class mingle with each other. For the reporters, their only goal is to get the story, even though they despise having to do it. For the Lords, their mission is to distract them long enough to allow their lives to go on. What happens is they begin to not only understand each other, but also work together as the plot unfolds. When certain information is revealed to the two reporters they start to see the pompous rich for more than what they thought. The rich, typified by Tracy Lord, begin to see the reporters as more than what they seem at the onset. Although a comedy, *The Philadelphia Story* is a shining example of personal growth, displaying that there is more to people than meets the eye.

Working from a terrific script, containing zany spots of rapid fire back and forth dialogue, *The Philadelphia Story* shines as one of the more mature screwball comedies made. Each character hates themselves just a slight bit or learns to by the film's end. This intellectual growth on the part of all embraces the notion that no one should take oneself too seriously. When one does, it always seems to spiral into mass confusion. In the face of all the confusion over ideologies, the prying eyes of the public seem to always want more, even when they are given much more than they deserve.

55

THE AWFUL TRUTH

1937

There have been a number of movies that try to hold the distinction of the best and original screwball comedy. One of those films was the recently discussed *It Happened One Night*. Another is the 1936 film *My Man Godfrey*, which should hold the distinction of being the first. The best of the bunch however, is *The Awful Truth*. Best is perhaps the only way to describe this prototypical screwball comedy. Coming one year off the heels of *My Man Godfrey*, *The Awful Truth* went that necessary step past it, producing a madcap romp of marital bliss heading toward the road of divorce and back again. From the opening set-up, where suspicions about the marriage are revealed, divorce proceedings commence. After that basis for the film, the comedy of errors begins.

The viewers are not given the actual happenings that led to why there was such suspicion. This adds to the eventual amusement by creating further suspicions during the film. Their divorce allows each party to pursue suitors, with the unspoken condition of the other party butting in and trying to cause problems. It is a clear indication that feelings still exist between them. From the moment that an outsider's feelings are shown, the audience is treated to the subtext that neither party wishes the other to be with anyone else. Rather than come right out and say it, a roundabout journey ensues. This incredibly hilarious set of events that masquerades as the journey inescapably leads the characters back to each other. Comedy is the method for their reconciliation. It is eccentric comedy at its finest, but there is also heart, longing and redemption. The focus will always be on the comedy and the comedic chemistry between the two principal characters.

To attempt to fully analyze a screwball comedy falls under the same heading as scrutinizing a magnificent lesbian porn movie. There does not have to be a grand scheme or great psychological undercurrent contained within the story for it to be enjoyable. Occasionally, it is simply better to sit back and enjoy the fun that is put upon the screen for the audience. That is what is so great about *The Awful Truth* and of course great lesbian porn. It is that definitive escapism of just relaxing and taking in the effort on the part of the performers. Cary Grant and Irene Dunne play their parts to perfection, with small but essential supporting performances by their scheduled fiancées to be.

The chemistry of not only the lead actor and actress, but also in their naturally flowing give and take dialogue fuels this treasure of a film. There is the definitive design that makes the viewer want to root for Grant and Dunne to get back together rather than be apart. A film such as this one allows you to find yourself as a participant, rather than merely a simple onlooker. Neither of the two fiancées is right for them. Grant and Dunne can only be right for each other. The two of them are of the same ilk, specifically seen through their background conversations with one another, while the other person is talking to someone. It is subtle, but the focused viewer will see that and appreciate the movie for its zany stylized format and just plain enjoyable quality.

54

DOUBLE INDEMNITY
1944

Film noir was born through the work of John Huston and Humphrey Bogart in *The Maltese Falcon*. While that classic shall always hold a sacred place in the heart of Hollywood, one movie took what they created and went one step further. *Double Indemnity* focused on the behaviors of the two main individuals, rather than merely spotlighting the crime as the primary element. It is their story, the lonely bored housewife with an air of mystery and the just as lonely and bored insurance agent who falls for her sexual charm, that the movie focuses on. The crime, a key element for a film noir, is almost placed on the back burner. It is the set-up and after affect that form the real basis of the film.

Fast talking insurance agent Walter Neff visits the house of a client whose auto insurance has lapsed. The man is not home but Neff is greeted by the man's wife. She immediately takes his breath away. Their first meeting is evocative of a well played tennis match, with sexual innuendo feverishly lobbed back and forth by both. Their second meeting is more of the same. That third meeting is where they both agree to murder her husband for profit. The trick now becomes how to do it properly and without arousing any unnecessary suspicion. More importantly, how can they get the most money out of the insurance company? Once the deed is done, that is when suspicion arises.

Although the steamy relationship between the main characters, how they come together, hatch their plot and the eventual conclusion of their association, is what the film is best known for, one overlooked aspect of this film is its originality The movie is told through a first person narrative voice over by Neff, played as if a detective novel is read to the audience. Neff's confession comes from his guilt and suspicions about fearing a double cross from his partner. The genius of the film is in reaching that final point with enough anticipation to answer why those suspicions exist?

Citizen Kane lost the Best Picture award to *How Green Was My Valley*. *Goodfellas* lost to *Dances With Wolves*. *Vertigo* and *Touch of Evil* lost to *Gigi*, because neither of these two films were nominated. It is not uncommon for the Best Picture winner to be a lesser film than one from the same year, yet the above examples are important because the difference in quality between the film that won and the film recognized as the far greater is such a large disparity. 1944 is of this variety. *Double Indemnity* is always named on any short list of the greatest films made, yet lost to such a lesser film, *Going My Way*, that it definitely belongs in that specific category of monumental upsets.

Tense in a uniquely peculiar way, *Double Indemnity* is one of the few movies that actually keeps you on the edge of your intellectual seat. The audience knows the truth, but the beauty is in how the plot unfolds. How will they get caught? The insurance detective, Keyes, knows the entire story behind the murder. He is unclear who the second person involved is. This is another brilliant plot element, as Keyes and Neff share a special bond. Keyes is Neff's friend and mentor. It is one of the unspoken delights of the film, how a man can be so low that he tries to get over on someone who unquestionably cares for him, yet ultimately reveals all to him as he embraces what he has done.

53

IN THE HEAT OF THE NIGHT
1967

What is the first thing the police in Sparta, Mississippi do after a white man is murdered? Find the first black man they can and arrest him. Even after it is discovered that the black man arrested for the murder is a police officer from the North, only the minutest of professional courtesy is extended at first. All those racial prejudices are still present. Prior to garnering the black detective's services, a preliminary symbolic metaphor for slavery and the mindset of Southerners, despite the plain fact that his skill and intellect are far greater than theirs, he is simply nothing to them. That is only in the beginning until one of them is ultimately able to evolve his thinking.

Racial stereotypes and prejudices aside, it should not be forgotten that *In the Heat of the Night* is a magnificently layered detective story. It is a uniquely crafted plot revolving around the murder of a Northerner and the two police officers who stop at nothing to solve the crime, despite their differing backgrounds. As the two main characters of the story, the racist white police chief and the black homicide detective from the North, maneuver through deciphering the case, they encounter numerous twists and turns. Standard to any great detective story, the twists help move the story along, which include red herring suspects and the implication of a police officer in the murder.

The relationship between Steiger and Poitier is the focal point of the movie. Progressing past their initial contempt for one another their desire and search for the truth brings them closer together. One thing that separates the white chief from the rest of the people in the town however, is his isolation. While others are perfectly content with their particular way of thinking, he is troubled by it. In one great scene he admits to Poitier that he is alone in the town. What this represents is that his ideals and beliefs are not of a similar nature to theirs. Where those people can never change, he can, because he is inherently different. This causes his loneliness. Their pseudo-friendship is not only extremely poignant, but helps show him that he is not like the rest and that it is for the better.

This incredibly brave movie challenged racial stereotypes, presenting a character that possessed the ability to develop in his thought process. Additionally, the movie showcased a character, what the townsfolk consider to be an outsider, who skillfully helps solve this peculiar and in-depth murder mystery. For the times it was incredibly tense subject material. It was a story that not only needed to be told, but also did not sacrifice story elements to tell it. The combining of these two polar opposites that inevitably come to work together, gather mutual respect and realize that they are not as different as initially believed, showed that separation by skin color is nothing but pure bigotry. Even though it was fictitious, *In the Heat of the Night* held a valuable lesson, one which unfortunately still has not reached as many as it should.

Despite its Best Picture victory in 1967, history has chosen to exalt other movies from that year as far more influential. *The Graduate* is generally considered the special film from 1967, yet even stranger is a movie that discussed and delved into the same themes, *Guess Who's Coming to Dinner*, which is also more revered than this great film.

52

THE LAST PICTURE SHOW
1971

The times, they are a changing. Despite all the side stories about relationships and the turmoil that goes into keeping and eventually losing one, the general theme of this film deals with having to move past a way of life that one has grown accustomed to. Change is never easy, yet for some it comes regardless of how much that tradition needs to be held onto. An absolute gem of a multi-generational story, *The Last Picture Show* shows both sides of the expanding horizons of life as well as exploring and challenging both the social and sexual morays of the time. Rich with great characters, old school traditional values and how those characters begin to deal with ever changing ideals on their natural evolution into a more modern world, this film has become a timeless classic.

Although there is no specific main character, the story is told through the interaction of one person, Sonny Crawford. All the townsfolk eventually come in contact with Sonny at some point within the story, revealing important insights about them in the process. Whether by direct contact or through association, Sonny affects all those around him, taking his place as next in line to the legendary character Sam the Lion, played by longtime Western actor Ben Johnson who gave an Oscar winning performance. Sam is the emotional center of the small town, having an effect on everybody. He saw that special characteristic in Sonny, leaving him his pool hall in his will. The pool hall and the picture show were where the townsfolk congregated to become a community. That allowed Sam to be that one link between everyone, which he earnestly desired to pass on to Sonny.

The Last Picture Show takes place during the course of one year. In that year, the whole town is changed. The passing of a great man occurs, which brings about the beginning of real change in the town. It is somewhat of a subtle change, but one that is felt throughout the town. The story starts out upbeat, filled with the spark of hope and happiness. After the death of Sam the Lion the town dynamic changes, becoming dreary as everyone appears to be going through the motions. This is an element central to the story's theme. The one last thing, a mainstay of hope, the picture show, is about to close. Once that final movie is shown, the town is now emotionally empty.

Peter Bogdanovich, directing his first major movie, crafts a masterful tale from the Larry McMurtry novel. *The Last Picture Show* is about the passing of time and the isolation that comes along with it. However, *The Last Picture Show* might be more about loss than any other theme. The loss of the town's father figure, the loss of dreams and a realization that once the picture show closes all hope of the future may be lost. The townsfolk continue by turning their attention toward everything and anything else, specifically sexual encounters. These little trysts help to provide that meaning in an otherwise empty life for the simple people who inhabit the town. *The Last Picture Show* unfortunately ran into the juggernaut that was *The French Connection*, which swept the major awards it was nominated for. In most other years, this tender and heartfelt piece of small town Americana may have gotten the Academy recognition it so richly deserved. Luck was not on its side.

51

NORTH BY NORTHWEST
1959

The case of mistaken identity is such a clever plot tactic that it is used in numerous films. In *North By Northwest*, perhaps Hitchcock's finest film to employ this gimmick, an ordinary man is mistaken for a spy. That is the only thing needed to get the story rolling into a brilliant tale of espionage and adventure that takes the audience on a journey across the country. It is easy for a cinematic device such as mistaken identity to become stale, as it has been done before. In this fantastic thriller though, the action involved keeps the movie from falling under that boring theme.

Advertising executive Roger Thornhill is mistaken for a man named George Kaplan. Kaplan happens to be an agent of the government pursued by a gang of spies who intend to murder him if he does not cooperate with them. As Thornhill can not cooperate, they drug him with excessive alcohol and place him behind the wheel of a car. He narrowly escapes driving off a cliff but is soon arrested for driving under the influence. After explaining what has taken place and not believed, Thornhill begins his own search for the truth of what is going on to clear his name. That has him running and fighting for his own life, leading him on a tour of shocking revelations.

One of the true elegant traits of any Hitchcock movie is the fact that he reveals the problem almost immediately. Early to midway through the movie, the audience is given certain information about George Kaplan that not only enhances the mystery surrounding the mistaken man, but also helps add to the heightening suspense of the movie. Currently it is a commonality to use this method to reveal what is known as the twist, yet only reveal it at the end of the movie after the audience has been following the mystery the entire time. Hitchcock's directorial brilliance was in revealing the twist in the middle of the story, yet masterfully continuing the element of suspense throughout, one of his trademarks. Few have been able to reproduce it any film, let alone as a signature of their work.

1959 was the year of *Ben-Hur*. Every great film from that year was overshadowed by William Wyler's epic. *North By Northwest* is the film that, in my opinion, suffered the most. It is a much better picture than *Ben-Hur*, with Hitchcock expanding upon his visionary style in *Vertigo* while preparing the way for changing the face of cinema the following year with *Psycho*. It is tough to say which of these three movies Hitchcock should have won the Best Director Oscar for, yet look at how these three films are currently viewed and compare them to the actual Best Picture winner. In each instance, Hitchcock's film is far better. It is a shame the Academy never agreed with that.

What many remember about *North By Northwest* are its two famous scenes, the crop duster attack scene and the final fight atop Mount Rushmore. Filled with great intrigue and skillful plot twists, *North By Northwest* is a movie that was incredibly hard to leave off the main list, as its placement at number fifty-one indicates. It is a shame that fifty was the number, but perhaps it is better to end the book with a movie as great as this one, from a master of his craft without equal.

BIBLIOGRAPHY / MECHANISMS / RESOURCES

BOOKS

Atkinson, John. *The Oscars* (2001)
Ebert, Roger. *The Great Movies* (2003)
Ebert, Roger. *The Great Movies II* (2005)
Harkness, John. *The Academy Awards Handbook* (1993)
Kael, Pauline. *5001 Nights at the Movies* (1991)
Simon, John. *Reverse Angle* (1982)
Tanitch, Robert. *Blockbusters: 70 Years of Best-Selling Movies* (1998)

INTERNET SOURCES

www.greatestfilms.org
www.imdb.com – The Internet Movie database
www.nypl.org – The New York Public Library

TECHNOLOGY

JVC 32" HDTV Television
TOSHIBA HIFI combination VCR / DVD player

FILMOGRAPHY

2001: A Space Odyssey   190, 197-198, 210, 212, 231, 239, 261, 265

The 39 Steps   307

The 400 Blows   290

8 ½   312

About Schmidt   310

Adam's Rib   228

Adaptation   119, 126, 153, 155, 247, 249, 320, 336

The Adventures of Robin Hood   114, 146, 151, 156, 227, 235, 284

The Adventures of Sherlock Holmes' Smarter Brother   301

The African Queen   190, 196-197, 200, 203, 213, 231, 280

The Age of Innocence   170

Air Bud   2-3

Air Force One   251

Airplane!   10, 107, 133, 192, 233

Akira   248, 266

Alexander Nevsky   314

Ali   313

Alien   254-255, 265

Aliens   260, 267-268, 308

Alien 3   249

All About Eve   82, 142-143, 151, 154, 190, 195-196, 224, 230, 235, 255

All Quiet on the Western Front   149, 151, 155-156, 191, 207-208, 210, 231, 235, 247-248, 295, 303

All the King's Men   143, 151, 155, 235

All the President's Men   8, 107, 135, 205, 234, 315

All Through the Night   111

Almost Famous   309-310

Amadeus   132, 137, 152, 154-155, 191, 207, 230, 235, 259

Amarcord   264

Amelie   245

American Beauty   119, 127, 153-155, 245, 313

American Graffiti   191, 217-218, 231

American History X   127, 153, 155, 161, 253

An American in Paris   142, 151, 156, 191, 212-213, 225, 231

The American President   233, 318

Amistad   168

Annie Hall   134, 152, 155, 190, 200-201, 225, 231, 272, 293

The Apartment   139, 152, 155, 191, 194, 225, 231, 235, 262

Apocalypse Now   190, 199-200, 231, 247

Apollo 13   78, 128-129, 153, 156, 235

Around the World in Eighty Days   140, 152, 156

Arsenic and Old Lace   294

As Good as it Gets   161, 168

The Aviator   2, 98, 125

The Awful Truth   146-147, 151, 155, 234, 340

Bachelor Party   176

Backdraft   78, 180

Back to the Future   166, 278

Bananas   293

Barry Lyndon   322-323

Barton Fink   180

Batman   178, 269, 290, 300

Batman Begins   268-269, 313

Battleship Potemkin   314

Battlestar Galactica   265

Beautiful Girls   118, 163

A Beautiful Mind   78, 107, 126, 153-154, 199, 242, 313

Beauty and the Beast (1946)   299-300

Beauty and the Beast (1991)   72, 107, 129, 153-154, 206, 212, 234, 300

Before Sunrise   281-282

Before Sunset   281-282

Being John Malkovich   127, 320, 336

Being There 162
Ben-Hur 44, 139-140, 145, 152, 155, 191, 215, 231, 275, 294, 348
The Best Little Whorehouse in Texas 174
The Best Years of our Lives 144, 151, 155, 190, 201, 231, 235, 278
The Bicycle Thief 274
The Big Country 164
Big Fish 290
The Big Lebowski 305-306
Big Night 233
The Big Sleep 201, 235, 268, 296
The Birds 269
The Birth of a Nation 102, 149, 190, 203, 208, 210, 231-232, 239
Blade Runner 198, 265-266
Blazing Saddles 235, 301-302
Blue 306
Blue Velvet 220
The Boat 251
Bonnie and Clyde 190, 199, 214, 231, 235, 316
Boogie Nights 168, 291
Born on the Fourth of July 178
Born Yesterday 82
Bowling For Columbine 2
Boys Town 227
Boyz N the Hood 232

Braveheart 128, 153, 155, 264
Brazil 132, 152, 156, 306
Breakfast at Tiffany's 245, 304, 309
Breaking Away 14, 18, 107, 133, 152, 155, 162, 234
Breaking the Waves 289
Bride of Frankenstein 222, 311-312
The Bridge on the River Kwai 100, 107, 139-140, 152, 154, 190, 194, 230, 234, 254, 287, 332
The Bridges of Madison County 129
Brief Encounter 287-288
Bringing Up Baby 191, 227, 231, 293, 296
The Broadway Melody 149-151, 156, 200
Buck Rodgers 265
Bugsy 180
Bull Durham 164
Butch Cassidy and the Sundance Kid 50, 190, 206-207, 231, 276
The Butterfly Effect 278
Cabaret 90
The Cabinet of Doctor Caligari 296
Captain Blood 114, 146
Casablanca 106, 107, 145, 151, 154, 182, 190, 192, 230, 234, 240, 268, 294
Cavalcade 148, 151, 155, 221
The Celebration 289
Charade 309
Chariots of Fire 28, 133, 152, 155

Chicago (2002) 76, 126, 153, 156, 249
Children of a Lesser God 176
Chinatown 38, 46, 92, 107, 125, 135, 178, 190, 197, 230, 234, 249, 251, 317
A Christmas Story 172, 283
Cimarron 149-151, 156, 200, 217
The Cincinnati Kid 117
Cinderella 206
Cinderella Man 313
Cinema Paradiso 264
The Circus 150-151, 156, 263
Citizen Kane 96, 106, 107, 145, 151, 154, 190, 192, 198, 203, 227, 230, 234, 244, 314, 342
Citizen Ruth 310
City Lights 149, 151, 156, 191, 217, 231, 260, 263
City of God 242-243
City Slickers 163-164, 180
Cleopatra 322
A Clockwork Orange 190, 204, 214, 230, 235, 255, 280
Close Encounters 191, 211-212, 231, 290
Closer 324
Cocoon 166
The Color of Money 176
The Color Purple 134
Coming Home 134, 248, 266

The Conversation	42, 107, 125, 135, 163, 234, 287	
Cool Hand Luke	136, 274-275	
The Country Girl	52	
Crash	256	
Cries and Whispers	323	
Crimson Tide	251	
Cross Creek	172	
Crouching Tiger, Hidden Dragon	2, 270-271	
The Crying Game	184	
Dances with Wolves	98, 125, 130, 153, 155, 191, 216-217, 231, 342	
Daredevil	1	
Dark City	111	
The Day the Earth Stood Still	235, 295-296	
Dead Man Walking	204	
Dead Poets Society	178	
The Decalogue	306	
The Deer Hunter	131, 134, 152, 154-155, 191, 218, 220, 230, 235, 266, 275	
Deliverance	235	
Destry Rides Again	94	
Diabolique	297	
Les Diaboliques	297	
Dial M for Murder	269	
Die Hard	260, 285	
The Dirty Dozen	136	
Do The Right Thing	235	
Doctor Zhivago	28, 137, 152, 155, 190, 201, 208, 230, 235, 287, 321, 332	
Dodsworth	219	
Dog Day Afternoon	235, 294-295	
La Dolce Vita	312	
Donnie Darko	263-264, 292	
Double Indemnity	144, 151, 155, 190, 201, 230, 234, 256, 317, 342	
Downfall	250-251	
Dr. Strangelove	137, 152, 156, 190, 198-199, 230, 235, 243	
Dracula	202, 222, 291	
Driving Miss Daisy	130, 153, 156, 178	
Duck Soup	148, 151, 156, 191, 221, 230, 235, 275	
E. T.	132-133, 190, 198, 210-211, 231	
Easy Rider	136, 191, 222-223, 231	
Ed	3	
Ed Wood	300-301	
Election	310	
The Elephant Man	271, 293	
Elmer Gantry	162	
Enemies, A Love Story	170	
The English Patient	128, 153, 155, 163	
Eraserhead	271	
Eternal Sunshine of the Spotless Mind	247, 320	
The Exorcist	218, 235, 304-305	
Fanny and Alexander	322	
Fantasia	191, 209-210, 231	
Fargo	16, 107, 128, 153, 155, 191, 220, 230, 234, 265	
Fast Times at Ridgemont High	198, 309	
Father of the Bride II	111	
Fearless	170	
Ferris BuellerÕs Day Off	232-233	
A Few Good Men	184	
Field Of Dreams	130, 153, 155, 164, 234	
The Fifth Element	197, 250	
Fight Club	245-246	
Finding Nemo	265	
Finding Neverland	125-126, 153, 155, 283	
Firelight	64	
The Firm	170	
A Fistful of Dollars	241, 284	
Five Easy Pieces	136, 152, 156, 178, 209, 223, 235	
For a Few Dollars More	241, 284-285	
Forces of Nature	334	
Forrest Gump	12, 129, 153, 155, 191, 214-214, 231, 235, 264	
Fort Apache	305	

Frailty 111
Frankenstein 191, 202, 222, 231, 311-312, 318
The French Connection 135, 136, 152, 154, 191, 204, 213-214, 221, 230, 235, 346
Friday the 13th 255
From Here To Eternity 48, 88, 107, 141, 151, 154-155, 191, 207, 213, 230, 234
The Front Page 149, 217, 297
The Fugitive 68, 107, 129, 153-154, 234
Full Metal Jacket 266
The Full Monty 297
The Game 245
Gandhi 132-133, 137, 152, 156, 285
Garden State 323-324
The General 275
Gentleman Jim 114, 313
Gentleman's Agreement 143-144, 151, 155-156
Giant 140, 191, 219-220, 231
Gigi 58, 140, 152, 156, 342
Gladiator 78, 126-127, 153, 155, 215, 283, 294, 309
Glengarry Glen Ross 184
Glory 12, 164, 281
The Godfather 42, 70, 90, 107, 135, 152, 154, 190, 192, 230, 234, 239

The Godfather II 42, 70, 90, 107, 125, 135, 152, 154, 190, 201, 230, 234, 239, 279, 311, 314
The Godfather III 314
Gods and Monsters 312
Going My Way 144, 151, 156, 161, 317, 342
The Gold Rush 191, 216-217, 231, 235, 263, 281
Gone with the Wind 102, 107, 139, 145, 151, 154, 162, 190, 192, 230, 234, 239, 281, 286
Good Will Hunting 168
Goodbye Mr. Chips 62
Goodfellas 98, 107, 125, 130, 153, 154, 163, 191, 205, 217, 226, 230, 234, 245, 342
The Good, the Bad and the Ugly 241, 284-285
The Graduate 74, 190, 193, 231, 275, 344
Grand Hotel 148, 151, 156
Grand Illusion 303-304
The Grapes of Wrath 66, 107, 145, 151, 154, 190, 197, 230, 234, 283, 305
Grave of the Fireflies 301
The Great Dictator 263
The Great Escape 138, 259-260
The Great Ziegfeld 146-147, 151, 156
The Greatest Show on Earth 141, 151, 156, 194
The Greatest Story Ever Told 332

Greed 216
The Green Mile 127, 277
Grosse Pointe Blank 118
Groundhog Day 298-299
Guess Who's Coming to Dinner 191, 228, 231, 344
Gunfight at the OK Corral 32
Hamlet 143, 151, 156, 182, 200
Hard Eight 291
Harvey 292
Heat 311
Henry V 178
Hero 2, 283
High Noon 32, 107, 141, 151, 155, 190, 194, 201, 226, 230, 234, 269-270
Highlander 131, 153, 156, 163
His Girl Friday 149, 296-297
Hotel Rwanda 251-252
How Green Was My Valley 96, 145, 151, 156, 342
Hud 138, 152, 155, 176, 235
The Hurricane 78, 127, 313
The Hustler 111, 117, 138-139, 152, 155, 161, 176, 202, 235, 290
The Ice Storm 233, 271
Ikiru 254, 262, 299
I Never Sang For My Father 214
In the Heat of the Night 136, 152, 154-155, 193, 199, 234, 315, 344

In the Line of Fire 251	Jurassic Park 68	Lethal Weapon 285
In the Name of the Father 170	The Kentucky Fried Movie 10	Life is Beautiful 2, 257
The Incredibles 259, 265	The Kid 263	Life of Brian 278-279
Indiana Jones and the Last Crusade 104, 277-278	Kill Bill: Volume 1 129, 260-261, 270	The Life of Emile Zola 146, 151, 156
Indiana Jones and the Temple of Doom 104, 277-278	Kill Bill: Volume 2 129, 267	The Lion King 206
The Informer 147	The Killing 140, 280, 293, 322	Lock, Stock and Two Smoking Barrels 308-309
Inherit the Wind 116, 162	Kind Hearts and Coronets 285-286	The Lord of the Rings I 76, 241-242
The Insider 78, 127, 312-313	King Kong (1933) 150, 190, 202-203, 210, 221-222, 226, 231, 310	The Lord of the Rings II 76, 242, 279
Intolerance 235	Kiss of the Spider Woman 176	The Lord of the Rings III 76, 107, 126, 153-154, 239, 287
The Ipcress File 208	Kitty Foyle 30	Lost Highway 293
It Happened One Night 92, 148, 151, 154-155, 190, 201, 230, 235, 275, 334, 340	Kramer vs. Kramer 14, 133-134, 136-137, 152, 155, 235	Lost in Translation 314
It's a Wonderful Life 94, 107, 111, 144, 151, 154, 190, 194, 230, 234, 245	L. A. Confidential 46, 107, 127, 128, 153, 155, 254	The Lost Weekend 144, 151, 155-156, 298
Ivan the Terrible 314	La Femme Nikita 250	Love's A Bitch 276-277
JFK 22, 107, 129-130, 163, 180, 212, 232	La Jetee 302	M 253-254, 257
The Jacket 278	La Strada 282, 310, 312	M.A.S.H 191, 208-209, 231
Jackie Brown 129, 168	The Lady Vanishes 307	The Magnificent Ambersons 161
Jagged Edge 166	The Last Emperor 131, 153, 156, 232	Magnolia 291
Jaws 190, 205-206, 230, 235, 255, 262, 304	The Last Picture Show 135, 152, 155, 204, 214, 221, 234, 346	The Maltese Falcon 40, 107, 145, 190, 198, 230, 234, 253, 342
The Jazz Singer 191, 223-224, 231	Laura 317-318	A Man For All Seasons 136-137, 152, 155, 156, 235
The Jerk 113	The Lavender Hill Mob 142, 151, 156, 233, 285	The Man Who Knew Too Much (1934) 307
Johnny Belinda 182	Lawrence of Arabia 80, 138, 152, 155, 190, 192-193, 231, 235, 245, 287, 332	The Man Who Shot Liberty Valance 138, 233, 305
Judgment at Nuremburg 138		The Manchurian Candidate 88, 107, 138, 152-154, 161, 191, 212, 230, 234, 257
Julius Caesar 34		

Manhattan	292-293	
Manhunter	212	
Marty	141, 152, 155, 210	
The Matrix	246-247, 270	
The Matrix Reloaded	247	
Mean Streets	70, 205	
Melvin and Howard	233	
Memento	127, 244	
Metropolis	257-258	
Midnight Cowboy	74, 107, 136, 152, 154, 190, 201, 219, 223, 230, 234	
Midnight Run	131, 153, 155, 233	
A Mighty Wind	318	
Miller's Crossing	320	
Million Dollar Baby	125, 129, 153, 155, 253, 287	
The Miracle Worker	88	
Missing	198	
Mister Roberts	225	
Modern Times	191, 219, 254	
Mona Lisa	176	
Monsters, Inc.	300	
Monty Python and the Holy Grail	253	
Mr. Deeds Goes To Town	32	
Mr. Saturday Night	184	
Mr. Smith Goes To Washington	62, 66, 94, 107, 145, 190, 200, 230, 234, 261	
Mrs. Miniver	145, 151, 155-156, 229	
Mulholland Dr.	315-316	
Munich	255, 313	
Mutiny On The Bounty	20, 147, 151, 155, 191, 221-222, 231	
My Cousin Vinny	129	
My Dinner With Andre	163	
My Fair Lady	137, 152, 155, 191, 224, 226, 231, 304, 309	
My Favorite Year	174	
My Left Foot	130, 178	
My Man Godfrey	147, 151, 156, 219, 235, 340	
Mystic River	129, 286-287	
The Natural	115, 172	
Network	18, 36, 38, 48, 107, 135, 152, 155, 191, 212, 230, 234, 295, 322	
A Night at the Opera	147-148, 151, 155, 221, 235, 314	
A Nightmare on Elm Street	255	
The Night of the Hunter	20, 107, 141, 152, 155, 210, 234, 283	
Nights of Cabiria	282, 310, 312	
Nobody's Fool	129, 134	
North by Northwest	139, 152, 155, 190, 201, 230, 234, 245, 348	
Nosferatu	291-292, 296, 324	
Nothing in Common	176	
Notorious	269	
Ocean's Eleven	257	
Ocean's Twelve	257	
October Sky	119	
An Officer and a Gentleman	174	
Oldboy	273	
Old School	111	
Oliver!	60, 136, 152, 156	
On the Waterfront	34, 107, 141, 151, 154, 190, 193, 230, 234, 260	
Once Upon a Time in America	271-272	
Once Upon a Time in the West	136, 244-245, 271	
One Flew over the Cuckoo's Nest	38, 92, 107, 135, 152, 154, 178, 190, 197, 206, 230, 234, 241, 295, 334	
Ordinary People	84, 98, 133, 152, 155, 235	
Out of Africa	132, 152, 156, 166	
Outbreak	251	
Parenthood	78	
A Passage To India	287	
Paths of Glory	247-248, 293	
The Passion of Joan of Arc	324	
Patton	135-136, 152, 155, 191, 223, 231, 283	
Persona	323	
The Phantom of the Opera (1925)	216	
The Philadelphia Story	30, 66, 94, 191, 207, 227, 230, 234, 281, 338	

Pi	252-253	Raging Bull	84, 98, 102, 107, 133, 152, 154, 161, 190, 198, 205, 230, 234, 256	Roman Holiday	245, 304, 309
The Pianist	38, 249, 317			Romeo and Juliet (1996)	307
The Piano	170	Raiders of the Lost Ark	1, 28, 64, 104, 107, 131, 133, 152, 154, 191, 210, 230, 234, 243, 255, 277-278	Romeo is Bleeding	170
Pinocchio	206			Rope	263
Pirates of the Caribbean	316			Rosemary's Baby	317
A Place in the Sun	191, 213, 224-225, 231	Rain Man	131, 137, 153, 155, 318	Rounders	111
		Raising Arizona	320	'Round Midnight	176
Places in the Heart	134	Rambling Rose	232	The Rules of the Game	303
Planet of the Apes (1968)	321	Ran	261-262, 282-283	Runaway Train	166
Platoon	131, 153, 155, 176, 191, 220, 231, 266, 280	Rashomon	254, 262, 280, 283, 299	Run Lola Run	278
Play Misty For Me	286	Ray	2, 252	Run Silent, Run Deep	251
The Player	228	Rear Window	52, 86, 107, 141, 151, 154, 190, 202, 230, 234, 242	Ryan's Daughter	287
Point of No Return	250			Sabotage	307
Porky's II: The Next Day	222	Rebecca	30, 86, 107, 145, 151, 154, 209-210, 234, 260	Sabrina	304, 309
Poseidon	251			Salvador	176
The Poseidon Adventure	251	Rebel Without a Cause	191, 210, 231	The Sandpiper	322
The Princess Bride	12, 107, 131, 153, 155, 163, 192, 232-233, 275, 318	Red	306	Saturday Night Fever	201
		Red River	200, 211, 296	Saving Private Ryan	127, 255
Princess Mononoke	266-267	Reds	28, 107, 133, 234, 283	Scarface (1932)	315
The Private Life of Henry VII	148	Remains of the Day	316	Scarface (1983)	315
Prizzi's Honor	166	Requiem for a Dream	252-252	Scent of a Woman	184, 295
The Producers	136, 152, 156	Reservoir Dogs	129, 153, 155, 256	Schindler's List	64, 68, 104, 107, 129, 153-154, 190, 193, 230, 234, 240, 255, 259
The Professional	163, 250	Return of the Secaucus 7	233		
Psycho	86, 107, 139, 152, 154, 190, 194, 197, 206, 225, 230, 234, 245, 304, 348	The Right Stuff	172, 235	The Sea Inside	321-322
		Rio Bravo	211, 296	The Search	182
Pulp Fiction	129, 191, 226, 231, 235, 240, 243	Robin Hood: Prince of Thieves	146	The Searchers	191, 226-227, 231, 299, 305
The Quiet Man	121, 194, 211	Rocky	14, 18, 84, 102, 107, 131, 135, 152, 154, 191, 218, 230, 234	Searching for Bobby Fischer	233
Quiz Show	129			Sense and Sensibility	271

Sergeant York	32	
Se7en	245, 249-250	
The Seven Samurai	239-240, 254, 262, 270	
The Seventh Seal	262	
Shadow of a Doubt	284	
Shadow of the Vampire	292	
Shakespeare in Love	127, 153, 156	
Shane	164, 191, 213, 226, 230, 235	
The Shawshank Redemption	56, 107, 129, 153-154, 214, 234, 239, 277	
Sherlock Jr.	275	
The Shining	258	
Short Cuts	68	
Shrek	286	
Sideways	125, 310-311	
The Silence of the Lambs	72, 130, 134, 153-154, 180, 191, 212, 230, 235, 245, 334	
Sin City	256-257	
Singin' in the Rain	190, 193-194, 226, 231, 254	
Sitting Pretty	182	
The Sixth Sense	272	
Slapshot	134, 152, 156	
Sleeper	293	
Sleeping Beauty	206	
Sleuth	316-317	
Sling Blade	302	
Snatch	306-309	
Snow White and the Seven Dwarfs	190, 206, 231	
Some Like it Hot	190, 194, 230, 235, 256	
Sophie's Choice	211	
The Sound of Music	137, 152, 155, 191, 208, 226, 231, 332	
Spartacus	126, 293-294	
Spirited Away	248	
Splash	78, 176	
Stagecoach	191, 211, 216, 231, 305	
Stage Fright	263	
Stalag 17	82, 112, 259, 291, 303	
Stand by Me	288-289	
Star Wars: Episode III	318-319	
Star Wars: Episode IV	76, 134, 190, 195, 197-198, 210-212, 231, 240, 270, 285, 319	
Star Wars: Episode V	76, 134, 195, 235, 240-242, 272, 279, 319	
Star Wars: Episode VI	76, 272-273, 319	
State of Grace	1	
The Sting	50, 107, 135, 152, 154, 206-207, 218, 234, 260	
The String II	50	
Stir Crazy	1	
Strange Cargo	111	
Strangers on a Train	213, 234, 262-263	
The Straight Story	293	
A Streetcar Named Desire	34, 142, 161, 190, 196, 203-204, 213, 231, 307	
Sunset Boulevard	82, 107, 142-143, 151, 154, 161, 190, 194, 196, 230, 234, 245	
Swept Away	308	
Switching Channels	297	
Talk To Her	288	
Taxi Driver	190, 205, 230, 235, 248	
The Terminator	260, 267, 308	
The Terminator 2: Judgment Day	267-268, 308	
Terms of Endearment	132, 152, 154-156, 172, 235	
The Thin Man	235	
The Thing	319	
The Thing From Another World	319	
Things To Do in Denver When You're Dead	118	
The Third Man	60, 107, 143, 151, 154, 164, 191, 209, 230, 234, 250	
This is Spinal Tap	318	
Throne of Blood	282-283	
Throw Momma from the Train	263	
Thunderbolt	150-151, 156	
Titanic	128, 153, 155	
To Be or Not to Be	172	
To Catch a Thief	269	

To Have and Have Not	268, 296	
To Kill a Mockingbird	80, 107, 138, 153, 161, 190, 201, 230, 234, 248	
Tom Jones	137-138, 152, 156	
Tombstone	32	
Tommy	239	
Tootsie	132, 191, 210-211, 231	
Touch of Evil	44, 107, 125, 140, 164, 234, 260, 342	
Toy Story	235, 279, 298, 300	
Toy Story 2	279, 300	
Training Day	78	
Trainspotting	297-298	
The Treasure of the Sierra Madre	143, 151, 156, 182, 190, 200, 231, 235, 254	
Troy	251	
True Crime	129	
True Grit	74	
The Turning Point	134	
Twelve Angry Men	24, 107, 140, 234, 243, 295	
Twelve Monkeys	302-303	
Under Capricorn	263	
Unforgiven	129, 153-154, 184, 191, 228, 230, 235, 275, 286	
The Untouchables	163	
The Usual Suspects	243, 283, 303	
The Verdict	133, 152, 155, 174, 176, 198, 211, 295	
Vertigo	58, 86, 107, 140, 152, 154, 191, 210, 227, 230, 234, 247, 342, 348	
The V.I.P.'s	322	
Victor/Victoria	174	
The Virgin Suicides	314	
Viva Zapata	34	
Volunteers	176	
The Wages of Fear	279-280	
Waking Ned Devine	297	
Wait Until Dark	136	
West Side Story	138-139, 152, 156, 190, 202, 226, 231	
When Harry Met Sally	318	
When My Baby Smiles	182	
Who's Afraid of Virginia Woolf	322	
White	306	
The Wild Bunch	191, 218-219, 230, 235, 291	
Wild Strawberries	276	
Winchester '73	111	
Wings	150-151, 156	
Winter Light	323	
Without a Clue	120	
Witness for the Prosecution	287	
The Wizard of Oz	54, 107, 145, 162, 190, 193, 230, 234, 239, 262	
Woman of the Year	228	
Wonder Boys	127, 153, 156	
The World According to Garp	174	
Written on the Wind	140-141, 152, 156, 227, 233	
Wuthering Heights	145, 191, 200, 215-216, 231, 316	
Yankee Doodle Dandy	191, 229, 231	
Yojimbo	270	
You Can't Take it with You	146-147, 151, 156, 227	
Young Frankenstein	301-302	
The Zero Effect	111	

Printed in the United States
85093LV00004B/86/A